WARRIORS OF THE RISING SUN

WARRIORS OF THE RISING SUN

ROBERT B. EDGERTON

JAPANESE MILITARY

W. W. NORTON & COMPANY • NEW YORK • LONDON

For information about permission to reproduce selections from this book, write to
Permissions, W. W. Norton & Company, Inc., 500 Fifth Avenue, New York, NY 10110.

The text of this book is composed in Granjon with the display set in Trajan.
Composition by Tom Ernst. Manufacturing by The Maple-Vail Book Manufacturing Group.
Book design by BTD / Robin Bentz.

Library of Congress Cataloging-in-Publication Data

Edgerton, Robert B., 1931–
Warriors of the rising sun: a history of the japanese military / by Robert B. Edgerton.
p.   cm.
Includes bibliographical references and index.
ISBN 0-393-04085-2
1. Military ethics—Japan—History. 2. Sociology, Military—Japan—History. 3. Japan—Armed
Forces—History. 4. World War, 1939–1945—Campaigns—Pacific Ocean. 5. World War,
1939–1945—Atrocities. I. Title.
UA845.E33 1997
355'.00952—DC21   96-47472
                                                                                          CIP

W. W. Norton & Company, Inc., 500 Fifth Avenue, New York, NY 10110
http://www.wwnorton.com

W. W. Norton & Company Ltd., 10 Coptic Street, London WC1A 1 PU

2 3 4 5 6 7 8 9 0

FOR KAREN

CONTENTS

CONTENTS

ACKNOWLEDGMENTS

I turned ten the week before planes of the Imperial Japanese Navy bombed Pearl Harbor. The Pacific War gripped my imagination, like that of most American boys my age, for the next five years. So did news of Japanese atrocities that filled American media. I was also deeply affected by the internment of a close childhood friend who lived around the corner from me until he and his family were deported to a camp in Arizona because their name was Yamashita. None of my friends with names such as Schneider or D'Agostino were taken away.

My own turn at war came in January 1951. Courtesy of the U.S. Air

Force, I spent a year at Syracuse University learning Russian before assignment to a bleak island in the Aleutians, where I joined other fledgling Russian speakers in monitoring Russian radio and radio-telephone traffic in the Far East. At times, we flew "ferret" missions over the Soviet Far East and Manchuria, attempting to discover Soviet intentions concerning the Korean War. I have vivid memories of heavily forested landscapes of Siberia and the plains of Manchuria where much of the Russo-Japanese War was fought. I also saw a bit of Korea at close range and could not help being impressed by the dogged courage of all who fought there, including the Chinese, who lost a million men earlier in the century. Because many of these ferret flights either originated or landed in Japan, I saw that country's economic revival at first hand as U.S. and UN troops and governments poured money into Japan. I also met many kinds of Japanese people, including some former junior officers of the Imperial Army and Navy. All were gracious, but no one wanted to talk about World War II. It was thought of as something that merely happened to Japan, not something that Japan had caused; Japan's economic rebirth was all that seemed to matter to them.

Over the years I have maintained ties with many people from the Far Northeast, and I am most grateful for their help. Among those deserving special thanks are Bogdan Stuzyk, Lev Polinsky, Genadi Plotnikov, Elena Brandt, Takie Sugiyama Lebra, Joseph Yamamoto, Kazuo Nihira, Takami Kuwayama, P. K. Chang, and John Park; for the maps I thank Sharon Belkin. I am also in debt to the staffs of the East Asian Library and the Inter-library Loan Department at UCLA and the Bodleian Library of Oxford University, as well as many kind people at the Public Record Office at Kew. I am most grateful to my editor, Edwin Barber, for his astute editorial guidance. My greatest debt, in all ways, is to my wife, Karen Ito.

The orthography retains the place-name spellings in general use at the time in English. Hence, Peking rather than Beijing. Also, in keeping with Chinese and Japanese practice, individuals' last names are given first. I have kept the spellings of Russian names as they were usually written in English at the time even when phonetically inaccurate. Therefore, Semenoff rather than Semyonoff.

INTRODUCTION

D uring their 1930s war with China, and throughout World War II, Japanese soldiers, sailors, and airmen fought with fanatical courage. Although stalemated in China, Japanese forces moved rapidly east and south across the Pacific, taking Indonesia, the Philippines, a host of Pacific islands, and much of Southeast Asia, including Singapore and Burma. Their advance was not halted until the fateful naval disaster at Midway and subsequent defeats at Port Moresby and on Guadalcanal. As American and Australian forces slowly drove them back across the Pacific and British troops forced them out of Burma, they fought with grim determination, often dying to the last man in suicidal banzai charges. Before the atom bombs forced her surrender, Japan's still formidable forces were preparing a fight to the death in defense of their home islands; at the ready were four and half million armed men in uniform, along with boys carrying explosives strapped to their backs—human bombs—and grandfathers fighting with bamboo spears. Those who survived these dreadful times will never forget the bravery of Japan's warriors, but few of Japan's enemies will ever forget—or likely forgive—their often bestial cruelty. Many Japanese officers and men committed such hideous atrocities that the world still recoils in horror at the memory.

Thanks to war-crimes tribunals and numerous survivor accounts, barbarous acts by the Japanese military have been chronicled in great and sickening detail. Japanese atrocities in China, many witnessed and even photographed by Westerners, shocked the world. Japanese troops, often under orders, raped indiscriminately before bayoneting or burning their victims to death. During their notorious six-week-long "rape of Nanking" in 1937, they raped at least 20,000 women of all ages and sadistically murdered some 200,000 men, women, and children. Atrocities like these continued in China until the war's end, as the Japanese shot, bayoneted, and burned alive many thousands of Chinese and used poison gas against Chinese soldiers and civilians alike.

Throughout the Pacific War, Japanese treatment of Allied prisoners was appalling. Japan's original policy made no provision for prisoner care. Many were murdered, until Prime Minister General Tojo later modified this policy—as long as a prisoner was able to work, he might be allowed to stay alive.[1] Nevertheless, over 28 percent of the Allied prisoners in Japanese captivity died, compared with 4 percent of all Allied prisoners held by Germans and Italians.[2] They were starved, beaten, and forced to live in squalor and work under inhuman conditions. Often for no reason other than Japanese scorn for anyone who surrendered, prisoners were beaten, burned alive, forced to run barefoot over broken glass, hideously tortured, and used for bayonet practice, or as targets for rifle practice. Photographs show Japanese soldiers using Sikh prisoners for target practice after they surrendered with other British troops at Singapore. Other photographs show Chinese prisoners being used for bayonet practice.[3]

Japan also maintained a huge, expensive biological warfare program in Manchuria and China, where Chinese, Russian, and Allied prisoners, including Americans, were exposed to deadly microorganisms to determine the suitability of typhoid, cholera, anthrax, and other diseases as agents of warfare. Many died agonizing deaths from disease or surgery performed without anesthesia. Many Chinese villagers and townspeople also died when bacteriological weapons were used against them.[4] The inhuman treatment of American and Filipino prisoners captured in Bataan and that of the British, Australians, and Indians who surrendered at Singapore were not isolated incidents. Nor was it at all unusual for captured Allied air crews to be beheaded with both ceremony and enthusiasm. At least eight U.S. airmen shot down over Japan were killed by vivisection without anesthetic at Kyushu Imperial University.[5] Two others were killed by the same unspeakable procedure on Guadalcanal.[6] A few Japanese soldiers who killed Allied prisoners later expressed their concern and even regret in doing so, but others killed with great willingness, appearing to enjoy themselves, laughing and joking all the while.[7] One man who beheaded more than forty Chinese prisoners described his emotion at the time as "ecstasy."[8]

Many prisoners were massacred soon after their surrender. When the Japanese captured Alexandra Hospital in Singapore, they bayoneted everyone on the first floor, including an anesthesiologist and surgeon operating on a patient, then rounded up all the patients and nurses from parts of the building and slaughtered them as well.[9] Similar atrocities took place in Hong Kong, Soebang, Java, Johore, Malaya, Amboina Island, New Britain, New Guinea, Wake Island, the Philippines, and elsewhere. Nurses and civilian women were often treated as brutally as the men. Sometimes, female prisoners were tortured and sexually mutilated before being killed. Officers ordered most of the massacres.

With a few exceptions, prisoner-of-war camps epitomized sadism; civilian internment camps were little better. Women were degraded, raped, tortured, beaten, and killed. Virtually all prisoners were half-starved, disease-ridden, and subjected to every form of humiliation and degradation that prison-camp officers and guards could devise.[10]

At sea, Japanese conduct was no less dreadful. Submarines regularly torpedoed merchant ships without warning, then surfaced to kill all survivors, a policy instituted at the highest level of the Imperial Navy. Some survivors were picked out of the sea, only to be bayoneted on the deck of the submarine.[11] Others were beaten insensible and survived only because after the submarine submerged, a few men untied themselves, managing to stay afloat long enough to tell rescuers what had been done to them. Allied prisoners shipped to places like Korea for internment invariably found themselves crowded into tiny spaces, which forced them to sit with knees drawn up during the entire voyage. Many contracted dysentery. The only sanitary facility was a bucket that regularly spilled its contents on the men as it was hauled up to be tossed over the side. When the skeletal survivors reached Korea, they were paraded past crowds of Koreans, who spat on them.[12]

The many instances of mutilating male and female prisoners alike in sadistic ways before killing them do not bear description. Eyewitnesses recount that some Japanese units ate the flesh of downed Allied fliers who were beheaded, then sliced into bits to be cooked and eaten.[13] Some units in New Guinea often ate human flesh, including the liver of an American flier. The consumption of human flesh became a festive ceremony of the officers' mess. While most Japanese soldiers refused to eat the flesh of their fallen comrades, they did eat what remained of Allied dead as well as of some natives, practices that had official approval.[14]

The Japanese frequently brutalized the civilian populations that the Japanese had so often said would benefit under the "East Asian Co-Prosperity Sphere" as well. Some 200,000 Asian women, most of them Koreans, found themselves forced to serve as "comfort women," as sexual partners for Japanese troops. When the Dutch commander of the Balikpapan oil fields set the rigs on fire before the advancing Japanese could capture them, the entire white population of the area, except for persons already killed by sword-wielding officers, was driven into the sea and machine-gunned. Soon after the Tjepu oil fields in Java were similarly set on fire, all Dutch and Indonesian males were killed and all of the women were raped several times in the presence of the Japanese commander. Atrocities like these occurred during the first year of the war on at least twenty-six separate occasions in Borneo, Hong Kong, Java, Malaya, the Moluccas, New Britain, New Guinea, the Philippines, and Sumatra.[15] Later similar acts took place elsewhere, including Manchuria, where many citizens of the USSR were killed because it was thought they might be security risks. The Chinese inhabitants of Hong Kong and Singapore were singled out for execution on many occasions, apparently because they had supported the British. Groups of civilians deemed "undesirables" were routinely arrested, interrogated under torture, and killed.

A last and terrible massacre took place in Manila just before the city fell to Americans. Under written orders to kill all males, Japanese marines in fact slaughtered many women, children, and infants as well. For four days, Japanese troops raped, shot, bayoneted, and burned alive thousands of civilians. Large-scale massacres of thousands of civilians took place in many other parts of the Philippines, as is revealed by the diaries of Japanese soldiers and officers, most of whom wrote about the details of these slaughters without a hint of emotion. However, one soldier was sufficiently distressed to write, "Indeed the Japanese Army does extreme things," and another left this poignant entry: "The innocence I possessed at the time of leaving the homeland has long since disappeared. Now I am a hardened sinner and my sword is always stained with blood. Although it is for my country's sake, it is sheer brutality. May God forgive me. May my mother forgive me."[16]

There would be little forgiveness on the part of the Allies. Such unspeakable barbarity made the Japanese one of the most detested military forces in history. After Japan's surrender in 1945, many among the Allies insisted that the Japanese never again be allowed to bear arms. Some wanted to kill them all. In a Gallup poll taken in November 1944, some 13 percent of all those Americans polled wanted to annihilate the Japanese people.[17] The Pulitzer Prize–winning historian Allan Nevins concluded that no enemy in the history of the United States was so "detested" as the Japanese.[18] He was not alone in reaching this conclusion.

After this greatly abbreviated and sanitized review of Japanese military brutality, it may surprise the reader to learn that early in this century the West celebrated not only Japanese bravery and skill in war but also their chivalry and kindness. During the Boxer Rebellion of 1900, the soldiers of Japan fought with such exceptional bravery that their Western allies applauded them. When compared with the soldiers and marines from Austria, Britain, France, Germany, Russia, and the United States, these men from Japan were found to be the least likely to murder, rape, loot, or otherwise brutalize the Chinese. In 1904 and 1905, "plucky little" Japan, as she was often known, decisively defeated "mighty Russia" in a series of land and sea battles larger and bloodier than any yet seen on earth. Again, the Japanese scrupulously adhered to international rules of war during the fighting and afterwards treated Russian prisoners, whether wounded or not, with such kindness that a British observer wrote, "The

Japanese consideration for their prisoners is almost unparalleled in the history of warfare."[19] An American army surgeon who inspected Japanese prisoner-of-war camps concluded that their "treatment of prisoners had established a new standard of humanity for the nations of the future."[20]

The Western nations had only praise for Japanese conduct throughout this bloody war. The bravery of the Japanese often struck European observers as superhuman, but no one, not even the Russians, accused them of barbarism or bestiality. On the contrary, after the war, Japanese admirals, generals, and statesmen were lauded and fêted throughout Europe and the United States, and Westerners who spent the war years in Japan could not praise the Japanese highly enough. A British commentator, writing in January of 1905, was so impressed that he predicted a new triple alliance of Japan, the United States, and Great Britain that would "stand together as the guardians of international justice and morality."[21]

This book deals with the exceptionally humane conduct of the Japanese early in this century, and the sometimes less than humane actions of Chinese, Russian, and Western troops. This was a time of terrible killing by high-explosive artillery shells, machine guns, and massed rifle fire as well as bayonets, swords, fists, and even teeth. How soldiers and sailors of various countries behaved under such stress holds up a mirror for the Japanese—and for all mankind. The book also explores the forces that changed the conduct of the Japanese military so dramatically during the 1930s and early 1940s that the world would be shocked by its brutality. And, finally, the book asks questions: What lessons lie in this story? What role might Japan's growing military strength play in an increasingly complex Far East, where old animosities among the Chinese, Koreans, Russians, and Japanese simmer and where ever-growing tensions threaten to bring about new wars?

WARRIORS OF THE RISING SUN

THE CRUCIBLE
OF CONFLICT—
NORTHEAST ASIA

The transition from chivalry to brutality by Japan's military cannot be understood without a knowledge of the recent history of Northeast Asia, especially Japan's entanglements with China, Korea, and Russia.

When the warships of Commodore Matthew Perry forced open Japan's ports to Western trade in 1854, the Western world discovered an "unknown" nation, one almost completely isolated for over two hundred years, and almost defenseless. Except for a few muskets and some ancient brass cannon, Japan had no firearms for her samurai warriors. Because no oceangoing vessels had been built during her isolation, she lacked a navy as well.

So, not surprisingly, Japan offered little resistance to Western domination beyond some small incidents when samurai attacked and killed a few Westerners. Even these minor assaults ended when Western warships acted together to punish the Japanese, bombarding coastal cities and sending marines ashore to burn them. As fascinated Western observers watched Japan's frantic efforts to build a modern army and navy, few understood that when the more than two-centuries-long period of seclusion began, Japan had been one of the two or three greatest powers on earth, behind only Britain and perhaps China.

Before her self-imposed isolation, Japan had not been a major maritime power but her ships had sailed as far as India and perhaps the coast of America, and long before she received firearms from the West, her samurai warriors defeated a combined Korean and Mongol force in 1274, killing 13,000 of Kublai Khan's men. Seven years later, with the help of a typhoon—a "divine wind"—that destroyed 4,000 of Kublai Khan's ships, they killed some 70,000 Mongol invaders and drove the remainder back to China.[1] When the Portuguese first arrived in Japan, in 1542, they found, to their astonishment, a country five times as populous as Britain with swords the sharpest and strongest in the world. Before long, Japan produced improved models of European matchlocks and cannon, which her soldiers used to attack China in 1592.[2]

For centuries, Japan's samurai clans had waged civil war until they were finally unified under the rule of Hideyoshi Toyotomi late in the sixteenth century. Hideyoshi, a peasant, not a member of the dominant samurai class, nonetheless rose rapidly through the ranks to become a brilliantly victorious general. His well-trained and superbly equipped force of over 300,000 men would have been more than a match for the army of any nation in the world. Well aware of his strength, Hideyoshi in 1592 declared his intention to conquer China, saying, "I shall do it as easily as a man rolls up a piece of matting and carries it under his arm."[3] Because he planned to invade China by marching up the Korean Peninsula, he demanded that Korea promise neutrality. The Korean ambassador refused, scornfully telling Hideyoshi that the idea of Japan conquering China "was as absurd as a bee trying to sting a tortoise through its armor."[4]

Choosing to fight Korea as well as China, Hideyoshi loaded over

100,000 men, including cavalry, on a large fleet of small, flimsy oar-propelled boats and sent them off to land at Pusan, at the southern tip of the Korean Peninsula. Large numbers of high-spirited Korean soldiers confronted the Japanese, but they lacked muskets and were no match for the samurai in discipline or martial skill. Averaging an incredible thirteen miles a day, the Japanese fought their way north to Seoul, which fell nineteen days after Hideyoshi's men had landed. Despite mountainous terrain, the Japanese soon took the northern city of Pyongyang, only eighty miles from China, but they would get no farther.

Later that year, a huge Chinese army—perhaps 200,000 infantry and cavalry—armed with cannon, lances, swords, and bows and arrows, but without muskets, forced the exhausted and depleted Japanese warriors to withdraw slowly south. Hideyoshi's attempts to reinforce his troops were thwarted by Korea's ironclad "turtle boats," which much predated the ironclad *Monitor* and the *Merrimac* of the American Civil War. Bristling with cannon and protected by heavy planks and iron sheeting that gave them the appearance of a gigantic turtle shell, these ships overpowered the frail Japanese junks, sinking many and sending the survivors back to Japan. Although outnumbered, emaciated, and no longer hunting tigers with spears for sport, Japan's warriors nevertheless defeated the Chinese in pitched battles here and there, inflicting heavy casualties as they slowly withdrew from Korea over a period of several years.

After six years of alternating negotiation and war—the deadliest fighting the world had seen—Japan recognized a stalemate and withdrew from Korea in 1598. China's losses were so severe that her army never recovered a will to fight, and she soon fell easy prey to the Manchus.[5] Owing to his weakness at sea, Hideyoshi had to abandon his dream of conquest, but he did leave a singular monument to the war—40,000 pickled ears and noses taken from slain Korean and Chinese soldiers were on display in Kyoto, then the largest city in the world outside of China. These trophies were sent home by Japanese generals to convince Hideyoshi of a Japanese victory.[6] Chivalry was no hallmark of Hideyoshi's campaign.

Portugal's Christian presence in Japan had become increasingly worrisome to the Japanese, thanks in great part to the influence of a shipwrecked English sailor, Will Adams, who had gained the ear of the shogun. Adams missed few opportunities to accuse the Spanish and Portuguese of territorial ambitions and to warn that Catholic missionaries posed a menace to the samurai lords who ruled Japan. That firearms in the hands of peasants threatened samurai rule became increasingly clear too. To counter this growing danger, Japanese merchants were forbidden, beginning in 1635, to trade outside Japan, all Japanese were forbidden to construct seagoing vessels, and Christianity was made illegal. Except for a few Dutch traders, confined to a small island in Nagasaki Harbor, all Europeans were deported; those Japanese who refused to renounce their Christian faith were imprisoned or killed in ghastly orgies of rage. Many built their own crosses in anticipation of being crucified. They were not disappointed. In 1638, an entire Christian community of nearly 40,000 was killed, to the last woman and child. Ironically, the atom bomb dropped on Nagasaki in 1945 destroyed the largest Christian cathedral in East Asia and killed some 7,000 Roman Catholics whose ancestors had survived this original bloodbath and two centuries of harassment as a detested minority.[7]

The decision by Hideyoshi's successor, Shogun Tokugawa Ieyasu, to close Japan off to the world in 1635 was meant to protect the Japanese against the "big-nosed, smelly" barbarians they found so objectionable, and it did so with remarkable success for over two centuries. Clan warfare came to an end and the population grew. In 1700, Edo (to become known as Tokyo) held one million people, more than twice as many as then lived in either Paris or London. When the "barbarians" returned in the mid-1850s with weapons too powerful to resist, the Japanese immediately began to plan for the foreigners' destruction. In fact, when Perry forced his way into Japan, to be followed by the ships of other European powers, the emperor and his closest advisers swore an oath to destroy them, then expand overseas. The Japanese homeland would thus be buffered against further invasions. Next, the powerful Choshu clan called for Japan to unite, modernize, and drive out the European invaders. Despite vicious clan rivalries that led to a civil war in 1877, Japan did unite and then use all its resources as well as European advisers to modernize. In the ensuing thirty years, Japan made such phenomenal progress in industrialization that she could actually implement overseas expansion.[8]

Close to hand, the great natural resources of the Chinese province of Manchuria, together with China's military weakness, created an irresistible lure, but the same wealth would also attract Russia, whose interests in Manchuria were even older than those of Japan. The stage was set for a great war that would thrust Japan onto the world stage, culminating in a still greater war, fated to destroy her as a military power.

CHINA, MANCHURIA, AND THE WEST

China and Russia first jousted over Manchuria during the early 1600s, at a time when Japan entered her two-century-long seclusion. While the victorious Manchu armies that conquered China in 1644 solidified their grip over China to the south, Russian trappers, hunters, and explorers flowed east toward Manchuria in sufficient numbers to perplex the Manchu leaders. Tsar Peter the Great also resettled peasant families in Siberia and sent Cossacks to explore the well-wooded and mineral-rich Amur River basin separating Siberia from Manchuria. Armed clashes between Cossacks and Manchu cavalry became so common along the border that the Manchu court in Peking dispatched an overwhelming force in 1658 which routed the Russians.

Soon, however, the Russians returned. Once the Manchus had control over China, they dealt with Russian encroachment. When Russian troops seized a Manchurian frontier town in 1685, the Manchu emperor K'ang-hsi sent 15,000 men with over two hundred cannon to recapture the place. After killing all but a few of the Cossacks, the Manchu troops withdrew, only to have more Cossacks return, necessitating another Manchu army expedition to drive them away. These battles portended far more terrible conflict in Manchuria two centuries later, but at this time war suited neither combatant. The Russians were absorbed in conflict against Sweden in the Baltic, and the Manchus were preoccupied with Mongolia and the rebellious Chinese.

So in 1689 the two empires signed a treaty establishing the Amur River as the recognized boundary between Russia and Manchuria. Trade would flow freely from both sides of the river. To ensure Russian neutrality along its long, vulnerable northern frontier, China's otherwise profoundly xenophobic Manchu court exchanged diplomatic missions with the tsar's government; no other Western power enjoyed such recognition. Despite China's contempt for foreigners, Russia also received economic, religious, and educational privileges in Peking, including the right to have Russian children educated there for as long as ten years. This Russian monopoly on access to China and the Manchu court stood until 1860, when British and French troops forced their way into Peking.

The city wall of Peking. (A. H. Smith)

During the nineteenth century, then, Manchuria became a crucible for conflict between Japan, Russia, and China. Once-formidable Manchu armies soon lost their military edge as they succumbed to the soft pleasures of Peking's court life, ignoring the outside world and its detestable foreigners. Foreigners did not ignore China, however. The silk route was well traveled by traders of all sorts, and European visitors of various sorts visited the coast, some of them traveling inland to trade. Russian expansion in Siberia was particularly troublesome.

The first serious foreign challenge to Manchu rule, however, came not from the north but from the south, and it had to do with opium. Until 1620, when tobacco entered China (via Virginia), opium was taken only orally by the Chinese, usually as a medicine. With the advent of tobacco, the Chinese began to smoke opium and found its effects so pleasurable that the practice spread widely. Opium grown in India, much stronger than the sort grown in China, soon found an avid market.

China declared the opium trade illegal in 1729, an empty gesture. By then demand for opium was so great and so many Chinese were profiting from the bribes offered by European traders that opium continued to pour into the country. In 1757, the imperial Chinese government in Peking tried to control the trade by restricting all European traders to Canton, where they were confined to a small area of warehouses—or "factories," as they were known—along the Canton River. These traders hailed from France, Denmark, Holland, Portugal, Spain, the United States, and Sweden, as well as from Britain. All were subject to stringent restrictions. They could not, for example, buy Chinese books, learn the Chinese language, bring foreign women on shore, or hire Chinese women for any purpose.

Little equity existed here. Because the Chinese professed no desire for Western goods—"We possess all things," the emperor told King George III—the Chinese accepted only gold or silver in return for their traded tea, silk, and other products. A fine enough policy, but unfortunately for Chinese attempts to keep Westerners at bay, opium smoking had taken hold not just among the wealthy but also among the poor, who insatiably craved the drug. Portuguese traders took the lead in meeting their needs until 1773, when the British East India Company, which had perfected opium production in Calcutta, achieved a monopoly in the China trade.[9]

People throughout China became increasingly addicted. By 1838, in Fukien and Kwangtung Provinces, close to Canton in the south of China, opium shops were as common as gin shops in England; fully 90 percent of the population was said to be addicted.[10] British visitors, all too familiar with the ravages of gin among London's poor, agreed that the idiotic smiles and deathlike stupor of opium addicts were even more horrifying than the effects of drunkenness.[11] So much silver was being spent on opium that the Chinese economy weakened dangerously. Without an effective navy, a strong customs service, or honest officials, the trade in opium could not be stopped until an incorruptible imperial commissioner named Lin obtained the emperor's permission to take matters into his own hands. Facing fierce opposition, Lin's men confiscated opium and opium pipes, destroyed opium shops, and burned many thousands of opium chests. Lin also jailed corrupt officials, executing the worst offenders and addicts who refused to reform. He had amazing success even in Canton, where the trade originated, but the powerful British traders remained a problem. Lin wanted no war with Britain, but he also wanted no opium trade in China. In March of 1839, he ordered foreign traders to surrender all their opium within three days and to sign a bond swearing, on pain of death, to smuggle no more of the drug into China.

Despite protests throughout Britain by well-connected persons who profited enormously from the opium trade, Lin was on the verge of success when a dispute arose over the bond. The British Royal Navy captain Charles Elliot, nominally in charge of British trading interests, opposed it. No British subject, he declared, could be sentenced to death without trial. Even so, some British ship captains were willing to sign the bond, leading to an altercation among British ships when Elliot fired a shot across the bow of a ship whose captain had signed it. Hoping to take advantage of this dissension, the Chinese had concocted a plan to burn the British ships at anchor by tying firecrackers to the backs of monkeys before throwing the animals on British ships to start fires.[12] This plan fizzled. Instead, in an act of stupendous folly, a Chinese "admiral" sent his barely seaworthy junks to intervene. Elliot blew them to bits and soon afterward, on January 31, 1840, Britain declared war.

Sixteen British warships carrying 540 guns sailed into Chinese waters, bombarding coastal villages before landing some 4,000 troops. Ancient Chinese arms proved no match for British artillery. Serious combat was out of the question, though many Chinese fought bravely and several prominent men killed themselves rather than surrender.[13] Others killed their wives and children to save them from the barbarians. After the British destroyed Chinese forts around Canton, an even larger force of ships carrying 19,000 British troops arrived from India. These men easily occupied several coastal cities, including Shanghai and Chinkiang, which controlled grain shipments to North China. With its own troops incapable of effective resistance, the Manchu court capitulated. In what was called the Treaty of Nanking, China agreed to open five ports to British trade and to the residence of British consuls, ceded Hong Kong to Britain, and paid a whopping indemnity of $21 million.[14] Significantly, during the treaty negotiations, neither side mentioned the opium trade. By then, the British wanted free trade and the Chinese wanted to rid themselves of the "red-coated devils" who threatened to overturn the Manchu dynasty. The "Opium War" was over.

Like the Han Chinese earlier, the Manchu government closed itself off to knowledge of the West. Its ignorance of British and European law was near-total. The Manchus did not understand the consequences of agreeing to a fixed tariff or of extraterritoriality, both of which they readily accepted. The fixed tariff would greatly limit future Chinese income; granting the Europeans the right to govern themselves on Chinese soil opened the door to even greater concessions. But none of this should be surprising—even the most sophisticated Chinese, like Commissioner Lin, believed that the British could not live without tea or rhubarb. Lin was almost right about tea, but this rhubarb speculation was based on Lin's novel idea that without it, the British would die of constipation. Lin also believed that the British had deformed legs, could not see at night, and were fatally vulnerable to any attack on their feet.[15] Far more damaging for the Chinese than such whimsical ideas was a failure to acknowledge China's need for military modernization. Assuring themselves that the defeat by British troops was an aberration, China's government went on much as before. Despite their isolation, the Japanese quickly learned about the Opium War and realized that they too were in jeopardy. Japan's clan lords worried about their future; a few even began to melt monastery bells to make cannon.[16]

Wracked by rebellion, China staggered through the mid-nineteenth century. The Taiping revolution lasted from 1850 to 1864 and spread to sixteen provinces, destroying over 600 cities. It led to the deaths of perhaps 20 million people and was finally put down only with Western assistance. Through it all, European encroachment insidiously continued. Gunboats began to sail Chinese rivers, European soldiers occupied Chinese coastal cities, Western goods flooded even the hinterlands, and missionaries gained the right to proselytize more and more openly. The dress of British women offended the Chinese with unseemly displays of flesh; when in the mood, which was quite often, British men casually assaulted Chinese merchants, amusing themselves, as Prime Minister Palmerston once complained, by "making footballs" of them.[17] When the Chinese fought back, sometimes killing foreigners, British punitive raids killed indiscriminantly. American ships also found cause to bombard and capture Chinese coastal ports when their citizens were threatened.

In 1858 and 1859, Russia won territorial concessions along the Manchurian border, while Britain and France again came to blows with China. In 1858, an Anglo-French force took the city of Canton almost without bloodshed. This was the first step toward forcing China to comply with the provisions of the 1843 Treaty of Nanking—permission for European plenipotentiaries to visit Peking or reside there, receive reparations for damages, and obtain better opportunities for trade. Much like the Opium War, this conflict happened almost inadvertently. In March 1859,

British and French envoys were instructed to travel from Shanghai to Peking in order to exchange ratifications on a recent treaty. They traveled to the mouth of the Pei-ho River, which linked Peking to the coast, only to find the river blockaded against shipping with four massive Chinese forts guarding its mouth. The Chinese instructed the envoys to follow a land route to Peking that began well to the north of the river's mouth, but the imperious Europeans insisted that they had the right to sail up the river if they so chose. Eleven British gunboats were ordered to clear the channel. Chinese guns in the forts opened fire with surprising accuracy, sinking four ships and damaging the others. Close to a hundred British lay dead and over a hundred were wounded, including their admiral, Sir James Hope. There would have been even more if Commodore Josiah Tattnal of the U.S. Navy had not rushed to the rescue, saying, as would often be said in the years to come, that "blood is thicker than water."[18] In spite of what was supposed to be American neutrality, he also allowed his sailors to fire on the Chinese.[19] This bellicosity by Tattnal notwithstanding, the United States wanted no part of war with China. It was on the brink of its own civil war.

After this debacle, 600 British Royal Marines and some French sailors next attempted to storm the Chinese forts, only to bog down in thick mud and get shot to pieces, losing more than half their number. When British ships took the survivors back to sea, they counted 426 dead and 345 wounded, with nothing but ignominious defeat to show for their valor.[20] The Chinese had fought bravely under their Manchu general, Sang-ko-lin-chin, who became an instant hero. Certain that the Chinese could not fight so well on their own, the British concluded that Sang-ko-lin-chin must be none other than Sam Collinson, an Irish deserter from the Royal Marines, his name mispronounced. From now on, the Manchu general would always be referred to by the British as Sam Collinson. For the British and French, an embarrassing and costly rebuff like this demanded revenge. In the fall of 1859, Britain sent a strong expeditionary force to North China under the command of General Sir James Hope Grant.

With him as a staff officer was a boyish colonel, Garnet Wolseley, later the most famous British army officer of his time. Some British troops assembling in Hong Kong were Indian, but most were regular British infantry, artillery, and cavalry. Although Lord Elgin, Britain's ambassador accompanying the force, hoped for a peaceful settlement, British officers had other ideas. In fact, though Wolseley believed that the "Chinese were the most remarkable race on earth" and the "coming rulers of the world," he so eagerly wanted to fight them that he openly prayed that peace negotiations would fail.[21]

Both Grant and Elgin were Scots—indeed, brothers-in-law—but nonetheless a study in opposites. The clean-shaven Elgin descended directly from Robert the Bruce, and his father had brought the "Elgin marbles" to Britain. Holder of a first at Oxford, he was, at the age of forty-seven, a polished man of the world. Stoutish and bald on top with long white hair on the sides, Elgin looked the very opposite of Grant, a tall, pencil-thin, and ascetic-looking fellow with a scraggly dark mustache and chin whiskers. Although barely literate and unable to read a map, Grant was a fine musician and popular with his men, and he had done very well commanding troops during the Indian mutiny. Hardly close friends, these two agreed that Britain deserved an apology from the emperor, along with a large indemnity, both of which the Chinese immediately refused. The British promptly declared war and were joined by the French.

Unlike the well-equipped British, the French arrived without transport and had few cavalry or even horses for their artillery. They were also greeted coolly by the British, who regarded them as a nuisance if not worse. The British attitude was surprising, given that the two armies had fought together against the Russians during the Crimean War only five years before, when the efficient and brave French had earned British respect. Nonetheless, General Grant had no use for them or their commander, General Cousin de Montauban, a distinguished but domineering cavalryman who attempted to control events without great success. Even so, de Montauban was later made a count and headed the French government until 1871, when the Franco-Prussian war was lost. Despite British doubts, the French infantry were well armed and fought at least as well as the British troops, and their spahis, Algerian cavalry, although few in number, were generally conceded to be even better than the excellent Sikh cavalry of the British.[22]

The Celestial Kingdom, as the Manchu leaders called China, was still so mysterious to the West that neither British nor French knew what to expect when they landed in North China. The Chinese, in turn, knew as little about them. After the fighting ended, Prince Kung, the emperor's brother, expressed surprise to Lord Elgin that Britain ruled India; also, he believed Britain to be so small that more than half of its people had to live aboard ships.[23] Serene in their own ignorance of events to come, French and British troops set up advance camp on the Liaotung Peninsula of Manchuria. There they enjoyed the excellent weather and abundant food, little imagining that many thousands of Russians, Japanese, and Chinese would die there in the near future, and certain they could easily sweep away Chinese opposition.

Late in July 1860, now ready for battle, an armada of almost two hundred British and French ships steamed for the Chinese coast. This time they avoided the Taku forts at the mouth of the Pei-ho, landing instead somewhat to the north, where they struggled through almost a mile of knee-deep mud led by General Grant, who had removed his trousers and boots, making himself the object of amused scrutiny by his troops. Horses and wagons had an especially terrible time with the mud; the troops reached solid ground exhausted, every canteen empty. The next morning, the smoldering hostility between the French and British almost erupted into violence. The British were under strict orders not to loot, and anyone caught doing so was flogged, but General de Montauban pointedly ignored French looting. While the envious British soldiers built wharves and unloaded supplies in the humid heat, French soldiers strutted around and showed off their stolen silks.[24] British officers were hard-pressed to prevent violence.

After a pause of several days to bring supplies ashore and to reconnoiter, 11,000 British and 7,000 French troops finally set off for a city named Sinho, where they would turn sharply to the southeast and attack the Taku forts from the rear. All went as expected until an advance guard of British cavalry watched in amazement as perhaps 2,000 Manchu cavalrymen rode toward them on shaggy ponies, their high wooden saddles making them sit tall. Each man wore a round black silk hat, ornamented by two squirrel tails, a cuirass of chain mail or metaled leather, and blue trousers tucked into furry black boots.

As British infantry and artillery hurried into position, the Manchus lowered the tips of their red lances and broke into a gallop. Artillery fire burst among them, but they came on until close enough for rifle fire to take effect. With many saddles now empty, the Manchus finally wavered and the British commander at last ordered his eager Sikh cavalry and the King's Dragoon Guards on their huge English horses to move forward.

The Manchus stood their ground, but the disciplined British cavalry simply bowled over the smaller Tartar ponies and drove the survivors away. Even though the Manchu cavalry had done little damage, their magnificent—and unanticipated—courage was much admired by the British.

Nonetheless, the British were not sufficiently impressed that they felt obliged to treat the Manchu wounded with the same consideration ordinarily accorded European soldiers. For example, after the battle, Robert Swinhoe, a British civilian interpreter for General Hope Grant, walked over the battleground with a British officer, Major Dighton M. Drobyn, who later became a general and won a Victoria Cross for gallantry. A wounded Manchu cavalryman knelt before them in the mud, "all dirty and stained with blood and gore: one hand was hanging to the wrist by a shred, his legs were broken, and the back of his head, gashed by a sabre cut, revealed the brain pulsating." Finding that the man could speak, Swinhoe blithely asked him about "the strength of the enemy's force engaged that day" and other military matters. The suffering Manchu only pleaded with the British gentlemen to put him out of his misery, but unable to obtain any useful information and unwilling to shoot the wounded man, Drobyn and Swinhoe left him to die in what Swinhoe estimated would be a "few hours more."[25] Manchu prisoners fared little better. One "elderly" Manchu cavalryman, armed only with a rusty sword and spear, was roughly dragged away by an Irish soldier who contemptuously asked an officer, "Sure, and are these our inimies?"[26]

When the British and French moved on to take Sinho, they met the same sort of weak opposition. Chinese soldiers carried bows and arrows, some ancient matchlocks, nine-foot-long gingals that spewed sparks and smoke but were otherwise inoffensive, and some obsolete brass muzzle-loading cannon. British and French artillery easily smashed their mud entrenchments, scattering all the Chinese save those tied to their guns by officers who had much earlier left the scene of danger.

Unopposed, the Franco-British army marched on toward the Taku forts, only weakly protected against attack from the land side. Artillery easily swept away the outlying Chinese defenses, and heavy guns began to pound the thick dried mud and straw walls of the first fort. The allied troops had to attack across a maze of deep ditches filled with sharpened stakes, but with the help of ladders and pontoon bridges they made their way forward to the fort's massive walls, where they began to fight a battle more medieval than modern. Unable to escape, the Chinese defenders fought desperately, throwing everything they could lay their hands on at the French and British soldiers below. When the foreigners set up scaling ladders to climb the walls, the Chinese pushed them over, toppling French and British soldiers onto sharpened bamboo stakes. After the Europeans had finally fought their way inside, the Chinese soldiers continued to fight until all had been killed, most by the bayonet. As the victorious soldiers dragged away the dead Chinese by their pigtails, tossing them into shell craters, they laughed and ignored an Italian photographer, Signor Beato, who wanted the scene of carnage left untouched for his camera.[27] Beato's photographs of this unequal warfare were every bit as gruesome as Mathew Brady's of fighting in the American Civil War.

Young soldiers quickly grew accustomed to the sight of mutilated corpses of the enemy, but when the Chinese agreed to return British soldiers and several Chinese porters employed by the allies taken prisoner earlier, the troops were sickened and infuriated by what they saw.[28] The wrists and ankles of the soldiers had been terribly torn by leather thong bindings; one man had been driven mad by torture. The Chinese prisoners were in even more dreadful condition. One man's skull had been split open so that his brain was visible, and the wound was filled with writhing maggots.[29]

The allies quickly advanced toward a second fort, this on the north side of the river, a larger and more formidable obstacle. To their relief, the occupants of the garrison had taken off their uniforms and put on civilian clothes, ready to talk about surrender. The British and French had already suffered upwards of 500 casualties. Not keen to storm another fortress, they told the skeptical Chinese that if they surrendered their weapons, they could go free. This was an offer unique in Chinese experience. Expecting to be killed but seeing no hope in resistance, 2,000 terrified Chinese troops shambled out of the fort and to their amazement were, in fact, allowed to go free.[30] Such a startling contrast to their own cruelty in warfare galvanized those Chinese commanding the two forts on the south bank of the Pei-ho. In no time, they also surrendered, along with their 600 cannon and all other Chinese troops under their command between the coast and Tientsin, a city of a million people about thirty miles inland on the Pei-ho. The commander of all the forts had been none other than the Manchu general Sang-ko-lin-chin, who had earlier slipped away to Peking with 150 cavalrymen.

As General Hope Grant and his staff steamed upriver on a gunboat, his troops slogged their way through appalling heat, above 100 degrees Fahrenheit in the shade. No resistance arose along the way. The foreign soldiers were delighted to find ripe fruit and vegetables in the orchards and fields, and villagers happy to sell ducks, chickens, mutton, and beef so cheaply that the soldiers had seldom eaten as well. Better still, the ancient walled city of Tientsin held astonishing luxuries. Ice was so readily available that a large block of it could be had in exchange for an empty beer bottle, as could 200 pounds of delicious grapes. There was so much ice that even the horses were given ice water.[31] The Chinese preserved large chunks of ice cut during winter by packing them in straw and chaff.

The troops felt quite welcome in Tientsin this summer of 1860, and when smiling emissaries from the emperor arrived to negotiate a peace treaty, it appeared that the war was over. While the two sides conferred, the British found letters from Peking to General Sang-ko-lin-chin. An otherwise isolated Chinese court was surprisingly well informed about allied strength and intentions, apparently thanks to British newspaper accounts that somehow came to them. In these letters, the court ordered Sang-ko-lin-chin to use his "invincible" Manchu cavalry of 30,000 to smash the barbarians and capture Lord Elgin. The Manchu cavalry had already done its best, even though it had been 28,000 men shy of its reputed strength, and would not fight again.[32]

Lord Elgin, known to the Chinese as "that fat barbarian," worked out a treaty at Tientsin, which the Chinese "emissaries" obligingly agreed to accept, but when it was put in writing and they were asked to place the emperor's seal on the document, the mandarins blithely admitted they had been lying. They had no powers to negotiate; they were merely stalling for time. Understandably furious, the allies promptly marched out of Tientsin toward Peking, where they intended to deal directly with the emperor. While the French and British troops approached, a makeshift 20,000-man Chinese army under Sang-ko-lin-chin was digging in along a three-mile front across their line of march. The ever-political Manchurian general wrote a flowery letter to the emperor, telling him not to worry about the detestable barbarians, because if they had the temerity to march against him, he would annihilate them.[33]

Unaware of 20,000 Chinese lying in wait for them, the unsuspecting members of an allied peace delegation were captured by the Chinese as they went forward to negotiate. Two junior officers, Lord Elgin's private secretary, Sir Harry Parkes (who served as interpreter), a correspondent for the *Times* of London named Bowlby, and some forty British and French private soldiers were taken; other officers barely escaped, their scarlet jackets easily visible through British field glasses as they used their swords to cut their way through a crowd of gray-uniformed Chinese. The captives were hauled before a Chinese officer who ignored Parkes's indignant complaint that they had been taken in violation of international law. The Chinese officer ordered Parkes, the only member of the party able to speak Mandarin, to kowtow. When Parkes refused, he and many other prisoners had their mouths stuffed with human feces and their hands tied with wet leather thongs before they were carted off to Peking in pain, humiliation, and fear.

Not yet aware of this outrage, the allies pressed on. Their commanders soon learned the size of the entrenched Chinese army, but even though only 4,000 men of the advance guard were available, they unlimbered their artillery and opened fire. Infantry and cavalry advanced behind the barrage, and 20,000 Chinese ran away. Only a few dozen allied casualties occurred, and in spite of heat, fatigue, and a plague of flies, the French and British pursuit was relentless, pushing the Chinese back on Peking's walls. Most of the combat took place between Sikh cavalry and Manchu cavalry. Neither side could be accused of chivalry. When a Sikh fell into Manchu hands, his eyes were gouged out and he was hacked to pieces. After the battle, Sikhs rode over the field, prodding Manchu bodies with their lances. If a man showed signs of life, a Sikh would dismount and slowly saw his head off.[34]

The Forbidden City's massive red walls could not be breached with ordinary artillery, so General Hope Grant sent for his heavy siege guns and tried to reestablish contact with General de Montauban and the French. Wolseley finally found the general at the Summer Palace, outside Peking. For two hundred years a sacred residence of the emperor, it was a compound of many elegant palaces, government offices, pavilions, pagodas, and parks, all enclosed by a high granite wall over five miles around. While British cavalry watched, the French blasted their way into the unguarded compound, looting enthusiastically. The next day, Lord Elgin accused the French general of being a thief, an insult that did nothing to warm the already frigid Franco-British alliance. After exercising great restraint while the French pillaged in such a frenzy that they ran around in women's silks, wearing mandarins' hats and refusing to obey any orders, the British finally joined in, albeit with comparative restraint.[35] Both armies made away with unimagined riches.

With his siege artillery finally in place, Lord Elgin now demanded that the Chinese in the Forbidden City return the allied prisoners. These unfortunates had been so tightly bound that their hands had rapidly swelled to twice the normal size and turned black. Shortly before his death, the mortified hands of the British lieutenant Anderson actually burst, revealing hundreds of worms feeding on the dead flesh. Anderson and the others were also beaten, stoned, exposed to the sun, and otherwise hideously brutalized. Only thirteen of the twenty-six British, and six of the thirteen French prisoners survived. Chinese coolies who had worked for the Europeans were buried up to their necks and left to be slowly eaten by scavenger dogs and pigs. The head of the British captain Brabazon, an aide to General Hope Grant, was returned but his body was never found. The body of Bowlby, the *Times* correspondent, had been eaten by pigs. This was the kind of barbarity that the West had expected from the Chinese and all "Orientals."

Thanks to the Russian diplomat General Count Nikolai Ignatyev— his grandson would fight against the Japanese in Manchuria in 1904—the British buried their dead in Peking's Russian cemetery, performing a ceremony so austere that French officers who attended were shocked. The French burial ceremony, on the other hand, was deeply moving for British observers. General de Montauban praised his dead countrymen and commended their souls to God, emotionally concluding with "Adieu mes amis, adieu." Then a long line of French soldiers filed by the tomb, and each paused to fire a blank cartridge at it. When the ceremony ended, the tomb was covered with cartridge papers.[36]

Except for the luckless twenty-three-year-old Prince Kung, no Chinese authority existed for Lord Elgin to negotiate with in Peking. The emperor and his court had fled before the allies arrived. Lord Elgin's first inclination after learning about the brutalizing of the allied prisoners was to burn the Forbidden City and replace the Manchu dynasty with a Han Chinese government. Talked out of these extreme ideas by the French and Count Ignatyev, Lord Elgin burned the Summer Palace instead, over the objections of de Montauban, who took this opportunity to accuse the British of barbarism. Prince Kung was suitably terrified by the destruction of the sacred palace and parks, and due in large measure to the shrewd intervention of Count Ignatyev, the prince agreed to Anglo-French terms rather than face the total destruction sure to follow if he did not.[37] France and Britain shared a £24 million indemnity, Tientsin was opened to foreign trade and residence, Britain received the Kowloon Peninsula, and France won the right for Catholic missionaries to own church property throughout China. Count Ignatyev took full advantage of allied domination to win new territorial concessions for Russia along the Manchurian border. Escorted by a huge entourage, he rode triumphantly home to St. Petersburg in a palanquin carried by sixteen elegantly robed men.[38]

China's shocking defeat of 1860 convinced some influential Chinese that they could no longer ignore Western military superiority. Noting that the Japanese had already begun to acquire Western weaponry, provincial leaders sought out European help in constructing arsenals and dockyards. Leading the drive toward Westernizing China's military was Li Hung-chang, a six-foot-four scholar, soldier, and diplomat who was to become one of the most powerful men in China and was already a man of great wealth and importance. Li warned everyone who would listen—and most still would not—that China must arm or Japan would join the West in destroying her.

Some unfortunate mistakes followed, such as entrusting China's largest dockyard at Foochow to the direction of two Frenchmen who had never before built a ship, and an artillery-manufacturing program to a British expert who happened to be a medical doctor who knew so little about making artillery that the barrels burst when fired.[39] Nevertheless, China did send some students to the United States and some officers to Germany. A small coal and iron mining industry developed. China also produced a few steamships. More important, the government purchased more and better weapons. But without a strong industrial base or the national will to build one, China never developed enough military might to hold off European expansion. Russia continued to nibble away at Manchuria, France took Vietnam in 1884, and Japan, soon to become her most dangerous enemy, grew stronger every year.

JAPAN'S WESTERNIZATION

Thanks to reports by their seafaring pirates, the Japanese knew about foreigners for many centuries before these despised, "unclean barbarians" actually landed in Japan. Like the Chinese, they wanted nothing to do with them. But far better than the Chinese, the Japanese recognized the power of foreign firepower. Shortly after the Portuguese landed in Kyushu in 1542, a Japanese lord purchased two matchlocks for the staggering sum of $180,000. With a little help from a Portuguese gunsmith, the Japanese not only quickly learned to manufacture muskets, improving designs along the way by, for instance, covering the touchhole so that a gun would fire in the rain. Japan soon had the best-armed and best-trained infantry in the sixteenth-century world. The Japanese also manufactured their own cannon.

In 1575, a Japanese army of peasants equipped with muskets and cannon met a samurai army armed with traditional weapons. The samurai charged the peasants with their accustomed gallantry and were shot to pieces, leaving 16,000 dead on the field of battle. There would be other battles, including Hideyoshi's attempted invasion of China, but the lesson was becoming clear: peasants armed with guns were too dangerous to coexist with their samurai superiors. Armed with a musket, the most lowly peasant could kill the bravest samurai, even his most noble lord.[40] Peasants were expected to be docile, respectful, and tax-paying, not warriors who could challenge samurai rule.

At the end of the sixteenth century, the feudal lords moved to disarm the peasant armies and prohibit the manufacture or importation of guns. They succeeded so well that when Perry's armada arrived in Japan in 1853, belching black smoke from the first steamships Japan had seen, the only firearms in the entire country were a few antiquated muskets and antique brass cannon that fired solid round cannonballs. Perry's cannons fired thirty-two-pound explosive shells. Nevertheless, many brave samurai were willing to fight Perry with their antiquated weapons, even though they were virtually defenseless against European gun fire. One nineteen-year-old samurai named Yamagata Aritomo, so tall and thin that he was known as the "crane," swam out to Perry's flagship with a knife between his teeth, prepared to fight the entire ship's company.[41] He was not harmed and later became the general who modernized Japan's army and led it throughout years of victorious yet chivalrous warfare.[42]

As the trumpets and cymbals of a U.S. Marine Corps band blared out "Hail Columbia," Commodore Matthew C. Perry, known as Old Matt, rowed ashore from the USS *Susquehanna* in his most elaborate uniform

Field Marshal Yamagata, "the Crane." (Colliers)

topped with a cocked hat and plume, accompanied by 300 sailors and marines—including two tall African-Americans—armed with rifles and bayonets. Perry and his men were met by samurai foot soldiers clad in leather and iron armor. As a brisk wind stretched out their brightly colored clan banners, ranks of iron-helmeted, obviously agitated cavalrymen sat on restless horses. Well aware of their military disadvantage, the Japanese tried everything in their extensive bag of negotiating tricks to send Perry away. The discussions, held in Dutch, quickly revealed that Dutch traders in Nagasaki harbor had kept the Japanese abreast of world events. Japanese negotiators were well versed in geography and were even aware that the United States had recently fought a war with Mexico and was building a transcontinental railroad. The Japanese were gracious, pressing gifts on the Americans, but there would be no treaty. Perry left, as the Japanese wished, promising to return with an even larger fleet. While his men gorged themselves on delicious ripe peaches the Japanese had given them, Perry sailed to Macao, Hong Kong, and Okinawa, where he prepared for a return to Japan.[43]

The Japanese had been deeply troubled by Perry's first visit. When he returned in February of 1854 with his "black ships," as the Japanese called his smoke-belching steamships—seven powerful warships accompanied by three supply vessels—he made it abundantly clear this time that nothing Japan might do would drive him away. He demanded trading rights for American ships as well as access to coal, water, and food. The Japanese repeated their earlier tactics of delay, obstruction, and denial of landing rights, but the ever-stern Perry insisted that he would land where he chose and that he would not leave until he had a treaty opening Japan to trade. Boasting of his ability to summon a fleet of one hundred warships in three weeks (a fib of considerable magnitude) the commodore went ashore at Kanagawa with 500 armed sailors and marines in their dress uniforms. The Americans received a warm welcome and many gifts, and this time were met by an English-speaking Japanese interpreter who had learned the language from a shipwrecked American captain held in Japan for four years. The Americans were impressed by the exquisite courtesy displayed by the Japanese but baffled by many of their practices—the two sexes bathed nude together, for instance, and married women used a mixture of urine, sake, and iron filings to blacken their teeth.

To impress his reluctant hosts, the humorless Perry staged a minstrel show featuring sailors in blackface and a choir that sang popular melodies. The Japanese loved the music and amazed the Americans by quickly memorizing the tunes and some of the lyrics.[44] The Japanese reciprocated by staging an exhibition of sumo wrestling—a boring show, thought Perry—but he was amazed by the strength of these men, who easily shouldered two 135-pound bales of rice, while it took two U.S. Marines to carry a single bale.[45]

Muscle power, however, yielded finally to firepower, and on March 31, 1854, the Japanese signed the treaty. Perry's displays of technological superiority proved convincing. The commodore sent troops ashore to demonstrate their discipline and firepower, inviting Japanese dignitaries to witness an awesome exhibition of long-range fire by his heavy guns. Perry's men also set up a mile-long telegraph line and quickly assembled tracks for a small steam engine capable of going twenty-five miles per hour while pulling some forty passengers in a modern pullman car. The

Japanese were suitably impressed, but one young man, a careful notetaker, was able to assemble such an engine himself only a year later.[46]

Perry was promptly followed by a Russian fleet, whose Admiral Putilov was far more skillful than the Americans in winning Japanese acceptance; then, all too soon for the Japanese, the British landed as well. Several acts of samurai violence fueled by the xenophobic emperor Komei killed a few Europeans, leading inevitably to retaliation. Samurai bravery could not compensate for obsolete cannon, and when British long-range explosive shells devastated Kagoshima as well as Shimonoseki, home city of the proud samurai Satsuma clan, all but the most unreconstructed xenophobes conceded a need to Westernize Japan's military. The man who saw this need most clearly was a brilliant and ruthless nobleman, Iwakura Tomomi, who had once been Emperor Komei's principal adviser. Like Li Hung-chang in China, Iwakura linked his country's survival with the rapid development of a modern army and navy. And like Li, he had to contend with an emperor who refused to modernize. All foreigners were to be driven out of Japan. Sometimes called *damyuraizyu* by the Japanese (apparently after the British sailor's expletive "Damn your eyes, you"), the "smelly, big-nosed" barbarians were not loved, but they could not yet be driven away. With government support and heavy investment by private entrepreneurs, Japan's economy was transformed in thirty years from being a countryside of agrarian fiefdoms to being a modern industrial state. A new system of currency, new banking, transportation, communications, and, above all, modern manufacturing—these fundamental changes proceeded at a remarkable pace.[47]

Li Hung-chang could not overcome Peking's conservatives, but Japanese modernists were more successful. In 1867, Emperor Komei died, and in 1868 his son, Meiji, ascended to the throne. The handsome and intelligent young Emperor Meiji was as determined to promote Westernization as his father had been opposed to it. The young Meiji was joined by many influential men, a number of them inspired by a charismatic, brilliant leader named Yoshida Shoin. His face pockmarked by smallpox, his clothes filthy, his hair matted, Yoshida presented a slovenly appearance that masked an enormous intellect. His energy was totally focused on leading his students to revere the emperor and master Western technology in order to use it against Westerners. To stay awake and teach at all hours, he put mosquitoes up his sleeve in the summer and ran barefoot in the snow in the winter.[48]

The nationalist fervor took hold. Astonishingly, the feudal lords of Japan agreed to give up their fiefdoms and return their patrimony to the emperor. The samurai, only about 5 percent of the population, reluctantly relinquished their special rights to be well fed without defiling themselves by working or touching money, and to kill with impunity if they felt it necessary to do so to maintain proper behavior among the rest of the population. These revolutionary sacrifices by the proudest of men were followed by an imperial decree that a national army and navy would be conscripted from the entire population, not simply the samurai. All men over twenty would be eligible for three years of military service followed by four years in the reserves. To be sure, all officers would be samurai, but other samurai might serve in the ranks along with peasants. Even the despised *eta*, Japan's untouchables, would serve in the national army.

The attempt to include the *eta* leather workers in the army, even as boot and saddle makers, was opposed by samurai and peasants alike. The *eta*, or *burakumin*, as they came to be known, would remain so "untouchable" that no Japanese would dream of setting foot in one of their settlements. The life of an *eta* was reckoned to be worth about one-seventh the life of a townsman. Those *eta* conscripted by the army served almost entirely in all-*eta* transport units. Those killed in battle did not have their names listed among the honored war dead.[49] Widespread opposition to military conscription arose among the peasants, few of whom even knew that Japan had an emperor when Meiji was restored in 1868. That peasants should obey an emperor rather than a feudal lord was a new idea. Some samurai were having second thoughts about imperial obedience, too. In 1877, cultural and political conservatives, including the Satsuma samurai so battered by foreign ships, rebelled against the Meiji government and its new conscript army, but with the help of Iwakura and the other reform-minded samurai nobles in the court, Japan's new peasant soldiers defeated the conservatives in a bitter six-month civil war. A year later, former samurai officers and men mutinied against the new Imperial Japanese Army. Fifty-three were executed, not by honorable means such as beheading or seppuku but by a firing squad. Japan's immense energy was now single-mindedly devoted to creating a Western army and navy with the industrial strength to support them.

In striking contrast to China, where soldiers occupied the lowest social rank and government was inconceivably inefficient and corrupt, Japan was a country where the people revered their military men, and the government was focused on military preparedness as few have been. Orders for rifles and cannon went to France, and although some samurai initially refused to fight with such ignoble weapons, they eventually gave in. Japanese officers were first trained in France, where their instructors complained that the young samurai were "flighty, capricious, overconfident and careless."[50] When Germany defeated France in 1871, the Japanese quickly switched to the victors. Soon Japanese soldiers were goose-stepping and following Prussian infantry tactics. Japanese naval officers, most of whom were samurai from the once rebellious Satsuma clan, learned from the British Royal Navy, often after years at sea aboard British ships. Japan's new ships would be built in England, too, for Britain ruled the seas and the Japanese wished to learn from the best. Japan's Westernization was not confined to military matters. Western arts, literature, science, music, and fashion also flourished. University students feasted on anything Western, and as samurai became industrialists, railroad magnates, and bankers, they incongruously appeared in Tokyo wearing their traditional two swords, one long and one short, along with top hats and plus fours. Other men wore black mourning dress with black silk top hats, a costume imposed even on their very young sons.

As advice and training on military matters were being sought in Europe, a high-level diplomatic mission toured Europe and America to determine what political reforms Japan would have to make in order for the West to deal with her as an equal. Talk of parliamentary democracy filled the air, but the most lasting advice came during an audience in Berlin with Bismarck, who warned that international law commanded respect by Western nations only when it was to a nation's advantage to respect it. Otherwise, he said, it was ignored and nations relied on war. Bismarck also advised the Japanese not to depend on alliances with other nations. To survive, Japan should strengthen her economy and military with all her might.[51]

JAPAN'S FIRST MODERN WAR AGAINST CHINA

A modern army and navy are not built in a day, and despite an obsessional devotion to rearming, it was not until 1894 that the Japanese felt ready to test themselves against a serious opponent. Thanks primarily to Li Hung-chang, by 1894 China had armed several hundred thousand troops with modern German weapons, including machine guns and Krupp artillery, and had purchased a navy almost twice as large as Japan's. However, China's armies were poorly trained, seldom paid, and led by officers who specialized in avoiding danger while enriching themselves. Despite their impressive modern weapons, the Chinese often lacked ammunition, forcing themselves to use bows and arrows or swords, some of which had tin blades. Many of their explosive shells were filled with sawdust. Troops were wretchedly housed and dressed in a motley array of silk shirts and baggy pants; they wore huge conical hats and carried fans and umbrellas. Many were addicted to opium and gambling.[52] China's Western-built warships were modern, but her navy was even more poorly trained and led than her army. How China and Japan measured up in their military modernization would be determined in Korea and Manchuria.

Korea, isolated from world affairs, indeed widely known as the "hermit kingdom," enjoyed a fragile independence at best. China was determined to reestablish her past dominance, when Korea was her vassal state. Fearing a "Chinese" Korea—the Japanese often referred to Korea as a "dagger" pointing toward her—Japan moved to control the country herself. Both China and Japan used strong-arm tactics to influence the Korean government, including assassination and armed provocation. When a Japanese-supported rebel group defeated Chinese-supported government forces in an armed confrontation, the king of Korea appealed to China for troops. China sent 1,200 men, but Japan reinforced its legation guards by 8,000 troops, an incendiary act, a prelude to war. Japan also demanded that the king guarantee various reforms that would assure Korea's neutrality and Japanese rights, including the right to maintain troops on Korean soil. When Korea refused, Japanese troops forced the king to sign an order expelling the Chinese and setting up a cabinet favorable to Japan. Two days later, three Japanese ships exchanged fire with two Chinese ships off Inchon Harbor, beaching one and routing the other.

These Japanese ships were after Chinese troop transports that spies had seen sailing from Tientsin. A few hours after the Inchon incident, the Japanese cruiser commander Captain Togo Heihachiro (whose name meant "peaceful son"), saw one of these ships, the British-registered SS *Kowshing*, chartered by the Chinese. It carried 1,100 Chinese soldiers under the apparent command of a German major. A decade later, Togo would be celebrated throughout the West as a naval hero, but on this day he very nearly became a war criminal. Togo signaled the unarmed ship to follow him and the British captain agreed to do so, but Chinese officers on board ordered him to sail on, threatening to kill him if he did not obey.

After four hours of frustrating negotiation, Togo became furious over the Chinese obstinacy, afraid that Chinese warships might appear at any moment. He finally ordered the captain to leave the ship. When his order was ignored, Togo's cruiser fired two broadsides and a torpedo at point-blank range, sinking the ship rapidly. Few of the Chinese troops could swim, and many of those who could were pulled under by the ship's suction. There were few lifeboats, and Japanese machine guns apparently fired on these boats as well as at the few survivors in the water. Over 1,000 Chinese soldiers and sailors died. Later, Japanese lifeboats combed the area but suspiciously saved only three people, all of whom were Europeans, including the British captain, Thomas Ryder Galsworthy. Galsworthy later said that he did not see the Japanese fire on helpless Chinese, but he was in no position to see everything that happened, and he might have prettied things up in any event. Other witnesses, including Chief Officer L. H. Tamplin, reported that the Japanese did indeed fire, but so did Chinese still aboard the sinking ship, who may have fired first.[53] These men left on board could not swim and were furious that some Chinese and the German major managed to swim to an island almost two miles away.

The initial British reaction to the sinking of a British-registered ship was cold. But when the Japanese offered to have the matter adjudicated by a British court, British experts in international law decided that Togo had acted properly under the circumstances. He emerged from the episode as a hero to the Japanese, not a war criminal. Four days later, still without any declaration of war, Japanese troops attacked and dispersed Chinese troops guarding Inchon Harbor. On August 1, 1894, the Imperial Palace in Tokyo finally declared war on China, in the "interest of peace," it said, and a special war budget of 150 million yen was unanimously passed by the Diet.[54] By mid-September, Japanese troops of the First Army had driven the Chinese back to the walled city of Pyongyang, captured by Hideyoshi three centuries earlier, where the Chinese fought surprisingly well for a week before giving way after Japanese soldiers breached the main gate. The next day off Port Arthur, in what is known as the Battle of the Yellow Sea, a twelve-ship Japanese fleet routed a larger Chinese armada, sinking six of its major warships. The Japanese lost only 90 killed and 208 wounded, most of them on board the French-built cruiser *Matsushima*.[55] The *Matsushima* carried a 12.6-inch gun, one of the most powerful in the world at that time, but because it could be fired only once every five minutes, the ship played little part in the battle except to serve as a huge, slow-moving target. If the Japanese had not broken off action at dusk for fear of a torpedo boat attack from Port Arthur, the entire Chinese fleet, now out of ammunition, would have been sunk.

By the end of October 1894, the Chinese army had withdrawn across the Yalu into Manchuria, where it dissolved in the face of the Japanese advance led by the now General ("the Crane") Yamagata until he fell ill and had to return to Japan. The Chinese forces were led by a courageous and humane general named Tso Pao Kuei, who did his best to put up resistance, but his task was hopeless. Manchu reservists called up to reinforce Chinese forces had not trained in years, were poorly led, and devoted their energies to robbing foreigners in Mukden. While their Manchu officers, like those of the Chinese, sent reports of great victories back to Peking, very few men actually stood to fight the Japanese, who steadily drove them back. A Chinese observer said admiringly that the Japanese fought "as if they were at drill."[56] One of the few who fought well was General Tso, who died trying to rally his men. The Japanese buried him with full military honors before pursuing the demoralized Chinese and Manchu soldiers down the Liaotung Peninsula toward Port Arthur.

Some 20,000 Chinese soldiers manned the formidable fortresses surrounding Port Arthur on the tip of the peninsula. Built by German engineers over a period of sixteen years, Port Arthur was defended by seventy large Krupp guns in twenty-two interconnected concrete-and-steel forts. While Japan's First Army herded surrendering Chinese soldiers into camps to the north of Port Arthur, the Japanese Second Army, under the brilliant General Oyama Iwao, landed and besieged the fortress. Sure of their invincibility behind Port Arthur's fortifications, the Chinese high command plastered huge placards on walls throughout the city, offering a reward to anyone bringing the body of a Japanese soldier to the authorities. Soon, several Japanese corpses were displayed hanging by their ankles from a huge camphor tree, disemboweled and emasculated, their eyes gouged out. Severed Japanese heads were also displayed on pikes mounted at the entrance to the city, where they would be the first thing seen through Japanese binoculars. Although the Chinese were in a strong position, their resistance collapsed almost immediately. Only 19 Japanese were killed and no more than 300 were wounded, but many of those had been left naked and mutilated for the advancing Japanese to see. Enraged by the placards and the ghastly display of bodies, many Japanese soldiers ran wild through the city of Port Arthur, looting, raping, and killing Chinese men, women, and children.[57]

Most outraged Japanese officers looked the other way while their soldiers slaughtered Chinese civilians, and not until after the better part of a day was the mayhem brought under control. As if there had been no slaughter by either side, General Oyama then celebrated his easy victory with a cherry tree-planting ceremony and a poetry-writing competition.[58] Despite their contempt for Chinese soldiers and their distaste for Chinese civilians, whom they thought filthy—the Japanese accused them of being half-pig, half-monkey and willing to eat anything[59]—only on this occasion during the war did Japanese troops loot, rape, or kill civilians. In fact, even after the capture of Port Arthur, Chinese prisoners often reported that the Japanese treated them with great kindness.[60] Still, Japan had entered the war pledging to abide by the Geneva Convention, and Western opinion was important to them. Their conduct in Port Arthur was no more brutal than that of the Chinese whenever they could capture Japanese or mutilate the dead, but because it occurred on a large scale in front of Western witnesses, much credibility was lost.[61]

Early in 1895, General Oyama's Second Army sailed across the Chihli Strait to Shantung Province, capturing the fortified city of Weihaiwei. Even the ever-unrealistic Manchu court realized the Japanese could now march on Peking with ease. Li Hung-chang hurried to Japan to sue for peace, but with nothing except the humiliated remains of the Chinese army and navy behind him to strengthen his hand, Li had little choice but to agree to Japanese terms. China ceded Formosa, the Pescadores Islands, and Manchuria's Liaotung Peninsula to Japan in perpetuity, agreed to open seven ports to Japanese trade, paid an indemnity of over £35 million, and allowed Japan to occupy Weihaiwei until it had been paid. More than twice the annual income of the Chinese court, this indemnity could be paid for only thanks to loans from France and Russia, both pleased now to have China in their debt.[62] China also finally recognized the autonomy and independence of Korea, thereby removing her protectorate and opening the way for Japanese dominance. After 481 days of war, from July 25, 1894, to November 17, 1895, Japan had reduced China's navy to port-bound impotence and had scattered, killed, or captured about 150,000 Chinese troops at a cost of only 172 Japanese sailors and 1,005 soldiers killed in action. However, another 15,860 Japanese died of diseases, mostly enteric fever, dysentery, and cholera, and many suffered from the effects of frostbite.

When the one-sided treaty was signed in Shimonoseki, the same city the British had bombarded into rubble three decades earlier, three Western capitals immediately expressed alarm. France feared for the loss of her growing influence in China, Germany for her now substantial trade in weaponry with the Chinese (particularly Mauser rifles and Krupp cannon), and each was deeply suspicious of the other. Russia was appalled at the thought of the Liaotung Peninsula's falling into Japanese hands. She was on the verge of obtaining Chinese permission to extend the Trans-Siberian Railroad south down this peninsula to the warm-water port of Port Arthur rather than east to her own partially ice-bound port of Vladivostok.

In the "spirit of friendship," as they put it, the three powers advised Japan to relinquish the Liaotung Peninsula. In the spirit of anything but friendship, the tsar put Russia's Far Eastern Fleet on alert, threatening to bombard Japanese coastal cities and sink Japan's fleet if she did not comply. Enraged but realistic, the Japanese government understood that if it did not submit, it might not have the power to resist Russia, much less Germany and France as well. When the Japanese public learned about the capitulation, widespread riots erupted, causing loss of life and considerable damage. Troops had to be called out to prevent even greater disorder. Clear at last about how much the country was still at the mercy of the West, Japan used her bitter humiliation to create a fierce new nationalism. Rallying to the slogan, *Gashin Shotan* (suffer privation for revenge), the response by the Japanese government and the emperor was immediate and overwhelming—Japan must become even stronger, and as rapidly as possible.[63] A new budget passed providing funds for six additional army divisions and the Imperial Navy would have 4 more battleships, 16 cruisers, and over 600 smaller warships. Military expenditures would soar from 20.6 million yen in 1895 to 133.1 million yen in 1896, over half of the entire Japanese budget.[64] In 1898, when China leased the Liaotung Peninsula—

including Port Arthur—to Russia, an outraged Japan intensified her military preparations even more.[65]

As soon as Japan withdrew from Manchuria, Russia moved ahead on one of her greatest engineering projects, a 5,000-mile-long railroad that would link European Russia with Siberia and Manchuria. Its Russian architects—principally the tsar, the soon-to-be count Witte, and some well-placed businessmen—told one and all that the Trans-Siberian Railroad would benefit China as well as Russia, and it did bring impressive prosperity to parts of Manchuria.[66] But it also led to war against China in 1900, and against Japan four years later. These risks were known, but Tsar Nicolas II insisted on going ahead. He detested the Japanese, whom he referred to as "monkeys," in some measure, it appears, because during his visit to Japan in 1891 a crazed off-duty Japanese police officer attacked him with a sword, leaving a scar on his forehead. The tsar was not fond of the British, about to be allied with Japan, either. He referred to them as "Zhids," the derogative Russian equivalent of "Yids," and he also felt that the Chinese were contemptible. The tsar would hear nothing about the dangers of expansion in the Far East, insisting that no one would dare to go to war against Russia. Not Japan, not Britain, and certainly not China.

RUSSIA'S EASTERN EXPANSION—MANCHURIA

Sergei Witte was the original driving force behind the railroad's construction. Son of a wealthy Dutch father and a high-ranking Russian noblewoman, Witte did not share the tsar's prejudices, perhaps because he married a Jewish woman. However, his star soon fell, and the impetus to press the railroad project farther east came from a former guards officer, Alexander M. Bezobrazov, the son of a wealthy nobleman, and a field marshal. When the grandfather of the actor Yul Brynner put up for sale a huge timber concession along both sides of the Yalu River, Bezobrazov joined with Grand Duke Alexander and others close to the tsar to buy it.[67] If they were all to profit as richly as they meant to do, the railroad across Manchuria then south down the Liaotung Peninsula to Port Arthur would have to be completed.

More than one and a half times the size of Texas, Manchuria in 1895 was largely wilderness. Western Manchuria, extending toward Mongolia, was grassland, northern Manchuria was a thick forest that still provided a home to Siberian tigers, the Liaotung Peninsula was fertile but sparsely

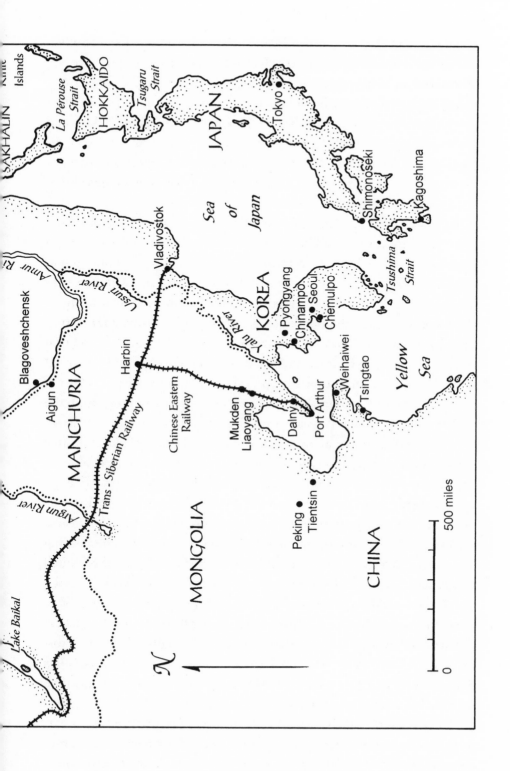

populated, and only the south of Manchuria, where most of the six million or so of its people lived, provided rich farmland. Much of the province was plagued by murderous mounted bandits, the Chunchuse, or "red beards," mostly former soldiers who now lived by plunder.[68] But this vast region was rich in the iron and coal that the Japanese home islands lacked, and its fertile farmlands beckoned to Japan's rapidly increasing surplus population. While Japan longed for the Manchurian riches her people thought they had won on the field of battle, Russia set to building a railroad that would make Manchuria theirs.[69]

Begun in 1891, the Trans-Siberian Railroad was built without apparent concern for cost; indeed, so few records exist that its total expense will never be known. We can be certain only that the figure was prodigious. Over 200,000 Chinese workmen had to be hired, fed, housed, and kept happy, the last being all too seldom possible because Russian workmen, also employed by the thousands along with Russian railway guards, routinely swore at the Chinese, pulled them around by their queues, and beat them. In addition to Chinese and Russian workmen, engineers and other specialists came from all over Europe, especially Italians adept at blasting tunnels through the mountains. Despite Russia's desire to profit from the undertaking, few large Russian firms shared in the contracting. Instead, Russia imported timber and cattle from China, tools, steel plants, bridge girders, and electrical equipment from the United States; and locomotives and sleeping cars from France, Canada, and the United States.[70] Even Japan provided coal and locomotives. As the Chinese Eastern Railway line, as it was called, snaked to the south down the Liaotung Peninsula, towns like Harbin, Mukden, Liaoyang, and Port Arthur became thriving cities that attracted missionaries from France, Britain, and the United States, shopkeepers from almost everywhere, as well as Greek bakeries, Tartar tobacconists, Japanese-owned barbershops and brothels, not to mention hordes of free-lance prostitutes from all corners of the globe.[71] The demand for skilled workmen of all sorts seemed unending; to the dismay of Russian engineers, Chinese had to be hired to operate complex machinery because they were able to learn the tasks far more quickly than unskilled Russian workers could.[72]

Security for the newly constructed railroad to Port Arthur lay primarily in the hands of a few thousand lightly armed and widely scattered railway guards, rather than Cossacks or regular Russian army troops, whose commonplace brutality had made them loathsome to many Chinese. Security became a major concern because the anti-Christian and anti-Western "Boxer" movement, which would soon lead to Japanese troops' being showcased for the world, spread south and west from Shantung to imperil the foreign missionaries, businessmen in Tientsin, and diplomats in Peking. The Boxers, who hated all foreign "devils," were also spreading north from Shantung into Manchuria, where their targets were Russians. At first, the Russians discounted the Boxer threat, believing it directed against missionaries or "ocean devils," as the British, French, and Germans were known, not China's longtime "friends" from Russia.[73] But months before the "ocean devil" diplomats in Peking were attacked, Russian illusions about Chinese friendship shattered.

In March 1900, things heated up. Anonymous posters calling for the extermination of all foreigners appeared on walls of inns and temples along the newly completed Chinese Eastern Railway. Boxers demonstrated their gymnastic and martial prowess before admiring crowds of Chinese. The telegraph line was cut and the track sabotaged.[74] Early in April, a Russian officer and two Cossacks were shot to death from ambush by imperial Chinese soldiers. It soon became apparent that the Boxers were not alone in their determination to kill the Russians. Imperial Chinese troops had joined them. By June 1900, attacks were taking place against Russian troops and railroad yards all along the line, and by the time the European legation quarter in Peking fell under siege by these same Boxers, Russian troops had to fight off large numbers of Chinese troops and Boxers in pitched battles that sometimes left hundreds of dead Chinese on the battleground. The Russian losses were smaller, but twelve Russians had been captured and sadistically tortured to death, their mutilated bodies left for all to see, many with crosses carved into their chests.[75] Almost 200 miles of railroad track were destroyed, some of it actually plowed under and turned into cultivated fields.

Russian reinforcements from Port Arthur moved north to relieve the railroad guards, taking unusual precautions not to inflame the situation by damaging crops, molesting Chinese women, or opening hostilities. Their precautions were wasted. Fanatical Boxers supported by Chinese troops eagerly sought them out and attacked. Bullets and bayonets proved the Boxers all too vulnerable, and as hundreds of them died, many Chinese army units lost their zest for battle. As the Russians heard more and more about Chinese atrocities involving the torture and mutilation of Russian wounded, their thirst for revenge grew. If a Russian soldier ducked his head when a bullet whistled by, another would shout, "Why do you bow, do you know her?"[76] In their quest for revenge, they often struck back against innocent Chinese civilians in ways that horrified their own officers. Their uncontrolled arson, rape and murder left several Manchurian towns utterly devastated.

Some seventy miles to the west at a place called An-shan, General Chin Ch'ang, the overall commander of Chinese forces in southern Manchuria, built up a force estimated at 50,000 while sending thousands more to fight as guerrillas along the railroad. They were ordered to do as much damage as possible before falling back toward An-shan, drawing the Russians with them. While General Chin's forces attempted to draw the Russians into a trap, fighting broke out in northern Manchuria along the Amur River, which separated China from Siberia at a place called Blagoveshchensk, a name that ironically meant "the place of good news."

In 1900, Blagoveshchensk held nearly 40,000 people. An American traveler was impressed by its wide streets, and although its buildings were entirely made of wood, he declared them fine, comparing the city favorably to towns of the same size in Europe or America.[77] Across the Amur River on the Manchurian side lay the city of Sakhalin-Ula, a far less modern place of 50,000 inhabitants, many of whom regularly crossed over to the Russian side to sell meat and vegetables. Despite the frequent passage of Russians to Sakhalin-Ula on business of various kinds, they did not notice the buildup of Chinese troops and artillery near the city. Early in July, Chinese residents of Blagoveshchensk who had been warned of an impending attack began to cross the Amur with all of their possessions. Only then did the Russians realize they were in danger.

Because of the Boxer Rebellion and the Chinese attacks along the Liaotung Peninsula, Russian troops had assembled in Blagoveshchensk. However, on July 12 they were ordered away to protect the railroad near Harbin, hundreds of miles to the south, leaving the defense of the city to a few Cossacks, one infantry company, some reservists who had no rifles, several armored steamers, and two artillery pieces. On July 15, Chinese troops using rifles and cannon fired across the river on Russian families out for a Sunday stroll. The steamers returned fire, and casualties fell on both sides. Had the Chinese chosen to cross the river, they could easily have done anything they wished to the city and its inhabitants, but they did not. Instead, the next day they intensified their bombardment, and the Russians were hard-pressed to keep their wooden city from burning. The shelling continued for the next four days, but the Chinese made no attempt to cross the river, and the Russian troops that had left the city for Harbin hurried back, arriving that night.

That same day, Boxer posters had been found in the Chinese sector of Blagoveshchensk. No actual poster appears to have survived, but the Russian authorities, led by the chief of police, announced that the posters warned of a Manchu invasion that night and urged the Chinese who remained in the Russian city to join in the attack. The military governor promptly ordered that all Chinese be removed from the city, and so began one of the worst atrocities in an atrocious war. Armed reservists and police rounded up Chinese in the city while Cossacks whipped Chinese families out of their homes outside the city. Several thousand Chinese and Manchus spent the night under guard before being driven six miles to a ferryboat station the following morning. Those who could not keep up in the fearful heat were shot or killed with axes. Any valuables they had were stolen. When the river crossing station was reached, no boats were available and none in prospect. The Amur River, at this point over 700 feet wide, carries a strong current, but the police officer in charge nonetheless ordered all the prisoners—the elderly, women, and children along with young men—to swim to the other side. Only a few tried, and the rest were whipped into the water. When Cossack whips proved incapable of driving most of the prisoners into the river, the Russians opened fire. Some 3,500 Chinese and Manchus drowned or were killed by gunfire, sabers, or axes. No more than 100 made it to the far shore. On the same day in Peking, a period of armistice for the beleaguered foreign legations began.

Few Russians in Blagoveshchensk expressed remorse over the deaths of these innocent Chinese, and no one tried to prevent authorities from soon afterward driving three other parties of Chinese prisoners to the same place and killing them in the same way. In fact, officials justified their actions by saying that the Chinese had refused orders to swim. They also issued sweeping new orders to kill all Chinese on the Russian side of the Amur, many of whom were slaughtered by ever-willing Cossacks. When the military governor of the Amur region, General K. N. Gribski, finally realized what was happening, he ordered that the killing cease and

Chinese victims of war in Manchuria. (L. L. Seamen)

all Chinese be protected or helped to cross the river if they wished. His orders were obeyed, but when news of the massacres leaked out, Gribski fell into disgrace, some other officers received punishment, although light, and the educated Russian public expressed horror.[78] A local Russian newspaper editorial noted that this message should be sent to the civilized world: "Do not consider us as brothers anymore. We are mean and terrible people; we have killed those who hid at our place, who sought our protection."[79] The tsar disagreed. He said that the Chinese "deserved the lesson they had been taught."[80]

On August 1, heavily reinforced Russian troops crossed the river despite gusting winds that threatened to capsize their boats. The Chinese put up little resistance when they came ashore, and their troops soon melted away into nearby mountains, abandoning the city of Sakhalin-Ula without a fight. As the Russian troops marched toward the city, they found the mutilated body of a Russian prisoner dangling from a birch tree; his severed head had been so hideously disfigured that he could be identified only by his uniform. Cossacks burned the city to the ground.

The imperial Chinese troops had now entrenched themselves in a mountainous area that separated the invading Russians from the town of Aigun, the oldest Chinese outpost on the Amur River. Even mediocre troops could have held this position indefinitely, but these Chinese soldiers were terrible marksmen who fired so high that Russian infantry and cavalry charges drove them back almost without any losses. After five hours of steady advances, the Russians were on the outskirts of Aigun, already burning in places as a result of artillery fire. The few Chinese soldiers left behind to defend the town gave the Russians an unpleasant surprise. Fighting from house to house, many killed themselves rather than surrender. When the fighting finally ended and Aigun was burned, the Russians gave thanks that such brave Chinese soldiers were so poorly trained and led. The Chinese left numerous cannon and machine guns, nearly 1,000 rifles, fifty banners, and large amounts of ammunition behind as they fled even farther into the mountains. After blowing up twenty-six ammunition depots, the Russians cremated or buried over 700 Chinese corpses. Their own losses amounted to only 12 killed and 41 wounded.[81] Led by General Rennenkampf, who played a controversial role that contributed to a disastrous Russian defeat in World War I, Cossacks drove the Chinese from one mountainous position to another, capturing hundreds of cannon, thousands of rifles, and immense amounts of ammunition, none of which had been put to good use by the Chinese, who by the end of August were unable to offer any organized resistance. Their commander took poison rather than surrender.

While the Chinese were being routed in northern Manchuria, Russian forces to the south in the Liaotung Peninsula defeated large Chinese forces with similar ease. In one encounter, some 14,000 Chinese had entrenched along a line of hills, where their banners waved, their cavalry galloped back and forth, and doleful sounds of horns reverberated across the plain toward the Russians. A patrol of 80 Cossacks had been sent to reconnoiter the Chinese position, but they misunderstood their orders and charged directly up the hill. The 14,000 Chinese fled. A few days later, about 2,000 Russian infantry, 200 Cossacks, and thirty artillery pieces easily drove 30,000 Chinese out of an extensive entrenched position, even though the Chinese fought with unusual tenacity. On the Russian side, no one was braver than the nurses who fearlessly tended to the wounded while under artillery fire, a pattern that would continue in all of Russia's subsequent wars.

After this defeat in late September, the Chinese fragmented into small bands of marauders, who lived by plundering local villages but posed no further threat to Russian forces. As the Russians gained control of cities like Mukden and Liaoyang, they freed some of their men who had been taken prisoner by the Chinese. The men had been forced to drink foul water and were beaten until they finally swallowed the human feces their jailors forced into their mouths. Their wounds were never attended to, and when they smelled so foul that their jailers were annoyed, the men were beheaded. The head of one of these victims was returned to the cell, where the surviving prisoners were told that they would be permitted to lie down to sleep only if they used the festering head as a pillow. After several days, the exhausted men had to submit, and one recalled that worms from the human cushion crawled over his own head and neck. From time to time, the prisoners were displayed to the public at the city gate, where passersby beat and spat on them, made them eat pancakes covered with feces, and forced them to kiss the genitals and anus of a piglet. One Russian soldier was cut all over his body and then chained near an open window so that flies would lay eggs in the shallow wounds and the worms would eat him alive. When the man tried to end his suffering by not eating, his guards forced porridge down his throat. They were disappointed because he choked to death before they could complete his torture.[82]

When descriptions of these and other horrors spread among the Russians, some soldiers took revenge on innocent Chinese civilians, but most officers controlled their men, and some went to great lengths to relieve the suffering of the Chinese peasants who crowded into the cities after their crops had been destroyed. Because no effective Chinese government remained, Russian officers took over the civil administration of Manchuria. In early October 1900, Manchuria had for all practical purposes become a province of Russia, controlled by 4,000 officers and 173,000 soldiers. But before that could happen, dramatic events took place to the south around Peking, where Japan's soldiers would for the first time display their bravery and chivalry to the West.

CHAPTER TWO

THE BOXER REBELLION— JAPAN IN THE WORLD'S EYES

The brutal fighting between Russians and Chinese in Manchuria during the spring and summer of 1900 attracted virtually no attention in the West, but simultaneous events in Peking were so dramatic that they captured headlines throughout the world. Western Newspapers breathlessly told readers that the ruthless Manchu empress dowager, Tzu Hsi, or "the Old Buddha," as she was usually called in the West, led tens of thousands of bloodthirsty Boxers, who first slaughtered missionaries and then besieged the foreign legations in Peking, where they killed all the "foreign devils"—men, women, and children.

Accepted as true for some time, the story was a fabrication. In fact, the besieged foreigners, protected by only a handful of legation guards, defended themselves while troops from eight countries fought their way inland from the coast in a last-minute attempt to save them. When they finally succeeded, the world hailed their heroism, reviled the Chinese, and supported the belligerent powers' demand that the Manchu government pay a huge indemnity. Among the foreign powers, which included Britain, France, Germany, Russia, and the United States, no people stood taller than the "little" Japanese, as they were always called, and none benefited as much as Russia.

Newspapers worldwide provided lurid speculation about the events as they unfolded, and soon thereafter eyewitness accounts by survivors found a vast reading audience. Hollywood later made a large-budget motion picture about the drama, starring Charlton Heston as a U.S. Marine officer, while journalists and scholars continue to describe and analyze the events to this day. These various sources provided a fascinating portrait of Boxer brutality, the determination of the Manchu court led by the empress dowager to kill all the foreigners, and the dazzling courage of the foreign civilians, soldiers, sailors, and marines. Not until better scholarship was published early in the 1990s did it become clear how distorted this picture actually was.[1]

It is now known that the Boxers were manipulated by xenophobic members of the Manchu court who saw an opportunity to use them against the hated foreigners without implicating themselves. The empress dowager, though indecisive at first, ultimately opposed the Boxers. Far from ordering the destruction of the foreigners, she actually ordered Imperial Chinese Army troops to protect them, and for the most part they did. The Boxers did not conduct the siege of the foreigners; they were no longer even in Peking when it took place. The siege of the legation compound was carried out by various Imperial Chinese Army troops, most of whom intentionally avoided killing the foreigners. The only serious attacks were made against Chinese Christian refugees who huddled miserably in a park area, defended almost entirely by the Japanese—the only non-Christians in the compound. In fact, with the exception of the Japanese, the legations treated the Chinese Christians abominably.

To be sure, there were heroics by many of the defenders, but there was cowardice, too, and more than a little stupidity. The first military expedition sent to save the foreigners in Peking failed thoroughly. And the second relief expedition did not take place for such a long time that if the Chinese had been serious about it, the besieged foreigners could have been killed many times over. When the allied troops finally reached Peking after brushing aside weak opposition, they behaved brutally. With the exception of the Japanese and most British and Americans, they raped and killed indiscriminately, and all the allies looted. Western headlines rarely mentioned the Japanese, but witnesses generally agreed that the best defenders of the surrounded legations and the bravest troops among the relief forces were Japanese, and many there called them the most humane.

Japan's chance to bask in international acclaim came thanks to the Manchu court. The Manchu dynasty had long been xenophobic to a fault, and it was never more so than in 1900. China's defeat by Japan five years earlier still rankled, and the continuing encroachment of the European powers became a growing embarrassment and a menace. The perennial impoverishment of the Chinese masses grew even worse as Western railway construction put Chinese barge workers and porters on the Grand Canal out of work. Western imports destroyed the market for local goods, especially in Shantung Province, the birthplace of Confucius and one of the poorest regions in all China and the one most subject to natural disasters. In 1900, drought turned the land into a dust storm. Many Chinese peasants were convinced that new developments like the railways and telegraph lines desecrated ancestral lands, disrupted the spiritual balance of their world, and brought about natural disasters. No new development troubled them more than the presence of Christian missionaries and their Chinese converts, now forbidden to practice ancestor worship, engage in religious ceremonies, or contribute financially to the rituals so important to most villages. The growing arrogance of the missionaries, the spread of their churches, hospitals, and orphanages (guaranteeing them new converts), and the preferential treatment they demanded for their converts in court cases created widespread resentment.

It was commonly believed that the Christians regularly ate Chinese children, drank women's menstrual blood, used the eyes and testicles of Chinese children for medical preparations, and concluded their church services with frenzied sexual orgies. Many of these beliefs were invented by sophisticated pamphleteers who gave away their clever propaganda leaflets in pawnshops throughout several Chinese provinces, including

Shantung and Chihli. Obviously the work of educated men, some of these pamphlets effectively combined fact with fiction, while others were simply outragious fabrications calculated to prey on the ignorance and fear of the peasantry. For example, hoping to encourage the widespread belief that Christians practiced sodomy and the fear that Chinese converts would sodomize helpless villagers, one widely distributed pamphlet assured readers that all Christian infants, boys and girls alike, had a hollow tube inserted in their anus in order to dilate them, thereby facilitating anal intercourse.[2]

Antimissionary riots became widespread and savagely cruel. For example, in 1870, Chinese set a French Catholic cathedral in Tientsin on fire. After killing two priests, the crowd dragged ten sisters into the square before the church. One after another, as her sisters were made to watch, each nun was stripped naked, her breasts hacked off, and a spear thrust through her vagina into her abdomen before she was thrown into the flames.[3] Most of these massacres were put down by the Manchu government in an attempt to placate the West. However, by 1900, a powerful conservative faction in the government no longer wanted to appease the West; its members wanted to kill all foreigners, including the missionaries, or at least drive them out of China. Led by Prince Tuan, an "overbearing, extravagant, licentious and idle" man whose son was the heir apparent to the throne, the "Iron Hats" (named after the original Manchu war helmets) hatched the idea of turning peasant unrest against the foreigners without implicating themselves.[4] The Iron Hats' passionate hostility toward foreigners grew after the sudden and unexpected decision of the emperor to emulate Japan by issuing a series of decrees that would modernize China, eclipse the Iron Hat conservatives, and encourage Western influence.

A decision of this magnitude was hardly characteristic of the Manchu emperor Kuang Hsu, a frail, timid young man who had lived his life under the shadow of his formidable aunt, Tzu Hsi, the empress dowager, dominant in the court for half a century. In addition to the painful debilitation caused by Bright's disease, he suffered from a rare urological condition that caused him to ejaculate repeatedly during his sleep as well as in response to any sudden stress, such as that caused by a loud noise.[5] Profoundly embarrassed and disabled by his affliction, he was incapable of sexual relations with a woman. Despite his physical disability and his timidity, in June of 1898, with his aunt's blessing, he issued some fifty well-intended modernization reform edicts affecting every aspect of Chinese life that he hoped would lead China into the modern world. The Manchu conservatives hoped for nothing of the kind. The Iron Hats eventually used fabricated evidence to turn the empress dowager against the emperor. She rejected his reforms, declared him ill, and assumed the regency.

During this period of turmoil, the Boxers emerged in Shantung. Their Chinese name meant "Fists of Righteous Harmony," but they became known as Boxers in the West apparently because the gymnastic movements they routinely practiced resembled those of boxing.[6] Recruited from unemployed, landless peasants, and other impoverished and aimless people available in growing numbers, the Boxers were descended from several secret societies such as the White Lotus Society, which had long preached revolution. They had no known leaders, yet they were united in their determination to kill all Christians and drive all foreigners out of China. They all wore red—usually a scarf, sash, or headband—and insisted that they were impervious to bullets. They were armed only with swords, knives, spears, and tridents, but there were many thousands of Boxers, all eager to kill Christians. Encouraged by Prince Tuan and the Iron Hats in Peking as well as the governor of Shantung Province, the Boxers began to attack Christians in Shantung, as they had already attacked Russians in Manchuria.

The Iron Hat faction had alienated the richest man in China, and one of the most powerful, Viceroy Li Hung-chang. Now over seventy, Li Hung-chang was still determined to modernize China. To do so he decided to use the Western powers to drive Prince Tuan and his conservatives out of favor in the court. He began by planting false stories of outrageous Boxer atrocities with Western newspapers, in the hope of provoking Western military intervention that could topple the government.[7] By the spring of 1900, no fabricated stories were necessary. As Boxers attacked Russians to the north in Manchuria, Boxers in Shantung destroyed railroads and telegraph lines, burning and smashing anything Western as they marched toward Peking, where they intended to kill the Christian devils in their legations and churches.

Missionaries in their isolated churches, hospitals, and schools in the countryside took alarm, and many prepared to flee to Peking while others worked to fortify their churches. Wisely, the French bishop Favier for-

Sir Claude MacDonald, British ambassador. (A. H. Smith)

tified the Catholic cathedral at Peitang, just north of Peking, against expected attack. But diplomats and other foreigners in Peking continued to believe themselves safe from Boxer attack. At that time, some 250 civilian foreigners lived in the legations or in private residences nearby. In addition to the diplomats and their families at the eleven legations representing Austria-Hungary, Belgium, Great Britain, France, Germany, Holland, Italy, Japan, Russia, Spain, and the United States, other foreigners worked in nearby banks, general stores, the Peking Hotel, or the newly established Peking University. Each legation also had a small number of armed military personnel as guards.

The senior Western diplomat was the Spanish minister, Cologon, but the leader of the diplomatic corps, especially once the Boxer threat emerged, was the British minister, Sir Claude MacDonald. A tall, pencil-thin forty-eight-year-old Scotsman with an elaborately waxed mustache,

Sir Claude initially pooh-poohed the Boxer threat, but once hostilities began, this former officer of the Highland Light Infantry proved to be a stalwart leader. The German legation was led by another former army officer in his mid-forties, the handsome Baron Clemens Freiherr von Ketteler. His American wife, Maud, was decidedly plain; as the daughter of a midwestern railroad millionaire, she had other charms, however. Von Ketteler was recklessly brave, but his brutal attack on a Chinese boy would help precipitate the attack on the legations and lead to his own death. The American minister, Edwin Conger, proved a thoroughly dull but unflappable former Union Army officer in the American Civil War. His wife, Sarah, a Christian Scientist, was as eccentric as her husband was solid. Throughout the siege, she persisted in assuring everyone that the bullets whistling over their heads were imaginary. The elegant young Italian minister, the Marquese di Salvago Raggi, ignored the distasteful military events altogether. He and his exquisite young wife kept to themselves during the day but dressed elegantly for dinner every night.

The least-liked minister was France's Stephen Jean-Marie Pichon. A portly man with a huge walrus mustache and sad eyes, he was a close friend of Clemenceau's. He would later rise high in French diplomatic circles and play a major role in negotiating the Treaty of Versailles. Intellectually, he stood above his colleagues, but he was no soldier. In fact, all agreed that he was a hopeless coward who would suffer any indignity to keep himself out of danger. As if to prove their point, he spent much of the siege mournfully telling others, "*Nous sommes perdus!*" A correspondent for the London *Times* referred to him as "the laughingstock of the whole place," an opinion that was reinforced when it became known that he slept in pajamas decorated with red hearts. Little is recorded about the other diplomats except that the same acerbic correspondent who criticized Pichon said that the Japanese minister, Baron Nishi Tokujiro, "resembled an anthropoid ape."[8] This racist attitude was widespread at the beginning of the siege, but the Japanese would do much to change Western views. Known as "dwarfs" and a "doll-like" race to the Europeans, who barely tolerated them in the life of the legations, the Japanese would earn great respect.

Bisected by a notoriously polluted canal, the legation quarter of Peking occupied some one hundred acres abutting the immense Tartar Wall on the south. The personnel of the eleven legations occupied spacious quarters, mostly in well-built two-story, stone-and-brick structures. In addition, there were innumerable stone walls that separated various buildings, as well as considerable parkland belonging to Prince Su, a member of one of the most prominent Manchu families. There were large stables for racing ponies and riding horses, several good wells, and large supplies of food. As the Boxer threat grew, the foreigners added to their food supply no less than 230 tons of grain taken from a nearby warehouse, and also appropriated an enormous number of bottles of champagne.[9]

Despite the considerable size of the legation quarter, when terrified missionaries and their Chinese converts began arriving in large numbers, it soon became plain that housing them was a major problem. For one thing, no legation wanted to have these unlettered, dirty, and all-too-peasant-like Chinese Christians in their residences; even if the legations had been more charitable, there were simply too many Chinese to house—several thousand by most estimates. All available housing was already taken by hundreds of Chinese workmen and coolies. Not knowing where to go or how to feed themselves, the bewildered and largely abandoned Chinese wandered about in their growing numbers, vainly searching for something to eat.

In casting about for a solution, British eyes fell on the palace gardens of Prince Su, a fourteen-acre expanse of beautiful trees, gardens, parks, and numerous buildings, including his own magnificently appointed palace. When a British emissary approached the prince to ask if he would mind making his park available to hordes of peasant converts to Christianity, the prince did not have to be told that this was a request he could not refuse. Taking only a few of his most precious possessions and half of his concubines, he reluctantly vacated his home, and the frightened and hungry Chinese moved into his park and his palace. In fact, he could have remained in his palace, since all the British wanted was the park for the converts, but he chose to leave, probably to avoid being identified with the Christians, which would, as events soon proved, have put his life at risk. As soon as he left, Westerners from various legations looted his palace of its treasures. All his silks and satins were made into sandbags, soon to constitute perhaps the most colorful fortifications in history.[10]

By May 26, the Boxer march on Peking had become so threatening that Sir Claude MacDonald requested Chinese permission to send for additional legation guards. While the court factions wrangled over whether to agree to this request, the Chinese Foreign Office reluctantly permitted him to send for a small number of men. He immediately wired the British admiral Edward Seymour for marines and sailors from the ships offshore. The largest contingent of troops available to assemble for the train trip inland to Peking consisted of several officers and hundreds of men of the British Royal Marine Light Infantry. However, because the Russian commander could only muster 3 officers and 76 men, he insisted—in an early and ominous display of allied disharmony—that the British forces could not outnumber those of the tsar. To avoid an open split, the British agreed. In addition to the Russians and British, Seymour dispatched 75 French sailors and marines with three officers, 30 Austro-Hungarians (most of whom were Yugoslavs) with seven officers, 51 Germans under only one officer, 39 Italians with two officers, 53 U.S. Marines with three officers, and 24 Imperial Japanese Marines under a single English-speaking officer, the remarkable Colonel Shiba Goro, who had been a military attaché to the Americans in the war against Cuba.[11] The reinforcements arrived in Peking on March 31, just before the Iron Hat faction was able to lock them out of the city. The men were lightly armed with rifles, bayonets, and a few machine guns, but no artillery, because the Russian commander, Lieutenant-Colonel Baron von Raden (one of many Russians of German

British legation in Peking with message board. (A. H. Smith)

ancestry to become nobles and serve in the army), in a not unusual example of Russian military ineptitude, had somehow managed to leave behind half his rifle ammunition and his only artillery piece. However, he conscientiously transported 1,000 cannon shells to Peking.[12]

As soon as the troops settled down after their tumultuous welcome, the work of preparing the defense began in earnest. In addition to the colorful silk sandbags, barricades of stone were thrown up, and able-bodied civilians, many of whom were brave young men, took up arms and looked around for opportunities for heroism. U.S. Marines assumed responsibility for holding the top of the Tartar Wall, a crucial position because it looked directly down into the legation quarter from its height of seventy to eighty feet, but a dangerous one fully exposed to Chinese fire. Other troops took up positions near their legations. Although their own legation was some distance away, the task of defending the Chinese Christians fell by default to Colonel Shiba and his two dozen newly arrived Imperial Marines, who joined thirty-eight Japanese sailors and civilians already at their legation. There was little love lost between most Japanese and Chinese, but Shiba was an exception. He had been a student in China, spoke Mandarin well, and, despite having fought against China in 1894–95, would defend these Chinese with uncommon devotion.

The foreigners in the legations prepared for the worst, still having no idea what forces might be brought against them. There were many thousands of Boxers still in or near Peking; however, they possessed no firearms except for a few ancient muskets. Even though the regular troops of the Imperial Chinese Army were also numerous, and many were armed with the most modern German rifles, machine guns, and Krupp artillery, for the most part their training and morale were dismal, as the war of 1894–95 with Japan had shown. With a few exceptions, their officers were hopelessly corrupt and incompetent. Part of the troops were known in English as Bannermen. They were the descendants of the original Manchu and Mongol armies that had followed their banners, similar to regimental flags, during the seventeenth-century conquest of China. The four original colors—red, white, blue, and yellow—were later supplemented by four "bordered" banners, red bordered with blue, and so on. There were 160,000 Bannermen in Peking alone and perhaps another 300,000 elsewhere in China, but for all their grandly ornate uniforms these men, who ranged in age from sixteen to sixty, were almost purely ornamental. They might still be able to provide some useful service as police or palace guards, but they were no longer soldiers. There were also provincial troops who owed their loyalty to the viceroy of their province rather than the government in Peking. Hence the loyalty of the men in Chihli, where the Peking was located, was to Viceroy Li Hung-chang, who, as we have seen, was implacably hostile to the Iron Hats.

In addition to these largely ineffectual troops, there were regular imperial soldiers organized into divisions and more or less well armed. Five divisions of these men were in Chihli, perhaps 60,000 in all, commanded by General Jung Lu, who opposed any attack on the foreigners. Finally, Muslim troops arrived from Kansu Province to the west. They were quite willing to attack anyone, especially "foreign devils" or "barbarians"; however, not all of these men were well armed. Some had only spears or tridents, and others relied on the gingal, a nine-foot-long oversized musket that required two men to fire it. Gingals were used against the legation, but to no appreciable effect except to produce a great deal of noise and smoke. By far the best troops in China were some 7,000 well-drilled men commanded by General Yuan Shih-k'ai, who refused to allow them to participate in any of the action about to take place.

On June 8, a throng of Boxers committed a terrible act of desecration in the eyes of the foreigners—they burned down the grandstand of the Peking Racecourse, the center of social life for the Europeans. Some young British civilians rode toward the flames out of curiosity and were charged by a crowd of Boxers chanting *sha, sha*—"kill, kill." Most of the British horsemen rode away, but one turned around and killed a Boxer with his pistol. This was first blood, and it undermined the already tenuous position of the moderates in the court. As a result, Prince Tuan and his Iron Hats took control, insisting that the empress dowager issue edicts urging the Boxers to attack the legations. When she refused, he issued bogus edicts himself. The next day, large numbers of imperial troops, including the men from Kansu under their brutal leader General Tung, marched into Peking and took up positions around the legation quarter. Without consulting the other ministers, Sir Claude MacDonald telegraphed Admiral Seymour, asking him to march immediately to the relief of the legations. The following morning, Seymour telegraphed that he was on his way; then the line was cut and Peking was isolated.

More and more Boxers gathered near the legation quarter while the foreigners waited nervously for Seymour's arrival. If all had gone well, the 110-mile journey by train should have brought the troops to Peking in a few hours. Exhibiting great faith in British efficiency, the Japanese embassy's chancellor, Sugiyama Akira donned his top hat and tails before asking to be driven to the railway station to greet Seymour's troops. General Tung's soldiers dragged him out of his cart and quite literally cut him to bits, leaving his severed head and genitals prominently displayed at the station. The next day the mercurial Baron von Ketteler rashly went for a stroll just outside the legation, where he saw a man who appeared to be a Boxer. Von Ketteler immediately flogged the man with his weighted cane, causing him to flee. He also beat a boy who had been with the man and dragged him back to his legation. The court demanded that the Germans return the boy, but von Ketteler could not, because he had already shot him to death during one of his many rages.

For the next three days, Boxers, General Tung's troops, and ordinary Chinese rioted, looted, and burned, focusing their wrath on Chinese merchants who did business with foreigners and Chinese Christians. As the disorder raged around the legation quarter, armed foreigners inside the quarter opened fire on the rioters, killing substantial numbers of them. One group of fewer than 20 U.S. Marines said they had killed 350 Boxers and imperial soldiers.[13] Other nations' troops and civilians killed Chinese with similar gusto. Von Ketteler claimed to have "bagged" seven Boxers himself. The rioters had not attacked the legation quarter, but they had done so much damage outside of it that on the fifteenth, orders were issued over the emperor's name to execute immediately all armed men shouting "kill"—namely, Boxers. The troops of General Jung Lu efficiently drove the Boxers out of Peking, killing many in the process, but the Boxers did not go peacefully. When the ruins of nearby churches were later inspected, it was found that many unarmed Chinese Christians had been massacred. Some had been roasted alive, and all were badly mutilated.[14] There had still been no attack on the legations, but the many provocations by the foreigners had strengthened the Iron Hats, and the empress dowager vacillated in her opinion of the foreigners, seemingly swinging more toward Prince Tuan's belligerency.

The Chinese court gathered in extraordinary meetings to discuss the best course of action. Business was often conducted over a 150-course lunch, which everyone but the empress dowager had to eat standing up.

Many of the dishes were Chinese, but there was no rice. The Manchus preferred their native wheat bread. Urgent discussions also took place in the legations. Admiral Seymour's relief army had seemingly vanished, and he was now referred to by the British in Peking as Admiral "See-no-more." Aboard his flagship off the coast near the Taku forts, Vice-Admiral

Young Manchu woman in Peking. (A. H. Smith)

Edward Hobart Seymour had received Sir Claude's plea for help at 11 P.M. on June 9. No one could accuse him of dithering while his countrymen and women were in danger. He had anticipated the need for a relief expedition and was ready to respond. Two short hours after he read the telegram, he put ashore about 500 British marines and sailors, who seized a railroad train. They arrived at the walled city of Tientsin twenty miles inland at 3:00 A.M. and quickly drove away some Chinese guards at the railroad station, where Seymour took command of several more trains to accommodate the 1,500 troops from other countries who were now following him. By 9:30 that same morning, he was on his way toward Peking, a mere ninety miles away, a trip of only four hours on a good day! Fifteen miles along the track, Seymour's men were waved across a steel bridge over the Pei-ho River by troops of the previously moderate General Nieh. Although Nieh's men appeared to be quite friendly, it was noted that some of them were dipping their bayonets into a pan of blood that was being drained out of an unfortunate dog. However, from this point on, Seymour began to encounter damaged track, and repairs went slowly.

The admiral has been accused of dashing off rashly without knowing what he would encounter, an accurate enough accusation but one that ignores the critical need for haste. Seymour has also been accused of thinking like an admiral rather than like a general by his refusal to leave his trains and set off on foot. These accusers overlook the fact that most of his troops—915 British, over 540 Germans, 312 Russians, 157 French, 111 Americans, 54 Japanese, 47 Italians, and 26 Austrians—were strung out along the railroad to the rear. His command over these forces was tenuous at best, and he had neither the water nor the food on hand to provide for this force during what could have been several days of marching and fighting in oppressive heat. His best chance of reaching Peking was to repair the track and press on, in the hope of encountering no serious resistance.

At Lang-Fang, a little farther along the way, those hopes were dashed. A large body of Boxers wearing their red sashes and carrying large swords and spears advanced toward the hastily detrained British sailors and U.S. Marines. The Boxers proved not to be invulnerable to bullets, as they had claimed, but they were very hard to stop. One British lieutenant had to shoot a Boxer four times with his pistol at short range before the man dropped. Captain Bowman McCalla of the U.S. Navy also complained that it took more than one rifle bullet to stop the onrushing sword-swinging Boxers. Machine guns turned out to be more effective, and eighty-eight Boxer bodies were left on the field, at a cost to the allies of only five dead. These five were Italian sailors caught unawares by the Boxers.[15]

Seymour now encountered the unpleasant facts of allied mistrust. When he requested the German and French commanders to move their trains to the rear and secure a line of retreat if necessary, they refused (a rare instance of Franco-German agreement). By the next morning, it was too late. The Boxers had cut the railroad in Seymour's rear, and imperial Chinese troops were gathering to oppose his advance.

While Seymour and the fractious commanders of his foreign contingents were arguing about what to do, the allied admirals aboard their ships anchored off the mouth of the Pei-ho River were trying to decide what action to take. They knew that attacks had been made against the railroad, that the foreign settlements in Tientsin had been attacked, and that there were unconfirmed reports that Seymour's force had been attacked as well. The admirals had seen reinforcements entering the four massive forts that guarded the mouth of the Pei-ho River, two on each side, and they had also observed torpedo tubes being sited to fire into the river. They guessed that the river mouth was being mined or very soon would be. Without access to the Pei-ho River, they could not control Tientsin, and this large city not only held many Westerners in their concessions outside the walled city but was the gateway to Peking. At 10 P.M. on June 16, a Russian officer delivered an ultimatum to the viceroy of Chihli at Tientsin, giving the Chinese exactly four hours—until 2 A.M. on the seventeenth—to surrender the four forts at Taku or have them attacked by Allied forces. Knowing that the Chinese would not capitulate, the allied commanders moved ten of their smaller warships across the sandbar at the mouth of the river in preparation for bombardment and landing. These ships held 900 sailors and marines, most of them British and Japanese, but 160 Russians and 130 Germans were also available to join in the assault, along with a few Italians and Austrians. The American naval commander, Admiral Louis Kempff, refused to sign the ultimatum or engage in the attack, on the grounds that it would be an act of war, which of course it was.

The proposed attack was so risky that it was downright lunatic. The four massive forts taken from the rear in 1860 had recently been modernized by German engineers, who installed rapid-firing Krupp artillery pieces to complement older but still dependable British Armstrong cannon. The allies would attack them from the seaside, directly into their firepower. Surrounded by moats and parapets, the forts seemed impervious to the small cannon on the allied gunboats. So hastily organized that there was no clear plan and little prior coordination, the landing parties would have to charge over open ground against Chinese cannon and machine guns. The men would also have to go ashore at night in small boats. It was a recipe for disaster, but the attack nevertheless went forward. As the small ships maneuvered in the river to land their troops, Chinese guns opened fire at 1 A.M. Inexplicably, the Russian commander of the gunboat *Gilyak* responded by turning on the ship's searchlight, making the *Gilyak* and its nearby sister ship such perfect targets that even the erratic Chinese gunners could not miss. Both ships were badly damaged and eighteen Russians killed and sixty-five wounded. As other ships exchanged fire with the forts, two British destroyers sailed upriver to the Tientsin dockyards, where their boarding parties seized four of the Imperial Chinese Navy's new German-built destroyers docked there. The Chinese crews offered little resistance, and the valuable ships were towed away.

As expected, the small-caliber allied shells made little impression on the forts until a lucky shot (claimed by a French gunboat) somehow hit the magazine of one of the forts, causing an immense explosion. At 4:30 A.M., the troops landed and began what appeared to be hopeless assaults, but after the demoralizing explosion, the sight of approaching British and Japanese bayonets was not welcome to the Chinese defenders, who abandoned their guns and fled. All four forts were taken with the loss of only seven allied dead and fifteen wounded, all except two of the casualties being British and Japanese. Chinese losses were not recorded, but they were probably not heavy, although some close order fighting took place and one British lieutenant gleefully reported that he had used his pistol to "bag a brace" of Chinese.[16] The Russians had suffered only two casualties during the attack on the forts, but after their losses at sea their blood was up and their smoldering hatred of the Chinese exploded into a massacre. When an unarmed Chinese lighter ferrying civilian goods landed near a fort the Russians had occupied, they not only sank the vessel but machinegunned the surviving Chinese workmen until all were dead. Somewhere between 500 and 1,000 innocent Chinese died.[17] All fighting ended about 10 A.M., and the way upriver to Tientsin was open.

As Seymour pondered his options, more and more Chinese troops took up positions between his men and Peking, and a Chinese messenger from the legations brought the news that he should expect strong Chinese opposition. Very soon thereafter, as Seymour was discussing matters with other senior officers, a large force of General Tung's Kansu Moslems attacked the Germans, and long-range Chinese artillery fire against the trains grew heavier. Seymour had too many wounded to carry, so he decided that he had no choice but to pack his wounded onto junks he found in the Pei-ho River and attempt to march back to Tientsin along the river. Captain McCalla led the U.S. Marines, followed by the British and French troops, along the north bank of the river while the other contingents trudged along the south bank. Progress was terribly slow, partly because the junks kept grounding themselves in the shallow water and partly because the Chinese made a number of small-scale but sharp attacks on the strung-out columns.

Soon the allies were surprised to come under fire from the forty-acre-square, fortified Hsiku arsenal, which barred their path toward Tientsin. Despite the size of this complex, the largest arsenal in North China, neither Seymour nor any other of the allies had any idea that it existed. Unable to bypass the arsenal, because its guns commanded the river and because of the helpless wounded men on the junks, Seymour decided to take the position by direct attack. When neither the French nor the Russian commanders proved willing to send their troops against such a formidable fortress, Seymour disgustedly dismissed them and relied on his own men. During the morning hours, British Royal Marines and sailors stormed the arsenal at bayonet point, and the Chinese defenders soon fled, only to be intercepted and mauled by German troops. The arsenal was a cornucopia of valuables. In addition to badly needed food and medical supplies, Seymour's men found no fewer than 250 modern artillery pieces, hundreds of machine guns, at least 14,000 rifles, and several million rounds of ammunition, most of which was the same caliber as the rifles of the allied troops.[18] Although the sound of artillery fire against the foreign concessions in Tientsin only three miles away echoed ominously, Seymour was unwilling to attempt an advance against what appeared to be several Imperial Chinese Army divisions. Instead, he remained in the arsenal, where his tired troops beat off several determined attacks by Chinese troops and Boxers, led by the now hostile General Nieh.

Tientsin was under heavy siege. Stretching for a mile along the south bank of the Pei-ho River and a quarter mile or so inland toward the ancient walled city, the foreign settlements at Tientsin with their well-built stone churches, hospitals, schools, stores, warehouses, clubs, theaters, tennis courts, and polo grounds were occupied by several hundred French, British, and American businessmen, teachers, and missionaries with their assorted wives and children. An uncounted number of adventurers from various European countries also lived in this colony. When Tientsin was first seriously besieged, on June 15, it was defended primarily by 1,700 Russian soldiers who had arrived from Port Arthur too late to join Seymour's expedition, but just in time to save Tientsin and its vital railroad station. They were soon joined by a few U.S. Marines and some Royal Welch Fusiliers, commanded by Colonel the Honorable Reginald Bertie. The British and Americans marched into Tientsin together, improbably playing bugles to the tune of "There'll Be a Hot Time in the Old Town Tonight."[19] Despite the potentially awkward fact that the Royal Welch regimental colors commemorated their charge up Bunker Hill, the Royal Welch (70 percent of whom were English) and the U.S. Marines became such fast friends that they supported one another throughout the bad days to come in China, and they drink an annual toast to each other to this day.

The European civilians were joined by Chinese Christians in building barricades around the six-mile perimeter that enclosed the settlement area. Thanks to thousands of bales of merchandise such as camel's hair, wool, peanuts, sugar, cotton, and rice, a sturdy wall was thrown together; with so few armed men available, however, only one man with a rifle was available to defend every hundred yards of the barricade. The work was supervised by a future president of the United States, Herbert Hoover, then a twenty-five-year-old mining engineer, while his wife, Lou Henry, worked energetically in a makeshift hospital that quickly filled with wounded as Chinese artillery systematically battered the settlements. In all, no fewer than 60,000 shells exploded in the settlements. Had it not been for the fact that few of these Chinese-made shells held heavy explosive charges—a result, apparently, of corruption—the defenders would have been annihilated.

It was obvious that the settlements could not be held against a concerted attack, which was expected at any time, so a young English civilian named James Watts rode for help. Leaving Tientsin during a moonless night with an extra horse, he and three Cossacks who spoke no English rode out of Tientsin, hoping to bring word of the town's desperate circumstances to the allied commanders at Taku. They were fired on repeatedly as they passed through hostile villages and twice had to swim the river to evade pursuers. Watts had been taught only three words of Russian—"left," "right," and "quickly"—all of which he mispronounced badly, but despite having one horse shot out from under him, after an exhausting twelve hours in the saddle, he and the three Russians reached Taku, where they described the dire situation. Very few troops were then available to be sent to Tientsin, so only a small U.S. Marine contingent of about 100 men set off immediately. As an eighteen-year-old lieutenant named Smedley T. Butler, who was soon to become a nineteen-year-old captain and eventually commandant of the U.S. Marine Corps, recalled it, they commandeered a train, threw in as many rails and ties as they could find, and chugged off. A few miles later, they encountered a column of about 400 Russian soldiers marching along the track while carrying their obese colonel, whose feet had given out.[20] The marines took the Russians on board, and the cheerful, brawny Russians proved to be enormously valuable in repairing the damaged track because two Russians could carry a rail that four marines had to struggle with.

After repairing the track, the troops deployed and advanced slowly against suddenly murderous Chinese fire. Soon, the fire was so heavy that the marines could not advance at all. Butler found himself lying in the dirt next to his formidable commander, Major Littleton Tazewell Waller, an imperturbable veteran who would eventually make a name for himself by his frequent use of water torture to extract information from Filipino rebels.[21] Waller casually commented, "I'm waiting to hear some poor fellow shot through the head. A bullet that hits the skull sounds like a stone splashing into a pond. I haven't heard that sound for many years."[22] Young Butler later wrote that he had never heard it and did not want to start then. The Chinese fire became too much for the Russians, who ran back through the prostrate marines, who soon decided to follow their lead. After retreating for seventeen miles, they met a large column of American, British, Italian, and Russian troops coming to join them.

Exhausted, half-blinded by a howling dust storm, and under continual Chinese fire, Butler's marines were feeling like anything but a triumphant relief force. In fact, Butler's feet were so badly blistered that if a friendly Russian soldier hadn't volunteered to rub them with bacon fat, he wrote, he probably would not have been able to go on. Wearily he made dinner that night out of a tough chicken leg while watching nattily dressed British officers being served what he called an "elaborate banquet" on linen-draped tables. The British officers did not invite the grimy Americans to their mess.

On June 25, most of the Russians, accompanied by some U.S. and British troops, marched to the Hsiku arsenal with little interference by the Chinese and led Seymour's men back to Tientsin. Seymour had buried 62 men and was carrying 232 wounded.[23] In addition to the 4,000 or so troops already defending the outskirts of Tientsin, substantial reinforcements continued to arrive, including portions of the Japanese Fifth Division and the U.S. Ninth Infantry Regiment. All of these men were under the nominal command of a newly arrived British brigadier general named Arthur Dorward of the Royal Engineers, who immediately found himself snarled in a web of suspicion spun by his alleged allies. The British and Americans got on with each other reasonably well, often declaring that "blood is thicker than water," but the French distrusted the British, the American army commander, General Adna Chaffee, had no use for U.S. Marines, and they even less for him, while the Russians trusted no one, least of all the Japanese, whom they suspected of harboring designs on Manchuria. All seemed bent on achieving the glory that would come to the first troops to reach Peking, but there was often little appetite for battle, and no taste at all for cooperation.

For example, the day after Dorward took command, the Russian lieutenant general Baron Anatoly Michailovich Stoessel, soon to become infamous during the Russo-Japanese war, decided to attack a fortified arsenal outside the walled city of Tientsin without bothering to inform the British general of his intentions. His men were met by a tremendous fusillade of what sounded like rifle fire, and they fell back asking for reinforcements. When a mixed allied force came to Stoessel's relief, the men discovered to their amusement, and Stoessel's mortification, that the Chinese "fire" had been firecrackers, not bullets. A fresh advance easily drove the Chinese away. On July 2, the enigmatic Stoessel abruptly withdrew his troops from the railroad station. Caught completely by surprise, Dorward scrambled to put together a force of replacements, but the crucial station was left

*General Baron
Anatoly M. Stoessel.
(Colliers)*

undefended for almost a full day before they arrived. The Chinese obligingly did not take it for themselves.[24]

For another week, there were nightly Chinese attacks against the barricades around the settlements. In one battle, Japanese cavalry, much
maligned by Europeans because its horses, like the men who rode them,
were so small, made a spectacular charge that scattered the Chinese. On
another occasion, a rumor spread among the exhausted and panicky
European civilians that they were being sniped at by Chinese Christians
within the settlement. Led by a British navy captain named Bayly (whom
Hoover referred to as "Bully" Bayly), some armed civilians arrested 600
innocent Chinese who worked under the supervision of Hoover. Bayly
was in the process of sentencing them to death when Hoover arrived with
a platoon of Russian infantry, which saved them.

Thanks to the railroad that was still intact, enough troops had arrived
by July 13 for an assault on the Chinese walled inner city of Tientsin. The
twenty-foot-high stone wall was so thick that only a very long barrage by
siege artillery could breach it, and the allies had neither the artillery nor
the time for that, so they resolved to make a direct attack over flat, marshy
land that would be swept by gunfire from the city's walls. Some 2,500
Russians accompanied by a few Germans attacked the east gate of the city

while something on the order of 1,500 Japanese and about 600 French, 900 American, 800 British, and a few Austrians prepared to attack the south gate. While the Russians maneuvered around to the east, the other allies stormed the south face of the wall, only to meet devastating fire and fall ignominiously on their faces in the muck. Pinned down, they suffered heavy losses, especially the Americans, who lost 150 men, including the elderly commanding colonel of the U.S. Ninth Infantry, Emerson H. Liscum, shot in the abdomen while trying to save the Stars and Stripes from falling in the mud when the flag's bearer was killed.

There was no forward movement, even by the intrepid Japanese. However, the easy-to-see, white-uniformed Japanese would attack again that night. Before doing so, the Japanese commander, General Fukushima Yasumasa, managed to persuade Dorward not to surround the walled city but to leave two gates free for the predicted escape of the Chinese troops. Fukushima was an intelligent and enterprising officer who had spent the entire year of 1892 spying in Siberia on horseback, after leaving an assignment in Berlin, and he had fought against the Chinese before. He was certain that they would run if given a chance, but he quite correctly feared that if the Chinese were trapped, they would fight to the end. At 3 A.M., Japanese engineers rushed the south gate, and a few survived to plant an enormous explosive charge. They returned to a safe distance, unreeling the wire that would allow them to detonate it electrically. As fortune had it, a bullet severed the line and the charge could not be exploded. While the allied troops lay in the mud wondering if they would live through another day of intense Chinese fire from the high stone city wall, a Japanese lieutenant named Inawe grabbed a box of matches and the only fuse he could find, a very short one. Surviving Chinese fire, he lighted the charge, which blew the gate to pieces. No trace of the lieutenant's body was found. The Americans, who owed their lives to Inawe's bravery, could not praise the Japanese too highly.

Even before Japanese troops swarmed through the gate, the Chinese had begun their retreat. When the other allied soldiers entered the ancient walled city, they threw themselves into looting with such enthusiasm that many greatly enriched themselves with large amounts of silver and gold, not to mention works of art. Some liberated so much of value that they could not carry it all. A British correspondent, the well-known Henry Savage Landor, remarked on the different styles of looting employed by the various nationalities. First, he noted that the civilians who knew where the wealthier shops were outdid all the soldiers in making off with valuables. The British were interested in souvenirs for their families, the few Japanese who looted did so in a "silent, quiet and graceful way," while the Germans, French, Americans, and Russians were said to be incapable of touching anything that was not solid bronze without breaking it.[25] A Japanese officer who observed the looting with horror asked an American newsman if international law had changed since he had been instructed about it. The American could only shrug.[26]

While some troops of the allied forces were stealing everything they could lay their hands on, others were killing with equivalent dedication. Chinese shopkeepers were shot in cold blood, as were other ordinary residents of Tientsin who were merely trying to avoid the deadly foreigners. Later, all the victims were said to have been Boxers. Other troops raped any more or less attractive woman they could find. One U.S. Marine wrote that Germans and Russians, in particular, bayoneted these women after raping them. Several U.S. Marines, hardly squeamish men, were so sickened by what they saw that they violently restrained some of their more rapacious German allies, leaving at least one wounded. But the carnage went on and on.[27] The West learned little of these horrors. The only newspaper correspondents on hand pulled their punches about what happened in Tientsin, just as they did about most of the similar outrages committed by the Western troops once they reached Peking.[28]

The only troops to be absolved of blame in this nightmare of savagery were the Japanese. This was quite surprising to the allies, who had expected the Japanese, like the Chinese, to be both militarily inept and sadistically brutal. Although praised by some Western observers, the Japanese victory over the Chinese in 1895 had been dismissed by most of the allies as one bad army fighting an even worse one. When the Japanese troops first arrived in Tientsin in their all-white uniforms, cooling themselves with small fans, they seemed absurdly effete, even effeminate to the Westerners. However, their courage in storming the walled city changed European minds quickly.[29] Fearful of being thought guilty of territorial ambitions in China, Japan had committed troops to the expedition only after repeated requests by European powers, particularly Britain, whose own troops were bogged down in the Boer War. Britain actually offered to pay the cost of sending more than one division of Japanese troops to

China, but Japan declined, saying modestly that the 22,000 men of the Fifth Division under Lieutenant General Yamaguchi Motoomi would be quite enough to deal with the situation. The Japanese had gained direct knowledge of the fighting qualities of Chinese troops only five years earlier and had no reason to believe that they had improved.[30] Not only had the Japanese fought more bravely than any other nation's men at Tientsin, they had behaved toward the Chinese with consistent decency. And despite fighting in mud and dark brown dust, they even managed to keep their white uniforms clean.[31]

While the savage, deadly, and almost totally unreported Battle of Tientsin was being played out and more and more allied troops arrived, the legation quarter at Peking was under a siege that was sometimes downright phony, and only now and then serious, but always dramatic. It began in earnest on June 19 when the ministers were debating a Chinese offer of safe passage to Tientsin. Confused about the situation in Tientsin, they asked for more details. When there was no immediate answer, Baron von Ketteler slammed his fist on a table and declared that he would go to the Foreign Office alone, and despite every effort to dissuade him, he set off in a sedan chair accompanied only by his interpreter. A Bannerman lance corporal recognized the German minister and killed him with a single rifle shot. There can be no doubt that von Ketteler was a marked man. In fact, the *Times* of London reported his murder four days before it took place.[32] A day later, the eccentric professor Huberty James, who was responsible for the idea that led to the eviction of Prince Su from his palace, was killed by Chinese sharpshooters. This apparent revenge killing also had been expected by the ministers.

The legation quarter was surrounded by two major armed forces. General Tung Fu-hsiang's red-uniformed Kansu regulars were relatively loyal to Prince Tuan and thoroughly hostile to the foreigners. However, there were relatively few of them in Peking compared with the imperial troops of General Jung Lu, who, unlike Tung, was determined to do everything he could to protect the foreigners. However, both Chinese forces attacked the Chinese Christians so often that all but a handful of their Japanese defenders were wounded at least once. The Italian sailors who were asked to support the Japanese were less than reckless with their lives. An American woman captured the prevailing opinion about them when she wrote, "One can only hope for Italy's sake her soldiers in Peking are the worst she has."[33] Some of the Chinese Christians who had been armed fought well, as did the Chinese-born British civilian volunteer Bertram Lenox-Simpson. Under the pseudonym of B. L. Putnam Weale, he wrote an account of his experiences in which he praised the discipline and valor of the Japanese as well as their kindness to the Chinese Christians, whom they alone among the foreigners did their best to feed. They even managed to find toys for the children.[34]

Except for attacks against the Chinese Christians, Jung Lu's men intentionally fired high, and although they made every effort to appear murderous by letting loose endless barrages, they seldom hit Europeans. Jung Lu's challenge was how to appear to be destroying the legations without actually doing so. The fortunate Europeans believed that the Chinese simply could not shoot straight and apparently never understood they were being spared. They also did not understand that heavy artillery could have been targeted against them at any time, because Jung Lu had large numbers of modern Krupp cannon, but they were shelled only very briefly, with relatively little damage. A few days of heavy shelling would have flattened the legations.

Life in the legation compound was hardly pleasant as bullets constantly flew overhead and now and then hit someone, but conditions were never truly desperate. There was always enough food that the foreigners in the legations did not go hungry; nor did they suffer from a lack of water or champagne. Meals became boring after a while, and toward the end of the siege the foreigners were reduced to eating sandy, uncleaned rice with their meals, but there was no real suffering. The same cannot be said of the wretched Christian Chinese. A young American woman referred to their condition as "the agony of relentless, hideous starvation."[35] Every one of the many trees in the heat-baked legation compound had been stripped of its leaves and bark for food. Now and then when a sentry killed a stray dog or one of the carrion crows that picked at corpses, it was given to the Chinese, who ravenously ate them "without a pretense of cooking."[36] Aside from the Japanese, the foreigners did not share their food supplies with the Chinese except for half of the "inedible parts" of the two horses that were shot each morning. No one, not even the missionaries, seems to have argued that the Europeans should share their supplies with the starving Chinese Christians.

This oversight was not the only evidence that many foreigners thought solely of themselves. Some able-bodied men remained barricaded in their rooms throughout the siege, and more than a few men and women alike remained so comfortably drunk on the massive supplies of liquor in the legation quarters that they contributed nothing to the defense or well-being of the quarter.[37] Some of the military personnel, too, were harshly criticized for their lack of fighting spirit. The Italians, Austrians (who were actually Yugoslavs), and some of the French (who were from Brittany) came in for such criticism. The other nationalities were not pleased when the French commander flatly refused a request to reinforce the U.S. Marines on the dangerously exposed Tartar Wall.[38] The U.S. Marines were also criticized—for their heavy drinking and lack of discipline, not for their lack of courage. Their alcohol intake was defended by many because their position atop the Tartar Wall was the most dangerous one occupied by any of the foreign troops. They were also acknowledged to be the best marksmen of any of the nationalities. The Russians earned high marks for their courage, and so did the British, but the Japanese consistently won the highest praise from the Europeans. Lancelot Giles, a young student in the British legation and one of many civilians who displayed heroism throughout the siege, reflected the general opinion of the Europeans when he wrote this about Colonel Shiba: "He is considered the best officer up here, just as the Japanese are undoubtedly the best soldiers. Their pluck and daring is astounding, our marines are next to them in this respect, but I think the Japanese lead the way."[39] In confirmation of Giles's view, Shiba would later receive a British knighthood for his heroism.

That everyone agreed about Japanese heroism was truly remarkable, for the Westerners could agree about little else. The British and Americans in the legation quarter got on reasonably well with one another but were seldom the best of friends. The Americans had their warmest relations with the Russians, whom they fondly referred to as "our Rooskis." It seems that the Russian commander, Baron von Raden—a superb marksman who enjoyed sniping at the Chinese every day—had ordered his poorly trained men to fight next to the U.S. Marines as much as possible in order to learn the trade of war, and although neither side could speak the other's language, they got along famously. The British, in turn, were enamored of the Japanese. The French, Belgians, and Austrians tended to interact among themselves and to avoid cooperation with the other forces, while the Germans were said to "fraternize with no one."[40]

One thing that all except the Japanese shared was contempt for the Chinese who had attacked them and an indifference toward the Chinese who endured the siege with them. Not only were the Chinese Christians not fed; Chinese women who were unwary at night were likely to be raped, and such acts were never prosecuted.[41] Even before the siege began, the troops and armed civilians of all nations had shown themselves willing to shoot Chinese outside the legations without first concerning themselves about their hostility or guilt. Killing them was considered akin to sport, and hunting metaphors such as "bagging" game were in general use. The queues of dead Chinese were kept as trophies. Civilians joined military men during midnight raids outside the legations in search of Chinese to kill. All Chinese were considered to be Boxers and fair game, as Bertram Lenox-Simpson recounted: "I marked down one man and drove an old sword at his chest. The fellow howled frightfully, and just as I was about to dispatch him a French sailor saved me the trouble by stretching him out with a resounding thump on the head with his Lebel rifle. The Boxer curled up like a sick worm and expired."[42] The young braves inside the legations killed many Chinese in this cavalier manner. That the Chinese, Boxers or not, might be human seemed not to enter anyone's mind.

Captured Chinese were almost invariably shot as Boxers without the necessity of proof or trial. Many of these executions were cruelly callous, but none could match those carried out by the French after a patrol captured eighteen Chinese in a temple near the legations, tied their hands, and led them to the French legation. The prisoners vehemently denied that they were Boxers, and as this was July 10, well after the Boxers had been driven out of Peking, it is likely that they were telling the truth. If so, the French were not listening. After executing three men with rifle shots, a French corporal decided not to "waste" ammunition on the rest. Instead, he bayoneted each man in the stomach, leaving all to die a very slow, excruciatingly painful death. We are left to imagine their screams as well as the state of mind of their executioner as he impaled one after another while the remaining victims looked on in terror.[43]

The siege of the Peking legations was not intended to kill all the foreigners. If it had been, nothing would have been easier for the Chinese than to use their many heavy German artillery pieces to batter the barricades and buildings to rubble, then send in thousands of infantry. Nothing of the sort happened. The occasional artillery fire that took place was always terminated before any significant damage had been done, and all-out attack by infantry never took place. The world was given to believe otherwise, however, as blaring headlines announcing the massacre of all foreigners appeared around the world. As early as July 4, the *New York Times* reported that all the foreigners had been killed, and on the sixteenth the London *Daily Mail*, followed presently by the *New York Times,* graphically described how Chinese artillery had battered the British legation to pieces before Chinese infantry closed in. Out of ammunition, the foreigners were said to have used their revolvers to kill their women and children before fighting to the death with their swords. Eventually all were slaughtered, their heads paraded through Peking on the bayonets of Chinese rifles.

This apocalyptic scene might have happened, of course, but it did not. The news services received this and other misinformation from Li Hung-chang, whose ownership of the Chinese telegraph service served him in very good stead as he once again did all he could to visit the wrath of Europe and Japan on his enemies in Peking. He succeeded brilliantly. Newspapers throughout Europe printed obituaries, funeral plans were made at St. Paul's Cathedral, and heads of state vowed vengeance, none more vehemently than Kaiser Wilhelm, who backed up his words by immediately dispatching 30,000 German troops bent on terrible revenge.[44] That Li Hung-chang's dispatches were entirely false mattered not. When the siege of Peking ended after fifty-five days, 66 foreigners had died of wounds and 3 of disease, and over 150 had been wounded, most not seriously. How many Chinese Christians, Boxers, and Chinese soldiers were killed or wounded will never be known. It was seldom noted that many more European lives had been lost during Seymour's abortive rescue attempt, and still more during the battles at Tientsin. Allied casualties at Tientsin were close to 1,000, and the loss of Chinese life was certainly much greater. But the killing of Chinese had just begun. Now they would be killed with impunity on a grand scale.

Impressed by the vast numbers of well-armed Chinese troops that opposed them, the second relief column would not repeat Seymour's rashness. For one thing, many of the troops were sick. Sanitation was terrible, diarrhea spread rapidly, and flies were so abundant that men could not sleep at night without mosquito nets, of which there were enough only for officers. Seemingly no one was eager to push off for Peking. There were too few Germans, Italians, or Austrians available to matter, and the French had so little confidence in the poorly trained Indo-Chinese infantry, which represented almost all of their force, that they were in no hurry to start. The Americans were worried about their lack of artillery and the Russians about their lack of cavalry, and General Dorward, who had seen modern Chinese weapons exact a heavy toll of his troops at Tientsin, argued that the allies should build up to 60,000 men before marching. The allied delay in getting under way to rescue the legations in Peking was not due solely to disputes about the shortage of troops; locating transportation for supplies was a major problem. There was a shortage of horses not only in China but worldwide in the aftermath of the Boer War, in South Africa, where 350,000 horses had been killed. Because so few Chinese would cooperate after the Russians had slaughtered so many civilians—shooting at every Chinese they saw, as one newsman reported—there was also a shortage of porters.[45] To make matters worse, the railroad had been torn to pieces, and junks that could sail up the Pei-ho River had been either sunk or taken inland by the Chinese.[46]

As the allied army slowly grew, the question of selecting an overall commander became a point of increasing contention. General Yamaguchi was the senior officer among them, but the European forces had little enthusiasm for serving under a Japanese, and the Germans found the idea to be out of the question, insisting on a Christian commander. After much dispute, it was finally decided that all would serve under Alfred von Waldersee, but the field marshal and his 30,000 men were inconveniently still in Germany. With the arrival of an Indian army brigade commanded by Lieutenant General Sir Alfred Gaselee, Dorward would step aside for the more senior British general, who would serve as interim commander. In addition to a few Germans, Italians, and Austrians, Gaselee would command a naval brigade of almost 600 British marines and sailors, 300 men of the Twenty-third Royal Welch Fusiliers, 1,300 men of the First Indian Brigade, a small force of Gurkhas, 200 Chinese under British officers, and various engineers and signalmen—almost 3,000 all told. He would also have over 2,000 Americans, including the newly arrived Ninth and Fourteenth Infantry Regiments from the Philippines, where they had been in combat against Filipinos; 1,200 French; and nearly 3,000 Russians, principally the First East Siberia Regiment. But Gaselee's major strength was the Japanese; they provided nine battalions of infantry, six batteries of artillery, and four squadrons of cavalry—9,000 men and twenty-four guns, almost twice as much firepower as the artillery of any other nationality. Another 25,000 Russian and Japanese troops were left behind to protect the Taku forts, the railroad, and Tientsin.

Young Smedley Butler of the U.S. Marines, just promoted to captain, marveled at the pageantry as the fresh troops finally marched out of Tientsin on August 4. The Japanese were still dressed all in white (very clean, he noted), the Russians wore white blouses over black trousers tucked into long leather boots (not so clean), while the Americans were in nondescript khaki trousers and blue shirts (filthy). He was especially taken by the newly arrived French Zouaves in blue jackets with flaring red pantaloons, blond Germans in spiked helmets, turbaned Sikhs, Bengal Lancers mounted on Arabian stallions, and Italian Bersaglieri with long black plumes on their hats.[47] Unfortunately for parade-ground pageantry, the Germans and Italians would soon turn back for lack of transport, the French would contribute nothing, except to mistakenly fire on their allies now and then, and the Bengal Lancers would be sharply criticized for not pursuing retreating Chinese forces.[48]

With the partial exception of the Japanese, who sometimes marched at the head of the allied forces very early in the morning, all the men suffered terribly from the heat, dust, flies, and mosquitoes. The temperature reached 140 degrees Fahrenheit in the sun, prostrating men of all the armies, even the Indians, who had never felt such heat in their often scorching homeland.[49] Artillery horses actually dropped dead in their traces. When dehydrated infantrymen shoved aside their protesting officers to drink from polluted wells, their indiscipline was ignored.[50] Butler estimated that half his men fell out because of the heat and dropped behind in search of wells. As the young marine captain learned, the Chinese turned this into a dangerous activity. While resting in a village where he found some welcome melons, Butler was horrified to discover two Japanese soldiers nailed to a door, their eyes and tongues cut out. Butler hurried back to the relative safety of his marine company.[51]

Unlike soldiers of several other armies who delighted in whipping Chinese villagers for the apparent sport of it, the Americans and Japanese rarely engaged in gratuitous violence. However, when they felt justified, both could be deadly. When a Chinese prisoner deserted his position and offered to fight with the Japanese against the Chinese, they regarded him with such disgust that they kicked him to death.[52] Regarding sniping by civilians as an unlawful as well as a deadly act, they sometimes took extreme measures. As an American officer from the Ninth Infantry looked on, after heavy sniper fire came from a nearby village, the Japanese rounded up twelve Chinese men thought to be guilty and shot them. Still, the Japanese were not perceived by the other allies or by most Chinese as brutal.

The same American officer from the Ninth Infantry was astonished by Russian disciplinary practices. Through no fault of his own, a Russian soldier lost control of a cart, dumping it off a bridge into a river. The man dived in and managed to save the horse from drowning and retrieved the cart. His reward was to stand at attention holding a salute while an officer screamed at him and repeatedly punched him in the face.[53] Russian soldiers were often guilty of casual brutality, kicking and whipping any Chinese they met before impressing them into duty as porters who carried their equipment while being steered by their pigtails. An American correspondent was appalled when he saw a Russian soldier crush the skull of a four-year-old Chinese boy for no reason, and Cossacks sometimes killed children just as casually.[54] The Japanese were shocked by the brutality of the Russians, who regularly shot Chinese as if they were rabbits and frequently fired heavy artillery at harmless Chinese houses for no reason that their allies could discover.[55]

The allies were opposed by somewhere between 50,000 and 100,000 Chinese troops, most of whom were well equipped. However, the majority were poorly led, and almost all were angry because they had not been paid for months. Nevertheless, large Chinese forces dug in on both sides of the river at a place called Peitang, about five miles north of Tientsin. The Chinese fought with determination, and the fighting became hand-to-hand before an attack by Japanese troops drove them back. An observer close to the action was shocked by the thudding sound made by Japanese bayonets as they were driven into the chests of Chinese soldiers and by the burst of air that followed as the lungs were pierced.[56] The Japanese lost close to 300 men; the Chinese, many more. The next day, the Chinese made another stand, and this time it was the Americans and British who drove them back. After this, there was only desultory fighting until August 14, when, after the Russians stole a march on the Japanese in an attempt to be the first into Peking, they managed to get lost. British-led Sikhs walked in to the city through an unguarded gate while Japanese, American, and Russian troops had to shoot their way in.

The allied forces had little difficulty with the Chinese troops, but they encountered many difficulties among themselves. The main thing they all agreed on was that being the first to relieve the legations was an honor that should fall to them. Although there was little camaraderie among the men of different armies, the American, British, and Japanese generally got along well. In addition to the close friendships that developed between the men of the Royal Welch Regiment and the U.S. Marines—but not between British and American soldiers in Peking—those in the relief columns often shared their canteens, helped men who had fallen out because of the heat, and commented on their Anglo-American kinship. Officers exchanged dinners, singing and laughing together. One British officer wrote that he was "very taken with the simple, homely hospitality and cheeriness of the Americans."[57]

Everyone was impressed by the Japanese. The same officer wrote this: "The Japs are perfectly splendid, like little terriers, as keen and plucky as they can be. Their wounded never uttered a sound, and I saw lots carried past me with terrible wounds, some actually joking with the stretcher bearers. Their whole arrangements are so wonderful. If a Jap is hit, there's always a doctor on the spot, mounted well, with the latest surgical jinns [magic cures]."[58] All the others came in for criticism. The British and Americans complained that the Russians were slow to move, and the French were considered to be shirkers.[59] The Indian troops did not like the French or the Russians, and the Germans were unpopular with everyone. Some men of the Royal Welch Fusiliers had such a serious brawl with German troops that four Germans were killed. It was said at the time that the British commander jailed the men not for fighting and killing four men but for failing to kill all the Germans.[60]

When the red-turbanned Sikhs entered the legation quarter, one of them was startled to receive a hug from an overjoyed Englishwoman who temporarily forgot her racial superiority.[61] The always kind and considerate British general Gaselee later rode in to find most of the foreigners safe. He was so relieved that he wept for joy. When the U.S. infantry finally arrived, the legation women found them too dirty and sweat-soaked to be hugged. The Americans were not just filthy; after two months in China, their uniforms were in such tatters that most men wore brightly colored

Chinese silk shirts and all wore Chinese red silk boots. The pretty Lady MacDonald went from group to group of allied soldiers, saying that she didn't know who they were but that she was delighted to see them.[62] The American civilians in clean tennis trousers and their wives in lawn dresses managed to do next to nothing to welcome the exhausted U.S. Marines and infantry who had "saved" them.[63]

Everyone in the legations knew that a large number of Europeans and Chinese Christians had been besieged in the Peitang cathedral, two miles north of the legation quarter. There had been no news from them since the siege began, and recently no gunfire had been heard. There was every reason to fear the worst. Bishop Favier had the foresight to fortify the sprawling Catholic compound, which contained a number of substantial buildings in addition to the cathedral itself. But he had only 2 officers, one French and one Italian, along with 43 French and Italian marines to guard 50 European church workers, including 22 sisters, as well as about 3,400 Chinese Christians. Unlike the legations, where days passed with only halfhearted attacks or none at all, Peitang was attacked every day, often several times, and was continually showered with flaming arrows and pounded by artillery. Food was so desperately scarce that all the besieged

American legation with stone barrier. (A. H. Smith)

were very weak and some actually starved. The civilians were not armed, but some of the women did what they could to fend off the Boxers. In fact, the Boxers, who were joined by imperial Chinese troops in the attack, later said that the only reason they failed to take the compound was that their magical powers were counteracted by the Chinese Christian women who stood on the barricades, boldly exposing their genitals to them.[64]

The success of the Christians' fight against the determined Chinese forces testifies to the courage of all these besieged people and to the inspired leadership of a marvelously brave and dedicated twenty-three-year-old French navy lieutenant named Paul Henry, who was killed near the end of the siege. Against seemingly hopeless odds, the young Breton lieutenant tirelessly urged his men to defend their barricades, and more than once led French marines on sorties against the Boxers that led to the capture of a cannon. He instilled discipline and the spirit of defiance so well that, even after he was killed by a rifle bullet on July 29, the defenders were able to hold out until August 16.[65]

General Chaffee and the U.S. Fourteenth Infantry were the second to reach the legation quarter, but Chaffee was determined to be the first into the Forbidden City. Early the next day, without a word to any of the other allied commanders, Chaffee ordered his men to blast down the huge doors to the sanctum. As they did so, they came under heavy artillery fire, not from the Chinese but from the French, who, instead of hurrying to rescue their compatriots and coreligionists in the Peitang compound, were determined to beat Chaffee into the Forbidden City. The French commander later explained that he mistook the Americans for Chinese, an explanation that did nothing to satisfy Chaffee, who broke off the attack after fifteen Americans had been killed and others wounded by the French fire.

At a meeting of the allied commanders, Russians convinced Chaffee that the destruction of the Forbidden City would serve no purpose. Although there was still time that afternoon after the conference to march the short two miles to Peitang, the only European to make an effort on behalf of the starving Christians was an elderly priest, Father d'Addosio, who rode off alone on a donkey to do what he could. He was killed before he could get halfway there.[66] The following day, a French-led multinational force finally made its way to Peitang, against no opposition. To their profound embarrassment, they discovered that the Japanese had liberated the cathedral's survivors the previous day. They also discovered that over

300 Chinese Catholics had died, along with close to 100 orphans and 60 Europeans. Some had starved to death only the day before. Nevertheless, Bishop Favier led the survivors in a patriotic welcome of the liberators. Minister Pichon, who accompanied the force, wept as usual.[67] Everyone ignored the Japanese, who looked on silently.

Many of the allied attitudes of rivalry and hostility were of long standing, whereas others sprang up during the campaign, only to persist in later years, but however much the allies mistrusted and disliked one another, they were eager to loot. Most of the Chinese in Peking had fled, leaving their homes, stores, warehouses, temples, and offices empty. Men of all the allied armies carried away everything of value not already stolen by the more astute diplomats who knew where to look for treasure. Led by what one observer called "the curs who never raised a finger to touch a gun" during the siege, these representatives of their governments made off with priceless jade, gold, silver, furs, and silk.[68] Restrained by Generals Gaselee and Chaffee, who hated looting, the British and Americans looted the least (they were under orders not to do so at all), but the Japanese did very well by themselves. They tunneled below the Treasury Building, and before any of the other allies could break into the building, made off with silver bullion worth one million pounds. All that the disappointed allies found inside when they arrived was a huge silver ingot that was too heavy to carry. What the foreigners could not take away in commandeered carts they smashed. As the plundering was well under way, the Prussian field marshal Count von Waldersee arrived with his 30,000 German troops, wearing jaunty straw hats that made them seem more like summer vacationers than avenging Huns. General Gaselee had done his best to prevent looting, but Waldersee changed all that! Complaining that the Americans apparently wanted to prevent everyone from making a profit from the war, he encouraged his men to loot.

While von Waldersee established himself in the Winter Palace with a lovely Chinese courtesan, his men made up for lost time by methodically looting everything that had not already been carted off. The kaiser had, after all, ordered his men to behave "just as the Huns of a thousand years ago."[69] Inspired by the kaiser's orders to take no prisoners and give no quarter, von Waldersee's men killed Chinese in wholesale numbers, as the count himself freely admitted, saying in a letter to the kaiser, "That many Chinese are shot is quite true."[70] This was hardly surprising, given von

Waldersee's declaration that he would deal with the Chinese by using "as strong and relentless measures as possible."[71] He went on to write that he had personally witnessed "countless executions." When we consider that he spent most of his time in Peking, not in the countryside where his troops were executing any Chinese who seemed even remotely troublesome, he may well have understated the number of executions that actually took place.

The Germans methodically shot Chinese, usually claiming that they were Boxers, and the Russians, as we noted earlier, did the same. A Royal Welch soldier shot an innocent Chinese with a dumdum bullet just to witness the effect,[72] and when the U.S. Fifteenth Infantry entered Peking, it posted men to lie in wait at the head of each street to shoot any Chinese who appeared.[73] In addition to the slaughter in Peking itself, allied troops carried out raids into the countryside, where they continued to kill anyone they could possibly link to the Boxers. These punitive raids, particularly by the Germans and Russians, continued for well over a year after the siege was lifted. Few prisoners were taken, and Chinese wounded were almost always killed, seldom humanely. Although some of the allies were much more given to rape than others, one eyewitness reported that soldiers of all the Western nations sometimes raped and then bayoneted Chinese girls and women.[74] In addition to these raids, the Americans and British paid General Yuan Shih-k'ai, leader of China's best troops, whom he had kept out of action against the allies, to cleanse Chihli Province of any taint of Boxer influence. It is estimated that Yuan's men killed over 45,000 people in Chihli alone and many more in Shantung.[75] The European forces may have been able to plead revenge as a motive because some 240 missionaries, along with their wives and children, had been tortured and killed by Boxers and imperial troops, but the killing by Yuan's men was simply professional butchery on an immense scale.

While this slaughter was taking place, the troops billeted in Peking had a great deal of time on their hands. They staged parades, which the troops heartily disliked, and the French, now reinforced by troops from metropolitan France, put on a dramatic evening festival under strings of bright lights. While military bands played, chasseurs on all-gray horses pranced by, followed by artillery caissons and infantry singing martial songs. Even the British were favorably impressed. For their part, the British played soccer and arranged several days of competition in infantry drills, rifle calisthenics, bayonet exercises, and tug-of-war contests. The only contribution by the Americans was to play baseball games, in which British officers were said to have taken "some" interest. What they used as bats, balls, and gloves is not recorded, but the camp championship was won by the Ninth Infantry enlisted men over their officers by a score of four runs to three. Also, a comic opera lampooning the empress dowager was staged to the obvious delight of all who saw it.[76]

The Japanese were the first of the allies to establish order in their sector of Peking, and it was to this sector that the Chinese first felt it safe to return. Japan's behavior in her district of Peking was called "exemplary." For instance, when Russian troops entered the district to loot or rape, they were arrested and returned to their units.[77] Hoping to distance herself from the European powers, all of whom had given the Japanese abundant evidence of the "lurking evil intentions" Japan tried not to express, she was the first nation to withdraw troops from China, and by accepting a Chinese request that she act as a mediator, the only nation even partly to put forward Chinese interests.[78] The Japanese hoped that expressions of friendship might win their country what victory on the battlefield five years earlier had not.

The negotiations between the Manchu court and the various powers could hardly have been more complicated. The court did not know whom to punish—although it finally agreed to strip the conservative Prince Tuan of his rank and exile him to Kansu—and each allied power had different demands. Germany wanted Chinese blood for the murder of von Ketteler; Japan wanted Chinese friendship to counter the Russian occupation of Manchuria. The other powers wanted an indemnity and trading concessions. After much controversy among the allies, they set the indemnity at the stunning sum of £67.5 million. Based on a formula for lives lost and property damaged, 29 percent was to go to Russia for her brutal but often ineffectual efforts, and 20 percent to Germany, whose troops did nothing to relieve the legations but later expended considerable amounts of ammunition in killing Chinese. For her feeble efforts, France would receive 15.75 percent, while Britain, which played such a crucial role, got only 11.25 percent. Japan, whose men did the most to save the legations, received a mere 7.7 percent, while the United States received 7.3 percent. Italy, which contributed virtually nothing, nevertheless received 5.9 percent.[79] There were other, relatively minor stipulations, but the sticking point for China and the allies was Russia's insistence that China sign a treaty that would not only indemnify Russia for damage to the Chinese Eastern Railroad but give her the exclusive right to maintain troops in Manchuria and exploit its wealth.

While the slaughter around Peking to the south was still taking place, and long before peace talks began, the Russians in Manchuria were consolidating their gains. Many Russian leaders had been openly elated when the Boxer-led hostilities in Manchuria broke out, recognizing that it gave Russia a perfect opportunity to seize this Chinese province. Now that the riches of Manchuria in timber, gold, coal, iron, and agricultural produce could be Russia's, and the ice-free harbor of Port Arthur gave Russia year-round access to the sea, there was no thought of returning Manchuria to the Chinese. At the cost of only 22 officers and 220 men killed, plus 60 officers and 1,223 men wounded, Russia had added an enormous asset to her empire. Thousands of Russian workmen aided by hundreds of thousands of Chinese "coolies" rapidly transformed ancient Manchurian towns into modern cities with parks, banks, churches, electric lights, and innumerable European-style offices and houses of red brick and stone. In a single year, Mukden's population trebled, transforming a relatively small Chinese city into a cosmopolitan city complete with American prostitutes and at least one African-American businessman.[80] An English observer of this remarkable development worried that it would prove as difficult for the Russians to abandon their new cities and the mineral and agricultural riches of Manchuria as it was for the British to leave Egypt. However, that is precisely what officials of several foreign capitals insisted that Russia do, none more vocally or threateningly than the Japanese, who continued to think of Manchuria as their future.

Many prominent members of the Japanese oligarchy had called for war with Russia as early as 1900, and Japanese newspapers, which already had large circulations, had become even more passionately chauvinistic than the country's leaders. Yet Japan's leaders were aware that war against Russia might well lead to defeat, and that war against both Russia and France, then Russia's ally, could be catastrophic. In an effort to even the balance of power, Japan had long coveted an alliance with Britain. Britain's sphere of interest in China was to the south in Hong Kong and the rich Yangtze River basin, not north in Manchuria or Korea, but Britain was increasingly concerned about the extension of Russian power in Asia, as well as the long-standing and growing threat that imperial Russia might move south toward India. In January 1902, while Russia was investing massively in developing Manchuria, Britain agreed to a five-year mutual defense treaty with Japan. Each party was to take any steps it deemed necessary to protect its interests in China and Japan, yet was free to remain neutral in the event of war unless that war involved a third party, in which case both Japan and Britain would be obliged to come to the other's aid. A few months later, under growing pressure from Tokyo and other foreign capitals, Russia agreed to withdraw her troops from Manchuria in three stages over a period of eighteen months unless there were further "disturbances," a clause vague enough to give them wide latitude for maneuver.

Despite the continuing international pressure, instead of leaving Manchuria, 30,000 Russian troops were declared to be "railroad guards," not soldiers. In April 1903, more Russian troops began moving to the Yalu River valley, where they built permanent settlements and began to cut timber for the Bezobrazov concession on the Korean side of the river as well as in Manchuria.[81] Japan responded angrily, as might be expected, demanding that at the very least Russia guarantee Japanese suzerainty over Korea. Russia flatly rejected this demand. Within twenty-four hours of its receipt, the tsar appointed the fervently anti-Japanese admiral Yevgyeni Alexeiev—believed by members of Russia's nobility to be the illegitimate son of Tsar Alexander II and an Armenian mother—to the post of viceroy of the Far East with supreme civil and military powers. This clear signal of Russian intransigence was followed by a Russian demand that Japan recognize Manchuria as being outside her sphere of influence and, moreover, that she restrict her interests in Korea to the area south of the thirty-ninth parallel. Despite angry calls for immediate war by many powerful Japanese leaders, the government, including General Yamagata, continued to seek peace and responded with a compromise offer. Repeated Japanese inquiries notwithstanding, the offer elicited no Russian response whatsoever. The tsar and most of his advisers were convinced that Japanese war preparations were a bluff. The "monkeys," Nicholas insisted, would never dare to confront the might of the Russian empire. Even Japan's British allies were far from certain that Japan would go to war or that she could defeat Russia if she did.[82]

On January 5, 1904, the U.S. secretary of state, John Hay, wrote in his diary that there was no hope of peace, because Russia was determined "to crush Japan and to eliminate her from her position of influence in the Far East."[83] Japan had reached the same conclusion. As January dragged on without a Russian response, Japanese military leaders became convinced that Russia was merely stalling for time to improve her military readiness. Even so, Japan was reluctant to risk world censure by striking the first blow, being well aware that European powers would be quick to condemn Asian aggression.[84] So concerned were Japanese leaders about what they saw as European racism, that the prime minister sent an urbane, British-educated envoy to Britain. Baron Suematsu Kencho (Law Trypos at Cambridge in 1885) had earlier served in the Japanese legation in London. A former high-ranking member of the Japanese government, he was openly pro-British. His assignment was to use the press to convince the British people that the Japanese had acted against Russia in self-defense, because, he was told, "the so-called doctrine of the Yellow Peril readily moves the hearts of western peoples and is nowadays popular on the continent. If we do not combat this doctrine with all our power, there is a danger that European countries will actually join together against us."[85]

Japan's military preparations were already complete, and her military advisers believed that the passage of time could only lessen her chances of success should war come. Japan's chief of the army general staff was Field Marshal Oyama Iwao, who had led Japanese forces against China in 1894–95. He was a large, hot-tempered man married to a dainty Vassar graduate who had spent twelve years in the United States, one of the first five Japanese women to be sent abroad.[86] On February 1, 1904, satisfied that a Harvard-educated classmate of Theodore Roosevelt's would be sent to America to obtain the president's good offices if the war went badly for Japan, Oyama urged the emperor to make war quickly and to strike first. Even with a first strike, he could promise the emperor no better than an even chance of defeating the Russian army. Naval advisers were a little more sanguine. They estimated that they could sink the Russian Far East Fleet but would lose half of their own ships in doing so. Reluctantly, Yamagata agreed the time for war had come, and the emperor gave his approval.

Japan had been preparing for war against Russia ever since Russian intervention in 1895 had cost her the Liaotung Peninsula and Port Arthur. The emperor understood that Japan could not increase her military preparedness any further and that Russia's forces in the Far East could be reinforced almost without limit. On February 6, Japan broke diplomatic relations with Russia. Two days later, she struck the first blow. During peacetime, every evening naval officers bathed, donned kimonos, and were served dinner by servants. Sailors decorated their ships with realistic paper flowers and trees, looking forward to their regular fifteen-minute smoking break each morning. On February 8, peace ended. Just before midnight, Japanese ships under the command of Togo Heihachiro, now an admiral, attacked the Russian fleet at anchor in Port Arthur. Under the cover of night, fast Japanese destroyers launched torpedoes at Russian ships, leaving a cruiser and Russia's two most modern battleships grounded near the harbor entrance. There had been no warning. Newspapers in France, Russia's ally, were critical of this attack without declaration of war, but newspapers and politicians in America and Britain roared their approval of this "stunning" and "masculine" victory, which they declared to be well within international law and common military practice. So began the largest war the world had yet seen.

CHAPTER THREE

"AND WHERE MAY JAPAN HAPPEN TO BE?"

F ew Russian officers believed that Japan would attack. As one put it, "Our giants would make short work of the little fellows from Japan. But Japan will not be so foolish—never!"[1] Most Russian officers were surprised by the outbreak of the war but not concerned about its outcome. When a senior general who was the former commander of Russia's elite cavalry regiment, the Chevalier Guards, was informed that war with Japan had broken out, he asked sarcastically, "And where may Japan happen to be?"[2] As a noble Russian officer who fought in the war recalled, most Russians, including most army officers, "laughed at the idea of little cheeky Japan daring to stand up to invincible Russia."[3] They expected the war to be no more than a brief and enjoyable punitive expedition.

To many observers, their confidence appeared to be justified. There were 1,100,000 men on active duty in the Imperial Russian Army, with another 2,400,000 reservists. With characteristic ineptitude, Russian military intelligence estimated that Japan had only 180,000 men on active duty and few trained reserves. In fact, she had 380,000 active duty soldiers with another half million reservists. Even so, they were badly outnumbered. However, although the Russian advantage in numbers was large, the vast majority of those men were in European Russia, over five thousand miles away by a single-track railroad, and the best of these troops would remain in the West to prevent a Polish rebellion or a German invasion.

Russia's Far East Fleet was about the same size as Japan's, but the Russian ships were in two ports separated by 1,100 miles. Russia also had large Baltic and Black Sea Fleets, but the Black Sea Fleet was trapped by a hostile Turkey, and the Baltic Fleet could not arrive in the Far East for many months. Few Russians understood that their ships were not as modern or as well manned as Japan's. Japan's navy had somewhat fewer battleships and heavy cruisers than the Russians, but more destroyers and torpedo boats; its sailors were superbly drilled and led by experienced officers trained to the highest British standards. Russia's ships were not as well armored as Japan's, many of their crews were poorly trained, and though the Imperial Russian Navy had a few excellent commanders, most were the products of a bureaucratic system that promoted not the best officers but those who had never displeased any of their senior officers.

Ever since the Tartar invasions from the mid-thirteenth to the mid-fifteenth century, which had cut off Russia from the great events of the European Renaissance, Russia had earned the reputation of being the most backward state in Christendom. After the fall of Rome and Byzantium, Russians believed that they were the last bastion of orthodoxy, the defenders of the only true faith, and hence morally superior. They actively persecuted non-Christians, especially their large Jewish population, spurned Western ideas, and developed a police state that forbade all dissent. Despite the Russian passion for drunken revelry and debauchery that had astonished foreign visitors for centuries, Western visitors usually characterized them as the most unhappy and unfree people on earth.[4] Russia's peasants, Jews, and subject peoples were decidedly unfree and

St. Petersburg on the eve of war. (Underwood and Underwood)

often miserable, but her peasants nevertheless loved their land—"Mother Russia"—their church, and their tsar enough to fight for them, and Russia's conscript soldiers from her many conquered peoples had no choice but to do so as well.

Even though Tsar Alexander III greatly intensified political repression after the assassination of his father in 1881, Russia's strength (like that of the new tsar, so powerful he enjoyed straightening out horseshoes with his bare hands) grew rapidly during the last two decades of the century. Oil literally oozed out of the ground at Baku, and supplies of coal and iron from the Donets Basin made Russia a major producer of steel. When completed, the Trans-Siberian Railroad would allow her to extend her growing strength to the Far East. From 1890 to 1914, Russia had the highest rate of industrial growth in Europe, and her military power grew enormously during this period. The Russian army was huge, brave, and surprisingly well equipped. During the nineteenth century, it had beaten Napoleon, held its own in the grim Crimean War against France, Britain, Turkey, and Sardinia and later defeated the formidable armed forces of Turkey. It had spent immense sums modernizing and was by 1904 a tremendous force. This was an army that would thrash Austro-Hungarian forces in World War I and even hold its own against Germany, despite such desperate shortages of ammunition that its artillery often could not fire at all, and such a shortage of rifles that unarmed soldiers huddled in trenches waiting for a comrade to be killed so that they could use his rifle. The army's eventual collapse in 1917 resulted more from governmental corruption and a groundswell of revolutionary ideology than from military incompetence.

The quality of the Russian officer corps, far more uneven than that of France, Germany, or Britain, was a major weakness. Many officers were high-ranking nobles whose foreign nannies had taught them to speak both French and English before they learned Russian; these men were also capable of discussing technical military matters in German. Educated at cadet schools and the General Staff Academy in engineering and science as well as military knowledge and tactics, many were furthermore devoted to the arts as painters, musicians, and poets, or at least as patrons of these arts. Most were also physical-fitness zealots, superb swordsmen, and brilliant horsemen, and some were even willing to entertain ideas of social betterment for the Russian people.[5] Nevertheless, it was still perfectly legal for an officer to order soldiers under his command to do agricultural work on his own estate, and many did so.[6]

Unfortunately for the army, these educated officers were outnumbered by the younger sons of the lesser nobility who were so badly educated that some were wholly illiterate. Many were also lazy, corrupt, vicious, ignorant, and so uncaring of the men they commanded that they enriched themselves by pocketing government funds meant for the soldiers' food, clothing, or weapons. Others openly took bribes and sold army property for their own profit. During the upcoming war, some officers would become wealthy by manipulating accounts to their own benefit.[7] Officers like these indulged themselves in gambling and drinking, often drinking vodka and champagne while playing cards for hours every day even in the front lines.[8] They also pursued women at every opportunity and played a game called coo-coo, in which bored and drunken officers took turns firing their revolvers at the sound of other officers' voices in a darkened room.[9] Some were brave in battle, but a good many avoided combat at all costs, and most were hopelessly lazy and inept by Western standards.

Officers like these served in Russia's many cavalry and infantry regiments. Officers from lesser noble families, like some of the higher nobility, often came from families with German and Polish ancestors, and some spoke Russian poorly. The far more demanding challenges of commanding the artillery and engineers were met primarily by well-educated men from Russia's growing and largely German middle class. Many others were Jews, despite the army's deep-seated anti-Semitism. A British observer in Manchuria was struck by the intelligence and drive of several artillery officers, including one man who worked day and night while singing poems by Lermontov.[10] Russian officers who were sent to Europe to observe foreign armies were amazed by the uniformly high quality of their officers. Except for a reliance on a loud authoritarian voice to cow their subordinates, there was nothing uniform about Russian officers, who included the best and the worst of men.[11]

Except for Jews, most of whom could read and write, the soldiers these officers commanded were largely illiterate peasants or the sons of impoverished ethnic minority families. Wealthy families routinely bought their sons exemptions from conscription. Whatever their origins, conscripts were uniformly treated as rude, ignorant children. Many peasants did not have surnames when they were conscripted and were given names by their officers. Officers addressed them as "little children" or "little brothers," expressing a mixture of concern for the well-being of these unsophisticated former serfs and exasperation at their inability to behave responsibly. The men addressed their officers as "Little Father," "Your Honor," "Your Excellency," and even "Your Illustriousness." They revered good officers, whom they honored on formal occasions by howling like wolves while standing at attention, but frequently refused to serve under bad ones.[12] Officers complained endlessly about the necessity of watching over their soldiers' every move to prevent them from fighting, from drinking polluted water or locally brewed alcohol, from harming civilians or being too familiar with them, from misusing their weapons or losing parts of their equipment. Many punched any soldier who displeased them.

Most officers nevertheless defended their men's courage and their kindly, simple nature, so often expressed in melancholy song. They also enjoyed the soaring melodies sung by Jews, who were admired for their musical abilities. Sometimes, especially after drinking, officers and men alike sang gay Gypsy melodies. Singing was so popular that one officer went so far as to teach his company of elite guardsmen to entertain visiting dignitaries by singing while marching on their hands.[13] The act was a hit. Despite this kind of merriment, officers seldom failed to complain about their soldiers' stupidity, a conclusion that many, if not all, foreign military observers found apt. The ineptitude and lack of initiative that foreign observers commented on was made worse by Russian army regulations that allowed all officers to choose at least two and usually three soldiers as their servants. Officers predictably chose the brightest men they could find, with the result that most of these men were not available for combat. At the height of the coming war, there were 40,000 soldier servants in Manchuria, few of whom were involved in the fighting.[14]

A Russian General Staff officer who marveled at the capacity of Japanese soldiers to make quick and effective decisions, without the aid of their officers, had this to say about Russian soldiers whose answer to any officer's question was a formulaic, but honest, "I cannot know":

> Of what use is it for the General Staff to prepare an ideal system of communication in battle if its organs are blind, if our soldiers in their ignorance and lack of education interrupt telegraphic and telephonic communications at the critical moment by using the wires for mending their boots or binding bundles of kaoliang (millet)? Of what use is the best preparation of a reconnaissance when the greater part of the reconnoitering troops can not distinguish between our own troops—not to mention Japanese troops at all . . . ? Of what use is it to furnish to noncommissioned officers a map which to them is a book with seven seals?[15]

Western observers sometimes disagreed with this view, saying that Russia's soldiers were uneducated and wholly lacking in initiative, but not unintelligent; they referred to them as "lions led by asses" (the French said the same thing about British troops). They also called many of their offi-

cers contemptible, dishonest, drunken, and incompetent.[16] Russian soldiers were large men, larger than most men in other European armies at
that time.[17] For example, Russia had no difficulty finding over 30,000 men
who stood well over six feet in height for her Guards Regiments, and the
average Ukrainian and Siberian conscript stood about five feet ten. This
war would initially be fought mainly by Siberian troops, and as U.S.
Marines observed on their way to fight at Tientsin, they were not only
large men but also strong. These descendants of Russian trappers, hunters,
adventurers, political prisoners, criminals, and runaway serfs had begun
to settle the vast, boggy forests of pine, spruce, alders, birch, and poplars
that stretched 3,000 miles from the Ural Mountains to the Pacific in the
sixteenth century. Since then they fished for salmon in Siberia's many
rivers, hunted sable, mink, fox, beaver, and bear for their fur, and labori-
ously carved out small farms.

   These Siberian soldiers were so uneducated that even their sergeants
were illiterate and superstitious, and all loved to drink even more than
European Russians, who, themselves, drank more than men of any other
Western country. They would die for "Faith, Tsar, and the Fatherland,"
but they did not readily submit to authority, a problem that would bedev-
il Russian commanders throughout the war. A Russian officer gave this
description of the Siberian troops he commanded: "Such a lot of cutthroat
brutes you never saw. No jail-yard of criminals could match my Siberian
riflemen. All had bullet heads and retreating foreheads—prognathous
skulls, and nothing in them—eyes like elephant's eyes. . . . I am not sure
they have souls. They seemed no higher in the scale to me than horses or
camels—camels that talk, and can scratch—and get drunk, if there's any
bad vodka around."[18] The Siberians were often described by Russian officers as inferior troops, soon to be replaced by much superior "European"
regiments. In fact, foreign military observers concluded that the Siberian
troops were better soldiers than their European counterparts.[19]

   Russian infantrymen and cavalrymen alike exuded a distinctive smell
of the tobacco that they smoked whenever possible and the leather from
their long black boots, belts, and pouches. No steel helmets were worn in
this war. The troops wore white or brown caps with such small visors that
they offered no protection against the sun during the summer. Their
loose-fitting white, green, or brown cotton tunics were worn over black
trousers stuffed into black leather boots so badly made that they quickly

fell apart, and so poorly fitting that men's feet slipped inside them, making quick movements difficult.[20] During the summer, many men replaced their boots with thick-soled Chinese slippers, while others actually fought in their bare feet. Foreign observers believed that their slowness in maneuver was a result of these heavy, ill-fitting, water-retaining boots.

Each man carried a gray blanket roll over his left shoulder and a large canvas haversack called a clothes bag containing his extra clothing, as well as a heavy wooden canteen, several day's rations, salt, bread, and tobacco. The bag hung from a man's left shoulder and bounced against his left hip. In winter, the men wore fur caps and long gray greatcoats that reached their ankles but were so surprisingly ineffective against the cold that soldiers coveted the far warmer winter gear worn by supposedly ill-equipped Japanese soldiers. Before the war, the Russian General Staff believed that the Japanese would be unable to tolerate the winter cold. In fact, they had less trouble with it than the Russians did.[21]

Each soldier carried an excellent, newly issued 30-caliber, five-shot magazine rifle with an effective range of over 2,000 yards, but many men had never fired the weapon before they arrived in Manchuria. A long, quadrangular needle-pointed bayonet was almost always fixed to the rifle, even when troops were marching many miles away from any possible enemy. The conviction that the bayonet was the key to victory went back at least as far as the Napoleonic Wars hero Field Marshal Suvorov's frequently repeated maxim "The bullet is a fool, the bayonet is a hero." Unfortunately for the troops of 1904, the steel in the current-model bayonet was so poorly tempered that if a soldier fired a hundred or so rounds with the bayonet fixed, it tended to bend from the heat. Its point was also a problem. Designed to be needle sharp, it was left so dull by hard usage that even the powerful Russian soldiers frequently could not drive it through the winter coats of the Japanese. In an uncharacteristic concession to concealment, Russian bayonets were browned so that they would not sparkle in the sunlight as men deployed for battle.

The Russians also had the latest-model Maxim machine guns, designed in the United States, but thought so little of them at the start of the conflict that only eight were allocated to an entire division. Totally misunderstanding the value of machine guns, the Russians initially used all eight guns together in a battery as if they were artillery.[22] However, the Russians did have large numbers of "quick-firing" (the term for new artillery pieces that remained set on the target despite recoil) cannon capable of firing thirteen-pound shells a distance of 6,000 yards. Batteries were connected to command centers by telephone wires, but on at least one occasion early in the war, the single line available was so overloaded with voice traffic that the Russian artillery commander actually ordered hundreds of soldiers to lie on their stomachs and pass messages from him to his observer by hand. At the start of the war, Russian army doctrine required that these guns be emplaced on the tops of hills or crest lines, making them completely visible and vulnerable to Japanese fire.[23] The Russians painfully learned to deploy their artillery in hidden gun pits out of Japanese sight. Despite these problems, and a frequent shortage of high-explosive shells, longer-range Russian artillery was consistently superior to the shorter-range Japanese guns.

Early in the war, there were three regiments of regular army dragoons in Manchuria as well as mounted railroad guards, but almost all of Russia's mounted troops were Cossacks, some of whom were ethnic Russians whose ancestors had moved to the periphery of European control, where they lived as adventurous freemen and freebooters. Many Cossacks, however, were not Russians. There were Buryats and Mongols from Central Asia and quite a few Muslim tribesmen from the Caucasus, including Chechens who fought against Russia after the collapse of the Soviet Union. These men spoke a variety of Turkic languages and usually knew no Russian. Their officers formed a diverse lot, too. Many were Cossacks themselves, and these usually became very intimate with their men, but others had non-Cossack origins. One was actually of African descent, and another, a colonel named Bunting, was of British ancestry. He led a regiment against the Japanese.[24]

Cossack contempt for serfs, and later for peasants and other non-Cossacks, made them only too willing to enforce government edicts against students, Jews, and factory workers, giving them a fearsome reputation for cruelty. Their horses were small, but the Cossacks rode magnificently and were able to live off the land almost without effort; foreign observers frequently remarked that they carried nothing, yet lacked for nothing. The Cossacks were expected to have an easy time of it against the unheralded Japanese cavalry, but events would show that they shot poorly when dismounted, and cavalry in 1904 almost always fought away from their horses. However, on the one occasion that Cossacks fought Japanese cavalry on horseback, the Japanese were forced to withdraw with casualties.[25] But Cossacks were unwilling to attack while on foot, or even to defend a position against an infantry attack. They spent most of their time foraging instead of scouting as ordered; when they did scout, the inability of many of them to speak Russian was not helpful. Cossacks were required to provide their own horses, and few were willing to expose their animals or, for that matter, themselves to harm. The Russian commanding general found them so useless that he dismissed them as "old men on little horses."[26]

Each regiment of infantry was made up of men from a particular region, and they were known and cheered on by regional names—Yeneseis, Krasnoyarks, Petrovskis, and so on. Russian engineers, many of whom were Polish, were quite good but the signal corps was not, and transport in general was inadequate and poorly organized.[27] Fortunately, each Russian company was provided with a mobile field kitchen—large wood-burning kettles on wheels—in which water was kept boiling at all times. All manner of meat and vegetables were added to make a nutritious, hygienic hot meal available virtually at any time. Foreign observers were universally impressed. There was also a plentiful supply of hard-baked, dark rye bread that men carried with them. Quite literally their favorite food, the bread was a nutritious, mild laxative that relieved troops of the ills of constipation, but it had some unfortunate consequences when men were confined to trenches for long periods.[28]

Perhaps most surprising, given the overall corruption and inefficiency of army procurement procedures, the government purchased the services of the Russian Red Cross to excellent effect. Although doctors, many of whom were Jews, were treated indifferently by the army, which did not even accord them the rank of officers, they nevertheless performed well, and many Russian nurses were no less than heroic.[29] After the protracted battle before Mukden late in the war, doctors went without sleep for days on end and several nurses for so long that at least one actually died of exhaustion.[30] Some Russian base hospitals were surprisingly modern with excellent standards of hygiene, modern x-ray machines, and ample supplies of medications and chloroform for anesthesia. However, surgeons did not wear gloves, and fly-borne diseases were a problem.[31] Other rear-area hospitals would prove to be so horrifically ill-equipped and corruptly run that Russian surgeons wrote scathing denunciations of everything that was wrong with them.[32]

Few armies ever devoted themselves so visibly to religious ritual and paraphernalia. Although many regiments were 30 to 40 percent Jewish, every day began with mass, the men kneeling on both knees while chanting sometimes for twenty minutes or more, and each day ended with an evening hymn that rolled over the landscape like the sound of a gigantic choir. Railroad cars, converted into elaborate churches, made their way to Manchuria, complete with reinforcements of bearded priests who gave benediction to the men every morning and evening. Priests also carried portable altars complete with sacred icons as close to the firing line as safety permitted, and a few even led the troops in charges. One used his four-foot-tall crucifix to pummel soldiers who wavered as the Japanese advanced. Some priests also rode with Cossacks on their raids, even though many of these men were Muslims.

How well the Russian troops would be led was a question in most observers' minds, but no knowledgeable military men of any country doubted that most of them would fight bravely. They always had in the past, and their love of country and the tsar was still profound. Most of the regular soldiers were young clean-shaven, pug-nosed blonds with very short-cropped, almost shaved hair, but reservists, especially those from Siberia, were much older, bearded men, many of them fat and physically unable to cope with rigors of campaigning. The European regiments were made up of soldiers from all parts of the empire: Armenians, Finns, Georgians, Latvians, Estonians, Kazakhs, Lithuanians, Ukrainians, Buryats, Poles, and others—Jews, Muslims, and Christians. In all, there were fifty nationalities speaking close to 200 languages. Many of these men, especially the Poles, hated Russia, but most would fight nonetheless. Few had seen combat before, but as they neared the war zone, foreign observers noted, their songs became more plaintive, their deep voices singing the Lord's Prayer with even greater feeling. It was obvious to all that they had no burning hatred of the Japanese or any understanding of why they were about to face death at their hands. One soldier asked a foreign military observer if the Japanese fought in armor, and another was overheard putting this question to an officer: "Tell me little father, what made the Japanese get so angry with us?"[33] Another asked, "Why should I have to fight? I have got six children to support."[34]

Few Russian soldiers had any idea why they were fighting, but even reservists who hated leaving their families for another stint in the army nevertheless had a profound love of country. One thirty-three-year-old reservist who volunteered to go behind Japanese lines disguised as a Chinese peasant was captured by the Japanese and sentenced to death as a spy. Asked if he had anything to say before being shot, the illiterate Siberian peasant replied, "I am ready to die for my Tsar, my Fatherland, for my faith." He briefly broke down and cried but recovered, crossing himself and praying to the four corners of the earth before calmly walking to the place of execution. A Japanese staff officer was so moved by the man's courage that he sent a letter to the Russians, saying that the Japanese who were present wept openly in sympathy for the man.[35]

THE JAPANESE

In every respect, the Japanese army was smaller than the Russian. Except for one division from northern Japan whose men were as tall as most European soldiers, its soldiers and most of its officers stood only five two or five three. Its horses were smaller, too, its ammunition of smaller caliber, its artillery of shorter range, and its overall numbers fewer than the Russian army's. It could boast no victories over Napoleon or other modern armies, only one over the laughably inept Chinese. Russians who had seen them fight during the Sino-Japanese War or the Boxer Rebellion knew how formidable they were, but few officers or men in Manchuria had witnessed them in battle and, after all, most said, Russians were not Chinese; they were Europeans, and Asian "monkeys" could not hope to defeat white men.

The senior officers who led the Japanese army and navy in 1904 had begun their military careers as sword-wielding samurai on horseback, looking very much like the men who confronted Commodore Perry. Indeed, Admiral Togo, who was to become world-famous during this war, had fought against the British at Kagoshima as a seventeen-year-old samurai.[36] Junior army officers were almost all from samurai families as well, but they had been trained by Germans in modern warfare. In addition to mastering military practice, they attained a remarkable level of physical fitness by wrestling, running, and dueling with heavy bamboo stalks used to simulate swords. They also trained with real swords against bayonets, until the swordsman could disarm a bayonet-thrusting rifleman, something few Russian officers would have dared to attempt.[37] When the man who would command the Russian forces in Manchuria,

General Alexei Kuropatkin, toured Japan in 1903 on an official visit, he was received by the imperial family, given honors, and allowed to visit military training camps.[38] He was greatly impressed by the savage combat training of Japanese officers and by their physical toughness. "The physical exercises of the future officers [were] like nothing I had ever seen in Europe; it was really fighting of the fiercest kind. At the end of a bout with weapons the competitors got to hand grips, and fought till the winner had got his opponent down and could tear off his mask."[39]

Unlike the Russian army, the Japanese army tolerated no lazy, uneducated, corrupt, or bored officers. Regular Japanese officers were trained to a single, high standard, although reserve officers might be less effective. Almost all Japanese and Russian officers grew mustaches, but only very senior Japanese officers were bearded. Like soldiers of both armies, they had their hair cropped to about a quarter of an inch. Officers of both armies wore trousers with wide red stripes down the sides, had distinctive shoulder insignia, and carried swords and revolvers. Japanese officers could also easily be distinguished from their soldiers by their polished leather boots. All were proud men for whom death in battle was the greatest honor and joy. Nevertheless, the Shinto and Buddhist Japanese had rather vague beliefs about an afterlife.[40] Dying in battle did not necessarily lead to heavenly rewards, but it was thought to bring great honor to a man's family.

When not engaged in actual combat, the Japanese troops began their day by brushing their teeth and ended it whenever possible by bathing. They were no doubt the cleanest soldiers ever to go to war; oddly, though, their sanitation was poor by European standards. Trash and garbage were not regularly disposed of, and latrines were poorly designed. As a result, they suffered from dysentery and other fly-borne diseases. They also suffered greatly from beriberi, a B-vitamin deficiency disease caused by a diet too exclusively based on white rice. Although rice was the staple, Japanese rations included cans of fish, mostly salmon, as well as beef, and canned vegetables such as daikon, lotus root, and seaweed, all packed in soy sauce. Fresh vegetables were rare, but an American observer in Manchuria was surprised to find many bright yellow sacks of bacon made in Chicago.[41] Kirin beer was sometimes available, and sake was issued in cold weather. Despite these diverse rations, the men's diet was still so heavily dependent on rice that between July and September 1904 about 15,000 men developed the muscular atrophy, paralysis, anemia, and neuralgia of beriberi that led to their hospitalization in Japan.[42]

In Manchuria, unlike the Russians, whose officers as well as soldiers were frequently infected with venereal diseases, the Japanese had no access to prostitutes and did not rape Chinese women. Also unlike the Russians, they showed little visible sign of religion in their camps. They had neither priests nor shrines, except for special occasions, when a white-robed Shinto priest or two would officiate at a ceremony honoring the dead or a mournful Buddhist priest would pass by silently swinging an incense burner. European observers were surprised to discover that unlike Russian encampments, where men sang and bands played incessantly, the Japanese had almost no music. They also had very few bugle calls, and those few calls sounded discordant to Western ears.[43] Although the men often laughed and played animated games, their camps were much quieter than those of their very noisy Russian counterparts.

Japanese soldiers were short but very sturdy and powerfully built men who were chosen from the best of available conscripts and then trained almost brutally. But unlike the Russian officers, theirs were not condescending toward their men, nor did they consider them stupid. For one thing, almost all of these clean-shaven soldiers were literate, even if they were from peasant origins, and all had been trained meticulously. Surprisingly, unlike European officers, Japanese officers maintained very friendly, even socially intimate, joking relationships with their men, who would nevertheless obey any order they gave. British army observers, who permitted no such closeness with their own men, were amazed by this seemingly contradictory mix of strict discipline and close friendship.[44] Together with their officers, Japanese soldiers were willing to die for their emperor, even eager to have that honor, but they were not faceless fanatics. Like those of the Russians, Japanese regiments were made up of men from the same locality, and there were well-known differences between men conscripted from diverse regions of Japan. For example, those from Kyushu, the ancient city, were fiery, impulsive men who attacked impetuously. Those from Sendai were solid, imperturbable, but slow in the attack, and those from the city of Osaka were considered to be unlucky and not always intrepid, a stereotype that persisted into World War II.[45]

When the war began, the Japanese soldiers wore dark blue uniforms with white or khaki canvas gaiters on their calves in which they kept their chopsticks. Instead of boots, they often wore lightweight shoes or *tabi* sandals, with the big toe separated from the other toes for better traction. Their round caps with a brass star in front looked rather like those worn by French officers. Their winter clothing was superbly designed, and in summer they wore khaki, having learned from their experiences during the Boxer Rebellion that white made too fine a target. Officers were supplied with mosquito and fly nets, both of which were greatly appreciated during the Manchurian summer. Unlike European infantrymen, who usually carried equipment that weighed sixty to sixty-six pounds (the Russians carried at least seventy pounds), Japanese infantrymen carried only forty-two pounds, plus a nine-pound, eight-ounce, .26-caliber rifle with a five-shot magazine. Like the Russian rifle, it was effective at over 2,000 yards. The Japanese had their own modified design of a Hotchkiss machine gun. They did not use it often at the start of the war, but quickly added it to their armament in sizable numbers.

Japanese artillery was outranged by the Russians, firing a comparable thirteen-pound shell only 5,000 yards, compared with the Russians' 6,000, but they had excellent mountain guns that could be dismantled and carried on ponies in the rugged hills and mountains of eastern Manchuria. The Russians had no artillery that could be moved in this fashion. Like the Russians, the Japanese believed that the bayonet was a vital weapon, but theirs was not perpetually fixed to their rifles. When needed, the sword-shaped blade snapped onto the barrel easily, and in combat it was usually used to slash at and disarm the enemy before a thrust was attempted. The swords of Japanese officers were made of better steel than Russian swords, and few Russians were equal to the Japanese as swordsmen, as would be proven in combat. Officers would often fight with swords in this war.[46]

Japanese cavalry had little combat experience, and most of the men were not skilled horsemen, but they were very well equipped, fought well when dismounted, and more than held their own against the Cossacks, especially in the mountains, where the Cossacks hated to venture. In fact, the most audacious and effective calvary raid during the war was by the Japanese, not the Cossacks.[47] However, relatively few Japanese cavalry units were available. Japanese supply and transport services were very well organized, with a special transport battalion attached to each combat division. They utilized lightweight carts pulled by former jinricksha men who had phenomenal

*Yokohama on the eve
of war. (Underwood
and Underwood)*

endurance, as well as Japanese carriers—so-called coolies—who were
under military discipline. Still, given the virtual impassability of Korean
and Manchurian roads, the Japanese, like the Russians, often had to rely on
Korean and Chinese peasants to carry their supplies.

Japan's German-trained medical corps was excellent, too. Knowing
how badly outnumbered their troops would be by Russia in a long war and
quite aware that in all recent wars four men had died of disease for every
one killed in combat, the Japanese medical corps was determined to even
the odds by perfecting its means of preventing disease and treating the
wounded. Even though the failure of food supplies to reach troops led to
a serious outbreak of beriberi early in the war, this problem was overcome,
and the nutrition of Japanese troops as well as Japanese prevention of disease were much superior to those of the Americans in Cuba or the
Philippines, or the British in South Africa. In addition, the success of the
Japanese in treating their wounded was startling. Of the 9,862 wounded
admitted to hospitals by August 1, 1904, only 34 died, and this ratio continued throughout the war.[48] Unlike the Russians, the Japanese did not

allow female nurses near the fighting, but their nurses did superior work during hospital recovery. In addition to dressing wounds and comforting the wounded, they carried them on their backs when necessary.

The excellence of Japanese military intelligence, and the almost complete inadequacy of Russia's intelligence service, gave Japan a decisive advantage. The ordinary Japanese soldier knew why he was fighting Russia—Russia had humiliated Japan by "stealing" Manchuria from her after she had won it in 1895. He also knew that the Russians felt superior to him. Many men in the ranks hated Russia as a result. They were motivated by an intense love of nation and emperor; even beyond this, they believed that they were fighting for the very survival of Japan. Perhaps most important of all, they were proud men who were determined to prove that "laughable yellow monkeys," as they knew they were often called, were warriors who could defeat a European power.[49] These intangible factors gave them a mighty advantage.

PORT ARTHUR

Before Togo's midnight attack against the Russian fleet at Port Arthur put it on a war footing, "Arthur," as the city was known, had been a bustling, flamboyant place, a little like San Francisco during the gold rush. Named after British Royal Navy lieutenant William Arthur (also his Royal Highness, Duke of Connaught) during the campaign of 1860, Port Arthur was in 1904 occupied by almost 60,000 Russian soldiers and sailors, as well as some 56,000 civilians of many nationalities who seemed to be constantly on the move as carriages and rickshaws sped along its dusty, unpaved streets crowded with horses, cattle, goats, and geese, determined to outdo one another in the recklessness that Russians seemed to crave. It was a lively city where sounds of song and laughter could be heard above the ear-splitting street noises.[50] Closest to the port itself was the so-called Old City, consisting of a hodgepodge of Chinese shanties, some elegant mansions, a few businesses, and a large constellation of warehouses, machine shops, factories, and government offices. Most of the inhabitants were Chinese, but bearded red-turbaned Sikh guards watched over the valuables in the warehouses, a role they also incongruously played in some Chinese cities. Some 700 Japanese small business men with their wives and children had lived there too, and many of the men had spied openly, including Viceroy Alexeiev's Japanese barber, but after diplomatic relations were broken,

Port Arthur showing war damage. (Colliers)

they sailed away, taking all their portable goods and a remarkable number of pet dogs and cats. Their sudden departure did not alarm the Russian authorities sufficiently for them to put Port Arthur on a heightened state of alert.

About two miles to the northwest, a new town intended exclusively for Europeans had been built, complete with broad streets, ornamental trees, a huge Orthodox church, banks, shops, restaurants, theaters, gambling dens, a circulating library, a circus (soon to become a hospital), an ice rink, and the most elegant hotel in the entire Far East, which would also soon be converted into a hospital. In the evenings, dozens of cabarets were thronged with military men and civilians who ate and drank very well, enjoyed the performances of female singers and dancers from all over the world, and later paid for the privilege of spending the night, or part of it, with one of them. Others headed for one of Port Arthur's dozens of Armenian-owned small hotels occupied by strikingly beautiful prostitutes, most of whom were said to be Russian Jews or Americans.[51] One of the most popular of these brothels was called the American House. It was estimated that there was at least one prostitute for every officer in Port Arthur.[52] Dressed in dazzling white uniforms, officers also attended fancy dress balls, where they danced magnificently with beautiful women, some of whom were expensive courtesans. A circus and theater regularly performed popular Russian plays. A British visitor complained that a few tipsy Russian officers would invariably rush the stage to embrace the actresses exuberantly, firing their pistols in the air and slashing at the stage settings with their swords.[53]

British and American visitors to the city, accustomed to "blue" Sundays, were amazed to discover that Sunday in Port Arthur brought a dawn-to-dark revel. People ate and drank continuously, played lawn tennis, enjoyed horse races at a modern track two miles outside of town, watched hilarious drunken "slow" bicycle races, in which the last man across the finish line won, and listened to the gay music of large military bands. All this, followed by vast dinners, capped off by more dancing, singing, and a night of drunken coupling.[54] Some of these orgies would have taxed the strength of Rasputin.[55] The best restaurant in the old town was Saratov's, located in a long, low-ceilinged building, divided into five dining rooms noted for their filthy tablecloths and slovenly waiters. It also had a large billiard room and a bandstand. Saratov's was always packed with officers, soldiers, and sailors who drank tea from beer glasses and Roederer's extra-sweet champagne. There were also civilian diners, drinkers, and smokers who discussed business or war during the day and arranged trysts with the chanteuses in the evening.[56] A much more elegant restaurant in the new town, Nikobadze's, was just beginning to attract officers when the war began.

A good many of the foreigners in Port Arthur managed to sleep through Togo's attack without alarm. Persistent rumors circulated the next day that many naval officers were ashore carousing that night. When morning light confirmed that three capital ships had been put out of action, Viceroy Alexeiev refused to believe it. Instead, he issued a series of platitudes about the virtues of duty and prayer. As telephones rang piercingly, military officers rushed to and fro, turning confusion into chaos by their contradictory orders. One of the more inventive orders instructed the navy to be on the lookout for submarine periscopes in the harbor and, should one be seen, to either smash it with a mallet or tie a flag to it before putting a line around it and towing the submarine into captivity. In fact, the Japanese had no submarines until very late in 1904, and the submarine the Russians had in dock at Port Arthur was not operational.[57]

When the Russian naval commander Vladimir Semenoff arrived in Port Arthur a few days after the Japanese attack, he recorded these first impressions:

Heavy artillery wagons were succeeded by the light two-wheeled carts of the riflemen. Horses, mules, donkeys, were dragging about the clumsy native carts. Military escorts were marching at their sides, with their greatcoats buttoned up to the chin. Here donkeys were braying, Chinese and Korean drivers shouting at one another; there a coachman making full use of the wealth of the Russian language. Cossack orderlies, almost standing up in their stirrups, were trotting about busily. Then again came troops with bands playing. From the port one could hear the rattling of the steam winches of steamers unloading cargo. Sirens and steam whistles shrieked. Tugs were puffing and panting in front of strings of heavy lighters. Gigantic cranes stretched upwards into the clean air, like the antennae of some monsters. The penetrating sound of hammering on iron, loud shouts, and the hiss of steam made a wild concert.[58]

The fortress of Port Arthur was commanded by Lieutenant General Baron Anatoly M. Stoessel, the same Stoessel who had performed so bizarrely during the fighting at Tientsin in 1900. Except for his receipt of a wound in the Russo-Turkish war, his record was without distinction, but

Crates of vodka on wharf at Port Arthur. (Colliers)

his high social rank and influential friends propelled him to this command. Although some men admired his plump, buxom wife, no one could abide Stoessel himself. He was not only supremely incompetent; he was a viciously petty martinet who always shouted terrible threats at his subordinates. He once even whipped a civilian who failed to salute him.[59] His main contribution to Port Arthur on the morning of the ninth was to order that anyone spreading rumors about the garrison's obvious unpreparedness for war be arrested.

Stoessel insisted that the navy's lack of readiness was not his fault. An admiral named Stark was cashiered instead, although he was far less to blame than Alexeiev, who had written orders on a priceless jade table in his elegant two-story mansion forbidding full readiness, copies of which Stark retained (in an oddity of history, one of the American officers blamed for the lack of readiness at Pearl Harbor was also named Stark). Stoessel immediately busied himself with a series of actions almost unimaginably foolish. He allowed ships laden with food to leave the harbor, and he sent several trainloads of food and vital medical supplies north to Mukden. The trains returned filled with prostitutes and vodka—an excellent exchange, many officers concluded. One American visitor saw what he estimated to be 10,000 cases of vodka stacked on a wharf.[60] Although he had been in command for some time, Stoessel had done nothing to complete the partial ring of forts and entrenchments that German engineers had begun along the hills to the north of the city. Had this line been completed, Japanese artillery would have been out of range of Port Arthur. Instead, he ordered that a defensive line be constructed just north of the new town. Known to his subordinates as "Stoessel's Folly," this line was completely dominated by hills to the north. If the Japanese took these heights, Stoessel's line would be an expensive death trap.

In not the least of his mistakes, Stoessel allowed most of the city's Chinese population to flee aboard sampans, taking with them a goodly portion of the cash in the Russo-Chinese Bank and leaving the city without the labor necessary to carry on everyday life, much less build fortifications. Coal lay in piles everywhere because there was no one to deliver it, laundries shut down, shops remained closed, and transportation vanished from the streets. William Greener, correspondent for the *Times* of London, wrote, "Never in so short a time did the social organization of a civilized community go so completely to pieces."[61] Once the exodus had been halted, those Chinese who remained were treated with the utmost barbarity by the Russians, especially Alexeiev's brutal military police. Greener, who endured the entire siege of Port Arthur wrote, "I have seen men cruelly kicked because they could not lift heavy loads no man could carry, I have seen men beaten and mauled for no other offence, that I could discover, than that they were Chinamen. I have seen ears torn, and queues tugged until the scalp was ripped. . . ."[62] The jobs previously done by Chinese now had to be carried out by Russian soldiers and sailors.

On February 6, the day when diplomatic relations were broken off, Admiral Togo's Combined Fleet, made up of virtually every warship in the Japanese navy, sailed out of Sasebo Harbor, sped on their way by thousands of women and children in rowboats carrying lanterns. Others marched to war accompanied by lanterns and bands playing music that even Westerners could appreciate. Nurses marched like men, in step with their arms swinging.[63] A naval band on board a steamship played "The Battleship March." Composed in 1900, this same march was played daily by Japanese radio stations during World War II. The fleet was joined by transports carrying troops sent off to war waving small rising-sun flags to thousands of people, who waved back shouting "Banzai!" (may the emperor live ten thousand years). Togo's main fleet headed for Port Arthur, but the transports, accompanied by several cruisers, sailed for Chemulpo Harbor (now Inchon), near Seoul, Korea.

On the evening of February 8, the advance guard of the Japanese troops went ashore near Chemulpo Harbor in what was called the best-organized landing on record.[64] As the heavily laden troops marched through Seoul on their way north, they were greeted by friendly Koreans, including women with exposed breasts but shrouded faces. They were also greeted by some of the most appalling smells in all of Asia as they marched by Seoul's open sewers. The tigers that sometimes still prowled the city's back streets wisely stayed away.[65] There were no Russian troops in Korea to oppose them, but there were two Russian ships in Chemulpo Harbor, the modern cruiser *Varyag*, built in Philadelphia, and a small, slow gunboat, the *Koreyetz*. Because there were nonbelligerent ships from Britain, France, Italy, and Germany in the harbor as well, the Japanese commander, Vice-Admiral Uryu Sotokichi, a graduate of the U.S. Naval Academy, at Annapolis, sent messages to all the ships in the harbor, advising them of the outbreak of war and urging them to leave before 4 P.M. that day, at which time he would attack the Russian warships. The Russian commanders had no intention of waiting to be attacked. Throwing all excess gear overboard, with their drummers calling the ship's company to action stations in the traditional way, the two ships sailed out to fight to the sound of their bands playing the Russian anthem, the voices of their sailors raised in powerful choruses. As they passed the foreign ships, their bands played "God Save the King," the "Marseillaise," "Hail, Columbia," and other anthems, receiving loud cheers from the Russians in return.[66]

The Japanese ships quickly riddled the two Russian ships, which limped back to the harbor, where they were scuttled. This battle is more significant for signaling the beginning of the land war than for this naval action, but the tenor of those innocent days was demonstrated by the suicidal bravery of the Russian commander, Captain Rudnev, and his men, as well as the great respect that neutral ship captains gave to these gallant men. As the two Russian ships were scuttled to prevent their capture, a British ship played the Russian national anthem. Russian survivors sang along, and even wounded men struggled to their feet to join in the patriotic fervor that even carried over to foreign ships, where men and officers participated in the singing as best they could. Men of several European nations wept.

The Russian wounded who had been taken aboard neutral ships were taken ashore to Chemulpo, where the Japanese set up a special hospital to care for them. Japanese wives of officers and diplomats volunteered as nurses and worked around the clock alongside Red Cross nurses. A British correspondent for the *Daily Mail* wrote, "It is impossible to speak too highly of the great care and attention which the Japanese people showed these stricken enemies."[67] Another British source declared that the Russian wounded were "cared for with the utmost solicitude by Japanese Red Cross nurses." The Russian government was so impressed that it donated money to the Japanese Red Cross.[68]

Other examples of both heroism and brutality in naval warfare followed. Led by the *Rurik*, Russia's cruiser squadron based at Vladivostok soon sank two unarmed Japanese merchantmen. No attempt was made to rescue the survivors. Later, the same squadron sank another unarmed merchant ship, which was carrying the heavy siege guns the Japanese had planned to use in their assault on Port Arthur. These ships also stopped a Japanese troopship carrying men of the Thirty-seventh Infantry Regiment. When the Japanese refused to surrender and opened fire with their rifles, the *Rurik* sank her, then steamed away. A few men survived to tell their story. Subsequently, a powerful Japanese cruiser squadron encountered these Russian cruisers, sinking the now hated *Rurik* and badly damaging two others, but instead of pursuing these wounded ships, the Japanese commander stopped to assist in saving 625 Russian survivors. His chivalry contrasted sharply with the recent conduct of the *Rurik*'s commander, who, incidentally, was among the men saved.[69] A British newsman in Tokyo reported that the Russian squadron had been able to locate the Japanese ships because their location had been betrayed by a Japanese officer who accepted a bribe. It was reported that he was convicted of this unthinkable crime and beaten to death by fellow officers.[70]

The first battle on land was already on the horizon. When Togo's ships attacked Port Arthur, Viceroy Alexeiev had command of perhaps 80,000 men, almost five divisions, not to mention another 30,000 railroad troops, who had all they could manage to cope with the incessant attacks of Chunchuse bandits, whose long-standing hatred for Russians was fueled by Japanese money and advisers. Concentrated at Liaoyang, these Russian troops had to defend a peninsula that stretched over almost 500 miles. Without reinforcements, Russia could not hope to beat off the numerically superior Japanese forces already in Korea and others expected to land momentarily in Manchuria. The only troops left in nearby Siberia were aging reservists with no stomach for war, so Alexeiev had to telegraph St. Petersburg for more men. They would be sent, but so would an army commander whose freedom to act without interference by Viceroy Alexeiev would never be established.

General Alexei N. Kuropatkin was an intelligent and conscientious officer who had fought bravely against the Turks as well as with the French Foreign Legion in Algeria. By the age of thirty-four he was a major general. A short, thick-set man with a close-cropped brown beard and narrow, almost Asian eyes, he was a well-liked and respected commander. Although lacking in charisma and almost fatally indecisive, he was a reasonable and thoughtful man who since becoming minister of war in 1898 had opposed war with Japan, whose army he greatly respected. Viceroy Alexeiev, on the other hand, reveled in the thought of war. Five years older than the fifty-six-year-old Kuropatkin, and very well placed with the tsar (perhaps because, as was widely believed, he was his illegitimate brother), the admiral turned viceroy was a formidable adversary for

General Kuropatkin.
(Colliers)

Kuropatkin. Kuropatkin accepted command, but to establish his own status he demanded a huge salary of 100,000 rubles a month, an allowance of twelve riding and eighteen carriage horses, and an entourage comparable to that given Alexeiev before he agreed to travel east.

At each stop along the Trans-Siberian Railroad, he promised victory, but the crowds were apathetic. Troop trains that followed were showered with pamphlets urging the men to mutiny.[71] Kuropatkin's train, like many first-class trains on the Trans-Siberian and Chinese Eastern Railways, was elegantly appointed with fine sleeping compartments and superb meals prepared by a French chef.[72] Each member of the general's staff had a private compartment, while Kuropatkin had a bedroom and a study. One carriage had been made into a church.[73] The commander also traveled with a personal physician.

The troops who followed enjoyed none of these amenities. Most of the first troops to be sent to Manchuria were reservists in their late twenties or early thirties. As they waited for the trains that would carry them to a war they had no interest in, they hugged their wives and children, many weeping openly. Once aboard the cold boxcars, they found no food. There was vodka, however, and most soldiers stayed drunk much of the way to Manchuria, leaving the train only to steal food and rape women. They also sang, very sadly.[74] Their officers could do nothing to control or console them. One officer who tried to impose discipline on his men was badly beaten, while a British observer helplessly looked on.[75]

The trip was long and arduous, especially so because the railroad was interrupted by Lake Baikal, the largest body of water in Europe and the sixth-largest lake in the world. It was 368 miles long, north to south, and 29 to 50 miles wide. To detour the railroad around the lake necessitated a 150-mile bypass that required blasting four long tunnels through the 8,500-foot-high mountains that ringed the lake. Until this project was finished, in 1905, each train had to stop at the lake. During the summer, everyone was ferried 29 miles across its narrowest point. In winter, once the ice was frozen to a sufficient depth, a railroad line was laid over it, but until the ice could carry that weight, soldiers had to walk across the lake, pulling their equipment on sledges. Officers rode in horse-drawn troikas, a trip that took five hours. Happily for the heavy-drinking officers, there was a pub half way across the lake as well as a large mess hall where the men could warm themselves and eat.[76] In early winter, as the ice was just forming, and during the spring thaw, traffic could not cross the lake at all.

Kuropatkin arrived at Russian army headquarters in Liaoyang on March 28. Like Alexeiev, he set up his staff in an elegant train sheltered by a neatly made, patriotically decorated wooden shed to shade it from the summer sun. Kuropatkin had been appointed commander of the army, but the tsar had not removed his crony, the sixty-one-year-old bachelor Admiral Alexeiev, from his position as viceroy, a post that in principle gave him ultimate authority over all civil and military affairs in the Far East. It was a formula for disaster even if the men had seen eye to eye. They emphatically did not. Kuropatkin wanted to avoid war, but even though the tsar had ordered Alexeiev to avoid war at all costs, the viceroy had refused to compromise on any points during the negotiations. He was delighted to have the war on his doorstep, insisting that vigorous action would bring total victory. Kuropatkin, who knew the strength of the Japanese and the weakness of his own army, wanted to play for time until major reinforcements could arrive.

THE BATTLE OF THE YALU

While Kuropatkin and Alexeiev were at loggerheads, the Japanese First Army was marching through Korea toward Manchuria to put them to the test. Led by a fun-loving, charming, cigar-smoking sixty-year-old general named Kuroki Tametomo, who used his cigar box as a pillow whenever he napped, Japanese troops were trekking north along almost nonexistent roads made worse by incessant rain. Men slipped and horses floundered on muddy mountainous roads. Despite some of the most meticulous planning in the history of warfare for every contingency, such as the exact width of every river that had to be bridged and arrangements for rest camps at the end of each day's march, they could not have kept to their precise schedule if Korean porters had not been available. These men were unbathed and foul smelling to Western observers and even more so to the fastidiously clean Japanese, who had been horrified by Korea's filth when they fought there ten years earlier, but they were also larger and stronger than the Japanese transport troops. The Koreans were easily capable of carrying sixty pounds on their backs at the phenomenal rate of three miles an hour. Dressed in heavy blue coats with their sheepskin collars turned up, the Japanese Second Division, followed by the elite Imperial Guards Division and the Twelfth Division—in all, some 42,500 men—marched north, followed by small Korean children who gaily ran along behind them, excited by the spectacle and given candy by the troops. The Japanese dragged along heavy artillery, including massive howitzers the Russians had no idea they possessed. The Russians scornfully dismissed the possibility that the Japanese were capable of hauling heavy artillery to the Yalu River over Korea's mountainous terrain. [77]

Before the war began, Japanese officers and soldiers alike had prayed for orders to march, and when they came, these men were ecstatic. Fathers and sons had said patriotic good-byes, mothers had tried not to weep, and as each regiment marched toward waiting transport ships, thousands of people had lined the streets waving flags, singing war songs, shouting "Banzai," and bowing as the troops passed by. On board ships heading for Korea, officers and men together had whiled away the time by telling

ghost stories and jokes, reciting poetry, and singing popular songs, some
trying to imitate professional performers by dancing or waving a fan.
There was even a piano. Magic tricks were very popular, as were card
games, go, and wrestling bouts in which men stripped to loincloths, like
sumo wrestlers of today, and grappled with each other as fellow soldiers
cheered, waiting for their turn. When the troops landed in Korea, they
were all business.[78]

To defend against Kuroki's fast-moving First Army, Kuropatkin sent
the newly arrived General M. I. Zasulich, holder of the Order of St.
George, Russia's highest medal for gallantry, to take up positions near the
Yalu River. He was ordered to retreat slowly before the Japanese, avoiding battle with their superior numbers. Not surprisingly, Admiral

Japanese infantry before the Battle of Yalu River. (Colliers)

Alexeiev ordered just the opposite—a decisive battle and a victory. The aggressive Zasulich much preferred Alexeiev's orders and ordered his 26,000 men to dig in along the Yalu. He was supremely confident that he could defeat his contemptible yellow enemies. The Russian commander put his strongest forces closest to the mouth of the Yalu, where he appeared to believe the Japanese would try to bridge the river. His left flank, farther upstream where the water was deeper and the current faster, was comparatively weak. In accordance with Russian doctrine, the artillery was placed on hilltops in full view of the Japanese, some of whom posed as Korean fishermen and sold fish to the Russians while noting their positions with precision. A few skirmishes between Japanese and Russian scouts broke out. As an indication of what was to come, when a Russian lieutenant was killed, he was buried by the Japanese with full military honors.[79]

On the other side of the Yalu, Kuroki's troops placed screens of twelve-foot-high millet along miles of road to shield their movements. To screen off one crucial mile of roadway, Kuroki actually transplanted thousands of full-grown fir trees. As a result, Russian observers saw nothing as over 40,000 men maneuvered into position to cross the Yalu. They also saw nothing when the Japanese artillery batteries, including their huge howitzers, were emplaced in camouflaged gun pits. The Japanese proved to be masters of military deception, while, as a British observer noted, the Russians seemed to prefer to mass their troops where they could be seen by the enemy but could see nothing themselves.[80] Kuroki's undetected troops easily crossed the Yalu during the night and on May 1 began an assault that, supported by their artillery, tore through Zasulich's weak left flank and sent his entire force reeling back in a disorderly retreat. Some retreating units were trapped and virtually annihilated, but others counterattacked bravely, in one instance led by a crucifix-wielding priest. The Russian infantry had hoped to drive the Japanese away with a bayonet charge. To their dismay, however, the Japanese actually ran away from them, then turned and under perfect discipline shot them down before they could reach the Japanese riflemen. The Japanese were not reluctant to use their bayonets, but this tactic was sometimes more efficient.

When the Russian commander of the left flank, Colonel Gromov, requested Zasulich's permission to make an orderly withdrawal, he refused, ordering that the troops not "abandon their positions on any pretext whatsoever."[81] The rout followed, and Gromov honorably killed himself with his revolver. Zasulich later justified his orders by saying that he had been honor-bound to show the Japanese that he was not afraid of them. He added that, as a holder of Russia's highest decoration for bravery, he could never retreat. Kuroki did not order his tired men to mount a vigorous pursuit of the retreating Russians, a pattern that would be repeated by the Japanese throughout the war.

Japanese troops were angry when they found that some of their dead had been mutilated, but they still treated Russian prisoners correctly, even though they confessed to Western observers that they could not understand why Russian officers did not appear to be horrified by their capture, or why they embraced and kissed one another, a form of intimacy between men that was foreign to the Japanese. Much of the fighting had been hand to hand with swords and bayonets. When a Western observer examined a surviving Japanese lieutenant's sword, he was surprised to find that it was so nicked that it resembled a saw. He was also surprised that the Cossack swords that lay on the battlefield were quite dull. A Japanese soldier told the same correspondent that when the fighting came to close quarters, as it often did, he and other soldiers frequently forgot to fire, striking out instinctively with their bayonets even though their rifles were still loaded. The soldier explained:

> "You want to use your bayonet with your arms, not your body. The Russky uses his bayonet with his body. He sticks his head down and rushes at you. If he catches you, you are spitted for good. He is such a big fellow that he lifts you fairly off your feet. If you are quick on our legs, though, you can step to one side, and then you have him; the only way with little men with short arms is to get in close." . . . "The first time I struck a Russian I could feel my bayonet grate on his bone," he went on. "I did not think of it at the time, but when I thought of it afterward it seemed very awful. I had seen him coming like a big black shadow, and I had just time to dodge, and I felt his bayonet go by my cheek like a razor does over your face. I pulled my bayonet out and sunk it in his neck before he had time to strike me. If I had not killed him he would have killed me. It is that way always."[82]

The Japanese had won a smashing victory, but they were exhausted and had no cavalry reserves to pursue the disorganized Russians. So they cremated their own dead, buried the Russian dead, and wandered over the battlefield foraging among bullet-riddled mess kits, bent bayonets, slashed Japanese and Russian caps, bits of dark rye bread, bandages, cartridges, rifle butts shattered by shell fire, dead horses, battered drums and bugles, and hundreds on hundreds of small blue books, carried by every Russian soldier listing his name, age, time of enlistment, home, and next of kin. Then the Japanese army quite literally went fishing. Every Japanese soldier carried a collapsible fishing rod in his pack and went angling whenever he could. Led by General Kuroki himself, officers and men who had seemingly forgotten about the war packed the banks of the Yalu.[83]

Compared with the massive battles that would soon follow, this was little more than a large skirmish. Twenty-seven hundred Russians had been killed, wounded or captured, at a cost to Kuroki of 1,036 killed and wounded.[84] No Japanese appear to have been captured. The Russians lost nineteen wagons filled with ammunition, eight machine guns, and all but three of the artillery pieces that had been in action. Before the battle, many Russian officers had been only too eager to boast about the prowess of their troops. When the magnitude of the Russian defeat finally registered on Kuropatkin's staff, as a young staff officer (later a general) wrote, "none of us, not even on the Staff, was able to imagine how the Japanese could have contrived not only to cross an exceedingly wide river without punishment, and to defeat our vanguard, but even to capture several guns."[85] "Several guns" was an understatement.

Kuropatkin had wanted to avoid a morale-boosting Japanese victory at any cost, fearing its psychological impact far more than the loss of men or matériel. Now not only was Russian morale badly damaged; Japanese confidence soared. Newsboys in Tokyo rang bells that attracted crowds to buy "extras" describing the great Japanese victory.[86] Newspapers in Britain and America were exultant, and people in much of Asia expressed their elation over the Japanese feat of arms. It was the first time that an Asian army had achieved a decisive victory over a European power, and this realization "shot like a glowing meteor over Asia."[87] Proof that "yellow monkeys" could defeat "white giants" had effects that went beyond Asian pride and confidence; bankers in New York and London who had thus far refused to lend large sums to Japan to finance the war now eagerly signed loan agreements.

As usual, the Manchu court was divided in its reaction to the Japanese victory. It was galling to them to have a Russian tsar appoint a viceroy with life-and-death powers over Manchuria, China's richest province, and they had no doubt that Russia was in Manchuria to stay, but they had grave doubts whether Japan would prove to be a better neighbor. Most of all they feared an expanded war with Russia. When the imperial Chinese general Ma unilaterally threatened to invade Russian Mongolia with his large and relatively well-trained army, the Manchu court hurriedly ordered him to desist and removed about half of the army from his command to assure his compliance. Because she was so weak, China of necessity chose neutrality. As a result, the Russo-Japanese war is the only large conflict in history fought entirely on the territory of a neutral country.

Few Chinese in Manchuria had positive feelings about the Russians. Japanese businessmen in Manchuria had been at pains to develop cordial relations with the Chinese, while the Russians, whether civilian or military, had been paradoxical at best. Often good-natured and friendly, Russians would walk with their arms around a Manchurian's shoulder one moment and kick him the next, a pattern that amused an English traveler who observed that his countrymen might now and then kick a Chinese but would never put their arms around one. With the Russian military buildup, victimization of the Chinese became more frequent and more brutal. At least one Western observer reported witnessing Cossacks killing Chinese children for no apparent reason.[88]

Unlike the Japanese, many of whom had learned to speak Mandarin, all but a few Russian officers had to rely on Chinese interpreters, most of whom were sympathetic to the Japanese or actually paid by them. The Japanese also spent large sums of money to enlist the support of the infamous Manchurian bandits, the Chunchuses. Armed with modern Mauser rifles, and often led by Japanese officers in disguise, bands of Chunchuses had been disrupting the railroad for some time, and with the coming of war they increased their destructive raids against bridges, rails, and railroad guards, blowing up ammunition dumps and warehouses and killing Russians whenever they could. Unaware that the Chunchuses were Japanese-led guerrillas, and unable to find them, in any event, Cossacks raided ordinary Chinese villages, where they rarely found Chunchuses but regularly shot innocent Chinese.[89] Cossacks also lived off the crops and animals of the villagers, further embittering the Chinese. Any village unfortunate enough to be in the path of the Russian army had all the wood on its houses and farm tools taken for fuel, its crops and animals eaten.

The promised compensation was so rarely paid that Chinese peasants soon learned to flee with everything they could carry, including the wooden doors and window frames of their houses.[90] As they fled, they sometimes waved small Japanese flags.[91]

The first land action by the Japanese had taken place along the Korean-Manchurian border. Their next major effort would be directed against Port Arthur, 500 miles to the south. As long as the Russian fleet lay safely at anchor in the harbor, now protected against torpedoes, it posed a threat to the Japanese warships and to the vulnerable transport ships that had to deliver troops and supplies to Manchuria. The Japanese also realized that if they could capture the fortress of Port Arthur, its loss would deal a terrible blow to Russian prestige. Not least important, the Japanese were determined to regain what they believed had been stolen from them by the Shimonoseki treaty of 1895. The Japanese Imperial General Staff, led by General Baron Kodama Gentaro, expected Port Arthur to fall as easily in 1904 as it had ten years earlier. The usually brilliant Kodama was badly wrong. Port Arthur would not surrender until January 1905, and had it not been for the craven behavior of its commander, General Stoessel, it could have held out even longer. Port Arthur would also cost over 100,000 casualties, most of them Japanese, because the Japanese commander insisted on ordering one headlong attack after another. The siege of Port Arthur would not prove to be Japan's most significant victory—that would come at Tsushima Strait later in the war—but it was undeniably a supreme test of will that riveted the world's attention.

Japanese intelligence had excellent sources of information from agents within Port Arthur, but because the fortified areas were off-limits to all civilians, they had no direct knowledge of the actual strength of the defenses. As early as 1902, Japanese intelligence leaders learned that the Russians had used 200,000 barrels of concrete to improve their fortifications, but they preferred to ignore the implications of so much building in favor of their conclusion that the Russians had done nothing of significance to strengthen Port Arthur's defenses. They believed that the tsarist government's corruption would leave the fortress indefensible and, as their spies and European visitors repeatedly said, allow them to walk into the city virtually without opposition. In fact, there were over 40,000 soldiers and 17,000 sailors ready to defend Arthur. Their defenses were not complete, but they nevertheless mounted over 500 artillery pieces and hundreds of machine guns in four-foot-thick shell-proof concrete bunkers, connected by underground passages and surrounded by moats, electrified barbed wire, and minefields. Port Arthur would be anything but a pushover.

Despite the chaos and drunkenness in Port Arthur that led to public floggings all over the city, and despite Stoessel's and Alexeiev's incompetent leadership, Russian troops, aided by those Chinese who had been unable to flee the city, worked feverishly to complete the outer line of fortifications, a twenty-mile-long semicircle of forts outside the city that covered all approaches to it. Until early May, trains from the north arrived regularly, bringing everything needed to withstand a siege, although to several observers it still seemed that the most common cargo was vodka. One European observer marveled at the Russian system of unloading crates of supplies. The workers simply tossed them off ships or freight cars onto the concrete wharf or sidings, where they smashed open. Anything that survived the crash was then dumped into a cart and hauled away. Broken items were thrown into the harbor.

Along with tons of war and construction matériel, Lieutenant General Constantine N. Smirnov, a well-respected tactician, arrived with the tsar's orders to replace Stoessel as commander of the fortress. Stoessel simply ignored the orders by declaring that even though Smirnov was designated commander of the fortress, he, Stoessel, was commander of the "Fortress Area," a superior command. He also rejected Smirnov's plea that a more distant line of defenses be built. For some ten to fifteen miles to the north of Port Arthur, the terrain was broken by hills that could easily have been fortified. A few trenches had in fact been dug in this "Green Hills" line some years earlier, but they had been neglected while concrete fortifications were being erected closer to the city. The German engineers who designed these forts built them well, but they were so close to the city and the harbor that they allowed these to fall within range of heavy Japanese artillery. The Green Hills line was far enough away to put Port Arthur out of artillery range. Well-built trenches protected by barbed wire and minefields, supported by machine guns, would have been a major obstacle for the Japanese, just as they were for all armies in World War I. Even the few trench lines that were belatedly built there gave the Japanese great difficulty.

The whole point of these fortifications was to provide a safe haven for the Russian Far Eastern Fleet, but thus far the fleet had done little to jus-

Vice-Admiral Makarov. (Colliers)

tify its existence. Admiral Stark would be the scapegoat for the Russian unpreparedness that permitted Togo's war-opening surprise attack to succeed, but he was hardly to blame for the wretched training that limited the effectiveness of most of his officers and men. Early in the war, a British observer watched in astonishment as a contingent of Russian sailors detrained at Port Arthur. A smartly uniformed Russian officer gave a simple order to "fall in," but the men continued to mill about in total confusion. It was obvious that they had not been trained to respond to even this rudimentary command.[92] And Stark surely was not the architect of the red tape that made repairs to his damaged ships so maddeningly slow. But tired, slow, and depressed, a German-speaker uncomfortable using Russian, Stark was not the man to put matters right. Little was done to improve training, sharpen discipline, or enhance tactical efficiency. His ships seldom left the safety of the port; when they did, they accomplished little. Many of Stark's commanding officers appeared to believe that their primary duty was to preserve Russian ships, not to fight the Japanese.[93]

Late in February, St. Petersburg decided to replace Stark with perhaps the best officer in the Russian navy, Vice-Admiral Stepan Ossipovitch Makarov, who was such a renowned tactician that Admiral Togo kept his book on tactics in the office of his flagship. He was also an enormously popular commander, known to his sailors as their "little grandfather." There was nothing grandfatherly about his energy level or his demand that the fleet he was to command be transformed into an efficient offensive force. Makarov cut a striking figure, tall with a bald head and a massive forked blond beard that stretched halfway down his chest. His fellow officers referred to him as "beardy." Makarov arrived in Port Arthur on the same day that the powerful Philadelphia-built battleship *Retvizan*, sunk by Togo on the first night of the war, was refloated—an omen that cheered everyone. It is too much to say that Makarov transformed the fleet overnight, but he did cut through the red tape, reassigned the most inept officers, and instituted training programs that kept everyone jumping for eighteen hours a day. The admiral himself usually slept in his uniform and seldom for very long.

Makarov was appalled by the wretched training of his men, but their spirits were high and they did slowly improve their skills at gunnery as well as seamanship. Under Stark, it took an entire day for the fleet to get up steam and blunder its way out of port to the open sea. In a month's time, Makarov had them accomplishing the same maneuver in two to three hours, and although his ships often still came close to colliding with one another, the improvement gave pride to all. He also swept away Stark's defensive spirit, actually leading his ships out of the harbor to fight on several occasions. Togo and his officers were quick to notice the change. The newfound bravery of the Russian fleet impressed them. Togo's response to the now dangerous Russian fleet was to do everything in his power to bottle up the Russian ships in Port Arthur. He twice tried to sink blockships in the harbor's mouth, with the loss of life of brave Japanese sailors but no success. He also tried mining the harbor's mouth, with much better results.

On the night of April 12, Japanese destroyers laid forty-eight powerful mines across the harbor's mouth. A Russian searchlight saw the ships, and Admiral Makarov was notified but concluded they were a squadron of his own destroyers "pottering about" in front of Port Arthur. Without shipboard radios, which he lacked but the Japanese possessed, he could not

Grand Duke Cyril.
(Colliers)

contact them, so he left matters alone after making a note to check for mines in the morning, just in case the ships had been Japanese.[94] Later that night an actual Russian destroyer blundered into four Japanese warships, which pulverized and sank it. The hopeless fight was easily visible from the shore and the distraught Russians rushed out to the rescue, led by four cruisers and Makarov himself in the battleship *Petropavlovsk*. Forgetting to order that the area be swept for mines, Makarov led the Russian ships into battle, exchanging numerous shells with Japanese ships before returning to Port Arthur.

As his flagship neared the harbor's entrance, there were three tremendous explosions. After striking a Japanese mine, the *Petropavlovsk*'s own mines, boilers, and magazine exploded, tearing the ship apart.[95] White steam and fire mixed with clouds of brown smoke as the huge battleship's stern rose into the air with its screws still turning, its bright green-painted bottom clearly visible. In less than two minutes, the huge ship was gone. On board was a famous Russian painter named Vasili Verestchagin, a kindly sixty-five-year-old, who was famous for his paintings of the Napoleonic Wars as well as one of Teddy Roosevelt leading U.S. troops up San Juan Hill. A passionate opponent of war, he had nevertheless been commissioned by the tsar to paint pictures of Russia's battles at Port Arthur. He died along with 636 Russian officers and men, including Makarov. Nicholas II's cousin, handsome Grand Duke Cyril, was badly burned but, thanks to his skill as a swimmer, reached a lifeboat, where he ruthlessly used an oar to beat off sailors who attempted to climb into the overloaded boat. He then forced those sailors already in the boat to row away, leaving the men to drown.[96] While a few ships searched for survivors, virtually every gun in the fleet was being fired by hysterical sailors certain they had spotted periscopes.

To honor Admiral Makarov, Togo ordered his ships to fly their flags at half-mast and declared a day of mourning. In Japan, funeral processions honored Makarov as if he had been a fallen samurai. In St. Petersburg, the funeral service for Makarov and the other dead was attended by Madame Makarov, the entire diplomatic corps, many senior naval officers, and the tsar and tsarina, who were in tears.[97] Thanks to Japanese secrecy, the world did not know that two of Togo's six battleships also struck mines and sank with terrible loss of life.

While Makarov was attempting to reenergize the Russian navy, other authorities were readying Port Arthur for a siege. The cabarets were shut down, and their women pressed into service as Red Cross nurses, a less lucrative but soon needed occupation. Needless to say, their new duties did not prevent these "nurses" from ministering to the carnal appetites of sundry unwounded officers who had money to spare. General Stoessel thought to inspire the defenders by making repeated pronouncements that he would "never" surrender and that Port Arthur would be his "tomb." A friend, a railroad general named Fock, who would soon become controversial, did his part for the war effort by lining up his Fourth East Siberian Rifle Regiment and having the men repeat after him that the Japanese were "fools." While the generals were posturing, most available men were working on Port Arthur's defenses, and the already formidable fortress became very nearly impregnable to any infantry in the world. Lacking the heavy siege artillery lost at sea, the Japanese faced a bloodbath so terrible that even their seemingly fearless infantry would reach the breaking point.

The defense line in the Green Hills was never wholly completed, but there was another line thirty-five miles to the north that had originally been built in 1900 and was reinforced soon after the outbreak of the Russo-Japanese War. The so-called Nanshan line lay in a maze of hills and ravines that spanned the narrowest point on the peninsula, a mere two and one-half miles. With the help of 5,000 Chinese laborers—among them a Japanese colonel in disguise—the line was hurriedly reinforced atop steep barren hills with new dugouts, covered trenches, hidden artillery batteries, barbed wire, and mines. It included elegant living quarters for the commander. When the Japanese inspected the building after the battle, they were struck by its luxury and the unexplained presence of "night garments and toilet articles of a feminine nature."[98]

The position was under the command of General Fock with about 18,000 men, but he decided to defend it with only 2,700 men under Colonel Nikolai A. Tretyakov, while the rest of his men remained in reserve. On May 5, the Japanese came ashore to the north of Nanshan, as expected on the same beach they landed on during their 1894 war with China. Viceroy Alexeiev had been ordered north to Harbin, and on May 6, the day before Japanese troops managed to cut the railroad, he escaped from Port Arthur by hiding among wounded men on a Red Cross train, an effective if not conspicuously honorable way to assure a safe departure. General Fock was an oddity in the Russian army. Although proud of his Teutonic ancestry, he was not a nobleman. He was also not a veteran of combat where he would have seen heavy casualties, yet he was obsessed with the idea of retreat to avoid needless casualties. He continually preached this policy against the traditional Russian doctrine of holding a defensive position at all cost. He would soon have a chance to test his views in practice.

Screened by Japanese destroyers, thirty troop transports landed three full Japanese divisions by mid-May, with others soon to follow. After days of skirmishing and preliminary bombardment, the Japanese attacked all along the line, and everywhere they were driven back with heavy losses. After nine separate attacks, Tretyakov's undermanned defenses had stopped the Japanese cold, but at dusk he was vainly pleading with Fock for reinforcements because the Japanese had managed to turn the

Russians' left flank by wading through the surf along the beach. Pounded by heavy shells, the Russians on the left found themselves engaged in hand-to-hand fighting, some of it waist deep in a stream that turned red before the Russians finally pulled back.

Rather than sending reinforcements, Fock ordered a retreat but the order did not reach everyone in the front trenches. Unaware of the orders, Tretyakov single-handedly tried to restore order while cursing Fock, who had said to him, "I'm withdrawing, you can do as you like."[99] Tretyakov finally succeeded in rallying his men by ordering his band to play a popular military march. The courage of some Russian officers who refused to retreat and fought to their death also helped prevent a rout. The bravery of these men in fighting a rearguard action was all the more admirable in light of the Russian belief that the Japanese would kill all wounded (in fact, they cared for them as well as they did for their own men). The exhaustion of the Japanese also helped save the Russians, but even more important was the reality that they were almost out of ammunition. Amazingly, the Japanese used more ammunition in this small one-day battle than they had during the entire Sino-Japanese War—34,000 shells and 2.2 million rounds of rifle ammunition.[100]

The battle cost the Russians 1,100 men, eighty-two cannon, and ten machine guns, but the Japanese had 739 killed and 5,459 wounded, many badly. Kuropatkin had told Fock not to turn Nanshan into a last stand, but Fock's failure to commit any of his reserves, who could easily have stopped the Japanese, led to defeat in a single day and cost the lives of 600 Russians, killed as they attempted to retreat. Because of Fock's precipitate withdrawal, nearly 1,000 Russian civilians, including 150 women and children, had to flee the important port city of Dalny on only a few hours' notice during the night, leaving it open to looting by the Chinese. Dalny—which means "far away," in Russian—was an eastern port city north of Port Arthur, the jewel of Russian Manchuria with its fine harbor, huge wharves, charming buildings, large cathedral, fine park, swimming pools, bowling alleys, 200 tennis courts, modern hospitals, and lovely homes. The retreating Russian troops abandoned it without offering resistance. The Japanese took possession of an undamaged port and tons of useful supplies not yet stolen by the Chinese. Among the valuables taken by the Chinese were thousands of bottles of fine champagne, which they sold for ten cents a bottle in Port Arthur, thinking they contained sparkling water.[101]

Able to carry only a few possessions and without food or water, the Russian civilians from Dalny suffered badly on their march south to Port Arthur, and so did Tretyakov's survivors at Nanshan because General Fock had taken all the food and mobile kitchens with him when he left Tretyakov in the lurch. When Colonel Tretyakov and his men finally reached Port Arthur, just ahead of the Japanese, General Stoessel met them with harsh words, accusing them of cowardice and threatening not to allow them into Port Arthur, where they would "infect" his brave men, and to court-martial all of them.[102] Incredibly, Stoessel later ostentatiously awarded a medal to his friend Fock.

Baron Kodama, perhaps the most talented of Japan's generals, had little interest in Port Arthur, consistently pressing instead for a decisive battle against Kuropatkin's army to the north around Liaoyang. He urged that Port Arthur be screened off by a limited number of troops, that the Russian fleet be blockaded, and that all of Japan's military force be used to defeat Kuropatkin before he could be significantly reinforced. If this had been done, Japan would very likely have destroyed Kuropatkin's army in short order, but Japan's Imperial Headquarters did not agree. Its leaders feared that the Russian fleet would somehow manage to sortie and destroy Japanese supply ships and troop transports. They also wanted the international accolades and bank loans that they believed would come to them when Port Arthur fell.

The Japanese troops that had taken Port Arthur almost without effort in 1894 had been commanded by General Nogi Maresuke, such a true samurai that he had found the Germans frivolous when he trained with them earlier in his career. He also had a tortured conscience. As an imperial officer during the Satsuma rebellion of 1877, he lost his regimental standard to the rebels. Profoundly ashamed, he immediately attempted suicide, but his men restrained him. Nogi then asked the emperor for permission to kill himself, but it was denied. His career languished, and shortly before the war he retired. A fanatical believer in the power of his men's spirit, Nogi had always been more than willing to order them to do the impossible. Although he had been retired for almost three years and was out of touch with modern warfare, he was once again given command, because it was thought that the will to attack would be more than sufficient to take Port Arthur. When Nogi landed at Dalny on June 6 he learned that one of his two sons had been killed at Nanshan. Declaring

General Nogi. (Stereograph copyright 1905, Underwood and Underwood)

himself pleased by his son's achievement of a warrior's death, he led his troops south toward Port Arthur. On the march, they sang hymns to the memory of the men killed in the 1894 attack on the fortress—all nineteen of them!

While Nogi's newly named Third Army moved into positions just out of range of Russian guns at Port Arthur, General Oka's Second Army landed at Dalny and moved north to join General Kuroki's First Army, marching northwest from the Yalu across the mountainous east coast of Manchuria. Kuropatkin wanted to bide his time, but St. Petersburg insisted that he attack to relieve the pressure on Port Arthur, which the Russian command deemed essential as a base for its navy and for the morale of the entire Russian people. The task of disrupting Oka's advance was given to the commander of the First Siberian Army Corps, Lieutenant General

Baron G. K. Stackelberg, a cavalryman who enjoyed great favor at court. There was nothing austere about Stackelberg's lifestyle; along with his wife and her maid, he lived in a palatial train near Liaoyang, where a cow provided fresh milk daily. On hot days, Cossacks watered down the roof of the train to cool its interior. Unfortunately, his generalship was not as impressive as his style of living. His personal bravery was never questioned, but he believed in attacking by first building a defense line, then moving ahead to build another one, hardly the dashing approach one might expect from a cavalry officer. Stranger still, as he approached Oka's army, Stackelberg failed to protect his right flank, which extended out into the flatlands to the west.

On June 14, at a place called Te-li-ssu by the Japanese and Wa-fang-kon by the Russians, the two forces collided. After an exchange of artillery fire in which the Russians held their own, Oku's infantry attacked. The Cossacks on Stackelberg's right flank predictably enough rode away, and the Japanese infantry spilled into the Russians' rear, sending Stackelberg's confused Siberians reeling back. If it had not been for a tremendous downpour, their defeat would have been even more complete. As it was, the Russians lost sixteen field guns, some 500 dead, and another 3,000 wounded or missing. The Japanese lost only 217 dead and 946 wounded, a relatively inexpensive victory by the standards of this war, but the battleground looked horrible enough after the fighting to impress an experienced British military observer. General Sir Ian Hamilton had been wounded in the Boer War, but when he looked over the battle scene he "stood still with horror," noting, "Never have I seen such a scene. . . . How silent; how ghastly; how lonely seemed this charnel house where I, a solitary European, beheld rank upon rank of brave Russians mown down by the embattled ranks of Asia."[103] Later, he came upon the body of a Russian soldier lying in a path clutching his cap in his hand. "He was a very handsome boy of about twenty; singularly dark, and on his face was a slight smile as if he was dreaming some happy dream."[104] Hamilton observed that thousands of Russians and Japanese had marched by his body, but no one had covered his face or tried to bury him.

A month later, after repeated urging by Alexeiev, Kuropatkin agreed to defend an important railroad junction at the city of Tashihchaio against four Japanese divisions moving up from the south. The task of defending it against the central Japanese advance was again given to General

Stackelberg, whose posh railroad car had led many of his fellow officers to complain openly that he was a "German," because no "real" Russian would behave that way. They conveniently overlooked many more flagrant examples of luxurious living by generals with Russian names; in reality, Stackelberg was a brave, steady officer whom the Japanese would come to respect as perhaps Russia's best. It is true that his wife, the baroness, had her maid with her, but she devoted herself to caring for Russian wounded, working much harder than many of the staff officers who criticized her husband. And even the milk cow was not a frivolous luxury; Stackelberg's doctor had insisted that maintaining his fragile health required fresh milk.[105]

Leading his men from an exposed forward position, Stackelberg camouflaged his artillery so well that the Japanese artillery, on beginning the battle, could not find the Russian guns. On Sunday, July 24, the Japanese infantry had to advance against heavy fire in 100-degree heat. Surprisingly, the Japanese Sixth Division, which led the assault, did not fight with the skill or recklessness so characteristic of the Japanese. Stackelberg's men did not even bother to occupy their forward positions to deal with such a timid assault. Other Japanese divisions fought well, but the Siberians held and even drove back some Japanese units with ferocious bayonet charges. That night, however, the veteran Japanese Fifth Division—the same one that had fought at Tientsin in the Boxer Rebellion—attacked brilliantly, and Stackelberg chose to withdraw. Skillfully, as they would do throughout this war, Russian rearguard units held off the tired Japanese while an orderly retreat took place without further loss. It was not a great battle— each side lost only about 500 men—but the heat left men exhausted, and flies tormented them almost beyond endurance. A recently arrived Russian staff officer was shocked to see that the sweat-soaked backs of the infantrymen were "black with flies," and he would soon learn how difficult it was to fend the flies off wherever there was food, blood, feces, or sweat. Any food was instantly covered with flies, which for wounded men were a cruel plague.[106]

The critical position on the Russian left was a mountain pass whose defense had been given over to Kuropatkin's good friend General Count Fyodor Keller, a man more accustomed to the drawing rooms of Paris than the battlefield, but nonetheless a warrior and a principled man who did his best to see that his men treated the Chinese well.[107] Unfortunately for the Russians, Count Keller was about to collide with General Kuroki's veteran troops, who were, as Kuropatkin later lamented, much better mountain fighters than the Russians. After an initial reverse brought about by a spirited Japanese counterattack and poor Russian communications, the immaculately uniformed Keller was attempting to rally his men when a Japanese shrapnel shell killed him, inflicting thirty-seven wounds. Although Keller's replacement was willing to continue the fight, the shaken Kuropatkin was not. The Russians once again carried out an orderly but bloody retreat from what should have been an impregnable mountain position. They left behind many dead, including newly arrived soldiers from the Ninth European Division, slaughtered when Japanese artillery caught them crowded together in narrow mountain passes. Once again, the Russians managed to conduct a skillful retreat, but they gave up positions they should easily have held.

The first three battles were relatively small in comparison with those to come, but they revealed to foreign observers and to the combatants themselves some surprising truths about the two armies. Hoping to frighten their men into fighting to the end, Russian officers told them that the Japanese would kill Russian wounded and take no prisoners. The Russians quickly learned that the Japanese did take prisoners and that they treated Russian wounded very well. One veteran newsman wrote, "I found that the Japanese were kind to the Russians who were wounded or prisoners. They smiled in real admiration and tribute to the survivors of a Russian battalion which had stuck it to the death."[108] Another reported several instances of kindness to Russian wounded.[109] Several veterans observed that Japanese routinely shared their water and cigarettes with Russian prisoners, one of whom said, "I did not expect them to feed and fan me, put a cigarette in my mouth and light it."[110] One newsman was struck by the sight of friendly Japanese soldiers trying to teach Russian prisoners how to do gymnastic exercises on an improvised horizontal bar. The Russians could not master the exercises, so the Japanese good-naturedly began to teach the Russians to speak and read Japanese, two more tasks they could not master.[111] The Russians also learned that the Japanese fought bravely by any standard but that they could be repulsed and some would even surrender, including a few officers.[112]

Russians believed that the bayonet was the deciding weapon in any battle. They found, however, that it was more difficult than they had expect-

Japanese officers supervise Christian burial for Russian dead. (Colliers)

ed to close with the Japanese, whose intense fire killed at great distances and who sometimes chose to withdraw behind their trenches, using them as a ditch to slow a Russian bayonet charge while they shot the attackers down. Also, the Russians were terribly slow on their feet because of their boots, which were far too large, and the necessity of carrying all their food and spare clothing in a large cloth bag slung over one shoulder. The heavy bag not only slowed them down; it tended to throw them so much off balance that men often fell.[113] The Japanese left their extra clothing and other heavy gear in storage areas behind the lines, a practice the Russians did not take up until later in the war. When Western military observers witnessed bayonet fights, they commented on how much more quickly the Japanese moved.[114]

At this stage of the war, the Japanese excelled in all tactics except the carefully aimed fire of rifles. They fired prodigious numbers of bullets, but these typically flew well over the heads of the Russians, who came to fear Japanese artillery and machine-gun fire but largely to ignore long-range rifle fire. Except for this inexplicable failing in so disciplined an army, the Japanese were much better able to wage war. Their generals and other senior officers were far better prepared and coordinated than the Russians; their soldiers were uniformly brave, as were the Russian Siberian regiments, if not the reservists. The Japanese fought as well in the mountains as the Russians did badly, they willingly dug excellent trenches—something the Russians disliked doing and in any event could seldom do well, owing to a shortage of spades—and they used camouflage far better than the Russians. They also were regularly able to outflank the Russians, whose Cossacks proved unable to slow advancing Japanese infantrymen attempting to encircle the Russian defenders.

After witnessing what they regarded as the Russians' appalling brutality toward the Chinese during the Boxer Rebellion, the Japanese were anticipating much of the same directed at themselves. Very early in the war, they were angered to find the mutilated body of at least one Japanese soldier and enraged to find dumdum bullets in the saddlebag of a Russian officer's dead horse.[115] Prohibited by international law, these hollow-nosed bullets expanded when they hit a man, causing huge, mutilating wounds that usually led to death, even if they did not strike a vital organ. But the Japanese learned that mutilation of the dead proved to be rare, and dumdums were not in general use. Although Cossacks often killed Japanese wounded, Russian soldiers for the most part surprised the Japanese by treating Japanese prisoners well, except for a few incidents late in the war, such as one when Chinese reported witnessing 126 wounded Japanese soldiers tied together as they were forced to hobble through Mukden to the jeers of onlookers.[116] On another occasion, a Russian officer gleefully beheaded two Japanese captives who had been tied to a stake with their heads tilting forward. A Jewish Russian soldier described the atrocity:

> Our commander had drawn back far enough to give his horse a running start. Now, with a shout of joy, he came galloping toward the stake. One slash and both heads plopped to the ground. Some of the men started a make believe football game with one of the heads, while the other was picked up by a group now doing a Cossack dance and skillfully tossing it from hand to hand.
>
> I turned away. But I realized that I, too, had become brutalized, because I felt no more than a mild twinge of disgust.[117]

The war had just begun, and each side was surprised by the other. Those surprises would grow as the battles grew larger, more deadly, and more decisive.

CHAPTER FOUR

"BRUTE FORCE, ANGUISH, AND HUMILIATION"

W hile Russian and Japanese forces gathered for the great Battle of Liaoyang, where over 400,000 men would come to grips, in early August, Nogi began his assault on Port Arthur. Choosing the weakest part of the Russian defenses, where advancing Japanese infantry could move unseen through the tall millet until they were almost on top of the Russian trench line, he was able to seize a hill that allowed his artillery to fire into the harbor, although his gunners could not directly see the ships. Faced by this threat of destruction to his fleet, Alexeiev ordered Admiral Makarov's successor, Admiral Vitgeft, to sail the squadron away to Vladivostok. Never an intrepid leader, and now emotionally depressed and slightly wounded, the bald, gray-bearded, elderly Vitgeft had been so inactive since Makarov's death that a well-known joke in Port Arthur was that "for the remainder of the war the squadron would observe the strictest neutrality."[1]

The dispirited admiral tried to make his ships ready to run the waiting Japanese gauntlet. It was no small task. Many of his sailors had to be recalled from the trenches and forts where they had been fighting as infantry. Ships' guns that had been removed to fire from land-based forts had to be dragged back by sweating horses and swearing men, while the ships themselves had to be made seaworthy. Many of them were damaged by Japanese shell fire—most seriously, the unlucky U.S.-built battleship *Retvizan*, which had been holed beneath the waterline. She was the sister ship of the USS *Maine*, sunk in Havana Harbor as the cause célèbre of the Spanish-American War.

Despite a strong premonition of his death, the greatly superstitious Admiral Vitgeft got up steam in his now rusty ships, leaving Port Arthur's harbor on August 10. The Russian ships were soon intercepted by Togo's far more numerous fleet, although the Russians had an edge in battleships of six to four. Togo was reluctant to engage Vitgeft, because he wanted to husband his ships for the coming battle with Russia's Baltic Fleet, making ready to sail against him. Knowing that he could not afford more losses after losing two of six battleships to Russian mines, Togo hoped that he could bluff the Russian ships back to Port Arthur without a major battle; however, the Russians kept coming, and their opening fire was surprisingly accurate. In the exchange of fire throughout the afternoon, both sides suffered severe damage, but the Russians resolutely held their course for Vladivostok.

With darkness and likely escape from the Japanese only half an hour away, two 850-pound, twelve-inch shells hit Vitgeft's flagship, the *Tsarevitch*, destroying the bridge and killing Vitgeft. Only the bloody stump of one leg could later be found. Hit by still more large shells, the *Tsarevitch* spun out of control, and the Russian formation, predicated on following her movements, disintegrated. Still unwilling to risk more losses, Togo stood back as the Russians finally restored order, then rejoiced as the inept admiral Prince Uktomsky led most of Russian ships back to Port Arthur, not to Vladivostok. Badly damaged by at least fifteen hits from twelve-inch shells, the *Tsarevitch* made her way to the German treaty port of Kiao-chou, where she was interned along with several Russian destroyers that accompanied her. Other Russian ships were interned elsewhere, and the fast cruiser *Novik* had to be scuttled in shallow water when her boilers gave out and Japanese ships pounded her into submission. The remaining ships of the Russian fleet would spend the rest of the war in the harbor of Port Arthur, their guns once again emplaced in forts, their sailors fighting as infantry. But against Togo these sailors had fought at least as well as the vaunted Japanese. The performance of the barely trained peasants masquerading as sailors who manned many of these ships far exceeded the highest expectations of their officers. Many of Togo's principal ships had been badly battered. He knew it had been his lucky day. Vitgeft had very nearly made good his escape.

On August 16, Nogi sent an offer of surrender to Port Arthur, asking the fortress commander to avoid useless loss of life. Women, children, priests, foreign diplomats, and foreign military observers were offered safe passage to Dalny. Stoessel was so enraged that he wanted to make no reply at all, but Smirnov finally persuaded him to send this curt note: "The honor and dignity of Russia do not allow of overtures of any sort being made for a surrender."[2] Not for four and one-half more months, after 100,000 casualties, would Port Arthur actually surrender. Three days after his surrender offer, Nogi launched a general attack at dawn. His orders were simple: attack, attack, and attack again without thought of losses. Japanese troops fell in rows and bunches, blasted by artillery, torn by mines and grenades, and literally riddled by machine-gun bullets. Men were hit by so many bullets—forty-seven separate wounds in one man, seventy in another—that their surgeons coined a term for it: "whole body, bee-hive gun-wounds."[3] Other men were killed by rudely manufactured hand grenades and some disabled when they stepped on boards through which sharp five-inch nails protruded, just as American troops did three quarters of a century later in Vietnam. In narrow ravines, Japanese bodies lay eight deep.[4] The stench of rotting corpses became so unbearable that the Russian defenders wore camphor-soaked handkerchiefs over their noses.

Before each of these horrendous attacks took place, the Japanese bathed, changing into clean underwear so that their spirits would live on without blemish. No doubt the clean underwear reduced the chance of infection when bullets and shell fragments tore through their bodies, but they died nonetheless, and in staggering numbers. In one early battle, the Japanese attackers fought for fifty-eight hours without sleep, food, or water, except for the biscuits they carried with them, before driving the Russians out of their position. The victorious Japanese were so exhausted that they immediately fell asleep amid grotesquely mutilated bodies, pools of blood, and piles of feces, snoring like "thunder," as one of their officers put it.[5]

Most attacks were driven away at terrible loss, but a few managed to come close enough to Russian trenches that the Japanese soldiers saw Russian officers standing on top of their fortifications and urging their men on by waving their swords or revolvers before being shot down. When the Japanese survivors of these attacks actually reached the Russian fortifications, they fought with bayonets, shovels, rifle butts, and stones before being killed or they tumbled into the Russian trenches, where, to their horror, they found feces everywhere, because the Russian soldiers, most of whom had diarrhea, had been forced to relieve themselves. They also found dead Russian army dogs, with collars and insignia indicating that they were scout dogs or messengers, an idea that filled the Japanese with admiration for Russian ingenuity and pity for the dogs.[6]

Stoessel believed that General Nogi and his staff lived in a luxurious villa in Dalny, rather like the mansion Stoessel himself occupied in Port Arthur. In fact, the slight, gray-haired, gray-bearded Nogi lived unpretentiously in a small, two-room Chinese house close enough to the front to have been shelled if the Russians had suspected his presence. Nogi had just a single, rather shabby sentry, and officers who came to see him on staff business had to make their way through a maze of Chinese men boiling caldrons of rice, women grinding grain by leading blindfolded donkeys around a large stone mortar, and small children who frolicked while pigs, chickens, and goats scavenged for bits of food.[7] Nogi lived as simply as any commander could; yet he was shielded from the horrors of the unending assaults and streams of mutilated men who passed through the Japanese lines to the rear, where they were well cared for but failed to serve as inspiring models for the next day's attackers, or for their general.

Some Japanese troops could not go on. The soldiers of at least one regiment from Osaka refused to advance, even after their officers slashed at them with swords and their commander intentionally exposed himself to Russian fire and was killed. The Osaka men were called "soft city boys" by rural soldiers, but they had fought very well at Nanshan and earlier at Port Arthur. Like some other Japanese troops, they lost their willingness to die, because, as in World War I—whose generals did not learn from this war—men were sent to their deaths until they could do no more. Even the densest and most callous staff officers should have realized by then that the slaughter was senseless. It is worth noting that the men from Osaka who would not advance were not shot or sent home; instead, they were ordered to the rear with something almost like an apology, being told that next time their objective would be attainable. Contrite at last, General Nogi realized that he had ordered thousands of men to their deaths to no purpose. He finally understood that will alone could not take the fortress. It could be taken only if it were pounded to pieces with long-awaited eleven-inch artillery pieces firing 500-pound shells, and if mines were dug under the Russian forts so that they could be blown to bits by dynamite. As Nogi and his staff were forced to rethink their plans, Generals Oyama and Kodama were making ready to test Kuropatkin's forces around Liaoyang in a battle that would dwarf anything yet seen at Port Arthur.

The Japanese forces that attacked Kuropatkin at Liaoyang were led by Field Marshal Oyama but the tactics for the attack came from General Kodama, who had planned this battle for years, and General Fukushima, whose high spirits and prodigious intellect had been on display during the Boxer Rebellion.[8] Oyama was a good choice for command, because he had fought over this same ground in 1894, knew the terrain and the weather. Although his volcanic temper sometimes erupted with terrifying force, this large man with a face that resembled a pock-marked football was utterly imperturbable in the turmoil of battle and consistently gave his general staff the freedom and reassurance they needed.

Before Oyama could bring three separate Japanese armies together near Liaoyang, he had to solve his difficult supply problem. In early July, when Oyama first came ashore at Dalny, the only serviceable port available to the Japanese, his first challenge was to find means of moving huge piles of supplies north to the battle zone. The Russians had left 300 railroad freight cars in Dalny but had driven away the locomotives, and the Japanese had only two that would fit the wide-gauge Russian line. Until the railroad could be rebuilt to accommodate Japanese trains, Oyama had to rely on small hand-pulled Chinese carts and the reliable but slow expedient of hiring thirty Chinese men to push each freight car.[9]

*Field Marshal
Marquis Oyama.
(Colliers)*

Kuropatkin had a supply problem, too, but men and matériel were now being ferried across Lake Baikal or routed to the south of the lake up a 3,000-foot gradient and through thirty-nine just-completed tunnels in such abundance that he had no shortage of food or ammunition, and his forces already much outnumbered Oyama's. Kuropatkin's army had been reinforced by an entire corps from European Russia. His men were well fed, and although they often drank stream water and ate cucumbers and melons from the fields, they were surprisingly healthy. Their morale was also good, and if they were slow to carry out their duties—infernally slow, in the eyes of foreign military observers—they eventually did follow orders with unfailingly good humor. When away from the front, officers were known to drink themselves into oblivion for a day or two, but the troops had little access to alcohol, which was a good thing if their favorite drinking song (which rhymes in Russian) is any guide:

I don't drink honey,
I don't drink beer,
I drink sweet vodka made of cherries;
I don't drink out of a thimble glass,
I don't drink out of a beaker,
I drink out of a pail.[10]

What they actually drank during this campaign was any Chinese home brew they could get their hands on, as well as tea—in such gigantic quantities that even tea-addicted British observers were amazed. One young Russian officer wrote, "Our infantrymen have an abnormal liking for tea, and they find means of preparing it, even under fire, somewhere in the rear of a rock or in a hole, and they always very amiably offer some to the officers, who must never refuse for it hurts them. Moreover, no one and nowhere does a Russian refuse tea."[11] An American military observer was so struck by Russians' capacity for tea that he described one officer who drank nine tumblers of tea before going to bed and put three more near at hand in case they were needed during the night. He speculated that this extraordinary intake of tea might account for the well-known nervous and excitable quality of Russian officers.[12]

Kuropatkin's weakness was not his troops. True, his Cossacks were of little use, and most were detested by Russian troops for their brutality and cowardice, but his infantrymen were loyal and brave. They were poorly trained and almost entirely lacking in initiative, but when well led they were staunch fighters, and even when badly led, which was often, they would usually defend a position to the death. Except for Polish soldiers, who hated their Russian masters, and deserted at any opportunity, the ethnic minority troops also fought well. One Finnish regiment fought to the last man.[13] For the men in the trenches what mattered most was the bravery and reliability of their company officers. As one such officer wrote, "Each eyewitness of battle may confirm how continuously, how narrowly its men watch their officer."[14] Fortunately, Russia's junior officers seldom failed their men. Her soldiers were failed by her colonels and generals.

In addition to his conflict with Viceroy Alexeiev, Kuropatkin's greatest problems were the overall incompetence of his lazy, competitive, and sybaritic staff officers, as well as his own indecision. Alexeiev, who lived in an elegant train, was so adamant about not having his sleep disturbed by train whistles that he forbade the movement of any locomotives at night, no matter how urgently the train's passengers or supplies were needed. Russian officers uniformly detested him.[15] Kuropatkin himself was an abstemious workhorse, but most of his staff officers spent more time at champagne breakfasts or in one of the seven Russian bordellos in Liaoyang than at work. Most staff officers slept from 8 P.M. to midnight, then splashed themselves with cologne and repaired to their favorite nightclub-bordello, where they stayed until 5 A.M. or so. They then slept until noon or later. Kuropatkin's chief of staff, the egregious young General Sakharov did no work at all, preferring to spend his time with his mistress, whom he had brought along to Liaoyang in direct violation of regulations. While the city was falling to the Japanese, he found time to marry the woman.[16] Distrust and conflict among staff officers was not lessened by the presence of many wives of officers who volunteered to serve as nurses in order to be near their husbands. Most were useless as nurses, preferring to devote themselves to scandalous dalliances. Many of these women were sent home in disgrace.[17] When other officers courted them, as they did relentlessly, the potential for conflict was explosive.[18] Some duels were fought, and several women committed suicide. More than one commentator observed that if Russian officers had pursued their duties with half the zeal with which they pursued women, Russia might have won the war.

Women were not the only source of trouble. Distrust so permeated the Russian officer corps that requests for reinforcements during battle were routinely dismissed without inquiry or any attempt to determine their legitimacy. Junior officers were so fearful of making a mistake that they typically chose to take no action unless given a direct written order.[19] Some officers, particularly more-junior men, fought with exceptional skill and bravery, but many senior officers were cowards. Some surrendered when the opportunity arose; others malingered by bandaging themselves for nonexistent wounds.[20] Still others found compelling reasons to ride to the rear when fighting began, often not to return to their units for days. An Italian correspondent quoted a Russian colonel as saying that if it were up to him, he would have hanged 50 percent of the Russian officer corps.[21] Staff and supply officers compounded their lack of bravery and their incompetence by their unmatched dedication to petty regulations. Some medical officers refused to issue bandages for wounded men without a written order, even though no one had a pen or pencil. Another supply officer refused to accept a written request for food because it was in pencil, not pen, even though he knew that the supply depot was scheduled to be destroyed only twenty-four hours later to prevent it from falling to the advancing Japanese.[22]

The worst offender in Kuropatkin's immediate entourage was the tsar's brother, Grand Duke Boris. His drunken outrages before the war were notoriously frequent and dangerous. During one party, he drunkenly demonstrated the fine edge on his new saber by slashing off the head of his trusting borzoi with a single blow.[23] In Port Arthur before the siege, his escapades were so annoying to Stoessel that after he paraded outside the general's house one night, drunkenly singing while dressed in a nurse's uniform, he was sent packing to Kuropatkin's headquarters. When his continued debauchery forced Kuropatkin to order him back to St. Petersburg, the intoxicated grand duke drew his sword and narrowly missed the general before other officers restrained him.

As if the derelictions of many of his senior officers had not been trouble enough, Kuropatkin tended to be his own worst enemy, changing his orders so frequently that Russian commanders became hopelessly confused. Because he did not believe that he could defeat the Japanese, he did not try for victory but attempted instead to minimize the magnitude of his defeat. In a letter to the tsar, Kuropatkin tried to justify his decision to fall back on a defensive line just south of Liaoyang by complaining that he was greatly outnumbered, a conviction that arose as a result of his own wretched intelligence and a successful campaign of disinformation by Oyama. He also informed the tsar, this time accurately, that the Japanese were more accustomed to hills and heat than his men, were armed with better mountain artillery, and had superior morale because they knew what they were fighting for and the Russian soldiers did not. He also pointed out that Japanese leadership was intelligent and energetic. Although he did not quite say so to the tsar, privately he had no hope of victory.[24]

Oyama never doubted that his men would have victory, and neither did his staff officers, most of whom were as good as Kuropatkin's were bad. Almost all had been trained by the French or the Germans and spoke at least one of their languages. Many were brilliant tacticians and strategists, but their most important qualities were their unselfishness, their loyalty to one another, and their willingness to cooperate rather than compete for individual glory. Even the brilliant Kodama and Fukushima cooperated fully. At this stage of the war, the morale of the Japanese troops could hardly have been higher. Unable to match the singing voices of the Russians, they nevertheless sang lightheartedly on the march.[25] They obeyed orders instantly and snapped their salutes with parade-ground precision. Sometimes they removed their hats and bowed. They only rarely received an issue of sake, and on their salaries of three cents a day they could not afford to buy liquor from the Chinese traders who followed them on the march. When the Japanese took over Chinese villages previously occupied by the Russians, they immediately set to work to convert these fly- and rat-infested houses into clean billets. Soldiers swept the streets, pasted clean rice paper on the filthy walls, cut fir trees for decoration, and arranged stones into gardens. After washing their uniforms in streams, they bathed themselves as best they could.[26] At the end of a day's march, they went to great pains to bathe, and they began every morning by brushing their teeth at extraordinary length, chatting to each other all the while.[27] Neither bathing nor toothbrushing was a common practice with Russian soldiers.

After Keller's defeat, Kuropatkin withdrew his large forces north of the Sha-ho River, where he intended to defend Liaoyang behind three lines of fortifications. The city itself was protected by seven fortress complexes connected by trenches, elaborate wire entanglements, and minefields. Several miles farther south were more strong points, trenches, and minefields commanded by machine-gun emplacements. The fifty-five-mile-long outer ring of trenches some fifteen miles south of Liaoyang had not been completed, but it nevertheless would pose a serious obstacle to the Japanese. Throughout August, while Nogi's men were dying at Port Arthur, Japanese patrols sparred with Cossacks as the Russians scrambled to defend their outer line and Oyama's staff coordinated the buildup of Japanese troops.

Thanks to the presence of so many correspondents and military attachés, the world knew that a great battle was about to begin. Kuropatkin's headquarters were besieged by reporters and military attachés from America, Austria, Britain, Bulgaria, France, Italy, Germany, Spain, Sweden, Rumania, and even South American countries such as Chile.[28] Another twenty-five foreign correspondents and military attachés were with Kuroki and almost as many at Oyama's headquarters, although Japanese censorship was predictably far stricter than that imposed by the

Russians. Often without information, except that which they invented, these men had little to do but chat with staff officers or each other, try to arrange for reliable servants, and stare at the boringly bright green millet and cornstalks, the yellow houses that stood out here and there, and the vast flights of wild ducks and geese that could be seen overhead whenever the skies were clear enough.

In early August 1904, the two forces made ready for what was probably the third-largest battle in the history of the world. No battle in the American Civil War had involved as many men, and only Napoleon's battle against the allied armies at Leipzig and the Battle of Sedan had been larger. Thanks to zealous Japanese intelligence, Marshal Oyama knew what his men were up against. Kuropatkin, on the other hand, had no sense of what to expect. His intelligence sources were so poor—often consisting of rumors carried by Greek, Polish, and Armenian liquor traffickers—that he was forced to use volunteers dressed as Chinese to learn what they could and to offer large rewards for any Japanese prisoner, an offer that was seldom redeemed, and then usually only by the capture of wayward private soldiers who knew little of value. As Captain Count Alexis Ignatyev, who had finished at the top of his class at the Russian General Staff Academy, observed, Russian staff officers were taught nothing about gathering intelligence. When he was appointed an intelligence officer at Liaoyang, Ignatyev "felt as though lost in the middle of a forest, surrounded by all the volunteer Chinese informers and suspicious Chinese interpreters. Headquarters sat blindfolded at Liao-yang, waiting for something to turn up. . . ." [29]

While the Russians waited and wondered, the Japanese forces moved closer. Kuroki's men in the eastern mountains were well screened by cavalry and tall ripe corn, while the main force in the center of the line was hidden by ten-foot-high millet and torrential rain. When Japanese troops emerged from the blinding weather, Russian officers could see little because their field glasses were so inferior that they often had to rely on foreign observers with better glasses or telescopes to point out the details of the Japanese deployment.[30] Thanks to Japanese agents who led the Russians to believe that many of Oyama's men were ill and that others had been dispatched to Port Arthur to reinforce Nogi, Kuropatkin was a little less anxious than before, but he still thought that the Japanese outnumbered him. In fact, Oyama had about 115,000 infantry and 4,000 cavalry, with just under 500 artillery pieces. Kuropatkin had at least 135,000 infantry (some foreign observers said 200,000), 12,000 cavalry, and over 600 guns. He also had over 30,000 men he could call on in Vladivostok, a similar number in Harbin, and almost as many guarding the railroad against the attacks of the Chunchuses that were becoming increasingly bothersome. In addition to these raids, the same Chinese General Ma who had four years earlier threatened to invade Mongolia now mobilized 30,000 men on the western border of the war zone, posing a threat that diverted still more men from Kuropatkin's defense zone around Liaoyang.

Throughout August, Liaoyang's flat landscape was inundated by rains that swamped the few existing roads, while dense fog reduced visibility even more. Men could no longer see the clouds of wild geese flying over-head. They could scarcely see one another. Nevertheless, Japanese officers urged their men forward through the mud and oppressive heat, and the exhausted, rain-soaked men responded by somehow hauling themselves and their large guns toward the front. Russian soldiers huddling in their flooded trenches were equally uncomfortable, but at least their artillery was already in place. It seemed to foreign observers that a great battle was impossible under these conditions, but Oyama was determined to attack, in part because he knew that the growing number of trains carrying more troops to Kuropatkin would not be stopped by the rain and in part because he knew that he could not expect reinforcements from the embattled Nogi at Port Arthur. Time was on Kuropatkin's side.

On August 26, as the weather improved, the greatest artillery battle the world had ever known began. Oyama tried to distribute his guns along his thirty-mile-wide central front, but owing to the mud his heaviest guns, including Krupp cannon captured at Nanshan, could be moved only by railroad and therefore could not be spread along the front. Many Japanese infantry would have to attack with little artillery support, although they were now well provided with machine guns, which the Russians for the most part still lacked. The shelling was devastating. The Japanese, who called the whizzing shell fragments "humming birds," hugged the ground or made quick dashes between shell bursts while, to the astonishment of these veteran troops, Chinese peasant families could be seen plodding along the road "without apparent concern."[31] Even duds and empty shell casings did horrific damage. A Japanese lieutenant wrote that on one occasion he saw an empty shell casing strike a Japanese soldier with such force that it tore his arm off, killing him. "When we examined the empty shell later on, we discovered inside it, first a piece of overcoat, then a piece of coat, then, a piece of undershirt, then flesh and bone, then again under-wear, coat and overcoat, together with grass and pebbles stained with blood, the whole making a sort of horrible canned goods."[32]

Kuropatkin's plan was to stall the Japanese attacks with his artillery screened by infantry before falling back to his lines of well-prepared trenches and fortifications, drawing a battered Japanese army into a vul-nerable position before launching his 70,000 reserves against them in a crushing counterattack. It was a plan that could have succeeded, and as the battle developed, it appeared that it would. The Japanese artillery opened the battle with some well-directed shells that destroyed Russian guns and killed horses and men, as foreign observers looked on from nearby hills.[33] But the longer-range, now well-concealed Russian batteries more than held their own; as Japanese infantrymen rushed forward with their usual courage, Russian riflemen and machine gunners stopped them cold. Rain turned the battlefield into a morass of mud so deep that even as many as twenty-four horses could not move a gun. Nevertheless, all along the cen-tral front the two armies clashed, fell back and clashed again, day and night, almost without an hour's relief.

Japanese casualties were so great that some units were no longer will-ing to attack, but most still did and were almost always met by Russian infantrymen who leapt out of their trenches to charge at them with their long bayonets. A British military observer noted, "Instantly all firing would cease on either side, the Japanese cheering wildly in answer to the drums and bugles of the enemy. The Russians cheer 'Hoorah!,' the Japanese, on such desperate occasions, cheer 'Wa-a-a!'" [34] To him, the sound was more a wail of grief than a martial cheer. As horrible as the car-nage was at the front, the sight of mangled men as they were carried to the rear on blood-soaked stretchers was even more unnerving. Russian nurs-es, as always, cared for them tenderly, working around the clock even though they were exhausted and always tormented by hordes of flies. Some of their patients were Russian machine gunners driven mad by the seemingly endless numbers of smiling Japanese who fell under the muz-zles of their guns.[35]

As Kuropatkin correctly anticipated, the Japanese now attempted to turn his left flank, a task that fell to the indomitable Kuroki, whose confident men marched through the fir-clad mountains toward the coming battle, singing and joking while their comrades who had attacked the Russian center were still shocked into inaction. Kuroki's men successfully waded across a river that the Russians had left unguarded, and on September 1, after a hard fight, they seized strategic Rice Cake Hill, which overlooked Kuropatkin's railroad lifeline to the north. Defying the rain, mud, and steep terrain, Kuroki's men somehow manhandled heavy six-inch guns up the hill and began to shell the railroad and Liaoyang itself, causing considerable damage and creating panic. Tragically, the first shell to explode in the city blew both legs off a Russian nurse.[36]

Kuropatkin was forced to take immediate action to drive the Japanese off Rice Cake Hill. The task fell to Major General Vladimir N. Orlov, a portly former instructor of tactics at the General Staff Academy, a thoroughly obnoxious man detested by his fellow officers. Orlov commanded fully 14,000 men, but they were overage reservists, the least capable force in Kuropatkin's entire army. However, the Japanese shelling was continuing to cause damage, and there was no time to delay. Kuropatkin did not want to commit his huge reserve, which he was saving for the planned counterattack, so he ordered Orlov to take the strategic hill. Conspicuously

Russian infantry prepare to meet Japanese attack. (Colliers)

mounted on a horse, Orlov led his twelve full battalions toward Rice Cake Hill, but his officers soon became lost and disoriented in the tall millet. As they were floundering about attempting to resume their march, a small force of Kuroki's men was able to come upon them unseen before opening fire at close range. The Russian reservists panicked, firing in all directions at the invisible enemy and, in the process, setting off several hot battles among the Russian battalions. Orlov lost 1,450 men to Kuroki's 180, and his surviving troops were now a useless rabble. Unnerved, Orlov led his only uncommitted battalion back into the millet, where he was promptly shot off his horse, and his men were easily routed again.

Despite this disaster, Kuropatkin decided that he must retake Rice Cake Hill to secure his railroad line before he could order his surprise counterattack. The job next fell to Stackelberg's veteran First Siberian Rifle Corps, twenty-five battalions strong. Without maps, they again became confused in the dense millet and did some firing among themselves, but officers were nevertheless able to assemble a large force and attack up the hill at night against Kuroki's determined but badly outnumbered defenders. The Russians lit magnesium flares to light their way. At least one Japanese soldier courageously rushed into the open to put them out and survived the experience. In the moonless dark, some Russian infantrymen who were charging up the hill bayoneted one another by mistake. Still, they siezed the hill, captured fourteen mountain guns, and took many wounded Japanese prisoners.[37] At 2 A.M. the triumphant Russians were digging in when Kuropatkin's hopelessly confused system of communications struck again. Someone on Kuropatkin's staff mistakenly ordered Stackelberg to withdraw, and Kuroki's men cautiously but gratefully returned to Rice Cake Hill and once again set up their guns.

Kuropatkin had no idea how many Japanese were on the hill, what condition they were in, or even what the terrain was like, because he had earlier rejected as unnecessary a request to map the area. Perhaps because he was physically exhausted after fourteen consecutive days of combat with very little sleep, perhaps because he knew that time was on his side, Kuropatkin canceled his massive counterattack and ordered a general withdrawal to defenses outside Mukden, forty miles farther north. Despite panic by civilians in Liaoyang and epic bouts of drunkenness by some of his troops who found unguarded barrels of wine and vodka (many of his troops were so thirsty that they had been drinking muddy water from puddles along the roads), the Russians once again managed to disengage from the exhausted Japanese and make an orderly retreat. They took with them several hundred Japanese prisoners, including some officers. A German military observer was so impressed by the Russian retreat and by the recuperative powers of the uncomplaining Russian troops that he congratulated a Russian staff officer, saying, "No one but the Russians can pull themselves together so quickly." The staff officer said that he wished his troops had not so often been put in a position to earn this praise.[38] During the long battle, Russian soldiers had repeatedly asked their officers when the order to retreat would be given. They had come to expect every battle to end this way.[39]

It was a model retreat, to be sure, but it was nevertheless a defeat and shook the morale of Russian officers and men, who began openly to wonder whether they could ever defeat the Japanese.[40] The Russians had suffered about 20,000 casualties and the Japanese close to 24,000. Kuropatkin had not used his huge uncommitted reserves, but Oyama had committed almost every man he had, and two weeks of fighting left the Japanese too exhausted to fight their way through strong Russian rearguard forces. They were also almost out of artillery ammunition. Still, they had won a major victory, as the world press readily acknowledged. The press did not report that some Japanese divisions were poorly led, that others had been so badly mauled that they lost the will to attack the stubborn Siberian riflemen, that their artillery had been outgunned by the Russians, or that the heavy Japanese losses could not easily be made up. From a tactical point of view, Kuropatkin had botched the battle with needless and confusing orders. There had been no need for him to retreat when he did. In fact, it is not at all inconceivable that his reserves could have won the battle if he had used them, but strategically he made the right decision. His army was shaken but still intact, and it would only grow stronger. Japan's strength was almost at its limit.

This battle brought home some deeply troubling lessons. Neither army had fully appreciated how unsettling it would be to its troops to fight an unseen enemy. Except for bayonet charges, which occurred quite often in this war and probably produced up to 2 percent of all casualties, infantrymen seldom saw their enemies. Shells were fired from a distance of several miles and rifles often from a distance of a mile or more. Facing death at the hands of invisible enemies was unnerving for soldiers of both armies.

Exhaustion played a role as well. Neither army was prepared to cope with a battle that lasted for two weeks. Soldiers in the combat zone were under fire day and night, until they were so exhausted that they slept through artillery barrages and could barely be roused to face an enemy attack.[41] But the most critical effect was on Russian general staff officers. Japanese generals learned to sleep whenever they could and to delegate authority. Russian generals, especially Kuropatkin, refused to sleep, were reluctant to delegate authority, and lost their ability to make sound tactical judgments as exhaustion overtook them.

Nevertheless, so rapidly was the Russian army reinforced and so thoroughly did it recover from its reverses that on October 2 Kuropatkin addressed his men with the stirring news that it was time to attack. He thanked them for their stalwart service before declaring, "Now the moment to go and meet the enemy, for which the whole army has been longing, has come, and the time has arrived for us to compel the Japanese to do our will. . . ."[42] General Kuropatkin had under his command over 200,000 men, versus possibly 150,000 Japanese under Oyama, who had also been reinforced but only by reservists. The Russians were slow to understand the extent to which barbed wire, machine guns, and artillery gave the defenders a decisive advantage. For their attack to succeed, they would need either far more men than they had or brilliant leadership, something they would never have.

When the time to march came, the Russian headquarters staff drank champagne and ate well as they looked forward to the next day's advance. The troops listened to regimental bands playing martial music and popular tunes, sang their own songs, played cards, and told stories as they always did. The next morning saw them in full dress uniforms parading with banners held high and, along with priests and bands, marching forward with parade-ground precision as if out of an earlier century. As the bands and drummers urged them on, close to 200,000 men crossed the Hun River and moved south toward the Japanese in their positions near the Sha-ho River. After their first day's march of only ten miles, they stopped, ate well, sang, and fell asleep confident of victory. The next day, even though the area had been scouted from an observation balloon, the absence of maps again took its toll, as Baron Stackelberg became so thoroughly lost that the entire advance grew confused. One aristocratic, elderly general rode ahead of his hopelessly lost regiment, consulting a tattered old map while he inspected the terrain through a pair of opera glasses mounted on lorgnettes.[43] His regiment never found the battle. As this vast army was trying to decide where it was and how it could move forward to where it wanted to be, the breakdown in Russian leadership once again made itself the dominant force on the battlefield. Orders were lost, missent, returned, ignored, rejected, and countermanded as every officer groped forward alone, hoping for a clear order that would lead to victory.

Well prepared for the enormous but bumbling Russian advance, the Japanese abandoned their forward positions on the Sha-ho River, leaving behind neatly made trenches, rice bags, colored postcards, letters, and hundreds of cases of Murai Brothers' Peacock Brand cigarettes. They also left intricate overhead conduits made of millet stalks that provided clear water to the men in the trenches; by contrast, the Russian troops invariably polluted every well they came across. On October 11, the Russians attacked all along the front as they attempted to drive the Japanese from a line of low hills. Their failure was complete. Lacking either clear orders or the ability to fight on, one battalion and regiment after another withdrew from the battle. A Russian general was incensed when he saw a junior officer leading forty men toward the rear. Suspecting cowardice, he accused the officer of deserting. Shocked, the young officer saluted and said, "Sir, this is all that is left of my regiment"—40 men out of over 2,000.[44] Japanese fire left many regiments as depleted as this one, and Kuropatkin was forced to order a general retirement. After this dreadful combat, the only victory the Russians could claim was one single hill that they took thanks to a numerical superiority of 20 to 1. The offensive cost Kuropatkin over 41,000 casualties. The Japanese lost less than half that number.

After the Russians withdrew, they dug more deeply into the earth and awaited reinforcements. To the surprise of foreign observers, their morale appeared unchanged. They played cards endlessly and sang, sometimes accompanied by concertinas and even brass bands that made the rounds. Encouraged by the low prices for alcohol, they also drank all the vodka and Chinese homebrew that they could find. Vodka cost only ten cents a bottle, while rum, cognac, and champagne were almost as inexpensive. The Japanese also dug in but seldom drank alcohol. When the emperor's birthday was celebrated on November 3, all soldiers were offered a ration of sake, but two-thirds of them refused. Instead, Japanese soldiers drank tea and celebrated by listening to officers apologize for their many failings, something that would not happen in the Russian army. They also performed spectacular and dangerous sword dances and listened to Chinese villagers play love songs on an instrument that resembled a zither. Soldiers also dressed as geishas and produced remarkably skillful renditions of their traditional songs and dances. Japanese officers seldom drank either, but occasionally they let loose. A few days after the emperor's birthday, the Japanese staff officers celebrated King Edward's birthday with another troupe of entertainers and drank so much champagne that the British general Hamilton, then only forty-five years old, felt obliged to stagger off to bed while much older Japanese officers were still going strong.[45]

Hamilton, who would command the ill-fated British invasion of Gallipoli in World War I, had enormous respect for the Japanese commanders, especially Fukushima, a man so unfailingly jovial that he was convivial even on the day after he learned his son had been killed in battle. Hamilton also had great admiration for the Japanese soldiers' behavior both in combat and during periods of inactivity, but he noted that they were not always "immaculate lambs" when it came to relations with the Chinese. He pointed out that even though they did not rape Chinese women, they did shock them by bathing naked in their presence.[46] They also occasionally bullied a Chinese shopkeeper and stole chickens and sometimes wooden windows and doors as fuel to cook their rice. But these offenses were minor compared with Russian looting, rape, and brutality. The Chinese in Manchuria initially feared the Japanese, and in the early days of the war Japanese soldiers did commit some crimes, but their officers and civil administrators quickly restored order so thoroughly that the Chinese were greatly impressed by the "unexpected mercifulness and equity of the Japanese rule."[47]

PORT ARTHUR

Finally conceding that his suicidal frontal attacks at Port Arthur had achieved nothing but a bloodbath, General Nogi reluctantly began to carry out the oldest and least romantic means of attacking a fortress—tunneling or digging "saps," as they were called, and planting mines. Ordinarily a sap or a tunnel would be dug underground until it was close to the enemy fortifications, at which point huge mines would be emplaced. After the mine was detonated, infantry would rush forward to overwhelm any defenders who survived the blast. But at Port Arthur the solid rock formations were only about two feet beneath the soil, forcing the Japanese, who hated this form of warfare, for which they were untrained and psychologically unprepared, to cover their advanced tunnels with sandbags. European armies used thousands of miners to dig tunnels like these, but the Japanese had not conscripted their miners and had no military tradition that dignified this form of warfare. Nevertheless, before the siege ended, they had dug the astounding length of twenty miles of saps and covered them with 1,200,000 sandbags. The Russians watched these gopher-like tunnels approaching them with increasing alarm, and they tried everything to stop the sappers. Mortars dropped large shells on them, men rushed forward to throw grenades and even buckets of garbage and feces into the sap heads, and sometimes the Japanese and Russians wrestled with each other until more Russians with bayonets came out of their trenches to resolve the issue.

In late October, after being urged on personally by Emperor Meiji, who knew that Russia's Baltic Fleet had set sail and was expected to arrive in short order, General Nogi ordered another general assault. Those men who attacked from trenches some distance from the Russians were, as before, usually shot down as soon as they left their protection. Those who burst out of underground tunnels usually lived longer, sometimes long enough to fight with bayonets, fists, and hand grenades, only to be driven back eventually, leaving the shattered bodies of their comrades to rot outside the hillside entrenchments protecting Port Arthur. One battalion of Japanese infantry that managed to drive Russian defenders out of their trenches was surprised to discover that the fleeing Russian survivors had to retreat over about 400 yards of completely open ground. As bullets kicked up the dirt at their feet, the desperate Russians zigzagged in vain attempts to escape the growing hail of Japanese fire. A British observer likened them to "human rabbits" as they jumped "from side to side, describing strange angles and circles, in their frantic endeavors to avoid the marksmen eagerly lining the side of the trench the Russians had just vacated."[48] It usually took many misses before a man went down, but all finally fell except for one who had literally run in a circle trying to evade the bullets. Suddenly, perhaps exhausted, he sat down and awaited death, which soon came. The last Russian to leave the trenches was a wounded officer who slowly limped along, making no effort to dodge bullets and no doubt expecting to be killed at any moment. Impressed by his courage, the Japanese held their fire.

Nogi and the staff officers who advised him still did not understand how strong the Russian defenses were. Many fortresses had four- to five-foot-thick concrete walls, steel doors separating one fort from another, and interlocking fields of fire that made it impossible for the Japanese to attack a single position without coming under fire from others. Nogi's October assault accomplished nothing, at the cost of many thousands of casualties. The usual result of these Japanese attacks was a bloody hand-to-hand fight that ended in Japanese defeat. An observer recalled one fight:

> It was a splendid sight, and worthy of the best traditions of Russia, to see these bearded giants suddenly rise up on the skyline and confront the Mikado's soldiers who looked like dwarfs beside the Siberian peasants. The fight immediately resolved itself into a series of individual combats between men, only separated from one another by rows of sand-bags. A small figure, singling out some Russian champion, would heave at him with the bayonet, but generally with disastrous results for himself, for it seemed to me that the Russians were more than able to hold their own at such close quarters. Apparently the Japanese did not care, and every soldier fought wildly until he was killed. Every now and then an officer would wave his sword in the air and rush forwards a few yards, slashing furiously at some Russian, who defended himself with his bayonet to the best of his ability.[49]

The Russian defenders had suffered terrible losses from Japanese artillery, and their impetuous counterattacks with bayonets had cost them still more lives, but they had killed many Japanese. As the fighting raged on, the command structure in Port Arthur remained in conflict, with Stoessel and his ally General Fock aligned against all the other Russian generals, especially Smirnov and Kondratenko, the fortresses' most dedicated defenders. Nevertheless, life in the city went on. While men fought and died in the forts and trenches surrounding the city, some officers still found time to drink and dine at Saratov's and to find pleasure in the arms of their courtesans turned nurses or the many prostitutes remaining in the city. In fact, some naval officers spent the entire siege in drunken revelry, taking no part in the defense of the fortress.[50]

Most Russian soldiers and sailors were not subjected to heavy Japanese shelling or attacks. They managed to endure reasonably well. Although the absence of fruits and vegetables led to increasing numbers of victims of scurvy, most of the troops and civilians in Port Arthur ate quite well and slept without interference. The captain of the cruiser *Novik* maintained a herd of cattle, 150 hens, pigs, sheep, geese, and ducks as well as a large vegetable garden. His crew ate very well throughout the siege.[51] Little boys played by dividing the city into quadrants, making bets about where the next shell would fall. Despite this semblance of normal living, more and more wounded and sick men made their way to one of the several large hospitals, where everything possible was done for them, by some excellent surgeons and many dedicated nurses, but medical supplies were running short, and the lack of hygiene was appalling. Moans could be heard from the street outside, and anyone who visited the maimed, delirious men would be repulsed by the millions of fat gray lice that climbed over them despite the frantic efforts of their horrified nurses.[52]

It was even worse on the Japanese side of the lines. Because the Japanese had greatly underestimated the casualties they would suffer at Port Arthur, their frontline medical staffs of doctors and medical aides were hopelessly overwhelmed. Many wounded men died because doctors simply could not get to them in time, and those who did have their wounds bandaged often lay exposed to heat and cold for days before they could be moved to a hospital in the rear or shipped back to Japan. For most wounded men, summer was far worse than winter. A blanket or two could warm a man during the winter, but nothing could be done about the summer heat and the hordes of flies that swarmed over the men, leaving some of these suffering victims with worms in their mouths and noses, to the horror of overworked orderlies, who were too few in number to alleviate this last torment for dying men.[53]

Stoessel and Fock were still at loggerheads with the other senior officers, but the men in the forts and trenches fought on, thanks to their own tenacity and the great bravery of many junior Russian officers. A few of these men were joined by their wives, who dressed in uniform and fought alongside them. One woman left the front lines to nurse her husband after he was wounded, only to return when he was out of danger. After taking many risks that earned her the respect of her male comrades, she was killed.[54] Sailors, untrained for this sort of warfare, sometimes ran away and had to be rounded up to fight again, but when well led they fought with great bravery too. The Russian soldiers who defended Port Arthur were almost unfailingly valiant, although 200 men did try to desert to the Japanese, who, unfamiliar with mass surrender, thought they were attacking and mistakenly shot them down. When one Russian soldier carried a badly wounded

Japanese officer down a hill to the Japanese lines, he was received with such gratitude and honor that he decided not to return to his countrymen.[55]

Nogi's utterly inflexible approach to besieging Port Arthur was clumsy at best, but in his defense it should be noted that the general had expected to have a large number of heavy-caliber siege artillery pieces to smash the Russian forts, and these had been lost early in the war when Russian warships from Vladivostok sank the supply ships carrying them.[56] Until these heavy guns could be replaced, Nogi's artillery was ineffective. While waiting for these guns to arrive, the Japanese built forty miles of rail lines to move supplies and constructed twenty eight-foot-deep concrete gun emplacements for the long-awaited eleven-inch guns that finally arrived in mid-November. These enormous cannon, each weighing eight tons without its carriage, were off-loaded from ships at Dalny onto wooden sledges that were pulled along planked roads by 800 infantrymen for each gun. It took one hour to move a gun fifty yards.[57] Thanks to the absence of rain, the Japanese were able to manhandle these monstrous weapons into position and supply them with large numbers of the 500-pound shells they fired. Once these guns went into action, the siege took on a new dimension. The Russian forts that had been invulnerable to smaller shells now collapsed under the devastating explosive power of these immense missiles.

While Nogi's new guns were slowly pulverizing the Russian front lines, Oyama was at the end of his tether. Convinced that Nogi was incapable of anything but suicide attacks, he sent General Kodama to Port Arthur with orders to take control of the battle and to replace Nogi if need be. Kodama was horrified by Nogi's unceasing frontal attacks, but afraid that sacking the still popular general would dispirit the troops, he allowed the aging general to retain command with the understanding that he, Kodama, would decide the course of battle. As if infected by Nogi's spirit, Kodama allowed Nogi to order another assault in late November. As before, the troops steamed themselves in huge earthenware jars set into the earth, then put on clean underwear and uniforms. They wished to die clean, and they expected that however badly their bodies might be mutilated, a small bone from their Adam's apple would be saved and sent home, where it would be ceremonially burned, an act allowing the family to determine the future happiness of the deceased. And, as before, they went to their deaths without dislodging the Russian defenders. The toll in killed and wounded was huge, as always. One of the men who fell badly wounded was a Japanese colonel who as a teenager had fought as a samurai in chain armor, wielding a sword.[58] An American journalist was struck by the sight of a blond Russian who lay dead with his teeth still clamped on the jugular vein of a Japanese soldier who had managed to kill the Russian with his pistol before bleeding to death himself.[59]

Following this latest debacle, Kodama ordered an intensified bombardment of the key position of the Russian defense, 203-Meter Hill, which was actually two hills connected by a saddle that offered a direct

Japanese eleven-inch siege guns outside Port Arthur. (Stereograph copyright 1905, Underwood and Underwood)

view of the entire city and the port itself. The Russians were well aware of its importance and entrusted its defense to the same intrepid colonel, Nikolai Tretyakov, who had led the losing fight at the Nanshan Hill line. He led his men valiantly, wearing a silver cross around his neck as a charm and handing out medals like candy. The two hills that made up the critical position known as 203-Meter Hill (after the elevation of the lower of the two) were surrounded by deep sandbagged trenches, four feet thick and five feet high, defended by machine guns and several batteries of cannon sited to fire at attackers who might advance from any direction.

Although Kodama had ordered that general attacks along the Russian line be ended, after preliminary bombardment, he again sent infantrymen forward toward 203-Meter Hill. As usual, they carried only hardtack, dried fish, water, and 200 rounds of rifle ammunition, and again they were shot down as they struggled up the hills. Many huddled behind parapets made from the bodies of the slain. Those few who reached the Russian trench line were killed by bayonets and hand grenades. Over 7,000 hand grenades fell on them in a single day's fighting. When Kodama ordered night attacks, Russian flares and searchlights blinded the Japanese and silhouetted them as targets. The Russians fought desperately, and although they had no sleep for four days and little to eat, and were so covered with dust from exploding shells that they could not recognize each other, they stopped the Japanese cold, killing General Nogi's second and favorite son in one of the attacks. The Japanese Seventh Division, which had arrived from Japan only a few weeks earlier, was almost completely wiped out, and so was the Ninth Regiment of the Ninth Division, composed largely of Japanese who had emigrated to California before being called back as reservists.[60]

Elsewhere the fighting had stopped, and under flags of truce stretcher bearers carried away the dead and wounded while Japanese officers presented their Russian counterparts with bottles of sake, Kirin beer, and other delicacies; the Russians reciprocated with wine, champagne and small, sweet cakes.[61] After the wounded had been removed, Japanese eleven-inch guns crushed the Russian concrete forts and smashed their trenches with a thousand 500-pound shells per day, while the Japanese dug their saps closer. On December 5, when a small contingent of Japanese crept up to the summit of 203-Meter Hill, they found only three Russians still alive. A Russian counterattack failed to dislodge the Japanese, and by nightfall the pulverized hills, so covered with fine powder that there seemed to be no solid ground left, were in Japanese hands. Tretyakov, who survived the battle although badly wounded, praised the courage of his men, praise they assuredly deserved. However, he could not find praise for the Japanese, whom he characterized as poor tacticians and not exceptionally brave men. He predicted that Russian forces would "utterly defeat" the Japanese in future battles and "drive them off the Continent."[62] There were few Russian veterans who shared his assessment of Japanese bravery and the outcome of the war.

In the light of morning through an icy wind and snow, Japanese artillery observers looked directly down onto the old and new towns of the city. The harbor would now be wholly exposed to well-aimed artillery fire, not just to shells that were blindly lobbed at Russian ships, as in the past. It had cost the Japanese 14,000 dead to take 203-Meter Hill, and 5,000 Russians had died defending it. The Japanese rushed reinforcements up the hill all night long, and as foreign correspondents looked on, they also began to dispose of the dead, more perhaps than had ever before been killed in such a small space. Many were unrecognizable as human beings, others were scattered about, their torsos connected to their extremities only by yards of intestines. Fortunately for the Japanese, it was so cold that the bodies quickly froze and there was no stench or flies. As foreign correspondents forced themselves to walk over the moonscape that had once been two fortified hills and was now a single heap of dust and rubble, they were horrified by the carnage. Some of the bodies were intact, and the correspondents were moved to pity as they looked at the faces of young Japanese and Russian soldiers, many of them mere boys. The British newspaperman Ellis Ashmead-Bartlett, who was appalled to discover that the Japanese corpses had turned green, wrote that the wide-eyed faces of the dead were frozen into expressions of "determination, terror, joy, fierce resolve and immense astonishment."[63]

From the top of 203-Meter Hill, Japanese artillery observers lost no time in directing the fire of their heavy guns onto the Russian warships in the harbor. Most of the Russian ships, now manned by skeleton crews or abandoned altogether, were scuttled in the shallow water of the harbor before they sustained further damage, but the last remaining battleship, the *Sevastopol*, steamed to the outer harbor, where she was protected by a hill from Japanese artillery and against Japanese torpedo boats by makeshift submarine nets. Badly damaged by the 120 torpedoes fired at her over the nearly three weeks that she remained afloat, the *Sevastopol* was finally taken to sea in the dead of night and scuttled in deep water. One of the sunken ships, the Philadelphia-built battleship *Retvizan*, was later refloated by the Japanese and served them as a coastal defense ship until she was sunk for good during target practice in 1924.

The capture of 203-Meter Hill, which meant the quick end of the Russian fleet, could have meant the destruction of the city as well if the Japanese had wished it. As it was, although errant shells caused considerable destruction, neither the old nor the new city was intentionally targeted; the new city, some miles from the port, was hardly damaged at all.[64] The garrison had no hope of carrying on a prolonged defense, but when the Russian war council met, soon after the fall of 203-Meter Hill, Smirnov and other senior officers argued that there was enough food and ammunition for them to hold out for several months longer, and Stoessel was compelled to agree. In addition to warehouses that were still filled with food, a profiteering British ship ran the blockade on December 12 with another 800 tons of food. The Japanese continued to shell the Russian positions, and even tried wafting poison gas over the garrison by burning tubs of arsenic (an experiment that failed), but despite the hopelessness of the Russian situation, when the war council met on December 29 it reaffirmed the determination to fight on.

Fock and Stoessel, however, had had enough. There is some reason to believe that Fock sincerely cared about the death and suffering of Russian soldiers and sailors in what he correctly saw as a lost cause. No matter how enlightened his view may have been, however, to surrender an intact fortress was an unthinkable affront to the honor of Russia, and no one among the officers agreed with him except Stoessel, whose motives are cloudy. After the war, it was widely rumored that agents of the Japanese army chief, Yamagata Aritomo, who was appalled by Nogi's lack of progress in taking Port Arthur, bribed three Russian officers by offering to pay them $65 million after the war in return for plans of the Russian minefields. The offer appears to have been made, but whether the plans were actually provided or Stoessel was involved is not known. It is true, however, that after the war, when three Russians attempted to press their claim to the money, two were killed (one was shot while in Japan) and the third disappeared under suspicious circumstances.[65]

There is no evidence that Stoessel was involved in this bizarre plot, but there is also none that he was concerned about the welfare of his men, who in turn detested him as an incompetent, self-serving bully. While the war council of senior officers was demanding that Stoessel fight on, he was secretly sending messages to St. Petersburg that prepared the way for surrender by openly lying about conditions in the fortress. He claimed to have "hardly any ammunition left" (he had over 2 million rounds for his rifles and over 82,000 artillery shells) and to have only 10,000 men under arms, all of whom were ill. It was true that 16,000 men were in hospitals, but in fact he had 868 officers, 23,491 soldiers, and 8,956 sailors who were remarkably healthy and willing to fight on. There were also 3,465 civilians and 20 priests.[66]

Having done his best to cover his tracks, and with his pledge to make Port Arthur his "tomb" forgotten, he telegraphed the tsar on January 1, saying that he and his men had done all that was humanly possible. Before the tsar could answer, Stoessel sent an officer on horseback to the Japanese lines, bearing a large white flag. As he passed by, Russian officers joked about his mission, not imagining that he was on his way to offer Stoessel's surrender of Port Arthur. The preliminary negotiations were held in English by junior officers while Russian and Japanese soldiers looked on and good-naturedly teased one another. While the talks were still going on, a Cossack and a Japanese cavalryman staged a horse race down a rocky slope, "in imminent danger of breaking their necks," as a British observer recorded. They apparently finished in a dead heat.[67] Stoessel met with Nogi the next day, offering him his beautiful white Arabian horse as a present, but the general declined it, saying he could not make personal profit from the war. Stoessel then asked for generous terms, which Nogi firmly rejected. Most Japanese said that Stoessel, who was uniformed elaborately, cut a striking military figure, but the European correspondents were unimpressed. One likened him to an overweight Dutch farmer.[68]

As soon as they heard the unexpected news, Russian officers and men wept and cursed Stoessel; then the soldiers and sailors threw down their weapons and looted the town in search of vodka, which they found in great quantities and consumed so rapidly that their despair quickly turned into an angry drunken riot in which everything of value they could find was stolen or destroyed. Their officers could not control them and had to hide for self-protection. It was a period of tense disorder that could easily have triggered harsh measures by the Japanese, but there were none. Prince Radziwill had predicted a massacre if the Japanese took Port

Arthur, but the well-disciplined Japanese were able to restore order without the use of force.[69]

The Japanese then went far beyond the bounds of international law or custom to help the Russian wounded. Instead of the wanton killing that briefly took place in 1894, they displayed kindness that bordered on tenderness, did not loot, but did not hesitate to punish any Chinese who did. They also lovingly cared for the many dogs that wandered about the city searching for food and their missing masters.[70] They joyously released a few hundred Japanese prisoners but took no action against their guards. However, the Japanese were first amazed and then disgusted to find that the fortress was amply supplied with food and ammunition and that the Russian captives were well dressed, well fed, and obviously fully capable of continuing the fight. Their officers seemed drawn and depressed, but they were splendidly uniformed in light blue greatcoats and polished leather boots while the men "showed no signs of privation or starvation."[71]

After a surprisingly restrained celebration in which the men cheered and drank some sake, many senior Japanese officers became more than a little drunk, and various skits were acted out on stage (one soldier wowed the audience by dressing as a European woman on her way to the opera), the Japanese conquerors faced the difficult task of dealing with over 50,000 prisoners, some 16,000 of them sick or wounded. Japanese doctors worked side by side with Russians, and Japanese medical supplies were liberally shared. Nogi ordered that able-bodied Russian soldiers and sailors be taken to Japan, but officers received the choice of staying with their men in captivity or giving their word not to fight again against Japan and returning to Russia with a soldier of their choice as a servant.

The Russian prisoners spent the first night camped out around fires close to the railway station, where they waited for a train from Dalny that was to arrive in the morning. It was cold, but they had blankets and the Japanese fed them. After morning prayers led by a priest, the men began to board trains that took some 4,000 men a day to Dalny. Stoessel had thus far remained in his splendid mansion attended by staff officers and Chinese servants, but the day of his departure finally came and many of the women left in Port Arthur were scheduled to leave by the same train. Poorer Russian women sat huddled together, feeding infants as best they could, while the Russian men ignored their obvious misery. In contrast, young, elegantly dressed women, whose profession was not in doubt to the

Japanese, powdered their noses and arranged the veils on their hats while they ignored the wailing children.

When Stoessel and his hefty wife arrived carrying her pet dog, a Japanese spaniel, they were accompanied by thirty-four cartloads of their personal property, including gold vases he had looted during the Boxer Rebellion. When he arrived at the station along with Fock and other senior officers, the Japanese bade him farewell courteously, but many of his own officers turned away from him with expressions of contempt. These same officers, half of whom had accepted parole rather than remain with their men in captivity, then rushed to occupy seats for themselves and their many pet dogs, which also were quite well fed. The prostitutes and the poor women were left at the station, along with the beautiful widow of an officer killed in the fortress. Complaints by foreign correspondents led Japanese officers to force the Russians to make room for the women and children. A war correspondent for the *Daily Telegraph* wrote that these Russian officers were not worthy of their uniforms,[72] and another British correspondent overheard a Japanese soldier say in wonderment, "They treat their women like so many beasts."[73]

Nogi chivalrously did not raise the Japanese flag over Port Arthur until Stoessel's train departed. Foreign observers were impressed, but not everything the Japanese did pleased the newsmen. As they and the bulk of Nogi's men camped outside of the fortress, waiting for a small Japanese force to entrain the Russian prisoners, two Japanese officers became so insulting to the war correspondents that several Europeans asked Nogi to be allowed to leave. He apologized but nothing changed. When Nogi's army finally marched into Port Arthur, his men presented a shocking contrast to the clean, well-uniformed Russians. European observers were surprised that their bands played poorly and that the men marched indifferently, wore shabby uniforms and worn boots, and carried dirty rifles. But they were impressed by their battle flags, all of which had been torn by gunfire, and no men had fought more bravely than they had.

Nogi proudly took their salute at the main Russian bandstand. The next day, standing in a cold rain, he heard an invocation to the spirits of the dead, thanking them for their noble sacrifice. He had many to thank. Over 60,000 of his men had been killed or wounded, and another 30,000 had gone down with beriberi, dysentery, and other diseases. He wrote to the army minister, General Terauchi, "The feeling I have at this moment is solely one of anguish and humiliation that I have expended so many lives, so much ammunition, and such a long time upon an unaccomplished task. . . . I have no excuse to offer to my sovereign and to my countrymen for this unscientific, unstrategical combat of brute force."[74]

Honored nonetheless by the emperor and the Japanese people, Nogi went on to become the hero of the Battle of Mukden and the tutor of Emperor Hirohito. Stoessel and Fock returned to Russia by way of Japan, where they were treated with respect. They portrayed themselves as men of honor who could not sacrifice lives needlessly. However, when other returning officers told their stories, both men were court-martialed and Stoessel was sentenced to death. The execution never took place, but he would spend years in prison. Although found guilty, Fock was released. Smirnov, who had also been accused, was exonerated.

It took weeks for the Japanese to burn the bodies of their own dead and to bury the dead Russians. When Western military attachés visited 203-Meter Hill more than two weeks after the surrender, Japanese and Russian bodies still lay everywhere. It took far longer to restore the harbor to something like working order. While all of this was taking place, the divisions of Nogi's Third Army, still secretly commanded by Kodama, were riding trains north to join Oyama for the climactic contest of the war and the largest battle the world had ever seen.

The Japanese High Command considered Nogi and his staff to be so incompetent that they were a liability to their overall command, but paradoxically the Russians were in such awe of him that they greatly feared his arrival in the north. In an effort to slow down the approach of Nogi's army, Kuropatkin's staff persuaded their always overworked general, whose hair and beard had turned white since the war began, to order a large force of Cossacks under General Mishchenko, a gray-haired artillery officer with a bulbous red nose and little knowledge of cavalry, to ride down the undefended, flat west coast of the peninsula before moving east to destroy parts of the railroad line and deflect Nogi's troops from their northerly march.[75] The raid was a farce. It had been so openly discussed by drunken Russian staff officers in Mukden that the Japanese were well prepared to meet it. Their only surprise was that it was so slow in getting started, a result of Russian officers' taking their time about providing themselves with every imaginable provision—so many, in fact, that once the cavalry column did move off, its 7,500 men moved little faster than infantry. Lacking mobile artillery, when they did encounter a Japanese force, they were able to do little more than hit and run, a tactic that did no significant damage to the railroad and slowed Nogi's men not at all. Most Russian staff officers were not surprised by the utter failure of Mishchenko's raid. They openly accused him of being a fool—and a not overly valiant one at that.[76]

While the garrison at Port Arthur was holding out against the Japanese, Kuropatkin's army was receiving large reinforcements, which rode into Mukden through rolling green hills that reminded British observers of the south of England. By the time Port Arthur fell, Kuropatkin had assembled a huge army—almost 280,000 infantry, 16,000 cavalry, over 1,200 guns, and some 12,000 men to serve them. He also received more than ample supplies of winter clothing, medicine, food, and ammunition. To maintain this large army during the winter months, his men systematically tore down every Chinese village in the region to build underground bunkers, cut down all trees for firewood, and took possession of all domestic animals. About 100,000 now destitute Chinese peasants were forced to flee to Mukden to save themselves. The Russian soldiers, who earlier had usually respected the lives and property of the Chinese, now looted and raped with abandon, killing men and women who tried to stop them. Fully one-third of all Russians who had to be evacuated from Manchuria had venereal disease, often as a result of one infected man raping a peasant girl who was later raped by others.[77] Japanese soldiers had virtually no venereal infections, because they rarely committed rape and had no access to "comfort women," as they did in future wars.[78]

The resistance of the Chunchuses grew in response to Russian atrocities, and they attacked small groups of Russians with growing audacity. Lord Brooke, a British observer with the Russians, was almost killed in one attack. Brooke was quite sympathetic to his Russian hosts, who were unfailingly courteous to him, some even delighting him by speaking fluent English and discussing pleasant subjects like English horse racing, but he candidly reported that Russians now killed Chinese indiscriminately and that Chinese hatred knew few bounds. They remembered, he wrote, the slaughter at Blagoveshchensk only too well.[79] A Russian officer wrote in disgust about the slaughter that Chinese "were not counted as human beings."[80] The Japanese, on the other hand, continued to treat the Chinese with great courtesy, spent large sums to prop up the Chunchuses, and did their best to fuel Chinese hatred of the Russians.

While Russia was nearly paralyzed by strikes and civil strife, most of which had to be put down by the army, Kuropatkin decided to attack Oyama's men, who held positions near the Sha-ho River stretching almost one hundred miles from east to west. In the first battle along the same river, in October, Kuropatkin had attacked in the mountainous east and was badly defeated. Now, in late January 1905, he would reverse his strategy and send a newly arrived general, Oscar Grippenberg, with 75,000 men to attack in the west against the relatively weak Japanese left flank. Grippenberg was sixty-six years old, virtually deaf, epileptic, and a military nonentity. His initial enthusiasm for just such a flank attack had fled when he learned he would be facing the now legendary Nogi.

The Battle of San-de-pu, named after a village that Grippenberg's army attempted to take, was a tragic fiasco. Instead of making his attack as ordered by maintaining surprise, Grippenberg's men blundered ahead, alerting the Japanese in time for them to reinforce and dig in. Russian officers still had no maps or clear orders, and Grippenberg seemed incapable of giving any or even of comprehending what Kuropatkin wanted him to do. The fact that Grippenberg refused to leave his posh train even in order to ride a mile to confer with Kuropatkin did not auger well for a coordinated attack. Instead of a concerted assault by his 75,000 men, he allowed 15,000 men to meander forward on a thirteen-mile front into massed machine-gun fire. They suffered such terrible losses that Kuropatkin, who had come to the front to observe the fighting, had to call off the attack. Baron Stackelberg in the Russian center had engaged the Japanese in equally bloody combat, again dominated by the large numbers of machine guns now available to the Japanese. When enough men were able to reach Japanese lines, Russians and Japanese fought hand to hand with medieval savagery. The British general Ian Hamilton watched one such battle through his field glasses as some 60 or 70 men on each side fought with bayonets, swords, and clubbed rifles without firing their rifles more than a handful of times. He was shocked by the barbarity of the contest, which lasted fully five minutes before the few surviving Russians finally withdrew.[81] The Japanese survivors could not explain why they had fought by throwing stones at the Russians or by seizing their bayonets in an attempt to pull them off their rifles rather than by pulling the triggers of their own loaded weapons.

Grippenberg lost 20,000 men at San-de-pu and Stackelberg another

Japanese soldiers help wounded Russian. (Colliers)

8,000 or more. The Japanese probably lost about 9,000, often because the wounded men froze to death if they were not quickly helped. A British attaché with the Japanese was struck by the sight of the bodies of older, bearded Russian reservists lying next to their prayer books, presented to them by the British Bible Society. He did not fail to see the irony of a British policy that gave money for guns to the Japanese and Bibles to the Russians.[82] After close-quarter fighting, Japanese bodies lay entwined with those of Russians. A British correspondent with Kuropatkin was moved by the sight of a Japanese officer lying on his back with a radiant smile on his face next to a blond, curly haired Russian teenager, also lying on his back, cushioning his head with one arm. He appeared to be asleep, but his unseeing gray eyes were open.[83]

The same correspondent was also astonished by the willingness of Russian soldiers to show compassion and even tenderness for the Japanese once the deadly combat had ended. Soon after a Cossack and a Japanese had wounded each other with their bayonets, the Cossack befriended his recent mortal enemy, and another Cossack nearby sponged the face of a badly wounded Japanese as tenderly as a nurse could. These were Trans-Baikal Cossacks, men with an unusual reputation among Cossacks for kindness to all.[84] Other observers reported the same thing. Only minutes after Russian and Japanese soldiers were doing their best to kill one another, once taken prisoner they were giving one another water, dressing each other's wounds, and generally behaving as if they were long-lost friends.[85]

A U.S. captain, John F. Morrison, was especially impressed by the conduct of the Japanese: "I several times saw wounded Russians brought in and the Japanese soldiers invariably treated them with great kindness."[86] Thanks to word of mouth and letters from Russian prisoners flown over Russian lines on kites, the remarkable chivalry of the Japanese was known throughout the Russian army by this time.[87] It was even acknowledged by the Russian public. *Russ,* probably St. Petersburg's most influential newspaper, concluded that Russians' use of the term "monkey" to refer to the Japanese was "shabby." The paper acknowledged the bravery of the Japanese and the great sacrifices they were making for their cause. It added, "All the stories told of the brutality of the Japanese have been shown to be unfounded. Our soldiers who have been prisoners and escaped are unanimous as to the kindness shown them by the Japanese. And the same feeling is expressed in letters coming from our soldiers, prisoners of war."[88] These sentiments were strengthened by the truly unmatched scrupulousness displayed by the Japanese with regard to the personal property of dead Russian soldiers and officers. The Japanese did not take souvenirs. Instead, they carefully collected not only Russian letters and photographs but also valuables such as gold watches, jewels, gold cigar cases, and even money, and sent them to the French embassy, which returned them to the next of kin. The Russian General Staff in St. Petersburg was impressed in spite of its prejudices.[89]

When Grippenberg first took command, he told his assembled regiments that if they retreated, he would have them shot, adding that if he ordered them to retreat, they should shoot him. He had not ordered the retreat, but his blunders had forced Kuropatkin to do so. After the battle, Russian soldiers and officers again seriously doubted their ability to defeat the Japanese, a state of mind that was not improved when Grippenberg declared that Kuropatkin was a traitor, then boarded a train for St. Petersburg and abandoned his command.[90] There was serious grumbling and heavy drinking throughout the army, but the still resilient Russian infantry fell back on Mukden in surprisingly good order to take up positions that had been strengthened during the five months since the Russian defeat at Liaoyang. While Kuropatkin attempted to deploy the army that was far too large for his command structure to control, Oyama was intent on attacking as soon as he could organize Nogi's Third Army on his left flank and the newly established Army of the Yalu on his far right. In the center, he would place the First, Second, and Fourth Armies on either side of the railroad used to bring up eleven-inch guns as well as troops from Port Arthur. Late in February, when Oyama was ready to attack, he had about 200,000 infantry and some 7,500 cavalry. He had fewer artillery pieces than the Russians but outnumbered them in machine guns by about 1,000 to 56. By now, Kuropatkin had over 300,000 men.

Kuropatkin was convinced, again largely as a result of Japanese disinformation, that the Japanese advantage in hill and mountain fighting would lead Oyama to attack in the east. Oyama assigned some of Nogi's men to this eastern army and took care that their presence would be noted. The bulk of Nogi's army was in fact held well back on the left, ready for a wide left hook around Kuropatkin's weak right flank. The Army of the Yalu on the right was actually relatively weak because many of its men were newly called-up reservists from the Sino-Japanese War of 1894, literally the last reserves left in Japan. Yet, as this weak force advanced, Kuropatkin drew more and more battalions away from his right to oppose them. As always, Russian intelligence failed miserably.

The result was disaster. While Japanese eleven-inch guns pounded the Russian center, demoralizing the shaken Russian infantrymen, led by his cavalry, Nogi's Third Army rapidly swept around the Russian right. Without adequate reserves in the area, and with most of his men, including his cavalry in the east, over fifty miles away as the crow flies and several days distant by forced march, all Kuropatkin could do was try to slow Nogi's advance as his troops on the right fell back toward Mukden. While Kuropatkin attempted to withdraw men from the left and center to oppose Nogi, the Japanese attacked furiously all along the front and Nogi continued his rapid march, which threatened to envelop Mukden from the rear and once again cut off the railroad to the north.

The battle raged from March 2 through March 7, 1905. As casualties mounted, Russia's beleaguered medical corps proved to be totally inadequate. Several hospitals continued to be well supplied and staffed, but they were now placed so far behind the lines that the wounded never reached them, while doctors and nurses spent day after day in complete idleness. By contrast, hospitals and aid stations near the front were overwhelmed with horribly wounded men. Everything was lacking, even bandages. Surgeons worked day and night until they actually collapsed in exhaustion. A Russian doctor later wrote that the suffering of the wounded was "indescribable."[91]

Behind the Russian lines in Mukden, fear and despair had already swept away all signs of order. As flames from huge fires set to destroy supplies lighted the night, troops fortified by vodka looted and burned stores, sometimes killing Chinese and Greek shopkeepers, while thousands of men, horses, and wagons flooded into the already crowded city of 300,000 as they fled from the collapsing Russian right flank. Coming upon a vast store of tinned food, bread, and casks of vodka, the Russians fought one another to carry away more tins than they could ever consume. Hacking the preserved food tins open with their bayonets, oblivious to their own cut fingers, many men gorged themselves while others stabbed at vodka casks with knives, bayonets, swords, and axes. Much of the vodka spilled out onto the muddy ground where soldiers, including Muslims, fell on hands and knees to slurp it into their mouths. Many soon lay in the mud unconscious. Left behind as their drunken comrades staggered north to escape the Japanese, many of them were later tortured and killed by the Chunchuses.[92]

In the growing chaos, Kuropatkin's headquarters train was a rock of imperturbability. An observer fleeing the drunken disorder and the defeated soldiers who were struggling by was amazed to see a waiter

> in faultless evening dress behind his master's chair, his spine bent at an angle of well-bred attention. On the steps of the carriage stood Kuropatkin's adjutant, bold, smiling, suave, exceedingly well groomed, every brass button and gold tag on his uniform shining like a mirror. He was chatting pleasantly with somebody and seemed as serenely oblivious to the hordes of beaten men who were tramping past as if he were standing in one of the most exclusive drawing-rooms in St. Petersburg.[93]

Insulated against the chaos around him, Kuropatkin ordered counterattacks against Nogi, but his orders were almost as surreal as Hitler's at the fall of Berlin. A few units did their best, to no effect. Nogi's men continued to advance, and a patrol actually cut the railroad line north of Mukden before being driven off, causing Kuropatkin to send a fevered telegram to St. Petersburg saying, "I am surrounded." This was a great exaggeration, but Kuroki's First Army now launched an attack that appeared to threaten Mukden's rear from the east, and Kuropatkin's resolve began to waver. Train after train pulled out of Mukden filled with wounded and some deserters. One held Lord Brooke and two hundred Japanese prisoners, including four officers.[94] As the confusion grew, commanders lost all touch with their troops. One distraught officer rode up to his army commander, General Baron A. V. Kaulbars, a stout, aged man with a prominent white mustache, shouting, "Your Excellency! I must know where the Seventh Regiment of the Rifle Division is." Kaulbars disgustedly shrugged his shoulders: "The Seventh Regiment? I do not know what has become of my whole Army, and he asks me where my Seventh Regiment is!"[95]

On the evening of March 9, Kuropatkin ordered a general withdrawal to Tieh-ling, the next city to the north. He was still unaware of the threat that Kuroki's army posed, but some of his staff officers were influenced by a Chinese interpreter's warnings that the Japanese were about to surround Mukden. The interpreter, it hardly needs saying, was employed by the Japanese. The Russians burned and blew up their supply and ammunition depots, and wrecked the imposing steel bridge over the Han River to the south. While dozens of trains and thousands of carts made their way north, troops straggled along without officers or orders. Only when Japanese troops closed in on the fleeing soldiers would they rouse themselves to fire and drive the enemy back. One of the worst dust storms in Mukden's history reduced visibility so much that the Russian rear guard could not see advancing Japanese soldiers until they were only forty or fifty yards away, and in Mukden itself it was impossible to see farther than a few feet. But the Japanese were usually unable to take advantage of the situation, because the fine dust particles caused their weapons to jam.

Panic was everywhere as men abandoned everything in their rush to escape:

> On the shoulders of these bearded men still gleamed epaulettes of all the colors of the rainbow, their hands still carried rifles they no longer needed, but they ceased to be soldiers. The officer corps had vanished, it was trailing along somewhere, doing its best to escape notice. It was powerless to restore any sort of order to this elemental torrent, pouring northward, as far as might be from the nightmare of the dusty fields of Mukden.[96]

Many of these men were not simply retreating, they were finished with war. When an officer asked one of these men who, like many others, was marching along with two loaves of black bread stuck on his bayonet, where he was going, the answer was, "Home, Your Honour, to Tambov

Province. As our regiment's been completely bust [sic] to pieces, why, I've decided it's time to finish!"[97] The man went on his way.

When men like these saw officers retreating with a piano in a cart that could have been used to carry wounded soldiers, they turned on them in fury, killing some, rifling through their baggage, and stealing their horses and carts. European Russians in rearguard units retained sufficient discipline to hold off the exhausted Japanese long enough for the bulk of the Russian army to make its way to the mountains around Tieh-ling and safety. The most powerful forces in restoring some semblance of order to these shattered units were company cooks, who had—almost without fail, it seems—managed to carry their precious mobile kitchens to safety. As

Japanese troops march into Mukden. (1905, H. C. White London)

hot meals were handed out, men came together again to eat, talk, and sleep, and the mutiny that seemed unavoidable somehow did not happen. Oyama's infantrymen fell asleep where they stood, and he had too few cavalry to cut off the huge Russian army. Every order, every encouragement, and every threat was used, but the Japanese soldiers, many of whom were older reservists of inferior quality, would do no more. More men had fought at Mukden than in any other battle yet fought on earth, and again the Japanese had won. But it was not another Sedan, not a crushing victory that would lead to a Russian surrender.

Oyama had to settle for another victory; he could not destroy the Russian army in Manchuria. It was a bitter failure, how bitter no one could then fully anticipate. Two days later, the tsar removed Kuropatkin from command, replacing him with one of his own generals, the much loved, seventy-year-old "Siberian Fox," General Nicholas Linievitch, who had looted Peking so thoroughly in 1900. Linievitch could not read a map or a railroad timetable and did not even know what a howitzer was, but his soldiers trusted him. Kuropatkin handed over command to Linievitch with dignity and left for St. Petersburg, but when he reached Harbin, he telegraphed the tsar and asked to be allowed to continue his service in Manchuria, saying, "I may not be a good general, but I am at least as good as some of my corps commanders." The tsar agreed and permitted him to return to the army, where he replaced Linievitch as commander of the First Manchurian Army.

The Russians lost at least 20,000 dead, and another 20,000 had been taken prisoner. Fully 50,000 more men had been wounded. The Japanese lost 16,000 dead and had 60,000 wounded. As great as the Russian losses were, the imperial Russian pool of manpower was so vast that they would soon be replaced, in large measure by first-line troops from European Russia, including Uhlans and the Chevalier Guards, the most prestigious unit in the Russian army. At long last, they also received thousands of machine guns, improved artillery, and mountains of supplies and ammunition. Oyama's losses were not quite as severe, but they could not be made up. There were no more trained men in Japan. In the weeks and months to come, Russian strength would grow while, because of these losses and others from disease, the Japanese army would shrink.

"YOU CAN KEEP TOKYO FOR YOURSELF"

While the Russian army struggled to regroup its shattered forces north of Mukden, the large Russian Baltic Fleet slowly made its way toward the Far East, where it meant to give battle to Admiral Togo's victorious but worn and damaged warships. The most decisive naval battle since Trafalgar, and perhaps the most decisive of all time, lay ahead. It remains the largest naval battle ever fought by ships alone.

The era of battleships with their big, long-range guns was in its heyday. Experts declared these well-armored, huge ships unsinkable by gunfire alone, but admitted that they might be vulnerable to torpedoes. Submarines remained in their infancy, and there were as yet no military aircraft, but many fast torpedo boats and destroyers existed. Both of these posed a mortal danger to larger ships. The Russian and Japanese fleets each possessed a squadron of four battleships of about 15,000 tons, mounting twelve-inch guns capable of firing 850-pound shells for over ten miles. Unlike the Japanese, who had their battleships built in Britain, the Russians built many of their own ships. Although formidably armed warships, they plodded, being more top-heavy than the British-built Japanese ships, and they were less heavily and completely armored (some battleships had no armor on their bows or sterns, a fatal flaw for some of them). Japan also had more cruisers, destroyers, and torpedo boats than the Russians did. When the two fleets finally met, the Russians held an advantage in the number of large guns, but everything else about the two fleets strongly favored the Japanese.

The decision to reinforce Russia's Far Eastern Squadron at Port Arthur was made in June 1904, when the battle for the fortress was still in doubt and the fleet in its harbor still a powerful force. Russia also had a strong fleet in the Black Sea, but owing to continuing hostility with Turkey, it could not pass through the Dardanelles. That left the Baltic Fleet of some fifty ships, most far from seaworthy. Command of these ships was given to Vice-Admiral Zinovi Petrovich Rozhdestvensky, a foul-tempered minor aristocrat known to his men as "the mad admiral," and to foreigners as the admiral with the "terrible name." As a contemporary British rhyme put it,

> And after all this, an Admiral came,
> A terrible man with a terrible name,
> A name which we all of us know very well,
> But no one can speak and no one can spell.[1]

At fifty-three, Rozhdestvensky was a tall, handsome, physically powerful man of boundless energy. He would need all of it. Many ships in his command had not been to sea in years, most of his sailors were newly conscripted "peasants in sailor suits," as one officer scornfully described them, and too many of his officers were lazy and incompetent. Many of his wealthy, noble officers went to sea accompanied by their accustomed lux-

Vice-Admiral Z. P. Rozhdestvensky. (Colliers)

uries. They brought elegant armchairs, soft beds, and writing tables adorned with silks, while bearskins and Persian carpets covered their floors and framed portraits and leather-bound books adorned the walls of their cabins. When officers like these were not gorging themselves on every epicurean delicacy, washed down with champagne and vodka, they frequently cursed and bashed the filthy, badly fed, expressionless sailors who worked listlessly from 5 A.M. to 8 P.M.[2]

No one took his duty more seriously than Rozhdestvensky. Sometimes sleepless for two or three days in a row, he alternated between a black depression and a towering rage, shouting and shaking his fist at malefactors and sometimes assaulting them. The high-strung admiral faced every imaginable problem, from unready ships to a shortage of ammunition and supplies, as well as crews that knew next to nothing about their duties. He received no help from the grand admiral of the navy, the Tsar's brother, Grand Duke Alexei Alexander, who knew absolutely nothing about ships but possessed a prodigious appetite for food, drink, and women. According to one of his brothers, his downfall was "fast women and slow ships."[3]

No one ever imagined that the Baltic Fleet, intended primarily for coastal defense, would be asked to sail 18,000 miles. Unlike the British navy, which had established coaling stations throughout the empire, the Russian navy had none. The Russian sailors might not be up to the voyage either. The British recruited their sailors as young teenagers and trained them to "think" like sailors; the Russian navy did not conscript its sailors until they were at least twenty-one years old, and then only for active duty stints of seven years. Moreover, because of ice, the Baltic Fleet could train only six months a year at best. British officers who inspected Russian warships found Russian officers to be quite similar to themselves as men, if not as sailors, but thought the Russian sailors dull-witted, indolent, and filthy. Most telling, they reported that Russian sailors thought their lot in life was to be shot at, while British sailors firmly believed they existed to shoot at others.[4]

Rozhdestvensky's chief of staff was a charming man of French aristocratic ancestry, Captain Clapier de Colongue. Tall, blond, and noticeably effeminate, he did everything in his power to smooth over the animosities created throughout the fleet by Rozhdestvensky's tirades, but with little success. Seen as an extension of the mad admiral, he would never be loved, but he was brave and would play a highly controversial role when the Baltic Fleet finally met the Japanese.

Despite tensions among senior officers, most of them worked steadily to make the lackluster fleet ready to sail. Nevertheless, ships still ran aground during simple maneuvers, and when the fleet was asked to demonstrate its skill in target practice (Admiral Rozhdestvensky's great skill as a gunnery officer had brought him his rank and his command), the gunners managed to miss all the targets but did hit one of the ships towing them.

Rozhdestvensky was remarkably unconcerned about the battle being waged at Port Arthur or even the activities of Togo's ships. He single-mindedly worked to ready his own fleet. Supplies and ammunition continued to pour in; fully one-third of the shells would prove to be duds when battle finally came. The admiral tried everything short of executions to discipline his sailors. Many of them stayed quite tipsy on home-brewed kvass, a drink made from dark rye bread and malt, and others openly proclaimed revolutionary ideas. Some turned to sabotage to prevent the fleet from sailing, and most thought they were about to set out on the voyage of the damned. Rozhdestvensky had already resigned himself to a terrible voyage with no hope of defeating Togo, but his sense of duty drove him out of the Baltic ports no matter how unprepared.

The fleet's greatest fear was an ambush by Japanese torpedo boats. Rumors of Japanese torpedo boats lying in wait in Norwegian fjords and Swedish inlets were taken so seriously in St. Petersburg that numerous Russian scouts rushed to Scandinavia to locate them. From rented boats or standing on promontories, more than a hundred Russian agents anxiously peered through their binoculars in search of Japanese warships, to no avail. The Japanese had not even considered sending torpedo boats on the 18,000-mile voyage to the North Sea.

Even after his fleet put out to sea, Rozhdestvensky's central concern continued to be its gunnery. Russian guns, made in the Obukov works on the river Neva, were of such high quality that none ever proved to be defective, but the gun crews were slow and inept at range finding—hardly a surprise, because many of the new peasant sailors could not count to one hundred.[5] Most navies, including the Japanese, had already adopted telescopic sights, the Russian navy had not yet managed to install these by the time Rozhdestvensky sailed. Other navies fired their guns electronically by merely pulling a trigger, but the Russians still had to pull antiquated metal lanyards to fire theirs. These often broke.[6]

When the fleet finally embarked on its great voyage, in mid-October 1904, it consisted of forty-two ships. In addition to Rozhdestvensky's flagship, the modern battleship *Suvorov,* and its three sister ships, the *Borodino, Alexander III*, and *Oryol*, it included several modern armored cruisers, as well as older ships of the same tonnage, a dozen destroyers and auxiliary vessels, transports, two all-white hospital ships, one staffed by one hundred nurses who came from Russia's best families (two were Rozhdestvensky's own nieces), and an all-purpose repair ship called the *Kamchatka*, manned largely by civilians and captained by a heavy drinker named Stepanoff. Gray or cinnamon camouflage paint was used in most navies in 1904, but every ship in the Russian fleet had its funnels painted a bright yellow with a black stripe near the top, a virtual guarantee of visibility.

Known as the Second Pacific Squadron, the yellow-funneled armada made its way past Sweden and Norway into the North Sea without major mishap. But the flagship *Suvorov* managed to run aground while coaling, and around midnight, under a full moon, the captain of the *Kamchatka*, thoroughly drunk at the time, reported sighting torpedo boats. A few officers on other ships wondered why the Japanese had targeted this insignificant repair ship when there were battleships and cruisers to be had; even so, few doubted that an attack was under way. Drums and bugles sounded action stations; every ship that had guns fired them wildly, while searchlights tried to locate the small, fast Japanese boats. Many officers and sailors humiliated themselves by panicking, screaming that their ships were sinking and grabbing life belts and cork mattresses as they prepared to abandon ship. When the searchlights finally found targets, hundreds of guns, including the twelve-inch guns on the battleships, concentrated fire on a few small ships that shone like silver under the searchlights.

Not until the *Suvorov* was within a hundred yards did Rozhdestvensky see that his targets were British fishing trawlers at work on their traditional Dogger Bank fishing grounds. Marked by red, white, and green lanterns, and frantically firing green flares as the Russian ships approached, they could not possibly have been mistaken for warships by any but the most hysterical of seamen. Nevertheless, the Russian ships had fired for fully twenty minutes, killing two fishermen and gravely wounding scores of others. Somehow, even though the battleship *Oryol* fired over 500 shells and the *Kamchatka* fired 300 from its small-caliber guns, the fleet managed to sink one trawler. But they did hit two Russian cruisers, wounding several sailors and killing a priest, leading an anticlerical junior officer to declare it not a bad night's work.[7]

Without stopping to provide any assistance to the wounded fishermen, the Second Pacific Squadron sailed away down the British Channel, once again mistakenly opening fire, this time on a Swedish trawler and a German merchant ship, but managing to miss both. With daylight, British crowds, still ignorant of the killing, gathered to watch the passing parade of scores of yellow-funneled warships belching black smoke. When the battered trawlers later arrived in Hull Harbor, Britain's mood turned ugly. The king called the incident a "most dastardly outrage," Parliament was furious, crowds gathered in Trafalgar Square, and newspapers called for war. Britain's rights on the high seas were not to be violated with impunity, and the Admiralty sent orders to the Home, Channel, and Mediterranean Fleets. The ominous gray ships of the world's most powerful navy began to close in on the bumbling Russian fleet, still oblivious to Britain's rage or the fact that the world's press had already denounced the Russians as incompetent and cruel bunglers. British cruisers steamed circles around the Russians, flaunting their superior speed and seaman-

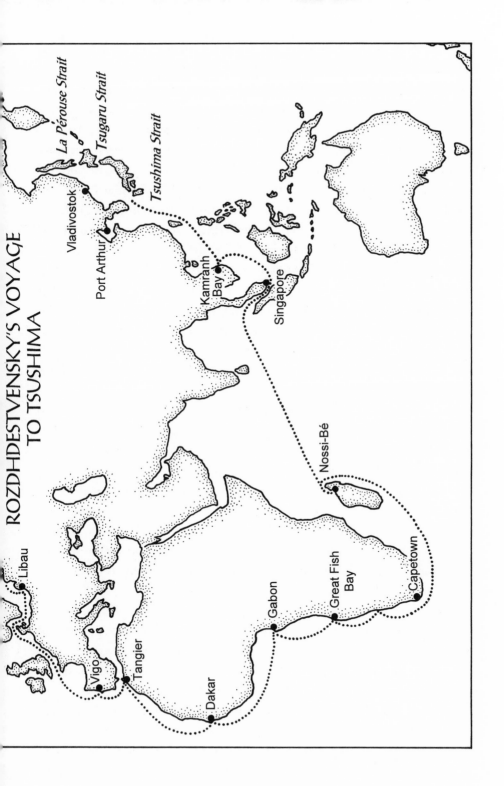

ROZDHDESTVENSKY'S VOYAGE
TO TSUSHIMA

La Pérouse Strait

Tsugaru Strait

Tsushima Strait

Vladivostok

Port Arthur

Kamranh
Bay

Singapore

Nossi-Bé

Libau

Vigo

Tangier

Dakar

Gabon

Great Fish
Bay

Capetown

ship, while no fewer than twenty-eight British battleships, all far superior to any Russian ship, rapidly closed in.

Still unaware of the threat of war, Rozhdestvensky anchored in the Spanish port of Vigo, where he learned of the international uproar he had caused. While London demanded apologies and St. Petersburg tried to sort out what had happened, the admiral staunchly defended his actions, blaming treacherous Japanese torpedo boat commanders, who he said had used the trawlers as shields, for the loss of British life. Germany was generally sympathetic to Russia at this time, but a German newspaper was almost as critical as the British press, referring to the action as "monstrous and inexplicable" and concluding, "The officers commanding these Russian ships must be all the time in an abnormal state of mind, and it is therefore not altogether unjustifiable to ask, as the English are asking, whether a squadron led as this squadron is led, ought to be allowed to sail the seas."[8] It also described Rozhdestvensky as an "exceedingly nervous gentlemen, who gets into a state of boundless excitement over trifles."[9]

This assessment was on the mark, but after the admiral issued a telegram that expressed "sincere regret" for the victims at Dogger Bank, the war fever of the British cooled, and they agreed to submit the matter to an international commission, which found Russia at fault and ordered her to pay an indemnity of £65,000.[10] It was finally safe for the Second Pacific Squadron to sail out of Vigo Harbor on November 1. Lord Beresford's cruiser squadron followed closely, taunting the Russians with exquisitely performed maneuvers, as Rozhdestvensky watched in admiration and frustration until he finally blurted out to Commander Semenoff, "Those are real seamen, if only we . . . ," before leaving the bridge in obvious anguish.[11] He had no idea how close he had come to meeting those seamen in unequal combat. Britain had very nearly declared war.[12]

After the British cruisers at last stopped dogging the Russian fleet, Rozhdestvensky was free to continue his voyage around the Cape of Good Hope, but only if he could find enough coal. British coaling stations were obviously off-limits; so were those of their Portuguese allies. But the French, sympathetic if not completely devoted allies, allowed the Russians to recoal at Dakar, where the temperature was 115 degrees Fahrenheit and the coal-blackened men could work for only a few minutes at a time. Many collapsed, but the only man to die was the young son of the Russian ambassador to France. With huge piles of coal stacked all over the decks of every ship in the fleet, Rozhdestvensky steamed along the coast of West Africa at a top speed of eight or nine knots. He was frequently forced to stop by mechanical problems, and all attempts to practice maneuvers were so hopelessly botched that the admiral screamed himself hoarse and arrested at least one hapless officer.

At his next stop, in Gabon, he was met by German colliers eager to make a sizable profit by supplying coal when no one else would. Many of the crewmen granted shore leave to escape the suffocating coal dust were dazzled by the tropical forest with its flowers, birds, and butterflies so different from anything in their experience. In German West Africa the ships again took on coal. On December 16, while the bored, sweating, filthy crewmen struggled with coal, a German major gave Admiral Rozhdestvenksy the dreadful news that 203-Meter Hill had fallen to the Japanese. The admiral asked, "And what is 203-Meter Hill?"[13] He shrugged the news off. He still had no interest whatever in military affairs, even those at Port Arthur that so much affected his own mission.

As the Second Pacific Squadron rounded the Cape of Good Hope, it encountered heavy seas, and several ships developed serious problems. At the height of the storm, the irrepressible *Kamchatka* signaled the *Suvorov* for permission to dump 150 tons of coal overboard, not because the coal made the repair ship top-heavy but because the quality of the coal was said to be poor. Already in a foul humor, Rozhdestvensky signaled back that every ship had the same coal and the only thing that should be thrown overboard was the fool who sent the signal. Soon thereafter, the *Kamchatka* signaled, "Do you see the torpedo boats?" Despite the terrible storm that made it impossible for torpedo boats to operate in such heavy seas, a general alarm sounded and everyone staggered to his action station before the hapless signalman on the *Kamchatka* explained that he had been using the wrong code. He had meant to say that the ship was all right.

A few days later, the ships reached Madagascar, where they received the news that shells from 203-Meter Hill had destroyed the Russian Fleet and that Port Arthur had surrendered. If worse news could be received, it soon came in a message that another group of ships—all the coastal defense hulks still in the Baltic—had set sail to join them, and Rozhdestvensky received orders to wait in Madagascar until they arrived, perhaps in ten weeks! This fleet was the brainchild of a bookish, pince-nez-wearing captain, Nikolai Klado, a longtime competitor of Rozhdestvensky's and his current nemesis.

The hospital ship Oryol, *not to be confused with the battleship* Oryol, *although both served in the battle of Tsushima Strait. (Colliers)*

Klado believed that these additional ships would thwart Togo by providing his gunners with so many targets that they would become confused and allow Russian battleships to destroy them. Rozhdestvensky knew that Togo would concentrate his fire on the Russian battleship squadron, no matter how many smaller ships were in the formation. He also knew that these unseaworthy ships—known as "self-sinkers" to Rozhdestvensky's men— would slow his progress beyond endurance. In despair, the admiral telegraphed St. Petersburg, asking to be relieved of his command.

Safely anchored in Madagascar's lovely bay of Nossi-Bé, the Russians enjoyed the hospitality of solicitous French officers who provided them with all manner of food and drink. Russian sailors were delighted to be away from coal dust and free to explore the beauties of Hellville—named after a French admiral, not the infernal region—which included grog shops. Even better, from their point of view, as word of the Russian fleet's arrival spread, prostitutes from all over Madagascar and South Africa began to appear at Nossi-Bé. A few officers joined in the merriment, find- ing some nurses from the hospital ship who were willing to meet them for clandestine bliss, but most shared their admiral's profound depression. Declaring their mission hopeless, many began to drink heavily. Sailors drank even more heavily, and several fell overboard.

On Christmas Day 1904, a haggard Rozhdestvensky climbed onto a twelve-inch gun turret, from where he addressed the 900 men of the *Suvorov*. Haltingly, he thanked them for serving their country well and wished them a happy and safe return to their families. Then he warned them of the danger that awaited them, and, with mounting emotion, his voice broken by audible sobs, he implored them to serve Holy Russia well. As he raised his glass of champagne, his powerful voice could be heard clearly above the dead silence of the crew: "To you whom I trust! To Russia!" The men roared approval, shouting, "Lead us, lead us," and many were in tears. A salute from the battleship's big guns ended the moving ceremony.

It was a rare moment of enthusiasm for the ill-starred Russian fleet, and poorly timed. No battle would be fought the next day, or the next month. The fleet would not fight for nearly five more months, and much would happen during that time. At first, Rozhdestvensky kept everyone busy by overhauling the ships and loading coal until the men collapsed in utter exhaustion. A few men died, and many came down with dysentery, but then fresh supplies of all sorts began to arrive from South Africa, and the French sold the fleet 1,000 bullocks as well as prodigious amounts of liquor. While the men were restoring their morale, the Russian Admiralty, ignoring Rozhdestvensky's request to be relieved, cabled instructions to the admiral that after being joined by the Third Pacific Reinforcing Squadron, as the "self-sinkers" were officially known, he was to reclaim "command of the sea" and cut communications between the Japanese troops in Manchuria and Japan. The admiral replied that at most he could hope to break through to Vladivostok and use that naval base to threaten Japanese supply convoys. He also requested permission to sail without waiting for the Third Squadron. His request was denied. Klado had the ears of the land-bound sailors in St. Petersburg.

By now, Hellville had absorbed an influx of foreigners from distant ports, and it soon lived up to its name, as drunken Russian sailors engaged in endless debauchery while their officers looked away. Many sailors lay comatose where they fell, as others crawled around on all fours. Those sober enough brought all manner of animals back to their ships as pets, including a large crocodile and a cobra that bit and almost killed an engineering officer. On one ship a favorite sport was getting monkeys and dogs drunk on champagne and inciting them to fight.[14] As indiscipline became worse by the day, Admiral Rozhdestvensky lay in bed, mysteriously indisposed. Rumors spread that he had suffered a stroke or a "nervous breakdown," but following two weeks of growing disorder, the admiral finally roused himself from his bed after a French administrator angrily complained to him that Russian sailors had been tearing down native houses and threatening their owners with violence. Enraged, the pale and weak admiral quickly restored order. Those pets not put ashore were thrown overboard, shore leave ended, and everyone set to work.

In mid-February 1905, newspapers arrived that provided shocking descriptions of riots, strikes, and uprisings throughout Russia, including the massacre of unarmed demonstrators before the Winter Palace. This news brought about an immediate revolutionary fervor throughout the fleet. To no one's surprise, the first actual mutiny broke out on the *Nakhimov*, whose officers had neglected their men shamelessly. The *Suvorov* trained its big guns on the ship to prevent further violence. Fourteen of the mutineers were chosen at random and shot by a firing squad; others were sentenced to long jail sentences, as Rozhdestvensky went on to smash other mutinies throughout the fleet. Finally, he packed the remaining ring leaders onto an old ship and sent them back to Russia, only to see the revolutionaries overpower their officers and guards. Once again, the *Suvorov* leveled her guns, and a boarding party had to retake the ship by force. With the mutineers at last under control, the entire fleet collapsed into indolence as the growing heat and humidity sapped everyone's energy.

Cigarette smoking was almost universal and constant on Russian ships, and the men's lack of energy was not helped by the new cigarettes they purchased in Madagascar. The Russians did not learn until after many cigarettes had been smoked that the tobacco was liberally laced with opium. Only the now energized Rozhdestvensky seemed unaffected by tropical torpor. He ordered gunnery practice, but even his own *Suvorov* missed the target, although it did hit the ship towing it on the bridge. Other ships milled about in total confusion because, it was eventually determined, they had not been issued the new signal code book used by the *Suvorov*. Torpedo practice was even more discouraging. According to Commander Vladimir Semenoff, "Seven torpedoes were fired. One never ran at all. Another began describing a circle, occasionally coming to the surface and threatening the boats, which speedily sought safety in flight. Two went off to the right, one to the left; finally two ran satisfactorily. And that in broad daylight, free from any disturbing factors, and with a smooth sea."[15] An earlier trial had been worse still.

When a local French naval officer told Rozhdestvensky that the Third Pacific Reinforcing Squadron was coaling at Crete on its way to join him, Rozhdestvensky insubordinately ignored his orders and set sail. No sooner he had done so than the irrepressible *Kamchatka* reported she was sinking. Rozhdestvensky ignored her, and after repairing what proved to be no more than a leaky pipe, the old repair ship caught up with the squadron. While Rozhdestvensky sailed east from Madagascar, the unwanted "self-sinkers" were doing all they could to join him. The fleet's sailors had drunkenly run amok on Crete, injuring many civilians, but had finally been brought back to their ships and the squadron put out to sea once more. Its commander was Rear Admiral Nikolai Nebogatov, an efficient sixty-five-year-old officer, but whose short stature, chubby body, and chronic eczema made him an unimposing figure. Known as "grand dad," he inspired no one. The old, 9,000-ton *Tsar Nikolai I* served as his flagship. It carried two twelve-inch and four nine-inch guns, but they had a short range and a very slow rate of fire. He also had an old cruiser and three 4,500-ton "flatiron" coastal defense ships never meant to go to sea. The Admiralty ordered him to join Rozhdestvensky but admitted it did not know where to find him. Nebogatov headed east nevertheless.

For three weeks, Rozhdestvensky steamed east toward Singapore without meeting a single ship, followed doggedly by Nebogatov's slower ships. On April 8, the forty-two-ship Russian armada steamed past Singapore as crowds gathered to watch while the yellow-funneled ships took fifty-five minutes to pass by, their decks laden with coal and their sides visibly covered by seaweed. Even though the ships were plagued by cockroaches and many men had come down with malaria and dysentery, thanks to the skill of ships' doctors and the toughness of the men, only eight died of disease after leaving Madagascar. Suddenly no longer a laughingstock, the Russian fleet impressed British observers in Singapore with its successful voyage; they began to write newspaper articles praising Rozhdestvensky's seamanship and speculating that the Russian fleet might give the Japanese trouble after all.

A Russian consul who came aboard the *Suvorov* from a small steam launch managed to inform the admiral that Mukden had fallen and Russian troops were retreating northward. Rozhdestvensky received

Artist's drawing of Rozhdestvensky's fleet near Singapore. (Colliers)

orders to wait for Nebogatov at Kamranh Bay. In a masterful piece of bad timing, the admiral was also informed that after he had successfully fought his way to Vladivostok, he was to hand over command of the squadron to Admiral Biriliov, already on his way there by rail. Rozhdestvensky detested Biriliov, who had never been in action but nevertheless insisted on referring to himself as the "fighting admiral." The voyage to Kamranh Bay was uneventful, although the fleet caused considerable perplexity among the crew of the passing British cruiser *Diadem* when it signaled that it wished to know the identity of the Russian fleet's admiral so that it could salute him correctly. The garbled Russian reply was "knives and forks," and the baffled British ship sailed past without saluting.[16]

The "mad admiral" had no intention of waiting for the "self-sinking" fleet. He took on coal from waiting colliers and, when the coal ships had been emptied, signaled his ships to report. One ship after another reported sufficient amounts of coal to allow them to steam to Vladivostok, but the battleship *Alexander III* reported only 400 tons, not nearly enough for it to steam that far. After assuring the incredulous Rozhdestvensky that the report was not a mistake, the *Alexander III* incurred his terrible wrath. Officered by high-ranking nobles, the battleship had always won prizes for coaling more rapidly than any other ship. It was now clear that it did so by deliberately loading less coal than it reported.

Rozhdestvensky had accomplished the miraculous. He had sailed his ships halfway around the world despite seventy major mechanical breakdowns, successfully coaling them in midocean in heavy seas on five separate occasions. Now he was trapped. He would have to wait in Kamranh Bay until more colliers arrived. By then the "self-sinkers" would be there. Falling back into a deep depression, Rozhdestvensky once again took to his cabin. He gave no orders to clean the bottoms of his ships; in fact, he gave no orders at all. The only activity was by his destroyers. On their own, they patrolled in search of the Japanese.

While Rozhdestvensky languished, the Japanese grew apprehensive about the approach of the Russian fleet. In the Japanese Admiralty there was anxiety. What might happen if a battle took place? Togo could not afford any major losses, and in the confusion of combat even poorly aimed twelve-inch guns and torpedoes could do great damage.

Unlike Rozhdestvensky, Togo fretted about the addition of Nebogatov's twelve- and ten-inch guns to the already powerful armament of the Russian fleet. Even more serious, what if the Russians managed to slip by Togo into Vladivostok? Japan knew she would soon have to sue for peace, and a functioning Russian fleet in the Far East would strengthen Russia's hand at the peace table. Wanting to force the Russians out of Kamranh Bay before Nebogatov could arrive, the Japanese pressured France to comply with international neutrality laws. The French grudgingly agreed, forcing Rozhdestvensky to anchor his squadron outside the bay in international waters. The French did allow the Russians to leave some unarmed transports and auxiliary ships behind. On May 9, Nebogatov's unwanted ten-ship fleet with its colliers miraculously managed to find Rozhdestvensky. Five days later, the combined fleet set off for Vladivostok.

For months, Togo had been supervising the overhaul and repair of his fleet. Many ships desperately needed refitting, and every day that Rozhdestvensky was delayed was heaven-sent. As it was, the *Asahi*, one of Togo's four remaining battleships, had barely been repaired in time for battle. Neither Rozhdestvensky nor any other Russian knew that two of Togo's six modern battleships had been sunk.

As a young man, Togo had displayed few intellectual gifts, but he became a brilliant swordsman and proved that, once he learned something, he never forgot it. In 1871, he went to England to train with the Royal

Admiral Togo.
(Colliers)

Navy. After riding a camel from Suez to Alexandria, he sailed to London with eleven other Japanese cadets. There he boarded with a middle-class English family and continued to study English, a language he would never learn to speak well. His problems with the language aside, he demanded respect. When British cadets on the training ship he soon joined taunted him as "Johnny Chinaman," the thin, five-foot three Togo challenged them to fight. They backed down. Slowly, he mastered his craft and earned the respect of his instructors.[17] His ability to make decisions and carry them through without hesitation was his greatest attribute.

Always confident to the point of pigheadedness, Togo assumed correctly that after the fall of Port Arthur, Rozhdestvensky would try to reach Vladivostok via one of three possible routes.[18] Togo ruled out two of them. The Tsugaru Strait, between Hokkaido and Honshu, was too narrow;

ships could easily be seen from the shore. La Pérouse Strait, between Hokkaido and Sakhalin, was a possibility but entailed a longer voyage, and Togo knew that coal was a problem for the Russians. He guessed correctly that Russian ships would take the most direct route, through the Tsushima Strait. Togo's navigational officers divided the waters of the strait into ten-mile squares, each with a number; Japanese scouting vessels need only report a single number to give the Russians' location. The Japanese had radios with a range of 500 miles; the Russians had few radios and rarely used the ones they had.

Rozhdestvensky tried to deceive Togo by leaking his actual route to a Norwegian ship captain, assuming that Togo would think the report false. But on May 25 he sent his supply ships and colliers to Shanghai. When this was reported to Togo by a Japanese scout ship, he knew that it would be Tsushima. If the Russians meant to take the longer route, the colliers could not be spared. As his battle fleet approached Tsushima, the Russian admiral ordered that everything inflammable, including the officers' expensive wooden furniture be thrown overboard, and thousands of first-aid packets were distributed while men stood at battle stations around the clock, sleeping beside the guns. On the night of May 26–27, the strait was wrapped in such thick fog that some officers began to think they would slip past Togo after all. But at 3:30 A.M. the mist briefly lifted, and a lookout on one of the Russian hospital ships got a fleeting look at a strange ship, which rapidly veered away. The Japanese armed merchant cruiser quickly transmitted the news to Togo that the Russian fleet had been sighted in section number 203. For Togo the number 203, reminding him of 203-Meter Hill, was an augury of victory.

Ninety minutes after receiving the report from section number 203, Togo's entire fleet sailed southwest to meet the Russians, who were heading north toward Vladivostok. After all unnecessary coal had been thrown overboard, each Japanese crew member dressed in clean clothes, washed his eyes with boric acid to reduce the chances of infection, and plugged his ears with cotton. The Russian ships were already at battle stations, but to commemorate the ninth anniversary of the tsar's coronation, all hands were issued a tot of rum or vodka, and the officers filled their glasses with champagne. After the requisite cheer for the tsar and a salvo, the men were led in prayer by a priest before returning to their posts.

Togo's flagship, the British-built *Mikasa*, named after a hallowed

Japanese mountain, was the most powerful ship in the world, and at this moment it was also the most important. Togo had been receiving regular reports from cruisers shadowing the Russian fleet about its formation, which consisted of two parallel lines of ships, the big-gunned battleships and heavy cruisers to the starboard, or east, and a line of weaker cruisers and battleships on the port, or west. Destroyers, auxiliary ships, and the two hospital ships followed. Togo had been told to expect this formation, which conformed perfectly to the plan drafted by his brilliant aide, Commander Akiyama Masayuki. Eccentric to a fault—he often worked all night, came to the bridge in bedroom slippers, and jumped overboard for a swim without removing his trousers—Akiyama had predicted almost everything the Russians would do.

If Togo stayed on a southerly course, his single line of powerful ships would pass quickly by the northbound Russians and would be able to fire broadsides for only a few minutes before steaming out of range, leaving the Russians free to run for Vladivostok. This was not an acceptable outcome for Akiyama or Togo. Togo decided that his twelve major ships, instead of briefly exchanging gunfire, would steam abreast of the Russian port line, then make a U-turn and sail north with them, enabling him to engage the Russian ships as long as necessary. The plan was risky because, in order to make the turn, the Japanese had to slow down while within the range of Russian guns. For roughly ten minutes, one Japanese ship after another would be a sitting duck.

When officers on the bridge of the *Suvorov* saw the Japanese ships making their leisurely turn, they were elated and expected Rozhdestvensky to open full fire, but the admiral simply stared through his binoculars as if transfixed. Precious minutes were lost before the *Suvorov*'s guns bracketed the *Mikasa*, hitting her a dozen times, and then hit the second ship in line, the *Asahi*, even harder. With surprisingly accurate gunnery, some 300 shells hit on or near the Japanese during a period of three minutes when they were unable to return fire. Fortunately for Togo, almost half of the heavy Russian shells were duds.[19]

Togo, though grazed by a shell fragment, never took his binoculars away from his eyes. On the *Asahi*, the damage was greater. An officer later wrote, "I was puzzled to know where to step as the shattered deck was bestrewn with pieces of human flesh and besmeared with fresh blood, while mutilated hands and feet and human bowels were scattered everywhere."[20] The British Royal Navy captain (later admiral) William C. Pakenham, an observer on the *Asahi*, was sitting on the deck in a white dress uniform calmly taking notes when he was struck by an object that turned out to be the right half of a man's lower jaw. Splattered with blood, the tall, monocled British officer left his chair and went below. Japanese officers thought that the notoriously unflappable Englishman had finally had enough, but in a matter of minutes, he returned to his chair dressed in a neatly starched, clean white uniform. He remained there throughout the battle. Togo later said that Pakenham was the bravest man in his fleet.

Twenty minutes after Togo's turning maneuver began, his lead ships were able to return fire, and they did so with terrible success. Before the Baltic Fleet entered the Tsushima Strait, the Russian ships' surgeons brought their operating rooms into readiness. Cupboards with glass windows and shelves, glass bottles, nickel boxes, and enamel pots were loaded with neatly packaged antiseptics, anesthetics such as chloroform, ether, and morphine, ointments for burns, surgical instruments, and silk-threaded suture needles in carbolic acid solution. The white walls and white linen-draped operating tables dazzled the eye under bright overhead electric lights. Throughout each ship, officers and men tensed for the first explosions of Japanese shells; some expected to be killed, whereas others later said that they believed their heavily armored ships could withstand anything the Japanese could fire at them.

Just before the first shells hit the battleship *Oryol*, its crewmen were surprisingly relaxed. Although they were at battle stations, some played checkers, others read, one man played a balalaika, and one group debated whether a single man could possibly devour 15 pounds of black rye bread at a sitting.[21] Officers took bets about whether there would be a battle that day. When the first four-foot-long, 850-pound shells from the Japanese battleships' twelve-inch guns hit the *Oryol*, the 15,000-ton ship shuddered so violently that no one any longer doubted the destructive power of Japanese gunfire. The Japanese had developed a new explosive called *shimose*, one substantially more powerful than the Russian explosive pyroxylin. Moreover, a Japanese twelve-inch shell contained 105 pounds of explosive while a comparably sized Russian shell held only 15 pounds of the weaker explosive.[22]

Fused to explode on the slightest impact, Japanese shells seldom penetrated Russian ships, but they did blow huge holes whenever they hit,

Battleship Oryol. *(Colliers)*

started fires, and sent large fragments of hot steel flying in all directions. Unlike the Russians, who, following French naval doctrine, tried to sink their enemies with armor-piercing shells, the Japanese followed British naval doctrine by first smashing the superstructure of their enemies' ships before attempting to sink them. When the first Japanese shells struck, sailors cried for stretchers as the acrid yellow smoke from the Japanese shells turned their beards yellow and caused them to cough convulsively. Steam billowing out of ruptured boilers and black dust from the coal that was still stacked on deck cut visibility to nothing. One of the first men to be hit tried to run on the stumps of his legs, severed at the knee, before he fell into a pool of his own blood. Before he died, he cried, "Brothers, the ironclad is flying up into the clouds, up into the clouds."[23]

And so it must have seemed as bodies were torn apart, blood flew like rain, and torsos without legs, arms, and heads rolled along the deck. One man silently tried to push his intestines back into his body before dying with an inhuman scream.[24] Many men bravely stood by their guns, firing at the Japanese ships with unknown effects. Others panicked, screaming that the ship was sinking, while officers did their best to calm them by saying that all would be well and they would live to see again the shore, where they could "have a drink and cuddle a wench."[25]

Below decks, fires blazed out of control and the temperature reached 140 degrees Fahrenheit as surgeons worked frantically by candlelight, amputating arms and legs that were tossed into piles on the floor, suturing wounds, and trying to comfort their screaming patients who, in shock from their wounds, complained that they were freezing to death. The smell of blood and antiseptics was so strong that even smoke and stifling gases could not overcome it. Priests knelt among the dying men, hearing confessions and giving sacraments. The *Oslyabya*, leading the Russian port line, sank at 3:30 A.M., only an hour after Togo's guns opened fire. Her huge superstructure disappeared as she keeled over with hundreds of white-clad sailors attempting to cling to her seaweed- and barnacle-encrusted bottom. Some 200 men of nearly 1,000 on board survived. She was the first armored battleship ever sunk by gunfire (her unarmored bow had been her downfall), but she would not be the last. By now, all the major Russian ships had suffered great damage, and no semblance of a formation remained. Togo later said that he knew the battle was won after the first thirty minutes of fighting. With the wounded Russian ships barely able to make headway in heavy seas, Japanese cruisers and destroyers moved closer for the kill.

Somehow, the infamous little *Kamchatka* had stayed very close to the flagship *Suvorov* and, with only one officer still alive, was still firing back bravely when at 6:50 she took a torpedo and went down, with no survivors. Ten minutes later, four torpedoes hit the *Suvorov* at once, and she sank at 7:00 A.M. with her remaining crew and her three pet dogs, a dachshund named Dinky, a mutt named Flagmansky, and a fox terrier puppy known as Gypsy. A few minutes later, her sister ship *Alexander III* went down, with only sixty survivors. Surgeons refused to leave their patients and went down with their ships.[26] Despite the carnage on the Russian battleships, Japanese ships were still taking some hits from Russians who stood by their guns. A young midshipman named Yamamoto Isoroku lost two fingers of his left hand.[27] He would survive to plan the attack on Pearl Harbor that began World War II.

The last ship to sink before darkness fell was the *Borodino*, the worst ship in the squadron, according to Rozhdestvensky. She had perpetual trouble with her boilers, engines, and steering gear. A significant number of her crewmen were outspoken revolutionaries, and her captain, Sevebrinnikoff, was suspected of having socialist sympathies himself. That Sevebrinnikoff used his own money to see that his men were better clothed and fed than those of any other ship in the squadron only increased Rozhdestvensky's suspicions. But when the battle began, the *Borodino*'s captain asked his men to do their best to maintain the honor of the ship. They fought until the ship sank beneath them; only one man of the Borodino's crew of 900 survived.[28] The Japanese who saw the ship go down respected the Russians' bravery, deeply moved as they watched crewmen being sucked beneath the surface as the great ship sank.[29]

Some of those trapped below decks in the *Borodino*, like the men in other drowned ships, probably lived in an air pocket for an hour or two, like the American sailors who went down with their battleships at Pearl Harbor. The fighting continued throughout the night, with the battered Russian ships listing more and more dangerously as men below decks tried to stuff mattresses and blankets into gaping holes in the ships' sides. During a lull in the action, the men were issued a tot of rum, some tinned beef, and biscuit before the dead were laid out on the stern and covered with Russian flags while a priest gave them absolution.

Before the *Suvorov* went down, Rozhdestvensky had been so gravely wounded that he could no longer command. As a result of a head wound, he often lost consciousness and a leg wound left him unable to walk. Clapier de Colongue was perfectly aware that the fleet was destroyed, along with Rozhdestvensky's career, but he resolved to save the admiral's life. With courage and determination that few thought he possessed, he mobilized a team of officers to carry the stricken admiral down to the deck of the listing battleship, while the destroyer *Buiny* gallantly stood alongside. Clapier de Colongue ordered the Russian sailors to lie down on the ship's side so that the admiral could be rolled downward over their backs. As a formidable young officer, Werner von Kursel, tried to predict when the next swell would bring the *Buiny* flush against the *Suvorov*, Clapier de Colongue, Semenoff, and others waited for the word to roll their admiral toward safety. At just the right moment, von Kursel bellowed "now" and Rozhdestvensky's inert body rolled down into waiting arms aboard the destroyer. It was an extraordinary feat.

Semenoff, Clapier de Colongue, and a few others stayed with the admiral, but the destroyer was so overloaded with survivors from other ships that most of the *Suvorov*'s remaining crew could not be saved. Von Kursel insisted on remaining with the ship as its sole surviving officer, and he and one hundred crewmen fought to their deaths. Despite his wounds, Rozhdestvensky was transferred to the undamaged destroyer *Bedovi*, soon afterward boarded by the Japanese. Rozhdestvensky regained consciousness only to learn that he was a prisoner and that four Russian officers were to be held as hostages against his possible escape. Deathly pale, with his head bandaged and his beard half singed off, the admiral struggled to a sitting position in bed to address the four men. All he could say was "poor fellows, poor fellows," before he began to sob.[30] The four officers looked on silently as the admiral's tears confirmed for them that their fleet had, as promised, died for Russia.

That night, the major Japanese ships broke off contact, giving the Russians two short hours to do what they could to make their ships more seaworthy. No one was busier than surgeons and priests, as piles of amputated arms and legs grew tall and the dead received absolution before being pushed overboard. Just before midnight, fifty-eight Japanese destroyers and torpedo boats swarmed to the attack, often approaching so close that the Russian ships could not lower their guns enough to hit them. At daybreak, most Russian ships still afloat wallowed, barely able to make headway. Only Rear Admiral Oscar A. Enkvist's fast light-cruiser squadron was largely unhurt, although during the night two of the cruisers had accidently rammed two others, sinking one of them. Enkvist's mission was to attack the transports at the rear of Togo's column, but the admiral chose to sail away, not to the north for Vladivostok and not to the main battle area to look for survivors but south for Manila, where his ships were interned by the U.S. Navy. Enkvist tried to justify his actions, but no one appeared more skeptical of his words than he. He became so depressed that he tried to take his own life and soon thereafter died of "shame," it was said.[31]

One of the trouble-making ships of the fleet was the old, slow light cruiser *Dimitri Donskoy*. Left behind by Enkvist, with six holes in her side, her boilers shot through, her captain dying, and most of her crew wounded, she was being abandoned by the crew when attacked by four cruisers and two torpedo boats. Somehow, the dying ship sank the torpedo boats and drove off the cruisers before it scuttled itself near the shore. The swift cruiser *Svetlana* was also too badly damaged to join Enkvist; instead of surrendering, though, it stood to fight against three Japanese cruisers until it finally sank with all hands.

Not all ships fought with such courage. To no one's surprise, the two unarmed white hospital ships surrendered, and the nurses were treated with great courtesy. In fact, the head nurse of the *Oryol* so cowed the English-speaking Japanese officer who boarded her that he felt personally defeated.[32] But on some ships, including the battleship *Oryol,* which had earned the most honors for her conduct on the voyage, men hid below decks rather than face Japanese fire. When Japanese came aboard after this ship raised a white flag, they were astonished to discover only 20 dead and 40 wounded: fully 850 unwounded men had spent the battle huddled below decks, trying to stay out of harm's way.[33] On another ship, the *Nakhimov*, three officers hid below decks and drank wine while the ship's crew fought on.

All that remained of the Russian fleet was the slow battleship *Nikolai I* and four slow cruisers under Admiral Nebogatov. When a line of Japanese cruisers made ready to shell them while still out of range of the old Russian guns, Nebogatov surrendered to avoid the useless loss of life. His fast, twenty-four-knot cruiser, *Izumrud*, refused to obey. Led by Captain Baron Ferzen and First Officer Patton-Fanton-de-Verraillon, another descendant of French nobility, the *Izumrud* outran two Japanese cruisers, but lacking enough coal to reach Vladivostok, was blown up by Ferzen in Russian territory, and his crew later reached Vladivostok safely.[34] The ancient coastal defense ship *Admiral Ushakov* also refused to surrender. After a hard fight, her once motley crew scuttled her and maintained their discipline so well that, even after hours in the water, 339 of 440 men survived.[35]

Nebogatov's other ships capitulated, however, to the annoyance of Togo, who later wrote of the surrender, "It was the strangest occurrence, and we were astonished and somewhat disappointed."[36] He made his disappointment perfectly clear: even though he recognized that the white flag had been raised on *Nikolai I,* he did not order a ceasefire. Akiyama was so horrified that he asked Togo whether the code of Bushido did not compel them to honor the flag. Without emotion, Togo said that he would stop only when the Russians stopped their engines. When the Russians did so and the firing finally stopped, Akiyama had tears in his eyes.

Twelve large ships had made up the Russian battle line. Eight had been

sunk and four captured. Of the cruisers, four had been sunk, one scuttled, and three interned; five destroyers went down, and four more were captured or interned. Two torpedo boats were lost as well. Only three small ships actually made it to Vladivostok. The Japanese lost only three torpedo boats, and although several other ships had received some damage, all could be repaired. The Russians lost 4,830 men, many of whom drowned. About 7,000 became prisoners, and 1,862 others were interned in neutral countries. Japanese losses stood in stark contrast: 110 killed and 590 wounded.[37] In the end, the epic voyage, with its terrible hardships and many displays of courage, amounted to the most one-sided defeat in modern naval history. President Theodore Roosevelt wrote that "neither Trafalgar nor the defeat of the Spanish Armada was as complete—as overwhelming."[38]

The Japanese treated those Russians who surrendered without a serious fight with disdain, but all the Russian prisoners received courteous care. The Japanese had been slow to pick up Russians after their ships sank, and many drowned needlessly, but some men, including one who spent sixteen hours in the water, were rescued. Once on board Japanese ships, Russian prisoners were stunned by the cordial reception they received. Everyone was given dry clothing, a glass of wine, and a package of cigarettes. The Russian sailors expressed amazement at the obvious trust and respect that existed between Japanese officers and men. When the survivors of the *Nakhimov* surrendered, their still intoxicated captain—one of those who had hidden below decks—humiliatingly attempted to drill them on deck as the Japanese looked on in disgust.[39]

When these Russian prisoners reached Japan, they joined the many thousands of Russian soldiers taken prisoner in earlier battles. Wounded Russian prisoners had been treated with exceptional courtesy at the time of their capture, being given water, food, and cigarettes, while delighted officers typically received large glasses of brandy. One Russian lieutenant who surrendered after Mukden proved to be a woman. Although dumbfounded, the Japanese also treated her courteously. Despite the disdain the Japanese felt for unwounded men who surrendered, most of these Russians did not feel like despised prisoners of war. And for their part, the Russians treated Japanese prisoners decently in Moscow. Japanese prison-

Russian sailors recuperate in Japan. (Colliers)

ers became objects of great curiosity but learned rapidly to speak a little Russian, and their captivity was tolerable.[40]

Russian wounded received every amenity, as did Japanese wounded in Russian hospitals. Many Russians said that, at last, they had found people who cared about them. The Japanese empress used her own funds to buy artificial limbs and eyes for wounded Russians, and in one hospital only 6 of 600 wounded Russians died, a remarkable record.[41] Russian prisoners waited for a peace treaty in camps throughout Japan. Those held in hospital barracks at Matsuyama, on a beautiful island in the Sea of Japan, found life especially bountiful. Officers were free to go among the Japanese people (albeit in the company of a Japanese officer), and some wasted no time in establishing intimate relationships with local women. Permission to shop in a nearby town, visit a hot spring, and stroll along the seashore was routinely given, and illiterate sailors received tutoring.

The head surgeon at Matsuyama was the epitome of kindness and competence, as were the many nurses who tended the wounded Russian prisoners. These men received any books and newspapers they wished, without censorship, but their letters home were censored, although rather ineptly. Japanese civilians felt such pity for the wounded men that they often gave them gifts of cigarettes and sweets. And although the Geneva Convention required only that prisoners be fed the same food given to Japanese troops, the Russians ate ample meals of European food. Officers received special favors. A badly wounded aristocratic Russian colonel was allowed to convalesce at the rented home of his wife, Princess Sophia von Theill, who had rushed from Russia to be with him.[42]

The Japanese, not anticipating the surrender of so many men at Port Arthur, or the capture of so many sailors, were hard-pressed to house and feed them all. Buddhist temples accommodated many, the pavilion of a zoo held others, while existing camps bulged with still others. When a contingent of officers arrived at Matsuyama, the Russians who greeted them were shocked at what they found: "A sad-faced, woe-begone, broken-hearted lot of sufferers? Not at all! There marched, there strutted forth, from the little white train station, the smartest lot of officers I ever saw parade the Nevsky!—a gala party in full-dress uniforms, clanking their swords and blowing smoke rings to the sun."[43] The Russians had expected gaunt, grieving men, not arrogant, well-fed fops who offered no excuses for their surrender. So had the Japanese, who were not impressed.

They ordered the new prisoners to surrender their swords, and although they treated these men properly, they disdainfully referred to them as the "surrendered" prisoners to differentiate them from the men captured in battle. The officers who surrendered with Nebogatov at Tsushima were accorded even less respect, but they were nevertheless treated with courtesy, if not the great sympathy shown earlier prisoners.

The British press was still capable of disparaging remarks about the stature of the Japanese, as in a caption entitled "The Pygmies Prevail," showing Japanese soldiers escorting large Russian prisoners,[44] but first-hand observers of Japanese conduct toward prisoners were unfailingly impressed. According to a British nurse who volunteered her services to Japan, the Japanese treated Russian prisoners more as "honored guests" than as prisoners.[45] Another British visitor wrote that Russian prisoners were treated "magnificently, with great generosity, and with every kindness and consideration."[46] A German diplomat commented that prisoners were treated "wonderfully well."[47] Still another British observer was struck by the sight of Russian officers on parole sightseeing in Nagasaki while they waited for a ship to take them to Vladivostok. "It was curious to watch the Russians enjoying the freedom of the enemy's country, sightseeing in rickshaws and on foot, shopping, and looking at war-pictures in the windows. The natives treated them with uniform respect and good-nature, and the Russians were loud in their praises of the considerate treatment they had received from the Japanese."[48] A fourth British observer wrote, "I have never, in the course of my many campaigns, seen prisoners, whether able-bodied, sick or wounded, so thoroughly well cared for as these Russians are by the Japanese at Matsuyama."[49]

An American army surgeon, Major L. L. Seaman, who had served in the Spanish-American and Philippine Wars as well as the Boxer Rebellion, was equally impressed by Matsuyama. He reported that the food was far better than the Russians had been accustomed to and that many prisoners told him they had never eaten better in their lives. The prisoners were also allowed to correspond with family and relatives and to read foreign newspapers. Dr. Seaman wrote that the Russians "had expected cruelties and were astonished to find themselves surrounded by what they were pleased to call paradise."[50] As arrangements were made to send the prisoners home, many requested permission to remain in Japan. When the men finally left Matsuyama, their spokesman said, "We have been treated everywhere as friends rather than enemies, and we shall always remember the kindness and humanity shown to us by the Japanese...."[51]

Throughout Japan, prisoners were well fed and clothed, and most were allowed to leave their camps to visit Japanese families, where they were so well received that even though they seldom spoke more than a few words of Japanese, many of these men were able to take Japanese "wives," as they referred to these girlfriends.[52] When a Russian sailor was repatriated to Russia and had to tell his Japanese lover that he was leaving, he wrote that he "felt as if the heart were being torn out of [his] living body."[53] Officers were treated even more indulgently, and once peace had been achieved, officers and sailors alike were given the free run of Nagasaki, where they gambled, drank, and "wenched" to their hearts' delight while waiting for ships to return them to Russia.

Togo treated Rozhdestvensky with great respect, seeing to it that his needs were met and assuring him that he had done his duty—which was all a warrior could ask of himself. The Russian admiral was moved by Togo's sincere words. Nevertheless, he remained depressed. He was housed in a beautiful temple in Kyoto, but his hair turned white and he ate little and refused the company of geishas.[54]

As fresh Russian regiments arrived in Manchuria from European Russia, it was anyone's guess whether they would stiffen the resolve of the veteran troops or become infected with their defeatism. After sustaining their own heavy losses, the Japanese forces were only slightly better off. Older reservists now made up a majority of the troops available, and they had little stomach for battle. Japanese Imperial Army General Headquarters had already scraped the bottom of the barrel for possible replacements from Japan. For Oyama to press on further into Manchuria would be to risk a destruction like Napoleon's in Russia, and Oyama was by no means sure that his weakened army would even be able to break though the increasingly formidable Russian defense line. German and Dutch military analysts believed that Japan could still defeat the Russians, but Oyama was unwilling to take the risk.[55]

Japan's desperate financial condition tormented the government. Her earlier victories had enabled her to seek foreign loans, particularly from Kuhn, Loeb and Company in New York, Jewish bankers who detested Russia for her mistreatment of Russian Jews, but by mid-1905 the war was costing the Japanese £11 million each month, and Japan's total annual budget amounted to only £22 million.[56] It was time to end the war, and with nothing but victories on land, the capture of Port Arthur, and the smashing triumph of Tsushima, the Japanese had every reason to believe that they could dictate favorable terms to the Russians. At the very start of the war, Viscount Kaneko Kentaro had been sent to the United States to renew his acquaintance with President Roosevelt, whom he had known as a fellow student at Harvard. Roosevelt had made it known that he was eager to act as an intermediary to bring about peace, and, better still from Kaneko's perspective, he was openly pro-Japanese.

Immediately after the battle of Tsushima Strait, Japan asked Roosevelt if he would bring the two combatants together to negotiate peace. Tsar Nicholas was indecisive, as usual. His country was torn by civil unrest, his fleet no longer in existence, and his government bankrupt, with no hope of securing a foreign loan.[57] However, the newly arrived elite army units had, in fact, revitalized the army in Manchuria, while the exhausted Japanese grew correspondingly more war-weary. The tsar's armies might not yet be ready to drive the Japanese out of Manchuria, but it was growing clearer with every passing day that Japan no longer had the power to defeat the Russian army. Tsar Nicholas's greatest fear was that Japan would invade nearly undefended Sakhalin. He decided to enter into peace talks in the hope of preventing it. On June 12, 1905, Russia agreed to meet with Japan under Roosevelt's auspices to discuss peace. While the interested parties argued over the site of the conference, Japan invaded Sakhalin and in less than a month of largely bloodless fighting seized all of the island—the only Russian territory to be lost to Japan. To strengthen Japan's hand even more, the Anglo-Japanese alliance was renewed for a period of ten years. It gave Japan a free hand in Korea and required each side to support the other militarily if attacked by any other power.

It appeared to the world that Japan held almost all the high cards as its delegation to the peace conference, now agreed on for Portsmouth, New Hampshire, set sail. Newport, Rhode Island, had been considered as a site, but Roosevelt feared that the "smart set" there would side too openly with the Russians. Led by Marquis Komura Jutaro, Harvard's first Japanese graduate, the Japanese were greeted with great enthusiasm as they made their way across the United States by train. When the two delegations first arrived at the massive, elegant Hotel Wentworth, a large crowd of local people cheered the Japanese delegates, who bowed and smiled in return, but did not cheer the equally smiling and bowing Russians.[58] Russia's delegation was led by none other than Sergei Yulyevich Witte, who got the job not so much because he was back in the tsar's favor but because no one else would take it. Unlike the suave, American-educated Komura, Witte was often abrasive and could not speak English. There were other contrasts too. Witte was six feet four, a massive dead ringer for Orson Welles, while the slight, reserved Komura was barely five feet five. Witte also made no bones about detesting American food, whereas the Japanese diplomat politely ate everything put in front of him. Topping it off, Witte complained that his room, and especially his bathtub, was too small, as it very well may have been.

The two sides had agreed not to talk to the press. Komura kept his side of the bargain, but Witte shamelessly chatted with every reporter he could find, and although it pained him to lower himself, he went far out of his way to treat all Americans as his equal. He was shocked, however, to discover that except for ten French waiters brought to Portsmouth from the Waldorf-Astoria in New York because the Russians could not speak English, the waiters at the hotel were American college students on summer jobs. Russian college students would never lower themselves by taking such menial work.[59] The two delegations were carefully protected by twelve Secret Service agents, but several of the Russians managed to slip away to meet some of the one hundred "summer girls" who were drawn to the hotel "dying to know celebrities."[60] The Japanese did not follow suit.

When it came to the negotiations, however, Witte was masterful. The war party in Japan insisted that their delegates impose humiliating terms on Russia—possession of Sakhalin, the Liaoyang Peninsula, and Korea, and a huge monetary indemnity. First, Witte adroitly characterized the Japanese as the aggressors in the war, which, he assured one and all, Russia was able to continue if she wished. He even convinced many neutrals that the Japanese demand for an indemnity proved that the Japanese had fought for money, not out of patriotism. True patriotism, he repeatedly put forth, lay with the battered Christian legions of Russia, whom Japan had treacherously attacked without warning. The "pagan" Japanese, as they often were portrayed, went so far as to attend church services on Sunday in an attempt to improve their image, a tactic that fooled no one.

Russian reinforcements on the way to Manchuria. (Colliers)

Witte also made much of the reception he received in New York by Russian Jews who, while remaining hostile to the tsarist regime of terror, nevertheless assured Witte that they still loved Russia and wished him the best in negotiations.

The tsar had instructed Witte not to agree to any indemnity. Indeed, one of his favorite expressions was "Our enemy together with their allies shall pay for all we have spent."[61] Now that American public opinion was shifting toward Russia, Witte flatly refused to hear about ceding Sakhalin or making any concessions at all. By the end of August 1905, it appeared that the two sides were deadlocked. Russia declared herself ready to renew the war, and the Russian delegation made plans to leave Portsmouth for home. When the Japanese government learned of this, key officials quickly met in the presence of the emperor. They knew from the banker Jacob Schiff that Japan could not expect any more loans unless the interest rates were unbearably high.[62] They also knew that two new army corps had just arrived in Manchuria from Russia, giving Linievitch over one million first-line troops, with more on the way. The Japanese saw clear signs of a coming Russian offensive, one the Japanese army had little hope of stopping. Komura was instructed to abandon his demand for an indemnity and offer Russia the northern half of Sakhalin. The two sides would agree to leave Manchuria, although Japan would be allowed to take over Russia's lease on Port Arthur. The Japanese had capitulated. After agreeing to these terms, Witte and the other Russians returned directly to Russia, but after distributing $1,000 in tips to the hotel staff, a courtesy the Russians did not match, Komura revisited Harvard, where he met faculty members he had previously known, and reacquainted himself with English and American poetry, his great love. A few years later, he would die reading Tennyson.

The Russian "victory" amazed the West. The German humor magazine *Jugend* printed a cartoon that depicted a gigantic Witte saying to a tiny, simian-like Komura, "You can keep Tokyo for yourself."[63] The *New York Times* wrote that the Russian "victory is as astonishing a thing as ever was seen in diplomatic history. A nation hopelessly beaten in every battle of the war, one army captured and another overwhelmingly routed, with a navy swept from the seas, dictated her own terms to the victors."[64] That was not the reality, of course, because the Russian army was now vastly superior to the Japanese, but that was how the world saw it and also how the Japanese public understood it. The Japanese had expected an indemnity large enough to pay the entire cost of the war, and they had received, as Witte boastfully declared, "not a sou!" Flags draped in black crepe appeared around Tokyo, leaflets denounced the government, newspapers bordered in black openly called for the assassination of cabinet members, Komura was hanged in effigy, and children contemptuously violated the Imperial Palace moat by swimming in it. Officials' houses were attacked, the American legation was stormed, Christian churches were burned and streetcars set afire. Before troops called out by martial law were able to restore order, over 1,000 people had been killed or wounded.[65] Komura had taken ill in Boston—with a diplomatic disease, some said, but Witte insisted that it was the result of the dreadful American food. Wisely, Komura did not return to Japan until the end of September, after the violence had ended.

This convulsion of the Japanese spirit reached its climax shortly after midnight on September 11, 1905, when the famed *Mikasa* blew up and sank in Sasebo Harbor, taking 251 crewmen with her, more than twice as many Japanese as died in the Battle of Tsushima. Many believed that this most samurai of ships, Togo's beloved flagship, had committed hara-kiri to erase the shame of the peace terms. The truth was less romantic. Some

Tsar Nicholas reviews Russian reinforcements.

sailors had been drinking industrial alcohol, and to remove its smell, set it on fire. The ship's nearby magazine exploded before the fire could be extinguished.[66] The Treaty of Portsmouth has not been forgotten in Japan. As recently as 1982, Japanese television produced an eight-hour dramatized documentary of the event, called "Flags over Portsmouth."[67]

Russia received the news of the peace treaty with near indifference. The war was almost forgotten, and with the eruption of revolutionary violence throughout the empire, the peace treaty afforded no reason for celebration. Witte, who received the rank of count on his return, had the last word as he surveyed the spreading violence of rebellion: "All this is trifling compared to what is going to happen one of these days."[68]

Rozhdestvensky and his senior commanders could not look at Russia or the war with such Olympian disdain. The emaciated, white-haired admiral returned to his homeland, only to be court-martialed along with Nebogatov, Clapier de Colongue, and others. Pressed to say whether Nebogatov had behaved correctly in surrendering even though his ships were still able to fight, he answered, "Certainly." When asked what he would have done if an officer had disobeyed the order to surrender and had continued to fight, he replied that he would have shot him.[69] He also took full blame for the defeat of his fleet. Rozhdestvensky was ordered to leave the navy but Nebogatov and Clapier de Colongue were sentenced to death. Although the tsar commuted the sentences, both men spent years in prison, as did several other officers. Rozhdestvensky lived in obscurity until his death three years later. Togo lived another three decades as Japan's greatest war hero. If he was tormented by the deaths of the defenseless Chinese and Russian sailors who perished under his guns, he did not say so. Just before he died, at the age of eighty-seven, he spoke his final words: "I am thinking of my Emperor—and of roses."[70]

CHAPTER SIX

"TO HELL WITH BABE RUTH"

Even before the Japanese victories at Tsushima and Mukden, the Western world had been captivated by the Japanese. A dyspeptic but influential correspondent for the *Times* of London, Dr. George E. Morrison, had found nothing to admire about the Chinese or anyone else while he was covering the Boxer Rebellion as one of those Europeans besieged in the Peking legations. But after observing the Japanese during their siege of Port Arthur, he wrote, "The marvelous smoothness with which the Japanese machinery of war runs is simply phenomenal, nothing has been seen before like it in this world."[1] It was not just Japan's military prowess that elicited superlative praise. This comment from the *Illustrated London News*, written before the Portsmouth conference, was repeated in similar versions by many commentators throughout the world:

> The Western world is trying, in a rather dazed way, to adjust its conventional modes of thinking to the discovery that the Japanese possess heroic virtues, which are not exactly spread broadcast in Christian Europe. They have a conception of public duty, not flagrantly obvious at every corner of other commonwealths; they have a dignity, a reticence, a patient forethought, a self-control— . . . Europe has not recovered from the shock of finding out the Japanese are a great people.[2]

Celebrated throughout the world for their moral virtues and their military prowess, and applauded by the American people during the Portsmouth conference, the Japanese might have expected that postwar world opinion would continue to be favorable. It was common for the Japanese to say what this prominent journalist wrote: "We admire Anglo-Saxon imperialism and hope our imperialism does not differ from theirs."[3] But as a prescient Japanese novelist, Mori Ogai, predicted when the war had just begun, in 1904, that was not to be.[4] The West would not tolerate Japanese imperialism, Mori said, and he was right. The United States was pleased to have Japan prevent Russia's expansion in the Far East. However, it, Britain, France, Holland, and Germany had no desire to see an imperial Japanese version of "Anglo-Saxon" colonial expansion replace that of imperial Russia, or to have a powerful Japanese fleet challenge their own in the Pacific. Military strength made Japan a threat not only to China and Korea but also to the European powers with major economic stakes in Asia and to the United States, which feared Japanese expansion into the Philippines and even Hawaii.

One positive note for Japan was her continuing military alliance with Britain. Soon after Portsmouth, the Japanese welcomed the British Far Eastern Fleet with a gala celebration. Geishas served free beer to British sailors; there were glamorous balls, parties, public celebrations, and not a few intimate encounters as well. A little later, Admiral Togo received a hero's welcome in England, where he was honored by Royal Navy officers who had trained him many years earlier. He was no longer an anonymous "Johnny Chinaman." Later that summer, he crossed the Atlantic on the ill-fated *Lusitania*, whose sinking by a German submarine would draw

America into World War I. While staying at the Knickerbocker Hotel in New York's Times Square, Togo walked through cheering crowds, often pausing to pat children's heads affectionately. An admiring crowd in Philadelphia surrounded him, demanding a speech. President Taft hosted him at a White House banquet, where he toasted the emperor, "whose sense of humanity and justice can always be counted on to contribute effectively to the peace of the world."[5] The U.S. Senate honored Togo by suspending business for an hour while all the senators stood in line to shake his hand.

After placing a wreath on George Washington's grave, Togo was enthusiastically welcomed by Theodore Roosevelt at his home. Togo admired a samurai sword sent to Roosevelt by the emperor, but when he unsheathed it he was horrified to discover that it was rusty. He promptly oiled it while lecturing the former president on the importance of maintaining the sword properly because, he said, for a samurai the sword is the materialization of the soul. At a State Department banquet, he was served nine vintages of wine and a forty-year-old sherry.[6] He then made a triumphal train trip through Canada to Seattle, where a U.S. cruiser saw his ship off on its voyage to Honolulu, where he received another rousing reception.[7]

Togo's grand reception in the United States and Canada was an authentic expression of public adulation of an international celebrity. It did not, however, reflect either governmental policy or the feelings of many Americans who lived on the West Coast. The Anglo-Japanese alliance was still alive, but the United States, long the silent third party in the alliance, as Russia well knew, was having second thoughts. Americans on the West Coast feared the growing "yellow peril" originally posed by the Chinese and more recently by the Japanese. William Randolph Hearst's newspapers had trumpeted that to the nation since the 1890s. Only one year after the Portsmouth peace conference, the San Francisco Board of Education ordered that all Asian children be segregated in special schools. President Roosevelt had been awarded the Nobel Peace Prize in 1906 for arranging the Treaty of Portsmouth. Now he condemned the action in San Francisco, but the board refused to rescind its order until he agreed to restrict Asian immigration to the West Coast.

The Japanese were profoundly offended by these measures, which reduced them to a category of "yellow" people not to be distinguished from the "despicable" Chinese or any other Asians. Tokyo's largest newspaper actually called for war, and the imperial fleet was put on a high state of readiness.[8] Roosevelt took Japanese talk of war seriously enough that he responded by sending the U.S. fleet on a menacing Pacific tour. When the armada arrived in Japan in 1907, most Japanese received the Americans coldly and there was even fear of violence, but the official reception proved to be courteous.[9] Well aware that she was outgunned and that her staggering war debt ruled out another major war, Japan cooled down the crisis.

Nevertheless, the anti-Japanese campaign in the United States was just beginning. Immediately after the Treaty of Portsmouth, a most improbable military personage pumped up anti-Japanese feeling even more. Homer Lea, an eighty-eight-pound hunchback with failing eyesight, began to write a book arguing that Japan could land 400,000 soldiers on the West Coast of America. Given the absence of American coastal defenses or an army of any comparable size, Lea held, Japan might easily conquer the entire West Coast, from Seattle to San Diego. Lea's book, published in 1909 (with a glowing forward by General Adna Chaffee of Boxer Rebellion fame), created a public furor in the United States. It alarmed military men while giving William Randolph Hearst ammunition to inveigh even more stridently against the "yellow peril" in his newspapers.[10]

Lea fancied himself a military genius who was denied the military honors he deserved strictly because of his physical handicaps. In a bizarre sequel to his book, Lea was actually appointed chief military adviser to Dr. Sun Yat-sen, whom some Japanese tried to groom to overthrow the Manchu dynasty and help them control China. With the aid of a former sergeant of the U.S. Fourth Cavalry named Ansel O'Banion, Lea trained several hundred Chinese in California whom he intended to use to lead the Chinese revolution.[11] Lea failed in this unlikely enterprise, but he did much to inflame America's fear of Japan by describing her plans to dominate China. Many prominent Japanese were convinced that Japan had a heavenly mandate to expand overseas. Since Japan's victory over China in 1895, Manchuria in particular and China in general had become primary targets for that expansion.[12]

Nor did Japan's ambitions stop with China. America also had good reason to study Japanese designs on the Philippines. The United States had just employed 70,000 troops to suppress Filipino rebels who had fought to regain their political freedom after the American defeat of Spain. The new American president, William Howard Taft, who shared none of Roosevelt's admiration for Japan, was determined to deny the Japanese a major role in China. Even so, in 1907 he signed an agreement with the Japanese offering them a free hand in Korea in return for a guarantee that Japan would honor U.S. sovereignty in the Philippines. When the king of Korea learned about this agreement, he sent a mission to The Hague to seek European protection against Japan. In swift reaction, the Japanese forced the king to abdicate in favor of his feebleminded son, a strong-arm act that led to widespread Korean resistance followed by brutal Japanese repression on the part of ultranationalist paramilitary groups and police. Many Japanese had never considered Koreans to be fully human, and there was nothing chivalrous about Japan's behavior in Korea, then, or later.

The tall, broad-shouldered, genial Marquis Ito, still a most influential leader, opposed annexation of Korea. He urged instead that Korea be made a willing ally rather than a vassal state. But in 1909 Ito was murdered. His assailant, whom Japanese police killed during interrogation, was said to be a Korean who had acted alone. The suspicion in some quarters that he might have been a Japanese agent sent to silence the peacemaker Ito was dismissed.[13]

In 1910, Japan annexed Korea, beginning a period of Japanese exploitation that ran until 1945. The period saw at least 700,000 Koreans forcibly shipped to Japan as workers, military conscripts, and "comfort women."[14] Japanese troops and civilians rarely displayed the courtesy and kindness to Koreans that they had shown to the Russians during 1904–5, nor were they any kinder on Taiwan, but at the time their conduct received little attention in the West. Neither did the fact that Russia and Japan had quietly reached an informal agreement to divide Manchuria into two spheres of influence. Chinese sovereignty notwithstanding, it was agreed that the Russians would control the north and the Japanese the south. Hardly an eyebrow was raised. More pressing matters on the world scene would soon lead to World War I, giving Japan a golden opportunity to dominate China—and to put her military chivalry on display once again.

JAPAN IN WORLD WAR I

In the early days of World War I, Britain warily watched her ally Japan. Would Japan take advantage of the European conflict to expand her Asian influence? Britain insisted that Japan enter the war only under rigorous restrictions, a condition Japan initially accepted. Soon, however, Britain became alarmed by the presence of powerful German warships in the Chinese port of Tsingtao and asked for Japan's help. Japan accepted with great alacrity, assuring England and the world that her entry into the war had nothing to do with self-interest or territorial expansion.

For Europeans from various nations, Tsingtao (literally "green island") was the most beautiful holiday resort in China, known rapturously as "the Pearl of the East" and "the Eastern Riviera." In response to the murder of two German missionaries (whose order was actually banned in Germany) three years before the Boxer Rebellion, Germany had forced an enfeebled China to grant her a ninety-nine-year lease and exclusive economic rights over a 500-square-kilometer area that included a strategic bay overlooked by Tsingtao and held huge deposits of iron and coal. By 1914, German-built Tsingtao boasted a modern harbor with a huge floating dry dock, numerous alpine resorts in the high hills ringing the city, and an urban character that looked altogether German. Its stone buildings would have blended into any German city, its streets and sewers were German-made, even its thousands of oak and pine trees were imported. Tsingtao's scrupulously clean beach and hilltop resorts were the envy of all the other colonial powers in China.

Tsingtao was more than a resort; it was also a military and naval base that housed numerous German warships under the command of Admiral Graf von Spee, as well as 3,500 German soldiers and marines there to defend it. An attack from the sea would be met by an impressive series of forts armed by dangerous but largely obsolete coastal defense artillery, and from the land side by five concrete forts with cannon and machine guns, all linked by deep, sandbag-covered trenches, protected by miles of barbed wire and minefields. When war broke out in August 1914, hundreds of German reservists from all over Asia were called to Tsingtao, and the port city was made ready for war. For Germany, the fight for Tsingtao would be more than a sideshow to the war in Europe. The kaiser could not abide the thought of a defeat by Japanese, still "yellow apes" for him. He declared fervently, "It would shame me more to surrender Tsingtao to the Japanese than Berlin to the Russians."[15]

The prospect of von Spee's powerful squadron of modern heavy cruisers, including the *Scharnhorst, Gneisenau,* and *Emden,* roaming free in the Pacific so alarmed the British that they asked their Japanese allies to enter the war to neutralize the Germans before they could destroy British merchant ships. Japan dispatched two squadrons of ships, including the fast, new 28,000-ton battle cruiser *Kongo* (which survived to play an active role in World War II). The Japanese ships failed to find the German cruisers, which shelled Tahiti and sank two British cruisers off Chile before sailing into the Atlantic; there they were destroyed by a British squadron. However, while the German squadron slipped away, Japan seized the undefended German possessions in the Caroline, Marshall, and Mariana Islands, including Saipan, Tinian, and Tarawa.

The Japanese also decided to take Tsingtao. Without naval strength in the Pacific to blockade the harbor or troops near China to capture the fortress city, Britain had to agree. Those ships and troops would have to come from Japan. However, Britain did insist that the 950-man South Wales Borderers Regiment, under Nathanial W. Barnardiston, fight with the Japanese. This famous Welsh regiment (previously known as the Royal Welch) had developed a violent dislike for Germans during the Boxer Rebellion, but during its long stay in Tientsin its men had also come to disdain the Japanese as an inferior race, calling them "coolies in uniform."[16] The British would in addition provide some 450 Sikhs, who disliked Germans and Japanese about equally. For their part, the Germans despised the Japanese for making an alliance with Britain, and they detested the British for many reasons, including, as they saw it, forcing Japan into the war.[17] Given so much animosity on all sides, there was every reason to anticipate a nasty siege.

The small British force would serve under Lieutenant General Kamio Mitsumi, a Japanese who had begun the war against the Chinese in 1894–95 as a forty-year-old sergeant and was now a charming, English-speaking sixty-year-old. For the first time in history, European troops would be under an Asian commander, and the British were decidedly displeased about it. Nor were the Japanese happy to have the British involved, thinking that these cloddish allies would only slow them down. In late August, before the British could arrive, Kamio landed north of Tsingtao with some 18,000 Japanese infantry, at least 5,000 cavalry, and 142 heavy siege guns. After battling heat, torrents of rain, mud, and mosquitoes, he began systematically pushing German outposts back on their main defense line. The fighting was not particularly heavy.

When Barnardiston's troops finally arrived, Kamio was almost ready to launch a major offensive. Courteous but distant, the Japanese general invited British officers to his staff headquarters, where the British visitors were amazed to discover an uncanny calm. Instead of their own customary flurry of staff activity, with dispatch riders arriving in a cloud of dust and officers anxiously bustling about, Japanese staff officers seemed to do absolutely nothing. While Barnardiston was there, Kamio spent the better part of a day wandering about in search of wild flowers or talking to his pet parrot; at the same time, one of his senior aides sketched.[18] Yet the Japanese were without doubt well organized, as one of Kamio's questions to Barnardiston revealed. The Japanese general asked how Barnardiston's men, who were uniformed in thin summer-weight shorts, kept warm in the winter. It was not an idle question; before Tsingtao surrendered in early November, snow would fall and the Borderers would suffer acutely from the intense cold.[19] Kamio had provided the Japanese with both summer and winter uniforms.

Before Kamio brought up all his assault troops, with their siege guns and ammunition, his troops had dug zigzag assault trenches forward toward the German lines. He also positioned artillery observers who could direct the fire of Japanese warships that would aid the assault, and his six-plane air force prepared for bombing raids against military targets. It carried out the first night-bombing in history with good accuracy, if little loss of life among the Germans, and helped sink a German merchant ship. None of the six planes was shot down, but the Germans' only plane, which busied itself by bombing the hated British and exchanging pistol fire with Japanese pilots, was eventually badly damaged while on the ground.[20] German artillerymen fired endless salvos and, thanks to eager-to-please Chinese spies, were told that the Japanese had suffered severe casualties. In fact, their losses were light except for one incident at sea in which a German destroyer put two torpedoes into the old heavy cruiser *Takashio*, the Japanese flagship during the Sino-Japanese War. The venerable ship carried one hundred mines, which exploded when the torpedoes hit, quickly sending it to the bottom. Only three men survived, but before some of the sailors drowned they were heard singing the Japanese national anthem.

Kamio planned a general attack that would culminate in a night assault. He calmly told Barnardiston that he expected to lose at least one entire regiment, a prospect that horrified the British general, who favored a long, bloodless siege to conserve the lives of his own irreplaceable troops.

The final assault began in cold rain and snow with a brilliantly accurate artillery barrage followed by Japanese infantrymen who rushed forward in small groups, making such good use of cover that they sustained few casualties despite mines, machine-gun fire, and German artillery fire. In one memorable encounter, a German lieutenant dueled a Japanese officer in a sword fight. While German and Japanese soldiers looked on, the German officer killed the Japanese. Shocked by this unexpected outcome, the Japanese troops then attacked with their bayonets, killing the German officer and all but one of his men, who was allowed to surrender.

The last battles were fought in the mountain forts, which fell with surprising ease, while Germans elsewhere spiked their guns and systematically destroyed everything of military value, including all the money in the bank and stamps in the post office. They even opened all the canned goods in their warehouses so that the food would spoil and be of no use to the Japanese or the British, who suffered from a severe food shortage.[21] Despite this wanton destruction, which the Japanese had hoped to prevent, and which would surely have led to brutal retaliation had it been done by the Allies in World War II, Kamio was remarkably gracious in victory. For fear of alarming the residents of the city of Tsingtao, 1,000 of whom were Japanese, Kamio ordered his men to stay out of the city while German officers kept their swords, maintained order, and prepared to move their men to hastily arranged prison camps. Japanese officers treated German officers with the utmost courtesy. Kamio even thanked them for the training he had received in Germany twenty years earlier as a junior officer.

Paradoxically, Kamio treated his British allies with almost studied indifference. He had given them only a small role in the final attack, and they had advanced with what the Japanese considered unnecessary caution. In fact, they had suffered only 13 killed (2 by accident) and 61 wounded, compared with 415 Japanese dead and 1,451 wounded. Despite the kaiser's feelings about losing Tsingtao to the Japanese, the Germans and their small contingent of Austrian allies had not exactly fought to the last man. They lost the comparatively small number of 199 dead and 294 wounded. Over 4,500 men surrendered. Nevertheless, the Japanese did not treat their prisoners with scorn.

While the Japanese scrambled to find transport for 4,500 prisoners—many more than anticipated—the British troops lived in German barracks, where they watched Japanese troops wandering through the city, doing a bit of looting when their officers were not looking. They did not rape or kill, but their indiscipline nevertheless shocked British officers, who had their own men under tight control. The British were also horrified by the Japanese lack of concern for sanitation. Japanese troops, normally zealous about their personal hygiene, were permitted to defecate where they pleased, leaving feces scattered everywhere around their campsites.[22]

Japanese contempt for the Chinese continued to be evident. Soldiers sometimes merrily beat heavily laden army-paid "coolies" over their heads and on their legs with bamboo clubs.[23] Still, Japanese soldiers treated Chinese civilians reasonably well and were perfectly correct with their German prisoners. They did not even search them for hidden weapons or inspect their belongings, which consisted of anything they could carry. The Japanese also permitted them considerable license. As the South Wales Borderers marched past a large column of German prisoners, the British troops began to whistle a popular song called "Everybody's Doing It." Insulted by what they took to be a taunt, the Germans turned their backs, dropped their trousers, and bent over. Their Japanese guards laughed uproariously but took no other action. Later they permitted German soldiers to insult foreign military observers whom they over-heard making critical comments about them.[24]

The Japanese had never wanted British military assistance and had done little to make their allies feel welcome. Before the British troops sailed out of Tsingtao, however, it was announced that a personal emissary of the emperor was coming to honor them. As the regiment stood at attention, each soldier expecting at least a medal and perhaps more, a small man approached wearing a bowler hat, a black evening jacket with tails, knickerbockers, brightly colored stockings, and yellow shoes.[25] Unsure whether the man was dressed for a state occasion or a round of golf, the British stared politely while he read a scroll expressing the emperor's gratitude, then disappointingly announced a gift of only cigarettes and cakes. Later, General Barnardiston fared much better. Invited to Japan with three of his staff officers, he was greeted by thousands of flag-waving children and lavishly entertained at balls and dinners. He also received a medal and, accompanied by the British ambassador, had dinner with the emperor and empress.

This signal honor, followed by a splendid round of dinners and speeches, took some of the bad taste out of Barnardiston's mouth, but the damage to Britain's prestige had been done. As intended by Tokyo, Japan emerged from the Tsingtao victory as a great Asian power while Britain was shown to be weak in Asia. Japan now had possession of Tsingtao and the German Shantung concession, a 500-square-kilometer area rich in iron and coal. This largesse could very nearly reverse Japan's previous reliance on foreign imports for 75 percent of her iron and steel.[26] The following year, Japan would present her infamous "Twenty-one Demands" to China, removing all doubt that her professed friendship for her neighbor masked intended territorial expansion. Much of the international goodwill Japan had earned was lost in the wake of this blatant political aggression.

As the world had come to expect, Japanese troops had fought bravely and treated their enemies well. During a truce after one battle, for example, they buried German dead with full military honors and placed wreaths on their graves.[27] They also treated the Germans well after they surrendered, although the prisoners' trip to Japan was not a pleasant one. The hastily summoned Japanese transport ships were old and small. The large Europeans were badly crowded. Sanitary facilities were primitive, and the food, consisting largely of tea and bread, was dreadful as well. The Germans made the best of things during the short voyage, convinced that German troops would soon enter Paris and they would be freed. Instead, they were imprisoned for over five years.

When the German prisoners arrived in Japan, civilians often greeted them warmly, but because the Japanese had expected the Germans to fight more resolutely in defense of the kaiser's honor, they had not anticipated more than a few war prisoners and had prepared no camps for them. The Germans had to be quartered in fifteen separate locations, including several small temples used to house Russian prisoners a decade earlier. Crowding was a continuing problem, but the food improved, cigarettes were made available, German newspapers were provided, and both men and officers were allowed to walk outside the camps with an escort.[28] Later, access to women was sometimes permitted, although not to the extent granted the Russians in 1904–5. Most camps were humanely run from the beginning, and some commandants were especially solicitous. One camp commander arranged for prisoners to be employed as well-paid mechanics and carpenters in a nearby town. There they also had access to women.[29] Only one camp stood out negatively—the largest one under the command of an officer who slapped German officers and men alike when they broke rules. In general, camp discipline was so loose that several officers escaped. Only one made it all the way back to Germany, but several reached China by posing as Dutch or Norwegian businessmen.[30]

In response to German complaints, the still neutral American embassy sent the twenty-three-year-old Sumner Welles to inspect all fifteen camps. He was presented with a twenty-six-page list of complaints, ranging from a lack of politeness by guards to poor dental work. Welles had sympathy for the prisoners but after a two-week tour reported them to be in excellent health, their European-style diets more than adequate, and conditions in general very good. He did criticize overcrowding in seven of the camps and noted that guards sometimes mistreated prisoners in two camps. On a later trip, Welles found that the government had made improvements, such as replacing commandants accused of mistreatment.[31]

The Germans were not treated as courteously as the Russians had been during 1904–5, but for the most part they could hardly complain. During five years of imprisonment, only 82 of the 4,592 prisoners died, almost all of them from the deadly influenza pandemic of 1918–19.[32] When the men were finally released after the armistice, a Japanese general bade them Godspeed, saying, "My dear gentlemen, you are now free."[33] One hundred and seventy-one Germans chose to enjoy their freedom in Japan instead of returning to Germany.

Japan began the war in debt by over 1.5 billion yen. Between 1914 and 1918, however, an expanding Japanese industry met needs that war-mobilized factories in Europe no longer could. By the time of the armistice, Japan had a surplus of 2 billion yen.[34] Japan had also fended off all Allied requests to send troops to the killing fields in France and Belgium—she did send a destroyer squadron to the Mediterranean to help the British against German submarines. A number of Japanese sailors are still buried in a British military cemetery in Malta.

THE SIBERIAN INTERVENTION

The Bolshevik Revolution of 1917 led to civil war and resulting chaos in Siberia. Caught in the disorder were 50,000 men of the Czech army, stranded on the Russian front when Russia surrendered to the Germans. At this stage of World War I, these men were badly needed by the battered Allies in France. No one wanted Japan to invade Siberia unilaterally, so the United States invited Japan to join with the Allies in sending troops to

Siberia to facilitate the Czechs' departure. Britain, France, America, and Japan each sent 7,000 men to Vladivostok to restore order. Japan responded with a vengeance, soon stationing 100,000 troops in Siberia.

Because Japan greatly feared the spread of communism, she hoped to strengthen the White Russian forces enough to topple the detested Bolsheviks. Japan also hoped to gain control of the Trans-Siberian Railroad, along with eastern Siberia, for her own economic interests. Thousands of Japanese businessmen arrived soon after the Japanese troops did. By May 1920 several of Japan's largest corporations had opened branches in major Siberian cities, bringing with them nearly 50,000 Japanese settlers, who began to buy mines, fisheries, forests, and railroads, moving to solidify Japan's control over the wealth of the region. The Bolsheviks could not stand up to Japanese troops, but their outrage was vividly displayed in the city of Nikolatevsk, where they tortured all 700 Japanese living there and raped the women before killing them.[35]

In retaliation, the Japanese occupied northern Sakhalin, with its mineral and timber riches, and took revenge against some Russian civilians. They also gave money, arms, and military advisers to a former tsarist general, the formidably named Baron Roman Nicholas Fyodorovich von Ungern-Sternberg, known to his men—not without reason—as "the mad Baron." When Russia capitulated to Germany in 1917 he was a thirty-three-year-old major general with a reputation for unsurpassed courage. He believed that he was the reincarnation of Genghis Khan and that it was his destiny to rule Russia. What is certain is that he was a sadistic killer who used his small army of white Russians and Mongols to kill as many Bolsheviks and Jews as possible. After a few victories accompanied by almost unimaginable slaughter, he declared himself the "Emperor of All Russia." Appalled by his depravity and less than sanguine about his future, his Japanese advisers had already left him, and soon thereafter Bolshevik armies closed in. The Mad Baron was captured, tried, and executed.[36] Even though her troops remained in Siberia until 1922, two years after the other Allied forces withdrew, Japan accomplished little in this Siberian foray except to antagonize the Soviet Union.[37]

THE POSTWAR QUEST FOR POWER

Japan played her hand in World War I to national advantage, but nothing in her actions dishonored her military men. Her political leaders clearly exposed their expansionist territorial designs on China, even though Japan later tried to repudiate these demands. Japan also took a principled position at the Paris peace conference of 1919, where as one of the "Big Five" nations, she proposed that the fledgling League of Nations could not hope to be effective on the world scene unless member nations agreed that racial discrimination must be abolished. Fearing an influx of Chinese, Japanese, and Indian immigrants, Canada, New Zealand, and Australia refused even to consider the idea. Other Western nations, including the United States, would have opposed the proposal too, but it died before it came to a vote. This rejection had far-reaching consequences. The Japanese proposal can easily be construed as self-serving because Japan would have been a major beneficiary of it. But when the West refused even to consider it seriously, the Japanese declared themselves a morally superior people, an idea with deep roots in Japanese culture and one of use to right-wing territorial expansionists. The idea of *kokutai*—the existence of national values and virtues that made Japan unique and superior—began to be emphasized in the Japanese Military Academy.[38]

Without doubt, the Japanese drive for territorial expansion owed much to this sense of divine destiny and inherent moral superiority, but population pressures also played a part. By 1936, Japan's population was growing by over one million persons per year. Japanese peasants lived in poverty, barely eking out a living on marginal land. Heavily taxed peasants still made up the vast majority of Japan's population, and their suffering did not lessen during the early decades of the twentieth century. From before the Tokugawa isolation until well into the 1930s, their lives were continually blighted by hunger that drove their sons into the army and their daughters to the textile mills or into prostitution. From 1590 to 1867, Japan recorded 2,800 peasant uprisings as a direct result of famine. Many peasants resorted to cannibalism to stay alive. A severe famine occurred in northern Japan as late as 1934.[39] Even in good years, peasants suffered severe ill health and malnutrition, as their short stature bore painful witness. Most peasant families rarely saw a bowl of white rice, and many struggled to stay alive by eating millet and barnyard grass. Plagued by flies, leeches, parasites of all sorts, fleas, lice, and bedbugs, they commonly fell victim to a host of diseases such as trachoma, tuberculosis, cholera, typhoid, typhus, diphtheria, dysentery, and smallpox.[40] When Japan's reservists were called to active duty against Russia in 1904, many of their families would have starved if other impoverished peasants had not helped them while their sons were away at war. Compared with Western countries, Japan had too many people and too little food. Westerners, including George Bernard Shaw, derided the Japanese government for not encouraging birth control, but in fact peasants regularly performed abortions and infanticide until shortly before the Pacific War, when infanticide was made illegal.[41]

When the Japanese army seized Manchuria in 1931, an army officer explained it this way:

> There are only three ways left to Japan to escape from the pressure of its surplus population. . . . The first door, emigration, has been barred to us by the anti-Japanese immigration policies of other countries. The second door, to world markets, is being pushed shut by tariff barriers and the abrogation of commercial treaties. What should Japan do when two of the three doors have been closed against her? It is quite natural that Japan should rush upon the last remaining door [territorial expansion].[42]

Another officer testified that the poverty of the peasant families who sent their sons to the army was so extreme that the young soldiers worried excessively about their family members, who survived only by eating rotten potatoes while enormously rich business corporations grew even richer. He argued that Manchuria had to be taken for humanitarian purposes, and many other officers agreed. It is more than a historical aside to note that in gratitude for Russo-Japanese War loans from Jewish banks, the Japanese allowed 5,000 Jews fleeing Nazi terror to settle in Manchuria, again for humanitarian reasons.[43]

When Tokugawa chose isolation from the world early in the seventeenth century, Japan's population was five times larger than Britain's, but her islands, although almost twice as large as Britain's, were so mountainous that only 15 percent of the land was suitable for agriculture. In many respects, preindustrial Japan had a successful market economy, but it was obvious to Hideyoshi, as it was to his successors, that Japan needed more land not only to prove her greatness but to feed her people.

As early as 1823, while Japan still shied away from the world, Sato Nobuhiro voiced a deeply held conviction that Japan was the foundation of the world; it was her destiny to expand. In what he titled "A Secret Strategy for Expansion," he called for dividing the entire world into provinces and districts of Japan, and he described in great detail how China should be conquered by launching the first attack in Manchuria.[44]

The West demurred. Plainly, Japan could not be allowed to operate in the world as a colonial power the way that Western powers still privileged themselves to do. Britain, France, and Germany had just carved up Africa among themselves. Along with Russia, they had staked their claims to portions of China. The Dutch held oil- and mineral-rich Indonesia, and the United States had annexed Hawaii, taken the Philippines first from Spain and then from the Filipinos themselves, and invoked the Monroe Doctrine. The Monroe Doctrine was tolerated when the Americans dominated Latin America, but when the Japanese invoked "Manifest Destiny" as they looked to Manchuria—which they had won in two previous wars—the West refused to hear of it.

America's racist treatment of Asians earlier in the century had almost sparked a military response by Japan, and the League of Nation's rejection of Japan's antiracism legislation did nothing to convince the Japanese that the West would ever treat her as an equal. When the United States passed a law in 1924 closing off immigration from Japan, the reaction was violent. Ten thousand people gathered in Tokyo to shout for war against America. The flag was ripped down at the American embassy, and a flood of books urged war against the United States.[45] Rabidly anti-Western nationalist groups sprang up all over Japan.

The 1920s, a time of severe economic depression in Japan and public resentment over large military expenditures, led the government to agree to restrict the growth of the military. As the spirit of democracy grew in Japan, the civilian government tried to weaken military power, actually cutting the standing army by 20 percent. However, Japanese peasants still starved while powerful corporations such as Mitsubishi, Sumitomo, and Mitsui made enormous profits. Rich businessmen routinely insulted Japanese military officers in public.[46] Chafing under the antimilitary mood in the nation and the Japanese government's acceptance of the Washington conference accord that restricted Japanese naval strength to only 60 percent of that of the United States and Britain, the military leaders seized on peasant suffering and overpopulation as issues that could restore their diminishing power.

Japan's army was conscripted primarily from the second and third sons of farming families. These men bitterly resented the poverty that humbled

their families while businessmen grew rich and corrupt.[47] By 1927, 30 percent of Japan's officers were the sons of petty landowners or small shopkeepers. Only about 15 percent were samurai. Their sympathies lay with
the lowly, not with the big businessmen whose taste for Western books,
music, and customs were seen as corrupting Japan's patriotic spirit.[48] Out
of these forces came the powerful "young officers movement," the
genkokuju, which challenged governmental and military authority, driving Japan toward war.[49]

In 1923, an earthquake laid waste to Tokyo; it was immediately said to
be supernatural retribution for Japan's Western-inspired frivolity and
individualism. With legal emigration blocked, militaristic extremists led
by these young officers renewed their calls for overseas expansion, a
refrain like that heard in Hitler's Germany a few years later. Combining
fascism with feudal autocracy, these militarists have been referred to aptly
as "superpatriots."[50]

Japan's Meiji constitution of 1889 made the military independent of
civilian governmental administration. Now determined to save Japan's
traditional values from its corrupt and degenerate civilian leaders, the
radical young officers began to seize absolute power over the government. Ultranationalist secret societies sprang up everywhere. For example, the Society of the Sword of Heaven supported war and territorial
expansion, terrorizing anyone associated with democracy. The military's
power over the government grew year by year, through threat and actual assassinations, until by the early 1930s Japan had become a military
autocracy. This virtual coup d'état had been driven largely by young officers, although they sometimes served as tools for senior generals and
admirals who used the militancy of the angry young men to intimidate
anyone who stood in the way of military dictatorship.[51] At the same time,
Japan stepped up its media program of hatred toward the West, particularly the United States. In 1935, a superpatriot stabbed to death the publisher of one of Tokyo's largest newspapers. The publisher's sin: he had
sponsored a visit to Japan by an American all-star baseball team led by
Babe Ruth. Overnight, "To hell with Babe Ruth!" became a national rallying cry. It took root so deeply that Japanese soldiers shouted it while
charging American lines in World War II.[52]

Inevitably, Japan seized Manchuria in 1931, then invaded North China
to safeguard Japanese rule in Manchuria. World War II loomed, but

despite the military's power, most Japanese were wary of military rule. As late as 1937, the year that Nanking was ravaged, a national plebiscite rejected military rule when it voted Prime Minister General Hayashi out of office. Some vocal opposition by socialists, communists, and liberal intellectuals appeared, too, but the Japanese government nevertheless remained firmly in the hands of the military. Emperor Hirohito replaced General Hayashi with a popular civilian, Prince Konoye, a tall, urbane, and sybaritic politician, who would be unable to stop the drift into war.

"STRIKE NORTH"—JAPAN AGAINST THE SOVIET UNION

The Japanese takeover of Manchuria in 1931 almost inadvertently led to a larger war against China. The Japanese called it the "China incident," not far from the truth. Japan's avowed enemy was the Soviet Union, not China, but the fear that Chinese communism would spread, eventually to engulf Manchuria, led to Japan's largely uncoordinated efforts to dominate China. Many in the Japanese military wanted not only to contain Chinese communism but to launch an all-out war to the north against their former foes, the "Russians," whose communist beliefs were seen as a mortal threat to the 800,000 Japanese who had moved to Manchuria, and even to Japan herself. Numerous armed clashes flashed along the disputed 3,000-mile border that separated Manchuria (or Manchukuo, as Japan renamed it) from Soviet Mongolia. These led to a series of large-scale border clashes in 1937 and 1938 in which the Japanese barely held their own, while suffering heavy losses; but there was no heavy and prolonged fighting until 1939.

Two years after the "rape of Nanking," in 1937, at a place called Nomonhan by the Japanese and Khalkhin Gol by the Soviets, a large Japanese force was almost annihilated. Even so, despite the terrible carnage and their hatred of the Soviets, the Japanese largely respected the international rules of warfare.

Troops serving in Manchuria in Japan's so-called Kwantung Army had been taught to hate Soviet soldiers for their communism and to have utter contempt for their military abilities. On the basis of their experiences in the war of 1904–5, Japanese officers published a manual describing the "Russian" soldier as stupid, lacking in all initiative, and capable only of blind obedience. They had time and again been driven forward by political officers who would summarily shoot any man who failed to advance as ordered.[53] In contrast, Japanese infantry were taught to attack in small groups, often at night, and to rely on their offensive spirit to bring them to hand-to-hand combat, which they believed they would inevitably win.

The fighting spirit of the Japanese troops was superb, but their weapons in 1939 at Nomonhan were no match for those of the Soviet soldiers. Japanese aircraft were superior to the Soviet, but few were available in northern Manchuria. Soviet artillery was longer-range, more numerous, and far more richly provided with ammunition than Japan's, while the Soviet advantage in tanks and armored cars was overwhelming. Because of Japan's limited industrial capacity, the Japanese army had to choose between concentrating on air power or tanks. It chose air power, and the few light and medium tanks it had at Nomonhan were no match for the heavier, far more numerous Russian armor. Without question the Japanese infantrymen with their rifles, machine guns, grenades, and especially bayonets were more than a match for Soviet infantrymen, but the Japanese foot soldiers were outnumbered almost two to one.[54]

When the first fighting began in July 1939, Japanese intelligence had no conception of the powerful forces amassed by the Soviet commander. That commander was Marshal Georgi K. Zhukov, soon to become the Soviet Union's most famous military leader against the Germans. Against Zhukov's nearly 70,000 men, over 1,000 tanks, twice that many supply vehicles, and hundreds of aircraft, the Japanese could muster perhaps 40,000 men, with only modest artillery support and a few score tanks and airplanes. For a month or so, the two infantry forces attacked and counterattacked, day and night, while Zhukov concentrated his armor for a decisive blow. Whenever the Japanese were able to reach the Soviet lines, their skill with the bayonet drove off Soviet defenders. On one occasion, a Japanese sergeant killed 12 men with his bayonet before being shot.[55] But Soviet trench lines and strong points were built in great depth, and there would be no Japanese breakthrough.

Combat in Manchuria took place under truly appalling conditions that pushed men to the limits of their endurance. The summer heat topped 100 degrees Fahrenheit. There was virtually no drinkable water; the flies were even worse than they had been during the 1904–5 war in Manchuria, a dust cloud hung over everything, food was scarce, and many men had dysentery or typhus. Japanese casualties were heavy, especially from artillery fire, and by the time Zhukov launched his massive tank attack on

August 20, the weakened Japanese positions had little support from their artillery, which had expended its ammunition faster than it could be replenished. They had also lost their tanks and air support. The Japanese had always prided themselves on their offensive spirit. To spend day after day hungry and thirsty, huddled in feces-filled foxholes, pounded by heavy artillery and overwhelmed by the stench of decomposing bodies was the very worst kind of hell.

In late August 1939, Zhukov's tanks encircled the Japanese before closing with the survivors. Most units had no weapons to use against Russian tanks except Molotov cocktails, which were lighted and then suicidally hurled against the machines by brave men. One Japanese officer actually attacked a Russian tank with his sword, and for some reason, perhaps astonishment, the tank commander drove away.[56] Despite reckless bravery like this, Zhukov's victory was total. Only about 5,000 Japanese survived, and few were in a condition to fight. Because neither the Soviet Union nor Japan wanted an all-out war in 1939, Zhukov pulled back and Japanese reinforcements were held up until peace was established.

An astonishing 79 percent of the Japanese force was killed or wounded in Manchuria. The Seventy-first Regiment lost 93.5 percent of its men. In contrast, the heaviest Japanese losses in the Russo-Japanese War were 18 percent at Liaoyang and 28 percent at Mukden.[57] Soviet losses, reported as 9,342, were probably twice that number. It was such a bloody, brutal battle, stretching men's nerves beyond the breaking point, that many Japanese had to be removed from combat when they became hysterical or catatonic.[58] And yet, with the exception of one incident in which a Japanese Red Cross tent was crushed by a Soviet tank (whose driver may not have seen its markings through the smoke and dust) and one in which a Japanese soldier may have bayoneted some Soviets who were trying to surrender, few atrocities were committed by either side.[59] It has been reported that the Japanese mutilated some dead Soviet soldiers, possibly while a few of them were still alive in an earlier border fight, but this horrendous battle was amazingly free of atrocities.[60]

The Japanese took about 100 Soviet prisoners, including two officers, while the Soviets took about 3,000 Japanese, almost all of them in the final tank assault. Since 1908, it had been declared a crime for a Japanese soldier to surrender, but many of these Japanese were too badly wounded even to kill themselves. Others tried but did not succeed, and several begged their captors to kill them. After attempts to "brainwash" the Japanese prisoners, the Soviets returned those who were severely wounded. Although these men never rejoined their own units, most were treated with embarrassed kindness and were not encouraged to kill themselves. Several officers, for whom the shame of surrender was even greater than it was for a soldier, did kill themselves either willingly or under duress after their return. Some noncommissioned officers received prison sentences as well. Many of the Japanese prisoners, at least 1,000 in all, chose to remain in the Soviet Union, where some married and became Soviet citizens.[61]

The Japanese found the shame of defeat almost unbearable, but their conduct during two months of dreadful combat, and afterwards while prisoners were being cared for and exchanged, was above criticism. The victorious Soviets were sometimes overbearing, but the two enemies managed to arrange for peace in a series of dignified meetings, and they cared well for their prisoners until it was time to exchange them. Few military forces in history have suffered a more complete, humiliating, and frustrating defeat by a hated enemy than the Japanese at Nomonhan, but their conduct throughout two long and miserable months would have passed muster at any war-crimes trial.

This "civilized" conduct under great duress is notable and puzzling because Japanese troops in Korea and Taiwan sometimes behaved brutally and because since the "Manchurian incident," in 1931, they had often behaved barbarically in Manchuria and in China. The first major clash that came to the attention of the West took place in the international city of Shanghai in January 1932 after five Japanese Buddhist priests were attacked by a Chinese mob. When one Japanese died, several hundred members of the Japanese Youth League took to the streets, where one was shot to death by a Chinese policeman, who was, in turn, stabbed to death. The large Japanese settlement in Shanghai was protected by Imperial Special Naval Landing Forces and civilian volunteers, backed by naval air forces. Opposed by China's elite Nineteenth Route Army, the Japanese forces opened fire indiscriminately; when the Chinese fought back, the battle escalated.

By the end of February 1932, Japan had deployed 50,000 army troops in Shanghai. The brutal fighting that followed in the narrow streets of the city was witnessed at first hand by Western media, whose newspaper accounts, photographs, and newsreels showed the world the horrors of bombing civilians and firing at helpless Chinese. American public opinion, already strongly anti-Japanese, became even more hostile, and Secretary of State Henry Stimson tried to persuade a reluctant President Hoover to institute sanctions. Japan won a sort of military victory by forcing China to accept a truce favorable to Japan, but her international image was damaged irreparably, as events would prove. That many Japanese troops wore gas masks as they advanced did not go unnoticed, especially considering that the Chinese had no poison gas.[62]

After this incident, Japan concentrated her attention on Manchuria and preparations for war against the Soviet Union. In turn, China began seriously to rearm. Support for China came from the United States and Britain, which provided military training as well as arms. Italy and Germany joined in. By 1935, Italy had set up a factory in China to assemble military aircraft, which, unfortunately for Chiang Kai-shek, proved to be obsolete. They also trained Chinese pilots, although with indifferent success. Many German military advisers and some civilians trained Chiang's Nationalist Army, eventually giving him an 80,000-man army with German coal-scuttle helmets and the goose step. As late as 1938, over thirty German advisers remained in China.[63]

While Chiang's army grew and Mao Tse-tung's Communist forces gathered strength in the northwest, Japan avoided major conflicts with the Chinese until July 7, 1937, at a place called Marco Polo Bridge, fifteen miles outside Peking. For reasons that remain mysterious, Chinese and Japanese patrols exchanged fire during the night. The fighting escalated despite efforts by both Chinese and Japanese commanders to end the affair. It seems likely that the firing was started and continued by a third party, probably Chinese Communists or radical students who wished to provoke an incident.[64] If so, they succeeded. Japan decided to crush China once and for all, estimating that only a few divisions would be required for the job. They believed the war would not last over six months.

As usual, Japan badly underestimated her enemy. The Soviets were anything but the pushovers the Japanese had expected, and the Allies would eventually prove to be far too strong for them as well. China, too, was a tough enemy. In the summer of 1937, Chiang had thirty well-equipped, German-trained divisions, and Mao had created a powerful guerrilla army in the northwest. However, Chinese leadership was poor and Chiang was often unwilling to risk his best men and weapons in battle, preferring to give up territory instead in a devastating scorched-earth policy. He was saving his strength for the coming fight with Mao.

By August 1937, major Japanese forces had landed in Shanghai and after ten weeks of street fighting would push toward Nanking. Most Japanese continued to regard Chinese civilians with the utmost contempt and often had even less regard for the Chinese soldiers of Chiang's Nationalist army or Mao's Communist troops. Japanese soldiers capriciously and ruthlessly looted, raped, burned villages, and shot, burned, bayoneted, and gassed Chinese peasants. The resistance of Chinese civilians hardened as their hatred for the Japanese grew, while the Communist Chinese armies not only treated the Chinese peasants well but fought the Japanese to a standstill.

Nationalist leaders continued to be corrupt but their forces nevertheless developed into formidable opponents. The Japanese had expected China's military to collapse quickly. Finding themselves surrounded by increasing numbers of well-armed, determined Chinese soldiers, they grew frustrated and atrocities mounted. Planes bombed and strafed civilians, rape and looting became even more common, and prisoners were routinely tortured for information before being killed. The Japanese also introduced huge amounts of opium into China, hoping to erode the people's will to fight—the Opium War renewed. Newspapers throughout the West carried eyewitness stories and photographs documenting these barbarities. One photograph in *Life* magazine of a Chinese baby screaming in pain and fear after being burned and wounded by a Japanese bomb in Shanghai was seen by 136 million people.[65]

These violations of what the West regarded as the international laws of war were so terrible and so common that, despite strict censorship, they aroused concern even within Japan. Nevertheless, Japan's atrocious acts not only continued, the 1937 "rape of Nanking" made the earlier barbarities pale into comparative insignificance. Because the Japanese military finally realized that Chinese resistance could not be overcome by the few understrength divisions thus far committed to battle in China, and because Japanese war plans now called for an attack to the south to acquire vital war supplies such as rubber, tungsten, tin, and especially oil, Japanese policy had to change. Chinese coastal cities would have to be taken as bases necessary for the southern expansion, and large reinforcements would be committed to the capture of Nanking, the Nationalist Chinese capital, in an attempt to force a Chinese surrender.

Nanking was an open wound for the Japanese. A decade earlier, in 1927, Chinese troops led by Bolsheviks had looted foreign consulates and threatened consular officials. U.S. and British ships opened fire in defense of their citizens, but the Japanese did not. Newspapers in Japan demanded explanations, but none were forthcoming.[66] In July 1937, Japanese forces took Peking and presently began their drive through the port city of Shanghai up the Yangtze River toward Nanking, some 200 miles inland.

The Japanese forces were under the overall command of a tubercular, five-foot-tall, 100-pound reservist general named Matsui Iwane, who had earlier been called to the Imperial Palace. There he received the emperor's mandate: break the Chinese government's will to resist by capturing Nanking. A devout Buddhist, and a kind and honorable military commander, General Matsui was saddened to assume the task. He considered the Chinese not his enemy but his brothers whom he was regrettably obliged to pacify.

Matsui's plans to pacify the Chinese went poorly at first. Shanghai was the fourth largest city in the world. Its vast slums harbored fiercely resisting Chinese soldiers who inflicted heavy casualties on Japanese troops caught in house-to-house combat. Matsui's five divisions became so bogged down in the city that the Japanese High Command was forced to stage amphibious landings of troops both north and south of the city, 80,000 men in all. After several brilliantly executed landings, Japanese troops fought their way inland with their usual audacity and skill. Nationalist troops, however, did not collapse. They fought on so courageously that the Japanese suffered over 110,000 casualties before reaching the walled city of Nanking. The troops were tired, hungry, and, as a result of their many losses, eager for revenge. Before the final assault on Nanking, thousands of Chinese soldiers surrendered, only to be machine-gunned down. One officer who tried to prevent the slaughter wrote, "Many of our men had lost good friends. The unit hated the Chinese and there was a feeling of wanting to kill every one of the bastards."[67]

From his sickbed a hundred miles east of Nanking, General Matsui called his commanders together. On entering Nanking, Japanese troops were to maintain the highest possible standards of conduct. Anyone plundering or causing fires would be punished severely, and military police would be posted to prevent unlawful conduct. Perhaps as a result of Matsui's orders, the first Japanese troops to enter Nanking were perfectly correct, according to a German witness in the city, General von Falkenhausen, a military adviser to Chiang Kai-shek. But later that night all semblance of civility vanished as rape and looting became widespread. The twenty-seven Westerners in Nanking, including eighteen Americans, who were secluded in the European safety zone around Nanking University, were now joined by thousands of terrified Chinese fleeing for their lives, among them many Chinese soldiers who had changed into civilian clothes. Whatever restraining effect Matsui's orders may have had was removed a day later when the ailing general was supplanted as the direct commander of troops in Nanking by a general named Nakajima—even Japanese officers called him a sadist—and by the emperor's uncle, General Prince Asaka.

While the city was being systematically ravaged, a Japanese colonel named Hashimoto, who belonged to an extremist antiforeign group, set up his heavy artillery to prevent refugees from escaping up the Yangtze River to the west. Among the vessels on the river was the British gunboat HMS *Ladybird*. Hashimoto's guns fired on the *Ladybird*, killing a British sailor and wounding others. At the same time, Japanese navy planes bombed and strafed the USS *Panay*, sinking her; everyone on board was wounded, and three Americans were killed. Although it was apparently a case of mistaken identity, the *Panay* attack created such a crisis that the emperor was warned the United States might declare war. "Abject apologies" were quickly offered, and a large indemnity was paid. The pilot who led the attack was reprimanded.[68] However, Colonel Hashimoto, who ordered the firing on the *Ladybird,* went unpunished. Indeed, he was later honored. After the war, the Allies sentenced him to life in prison.

The atrocities in Nanking grew in savagery.[69] Prince Asaka ordered all Chinese army prisoners in Nanking, whether in or out of uniform, to be killed. Other officers commanded soldiers to loot everything of value to defray the cost of the campaign. Some soldiers ran wild, drunkenly killing and raping on their own, but most of the atrocities were conducted under the orders and direct supervision of officers. Chinese men were tied to posts and used for bayonet practice, as officers and sergeants corrected their men's technique and urged them to "show their toughness."[70] Officers beheaded other victims while competing with one another in trying to cleave them in half with a single blow. Borrowing an ancient Chinese practice, the Japanese buried many victims with only their heads remaining above the earth, until they died of thirst or a tank ran over them. Others they doused with gasoline and burned alive. Rape was so well organized that any reasonably attractive Chinese woman was loaded aboard a truck and taken away to be raped until the troops found her so unappealing that she was bayoneted and tossed onto piles of other civilian bodies. Some were doused with gasoline and burned, but many bodies were simply left to decompose. The most attractive women were reserved for officers, many of whom raped as sadistically as their soldiers did.

A former Japanese soldier named Nagatoni recently related his experiences in Nanking, saying he recalled riding in a truck past piles of many thousands of dead Chinese. Wild dogs gnawed at the dead flesh. Later a Japanese officer approached a group of Chinese prisoners, unsheathing his sword. He spat on it and with a single blow beheaded a cowering Chinese boy. The head tumbled away, as blood spurted in two streams from the neck. The officer told Nagatoni to take the head home as a souvenir. "I remember smiling proudly as I took his sword and began killing people." Now seventy-nine years old, Nagatoni expressed regret for his past actions. He confessed that Japanese soldiers impaled babies on bayonets and threw them alive into pots of boiling water, gang-raped, then killed, women from the ages of 12 to 80. "I beheaded people, starved them to death, burned them, and buried them alive, over 200 in all. It is terrible that I could turn into an animal and do these things."[71]

All of this took place before the horrified eyes of Westerners. Some used their immunity from harm to save women about to be raped. One American even managed to come away from Nanking with a film of atrocities that showed Chinese infants thrown into the air, then caught on bayonet points. Later shown to a few select audiences in the United States, it was considered too ghastly for wider viewing. As the atrocities grew ever more outrageous, Westerners were insulted, threatened, and forced to watch sexual mutilations, rapes, and murders. When the organized butchery ended six weeks after it began, the raped bodies of grandmothers over seventy, girls under twelve, and women in their last month of pregnancy lay in the streets to be seen by Western witnesses. One of these recorded the rape of a young married woman who was so close to giving birth that she went into labor less than two hours after the sexual assault.

Chinese being beheaded as Japanese look on. (UPI/Corbiss-Bettmann)

Miraculously, her baby was healthy.[72]

When General Matsui grew well enough to travel to Nanking, the worst of the atrocities had ended, but he learned what had happened and scathingly rebuked the responsible officers. They openly laughed at him, and one divisional commander scoffed that he saw nothing wrong about Nanking.[73] Matsui soon afterward received orders returning him Shanghai. A postwar Allied tribunal concluded that 20,000 women had been raped. At least 200,000 men, many of them civilians, had been killed. The actual number will never be known, but Chinese estimates put the death toll much higher.

After the Japanese surrender in 1945, Matsui was accused of war crimes. To protect the imperial family, and to assuage his own guilt for the actions of men nominally under his command, the innocent Matsui was a willing scapegoat. Before he died on the gallows, he gave an interview to the *New York Times* in which he admitted that unlawful acts had taken place, and made it plain that the fault lay with senior officers. Lamenting the loss of a spirit of Bushido or humanity that had led to the atrocities, Matsui declared himself "really eager to die at any time."[74]

While awaiting execution, the frail old general praised those senior officers who had taught him the meaning of Bushido, saying that these men were not the "cut-throat or highwaymen type" that later assumed power with the rise of militarism. With militarism, he said, the nation changed. "I believe it was the young ones, acting impetuously and without restraint, who finally brought everything to the present pass."[75]

Prince Asaka, commander in Nanking during the atrocities, was not called as a witness, much less as a defendant. In 1944, the emperor's younger brother, Prince Mikasa, then a young officer in China, startled the Japanese by publicly condemning the Japanese atrocities in Nanking. He said that he was appalled to discover that, as late as 1944, Japanese officers used Chinese prisoners for bayonet practice to instill "guts" in their soldiers, and that other prisoners were gassed and shot. Authorities destroyed copies of his speech. Not until July 1994, fifty years later, did a surviving copy come to light.[76]

Despite confessions like these, many Japanese continued to deny that atrocities took place in Nanking. As recently as May 1994, Justice Minister Nagamo declared that the "rape of Nanking" was a fabrication. In fact, many smaller Nankings took place all over China. Looting, arson, rape, and killing of prisoners, usually by bayonet thrusts, was reported by the Chinese throughout the war, and many Japanese veterans have admitted that the charges are true.[77] One corporal boasted of killing a pregnant Chinese woman: "We stuck our bayonets in her huge belly, skewered her like a piece of meat." He was also proud of cutting a "coolie's" head off with one stroke of his sword.[78]

A timid new officer who initially thought that the eyes of the veteran soldiers he commanded looked "evil" soon beheaded a Chinese prisoner and ordered rookie Japanese soldiers to bayonet other helpless Chinese. He saw himself and his men transformed into "murdering demons." He later confessed that "everyone became a demon within three months."[79] A Japanese doctor routinely killed so many Chinese patients that for some time he could not remember doing so.[80] What is more, Japanese planes routinely bombed and strafed civilian targets, including such innocuous ones as peasants working in their fields. Japan's policy was called "The Three All's—Burn All, Seize All, Kill All." What made Nanking different was the Japanese attempt to use terror on a grand scale to force the Chinese to surrender and the awkward presence of twenty-seven Western eyewitnesses.

After the fall of Nanking, the Japanese took the important rail and canal center of Hsuchow in May 1938. Before the city fell, Chiang's troops, who were yielding land while inflicting losses, surrounded a major Japanese force, killing some 8,000 men. The next target was the Hankow-

Japanese soldier bayonets Chinese prisoners in rural China. (UPI/Corbiss-Bettmann)

Wuhan industrial complex, 400 miles up the Yangtze River from Nanking. Chiang continued to conserve his forces by a strategic retreat, all the while receiving major arms shipments from Germany and, surprisingly, from Stalin. Hankow fell with astonishing ease, but Chiang merely moved his army farther west to Chungking, a city the Japanese would never capture. Some Japanese learned a lesson from the international outrage over Nanking. The first troops to enter Hankow were thousands of military police, who maintained order. Also, the Japanese arrived with their own "comfort women"—Japanese and Korean women who took up their duties in brothels controlled by the army.[81]

As the war dragged on, the Japanese took Canton in October of 1938, but their drive to the West bogged down with heavy casualties and increasingly serious supply problems. The morale of Japanese troops was near collapse. In the rugged terrain of western China, Japanese tanks were of little use and infantry was no longer eager to fight the Chinese with bayonets. In fact, some Japanese now surrendered to the Chinese, and entire units were known to lose their nerve. A European businessman in North China reported observing a unit of some 500 cavalry and infantry flee in panic under Chinese machine-gun fire. Others surrendered.[82] By 1939, 588 Japanese troops had been punished by court-martial for threatening a superior with violence or being insolent, and 78 others for insubordination. There were only 120 such cases during the entire Russo-Japanese War.[83]

By the end of 1938, when most of the heavy ground fighting had taken place, Chinese casualties topped one million and Japanese reached 700,000. By the eve of Pearl Harbor, over 400,000 Japanese had been killed in China.[84] The Chinese theater of war would continue to bleed Japan, as one million men would be tied down there throughout the war, but early in 1941 it became increasingly clear to all concerned that the war could soon expand, and with it would go the full measure of Japanese bravery and brutality.

CHAPTER SEVEN

"REMEMBER PEARL HARBOR"

B efore bombs fell on Pearl Harbor, Japanese leaders agonized over the wisdom of attacking the Allies. The attitudes, like the events that led to Japan's attack on the British, Dutch, and Americans in the Pacific were complex, and their role in leading to war remains controversial. It was not simply, as many have written, that Japan had devised a plan to seize the raw-materials wealth of Southeast Asia and the East Indies, knowing that the Western powers were too weak to stop her, then negotiate peace from a position of strength. Neither was the war a result of a conspiracy on the part of Churchill and Roosevelt to save Britain—

and America—by luring Japan into an attack against the United States that would permit Roosevelt to unite war-leery Americans in the fight against "Axis tyranny."

To be sure, there is a modicum of truth in both of these claims. The Western powers were weak in the Pacific, and the Japanese knew they could take the area's riches with little difficulty. Churchill knew that Britain's very survival could depend on U.S. entry into the war, and Roosevelt had long wanted his country to join the fight against the Nazis. But what led the Japanese to attack Pearl Harbor was a series of diplomatic miscalculations and downright blunders, not, as some still claim, Churchill's callous decision to withhold from Roosevelt intelligence information that Pearl Harbor would be the target or, in turn, Roosevelt's cynical decision not to warn his commanders in Pearl Harbor that they were about to be attacked.[1]

Japan's atrocities in China since 1932 and her increased attachment to the Axis powers created growing American hostility, which resulted in a reduction of essential exports to Japan, increased lend-lease to China, and ultimately to a freezing of Japanese assets and an oil embargo. Many of Japan's army officers nonetheless opposed war in the Pacific, and even senior navy officers opposed war with America. In both services, there were "liberal" senior officers who tried to dampen the war lust of their younger colleagues. For the most part, Japan's major industrialists opposed broadening the war as well, and the government usually did its best to avoid a general Pacific War. Prime Minister Hirota made many attempts to prevent a widening of the war from China to the Pacific; he even attempted to end the "China incident." After the war, the Allies hanged him nevertheless. Tojo, who replaced him, was a general, but he too sought a compromise. And Prince Konoye, his successor, came close to treason in his attempt to end the war. Emperor Hirohito opposed the war as well but was warned not to speak openly or his advisers would be assassinated.[2]

With the Netherlands already occupied by the Nazis, Holland had little military strength available to protect the riches of her East Indian empire, and France's forces in Indochina—reluctantly to be sure—cooperated with Japan throughout the war. Britain was so embattled at home and in North Africa that she hoped to avoid conflict in the Pacific, while American public opinion was heavily opposed to involvement. Even Roosevelt, who saw the necessity of America's fighting the Axis powers, had been warned that the United States would not have the military or naval strength to contend with Japan before the spring of 1942 at the earliest. In Japan, many men in the government and military had come to realize that the country's adventure in China had proven to be a disaster. The easy victory the army had promised was nowhere to be seen. The war was a profitless, deadly drain on Japan's strength that endangered her hold on the wealth of Manchuria.

All these factors competed for supremacy as 1941 wore on, and the Japanese military planned intensely for a Pacific campaign, including a naval air attack on Pearl Harbor. For many in Japan, as in the West, war seemed unavoidable. Nevertheless, diplomats continued to search for a way around war between Japan and the United States by exchanging a series of proposals. Japan sent a delegation to Washington led by the six-foot, 200-pound ambassador, Admiral Nomura Kichisaburo. The Japanese did not realize that U.S. cryptanalysts had broken both their diplomatic code and their "unbreakable" naval code, JN-25 (the British and Dutch were reading Japanese coded messages as well).

Whether intentionally by war hawks, as some Japanese believe, or simply by mistake, a number of crucial Japanese proposals were made to sound far more threatening in English translation than they sounded in the original Japanese.[3] This, combined with code-breaking evidence that the Japanese navy was preparing for war action, led American diplomats, particularly Secretary of State Cordell Hull, to mistrust the Japanese. Despite Hull's refusal to acknowledge that a late November 1941 Japanese proposal for peace contained some concessions that were worthwhile negotiating points, President Roosevelt made a conciliatory reply that might have led to serious peace negotiations. However, Chiang Kai-shek complained bitterly that the Americans were appeasing—a dirty word since Chamberlain and Munich—the Japanese at Chinese Nationalists' expense, a point that Churchill mildly but effectively supported.[4]

On the basis of these complaints and further intelligence information about Japanese troop movements into French Indochina, Roosevelt's so-called modus vivendi proposal was not submitted. After the war, Tojo, already fated to die on the gallows as a war criminal, said with great sadness that the expected modus vivendi had led him to prepare a counterproposal containing new compromises that might have averted war. Instead of a modus vivendi, Hull presented an ultimatum one of whose provisions called on Japan to withdraw from China. Hull had not meant "China" to include Manchuria, but the Japanese assumed that it did. This demand was unthinkable for them—it meant war.

Had the Americans recognized Japan's right to Manchuria, negotiations would very likely have continued and war might have been prevented. At least it would have been delayed, because even short negotiations would have made the North Pacific's winter weather too inclement to permit the Pearl Harbor attack until the following spring, by which time the United States would have been far more ready for war.[5]

The climate of the times made misunderstandings like this tragic diplomatic mistake not only possible but likely. Japan detested Western racism and economic domination. Her large surplus population and shortage of raw materials made expansion essential if she were to remain a world power. The fear of spreading communism in China was intense as well. The West had its own fears and delusions. Japan was unwelcome as a competing economic or military power. Racial fears of the "yellow peril" were very much alive, and beneath much that the West did in negotiating with Japan was the fixed belief that her nearsighted, tiny military men were ludicrously inept. These attitudes, culminating in the attack on Pearl Harbor, did much to create the hatreds that led to the brutal fighting and many atrocities of the Pacific War.

Long before war erupted, the Allied economic encirclement of Japan was widely perceived by the Japanese as a threat to their existence. Young officers stridently urged all who would listen—and many did—that the demonic white men were determined to starve Japan out of existence. The purported American demand that Japan leave Manchuria convinced many that war was justified. If the divine Yamato race were to live, war would have to begin, and it would be war without mercy. The attack on Pearl Harbor was, in reality, only a limited military success, but it raised spirits throughout Japan. However, it also made the Japanese overconfident. Most important, this "sneak" attack on a Sunday morning, instantly made the Japanese the most hated enemy in American history. Japan's modest military victory proved to be an immense propaganda loss. In 1904, America's press joined other Western newspapers in praising Japan's attack on Port Arthur without prior declaration of war as "brilliant" and "masculine." Now they used Japan's "treachery" to whip up racial hatred and demand terrible retribution.

Admiral Yamamoto in 1934 at the Naval Limitation Conference in London.
(UPI/Corbiss-Bettmann)

The plan to attack Pearl Harbor was conceived by Admiral Yamamoto Isoroku, who as a young man had lost his left index and middle finger at Tsushima. During the 1920s, Yamamoto spent nearly three years in the United States. He returned, speaking good English, liking Carl Sandburg's *Lincoln*, enjoying American football, and understanding

America's vast industrial strength. Yamamoto did not drink, but the handsome five-three, 125-pound young naval officer had an eye for women. Married with four children, he was not a womanizer by the very high standards of the Japanese navy, even though he had several geisha mistresses, who were ushered on board ship with ceremony and gaiety. One, Kawai Chiyoko, his lifelong love, published his love letters to her in 1954. He was also an addicted gambler who bet on every Japanese and American game of chance and skill he could find, especially *shoji*, Japanese chess. His first gamble was Pearl Harbor; his second, Midway.

Yamamoto made no secret of his conviction that Japan could not hope to defeat the United States in war; he promised a year of success at most. Nevertheless, as commander of the Combined Fleet, he planned the attack on Pearl Harbor. Not everyone in the navy thought the proposed attack was a good idea. The chief of the staff of the First Air Fleet called it too great a gamble, while the leader of the Eleventh Air Fleet argued that, whatever happened in the war, Japan could not win. A negotiated peace would be necessary, and the Pearl Harbor attack would make the Americans too angry for negotiations.[6] Even Commander Fuchida Mitsuo, the tall, skinny naval airman who led the air strike on Pearl Harbor, initially had doubts about Yamamoto, accusing him of being too fond of England and America and of lacking "guts."[7] Many Japanese admirals deplored Yamamoto's faith in naval air power, pointing to the power of Japan's beautiful new 70,000-ton battleships, not ugly aircraft carriers, as the way to victory.

Undeterred, Yamamoto conducted meticulous training trials of air attacks at a bay on the Inland Sea that closely resembled Pearl Harbor. New shallow-running torpedoes were developed and dive bombing perfected. Even Fuchida and his movie-star handsome staff officer compatriot, the brilliant Genda Minoru, eventually became fervent converts. Admiral Yamamoto, who subscribed to *Life* magazine until the time of Pearl Harbor, did not plan a sneak attack. He insisted that Pearl Harbor receive at least a thirty-minute warning; when this did not occur, because it took Japanese embassy clerks in Washington too long to decode the message declaring war, he was distraught. So was Tojo, who had wanted war to be declared before the attack.[8]

Command of the Pearl Harbor task force was given to Vice Admiral Nagumo Chuichi, a man Yamamoto neither liked not trusted.[9] Nagumo was a competent sailor, but his appointment to command was a political

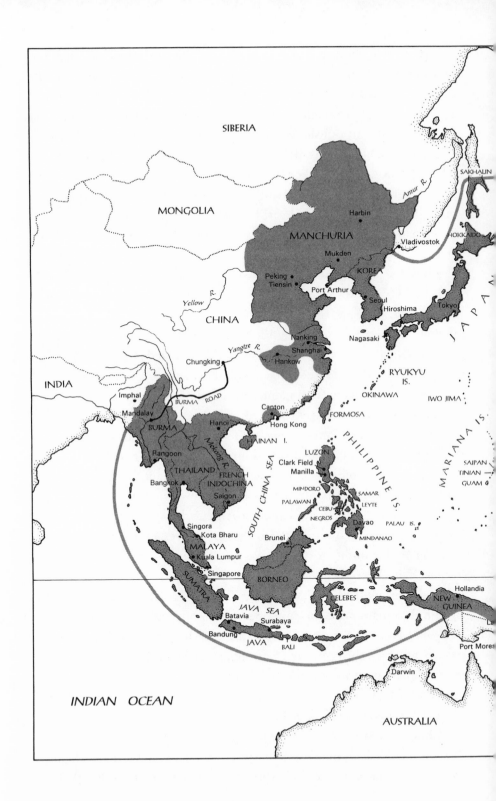

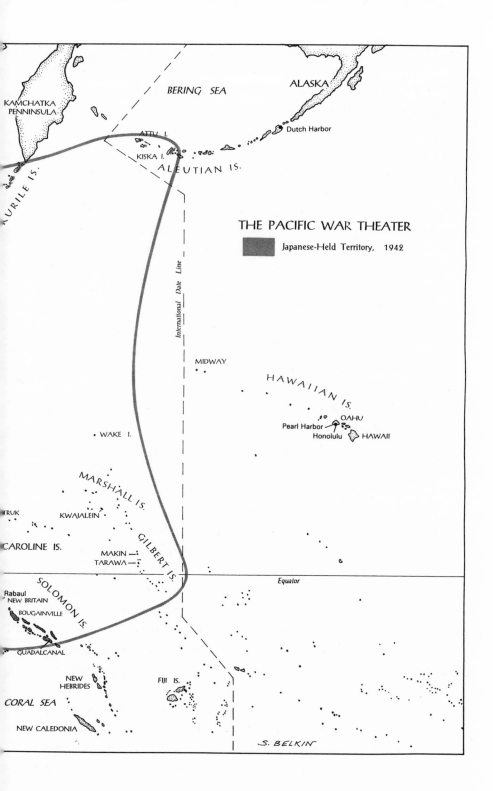

THE PACIFIC WAR THEATER

Japanese-Held Territory, 1942

KAMCHATKA PENNINSULA

BERING SEA

ALASKA

Dutch Harbor

ATTU I.

KISKA I.

ALEUTIAN IS.

KURILE IS.

International Date Line

MIDWAY

HAWAIIAN IS.

OAHU

Pearl Harbor

Honolulu

HAWAII

WAKE I.

MARSHALL IS.

TRUK

KWAJALEIN

CAROLINE IS.

GILBERT IS.

MAKIN

TARAWA

Equator

SOLOMON IS.

Rabaul
NEW BRITAIN

BOUGAINVILLE

GUADALCANAL

NEW HEBRIDES

FIJI IS.

CORAL SEA

NEW CALEDONIA

S. BELKIN

one. He had doubts about the wisdom of the mission, showing signs of acute anxiety and timidity to fellow officers on several occasions during the voyage to Pearl Harbor.[10] The night of November 25–26, 1941, Yamamoto checked into an elegant old inn with Chiyoko where he was seen playing a game of flower cards. The next morning, the task force sailed under strict radio silence.

Thanks in large part to the accurate observations of a Japanese spy, Fuchida and his men knew exactly where the American warships would be berthed. On the early morning of December 7, Fuchida's "Zero" fighter with distinctive yellow and red markings on its tail lifted off the carrier *Akagi*. Despite frantic radio messages such as "This is no drill," the Americans were taken completely by surprise. They managed to shoot down only 29 of the 353 Japanese planes, killing 55 men. The United States suffered 3,695 casualties and the loss of most of its Pacific battle fleet. Photographs of the destruction soon became an indelible part of the American memory. The Pearl Harbor Monument, with oil still seeping to the surface of the harbor, continues to bring tears to the eyes of many. However, the U.S. Navy's three aircraft carriers were not in the harbor, and its vital repair facilities were largely untouched. Its oil tanks, holding as much oil as Japan's entire oil reserve at the time, were not hit either.

When the planes of the first strike returned to their six carriers, Fuchida made ready for the planned second strike, intended to destroy those essential targets. As the planes were being reloaded and refueled, Nagumo called Fuchida to the bridge. Asked about the success of the raid, Fuchida reported that four battleships had been sunk and four others badly damaged. He saw no U.S. fighter planes at all. Fuchida was quick to mention that even the ships that had been sunk were in shallow water. Salvaging them would not be difficult. Nicknamed Hitler because of his small mustache and intense eyes, Fuchida strongly recommended that the second strike go ahead as planned.[11] Nagumo said nothing, dismissing the flier who returned to his planes only to discover the bombers being stowed away and the fleet turning north, away from Hawaii. Furious arguments burst out among the fliers, Fuchida, and Genda, all of whom wanted to strike again. Nagumo, however, was satisfied with the single attack and would risk nothing more to a possible attack by the missing U.S. carriers. When an appeal was made to Yamamoto, now sailing east in a battleship to escort the task force home, to overrule Nagumo, he declined, saying that "even a burglar hesitates to go back for more."[12] The chance to destroy Pearl Harbor as a useful naval base for at least a year was lost. Fuchida never forgave Nagumo. He continued to carry out his duties, but because of a bout of appendicitis, he was not able to fly at Midway, perhaps saving his life. After the war, this devoted warrior who felt the war entirely justified nonetheless converted to Christianity, becoming an evangelical missionary and a friend of Billy Graham.[13]

Pearl Harbor was not the first Allied target on December 7—that was Malaya, where Japanese troops went ashore hours before bombs fell on Hawaii—nor was it the only American target. Guam, Wake, and the Philippines were hit soon thereafter. Guam lay almost due south of Saipan, a Japanese-held island in the Marianas that would later be the site of one of the Pacific War's great battles. Guam had flown the American flag since the Spanish-American War. Japan had taken Saipan, and its sister island Tinian, from the Germans in World War I. For fear of antagonizing Japan, the Americans had not fortified Guam or built a military airfield there. Its garrison consisted of 153 marines, a few hundred sailors, and local troops aided by some small patrol boats. Three hours after the attack on Pearl Harbor began, 5,000 Japanese troops started to come ashore, accompanied by cavalry, actually on horseback. U.S. Marines, sailors, and Chamorro island guardsmen fought back with their only weapons—machine guns and rifles—for twenty-five minutes before Guam's governor ordered them to cease fire. There were few casualties on either side. American survivors, including navy nurses, would be the first to experience the horrors of capture by the Japanese. Wake Island, next to be attacked, would also feel the full fury of Japanese brutality.

Only a few minutes after Guam was attacked, Japanese planes bombed and strafed Wake atoll, a sandy flyspeck about halfway between Guam and Midway. Lacking fresh water or anything else of value except for hordes of hermit crabs and odd-looking hump-backed rats, Wake had been overlooked for centuries until 1935 when Pan-American Airlines thought it a good refueling stop for its clipper service from the Orient to the United States. Passengers who spent the night in Wake's new, if rather spartan, hotel often borrowed the hotel's complimentary pellet guns to hunt the rats. Wake's three small islands were largely covered by an almost impenetrable scrub brush standing ten to twenty feet tall. To the surprise of visitors, there were no palm trees. There were no military installations on Wake either until January of 1941, when the growing tension in the Pacific led the navy to send some 1,000 civilian construction workers and hundreds of marines to build an airfield and fortify the three islands. Wake's strategic location, only 620 miles almost due north of Japan's Marshall Island base of Kwajalein, and its potential role as a refueling stop for B-17's enroute to the Philippines made it an asset for the United States—and a threat to Japan.

As Japanese reconnaissance planes flew unmolested overhead, coastal defense guns were emplaced and machine-gun positions set up, and the airfield construction, featuring concrete revetments to protect planes, went ahead. The airfield was completed only days before the first Japanese attack. Nevertheless, its handful of planes and marine antiaircraft guns took a toll of Japanese planes. After several more raids, a small Japanese landing force arrived, only to be shot to pieces by the marines' five-inch guns, sinking two destroyers, and damaging two light cruisers and several transports. The Japanese suffered over 700 casualties at a cost of only 4 wounded marines.

When the Japanese returned just over two weeks after their first attack, it was with a large armada accompanied by two aircraft carriers. After an unequal exchange of gunfire, and heavy punishment by Japanese planes, Japanese landing craft put troops ashore during the night. Japan's well-trained Special Naval Landing Forces fought skillfully, firing light machine guns then moving close to marine positions to hurl grenades and use their flamethrowers. On Wilkes Island, their skill and bravery were not enough. Two Japanese officers and 94 men were killed—the only 2 survivors were taken prisoner. The cost to the United States was 9 dead and 5 wounded.

The battle for Wake was not so one-sided. In addition to the men who manned the artillery, there were only 85 marines plus a few civilian volunteers available for mobile, beach defense. While most of the civilians hid in the dense brush, refusing to take on a military role, these few men fought superbly. They inflicted hundreds of casualties before the landing of Japanese reinforcements convinced their commander, Major James Devereux, only five feet five, but a tough, resourceful officer, and Navy Commander Winfield Scott "Spiv" Cunningham, officer-in-charge of all naval operations, that it would be useless to sacrifice more lives. Devereux and Cunningham did not know that a U.S. naval task force with marine reinforcements had turned back, many of its marines in tears. At this stage of the war, aircraft carriers were to be protected at all costs, even including the lives of the men on Wake and the honor of the navy. Unaware of the marines' victory on Wilkes, the two officers forced their men to surrender, often over vigorous and profane objection. The first Japanese officer to confront Devereux's white bedsheet on a stick, offered him a cigarette, bemusedly telling the anguished major that he had attended the 1939 San Francisco fair. When the Japanese death toll became clear—over 800, with many more wounded—Japanese hostility soared.

Herded off for interrogation, the American officers were initially treated humanely, but the enlisted men and civilians—more than 1,500 of them—had their hands tied behind their backs with wire and were slapped and deprived of food and water until a navy doctor prevailed on a Japanese officer to remove the wire. After two weeks of barely acceptable treatment on Wake, a Japanese naval transport arrived and all prisoners were dumped unceremoniously on its deck from cargo nets. All prisoners, including wounded officers, were then forced to run a gauntlet past Japanese sailors who slapped, struck, and clubbed them gleefully. After a six-day voyage marked by bitter cold, starvation rations, and capricious beatings—one officer was viciously clubbed for talking too loudly—the ship reached Yokohama. Eight officers and 12 men were sent to a prisoner-of-war camp in Japan; the others were shipped to Shanghai.

Once at sea, Navy Lieutenant Saito Toshio, commander of the guards, ordered 3 sailors and 2 marines out of the cargo hold on deck, where 150 Japanese formed a semicircle around the bewildered men. After they were bound and blindfolded, Saito informed them—in Japanese—that because the Americans had killed so many Japanese on Wake, they would be killed "for revenge." Each man was then beheaded. After mutilating the bodies, the crew threw what remained of the men overboard. The rest of the prisoners spent the war in prisons near Shanghai, then in Korea, and finally in Hokkaido. A few Japanese guards and officers were kind, but most were brutal. The prisoners were routinely beaten and fed very little. Walking skeletons, they were still forced to work twelve-hour days. Four of the 5 Japanese who murdered the American victims on board ship spent nine years in prison. One was acquitted. Saito is known to have survived the war but was never found. Commander Cunningham's Annapolis class ring, however, was recovered from his home.[14]

Not all of the Americans on Wake had been sent off to prison camps. The Japanese commander, Navy Captain Sakaibara Shigematsu, had ordered 96 construction workers to remain on Wake to help strengthen the defenses. Dr. Shank, a civilian, volunteered to stay with them. When Wake surrendered in early September 1945, the returning Americans met a malnourished Sakaibara with a small surviving garrison near starvation. After inspecting the graves of the 49 marines, 3 sailors, and 70 civilians who had been killed during the sixteen-day battle for the atoll, they also found a long trench marked as a grave. They learned that as American air and naval raids against Wake increased in intensity through 1943, Sakaibara believed that an invasion was imminent. On October 7, 1943, fearing that if captured, the Americans would reveal the weakness of his defenses, he ordered them tied and blindfolded, then lined up and machine-gunned. No one survived. Sakaibara and several of his officers were hanged on Guam in 1947.[15]

Within an hour after the first bombs exploded on Pearl Harbor, General Douglas MacArthur's headquarters in Manila received a phone call warning the staff to expect an attack there at any time. General Lewis H. Brereton, commander of MacArthur's newly formed 200-plane Far East Air Force, rushed to MacArthur's plush penthouse hotel-suite head-quarters in Manila to request permission to bomb Japanese air bases on Taiwan. Permission was denied, and after epic confusion almost all of his planes were destroyed on the ground, some nine hours after Pearl Harbor was attacked. General H. H. "Hap" Arnold, soon to be chief of Allied air forces in the Pacific, telephoned Brereton in disbelief, demanding to know "how in the hell" such a disaster could have taken place.[16]

About the time that MacArthur was losing the United States' second-largest threat to Japan, his B-17 bombers, Japanese troops were slowly pushing back British forces on Hong Kong. Six battalions of Indian and Canadian troops, along with some 2,000 civilian volunteers, fought them to a standstill until Christmas Eve, when they finally surrendered with 1,200 men dead, twice the Japanese total. For no known reason, 50 British officers and other ranks had their hands tied and then were bayoneted to death.[17] Drunken Japanese troops then raped and looted in a smaller-scale replica of Nanking. Nuns were a special target.[18] At a hospital caring for British wounded, James Barrett, a Canadian army chaplain, watched Japanese soldiers bayonet 15 wounded men as they lay in their beds. The next day, he found the bodies of more than 70 men who had been bayoneted in their beds. Some had been horribly mutilated: "their ears, tongues, noses and eyes had been cut away from their faces." Four nurses told the chaplain that they had been raped and that they feared even worse the next night. One woman had been forced to lie on 2 dead bodies while being raped several times. He later found 3 dead nurses, one with her head nearly severed. All told, Barrett cremated 170 bodies.[19] A little more than two months later, Britain's "impregnable fortress" of Singapore would fall, leading to an even more terrible orgy of atrocities. But the stubborn courage of the men on Hong Kong was only occasionally duplicated by the much larger British army in Malaya.

The British fortress on Singapore Island, off the southern tip of Malaya, posed a naval and air threat to Japanese aspirations in the South Pacific. What is more, Malaya itself was the world's largest producer of tin and rubber. Thailand, just to the north, was the gateway to Burma and India. The task of devising an invasion plan for Thailand and Malaya fell to one of Japan's most fanatically radical young staff officers, Tsuji Masanoba. A few months earlier, Tsuji had conspired with other ultranationalist officers to prevent a proposed meeting between Prime Minister Konoye and President Roosevelt just before Pearl Harbor, by assassinating Konoye. The meeting was canceled, making assassination unnecessary. Young Major Tsuji also devoted his considerable intellectual abilities to the conquest of British Southeast Asia. First, the short, bald, round-faced, horn-rimmed Tsuji persuaded his radical friend Captain Aseada Shigehara—a fearless, athletic six-footer—to pose as a civilian while spying on British defenses. Aseada returned safely with copious, valuable notes. Then Tsuji persuaded a pilot friend to fly him over the area in an unmarked, unarmed plane to examine modern British airfields and to test their defenses. He returned vastly impressed by their size but confirmed what had been expected. There were only 50 obsolete combat planes in Malaya. British planning officers estimated 500 modern planes as the minimum needed to defend the country.

Thailand was the only Southeast Asian country to remain independent of a colonial power. Hoping to forge a treaty with Thailand without major conflict, Tsuji believed that a relatively small force of Japanese could persuade the Thais to accept a neutrality treaty. Malaya, on the other hand, was a jewel in Britain's colonial crown that would not easily be taken.

Tsuji estimated three months of hard fighting before Japanese troops could reach Singapore. To avoid heavy fighting on the borders of Malaya, he hoped to find a way through Thailand that would be less bloody. A dream came to him in which 1,000 Japanese troops wearing Thai uniforms would be packed into some 300 buses, along with a large number of Thai dance hall and bar girls. They would then drive past Malayan border guards, waving Thai and British flags while drunkenly shouting "Japanese soldier is frightful!" and "Hurrah for the English!" He was certain his plan would work.[20] Wisely, his superiors disagreed.

The next issue was how to cope with tropical heat. The British soon declared the Japanese "natural jungle fighters" because they fought in it so much more skillfully than the British. In fact, though, no Japanese soldier had ever fought in a jungle before Malaya, and few had even seen one. Tsuji insisted that they be issued tropical-weight uniforms, and prepared a detailed set of instructions for maintaining their health and weapons under tropical conditions. The Japanese planning staff thought it would be suicidal to pack men and horses into the holds of ships in tropical heat. To test this idea, Tsuji packed thousands of troops virtually on top of one another—three men to a six-by-three-foot mat—in the boiling holds of several ships, along with their steaming horses and equipment. After a week of this torture with limited water, the men carried out a successful mock landing.[21] Finally, Tsuji wrote a pamphlet titled "Read This Alone—And the War Can Be Won." In addition to giving instructions about the tropics, he wrote, "In the Japan of recent years we have unthinkingly come to accept Europeans as superior and to despise the Chinese and the peoples of the South. This is like spitting into our own eyes."[22] Tsuji hoped that Japan's soldiers would join him in a racial war.

Command of Japan's invasion forces was given to General Yamashita Tomoyuki, a large, burly man of fifty-nine who had been trained in Austria, Germany, and Switzerland. After fighting in China since 1937, he now came ashore with some 60,000 men, 400 guns, and 120 tanks.[23] Britain's hopes of thwarting the landing were crushed when her two major warships, the *Repulse* and *Prince of Wales,* were sunk by Japanese planes off the invasion beaches. The doomed British ships had no air cover. Malaya was defended by upwards of 130,000 military personnel, perhaps 85,000 of whom were combat troops. However, their leader, General Arthur Percival, was tragically indecisive, and many of his

Indian troops, so heavily laden that they could barely move in the jungle heat, would not stand up to the Japanese. Many of his best British troops were kept in Singapore until it was too late, leaving most of the fighting to the Australians, who battled ferociously but were often outmaneuvered by aggressive Japanese infantry tactics. The Japanese had air superiority, numerous light tanks, and superior initiative and mobility, thanks in large part to the thousands of lightweight bicycles they used to move rapidly down well-paved British roads, then carried across rivers and into the jungle. Averaging twenty miles with two battles and four to five bridge repairs each day, Yamashita's men smashed their way to the southern tip of Malaya in fifty-five days, not the ninety Tsuji had predicted. Yamashita had originally been given four divisions for the invasion, but after evaluating British power he disdainfully returned one. Events proved him right.

As Yamashita's army dashed south, now Lieutenant Colonel Tsuji rushed all over Malaya, first congratulating platoon leaders and then berating superior officers for their tactical errors. He regularly returned to staff headquarters to rail against colleagues whom he accused of corruption or laziness, even shouting at generals who did not measure up to his impossible standards of fanaticism. Several times he went into a total funk, disappearing for a week at a time before returning to duty as if nothing had happened. Thanks to his brilliance (and his prominence among radical young officers), everyone, including Yamashita, gave him enormous latitude. Yamashita also listened to what he said. When Tsuji complained to him that some Japanese troops were guilty of rape and looting in Malaya villages, Yamashita had their commander put under thirty-day arrest, a serious penalty. It was not enough for Tsuji. He wanted the soldiers shot. When Tsuji later complained about petty theft by soldiers, Yamashita lined up his senior officers and gave them a tongue-lashing about the need for discipline.[24]

Ill-treatment of Malays was not to be tolerated—they were to be liberated from the white man's yoke. Allied soldiers were another story. Among Yamashita's Japanese divisions were the elite Imperial Guards, heroes of the Russo-Japanese War, who once again proved to be excellent combat soldiers. However, after being held up for a week by badly outnumbered Australians at Muar, the guards herded 110 Australian and 40 Indian wounded who had been left behind into a small shed, where they were beaten, taunted, and denied food and water while the Japanese laughed at their suffering. That evening, all had their hands tied before being dragged outside, shot, bayoneted, and beheaded. A couple of the prisoners miraculously escaped into the jungle, later to tell the story. After the war, the guards' commander, Lieutenant General Nishimura Takuma, was hanged by the Allies.[25]

When the last Allied troops crossed the single, narrow causeway across the Johore Strait to Singapore Island—90 survivors of the Argyll and Sutherland Highlanders with their bagpipes playing "Highland Laddie"—they were stunned to discover what Yamashita had long known. Although the south-facing beaches of the naval base bristled with fortifications, the extensive north shore was completely undefended. General Percival had chosen not to fortify the area, lest his troops come to regard the island as a sanctuary and stop fighting in the jungles of Malaya. He also feared that the civilians might panic if they thought Singapore was in danger. Even after receiving direct orders to fortify, he did nothing.

Still, as Yamashita planned to cross the shallow strait, he had to confront the surprising but growing possibility of defeat. He had only 30,000 effective troops, while the British had over 100,000, including the newly disembarked Eighteenth Division. Moreover, he was almost out of ammunition. He knew that a dogged defense could defeat him, but he also knew that British morale made that unlikely. He crossed the strait, and the British fell back. Unable to call Yamashita's bluff, Percival on February 15 surrendered over 130,000 military personnel. Singapore had not been a cakewalk for the Japanese; they suffered 5,000 casualties, half of their total for the entire campaign. But they had won a great prize.

With planes flying overhead and 125 tanks rumbling through the streets, Yamashita put on a show of force to cow Singapore's civilians. His frontline troops also put on a show of terror. First, they bayoneted everyone in Alexandra Hospital, including a patient undergoing an operation, the surgeon, and the anesthesiologist.[26] They then ran wild, stealing valuables and raping women. Many Indian soldiers who had done little fighting now defected to the anti-British Indian National Army, led by Chandra Bose. Those Indian troops who refused to do so were tortured, even beheaded, yet the majority remained loyal.[27] Following Tsuji's frenzied urging, Yamashita personally ordered that all residents of Singapore be screened for such undesirable attributes as tattoos (signifying possible criminal-gang membership), wealth, education, status as government employees, and, indeed, anything that local commanders found distasteful. Some 6,000 Chinese were shot, buried alive, bayoneted, or, very often, taken to sea, bound, and kicked overboard. Yamashita was hanged by the Allies in 1946.[28]

On December 22, while Yamashita's troops were fighting their way south through the Malayan jungle, 43,000 men under General Homma Masaharu came ashore on Leyte, in the Philippines, without opposition. MacArthur had no air or sea power, and too few soldiers, to fight on the beaches. Hoping to mount a delaying action, he saw many of his untrained, poorly armed Filipino troops run from danger as Homma's armored columns moved swiftly toward Manila. Declaring Manila an open city, MacArthur took a boat to Corregidor on Christmas Day, while his army, including 15,000 Americans, escaped into the Bataan Peninsula, as war plans called for them to do. Because the Japanese failed to bomb the crucial bridges leading to Bataan, close to 80,000 men made it there with most of their weapons, but little food. At this stage of the war, most Filipinos were treated well, as Homma had ordered. He had served with the British army for eight years, including a year with the British expeditionary force in France in 1918. He had opposed the current war but would do his duty. His duty, as he saw it, was to win the war honorably, then win the affection of the Filipino people.

Homma's success in battle was so great that his best division, the Forty-eighth, was shipped off to the Dutch East Indies, replaced by a brigade of only 7,500 older men wholly unprepared for combat. Their commander was Lieutenant General Nara Akira, who had attended Amherst College and graduated from Fort Benning Infantry School, in Georgia.[29] Without hope of success, Nara dutifully attacked the dug-in soldiers on Bataan, and his men were cut to shreds. Continuing resistance on Bataan throughout January, February, and March left Homma embarrassed and Tokyo furious. Fifty thousand reinforcements had to be sent before the malaria-wracked, half-starved Americans and Filipinos, only 27,000 of whom were combat effective, would surrender. It came on April 9, the anniversary of the Battle of Appomattox. MacArthur was not among the captives. Earlier, he had been ordered to leave Corregidor by PT boat.

Soon after General Wainwright, MacArthur's replacement, surrendered, Japanese troops stole everything the 78,000 prisoners possessed, including their tooth brushes. Homma, who had expected 25,000 at most, had entrusted their care to Major General Kawane Yoshikata. Kawane presented a plan to Homma that would have provided transportation, food, and medical supplies for the prisoners in a model of humane treatment. Homma approved it, but everything went wrong. There were too few trucks and far too many prisoners, most of whom were too weak and sick to march any distance. What happened on the trail of death to Camp O'Donnell was as quixotic as it was ghastly. Some Japanese guards bayoneted prisoners without provocation. Others forced Filipinos to bury weak Americans alive—the image of one officer's living hand reaching out of his grave is unforgettable. Still others forced Filipinos to kill Americans too weak to march, then bury them. But some guards shared their canteens with prisoners, and others saw to it that they were well fed. A few prisoners rode all the way to Camp O'Donnell without any difficulty.

Many, however, perished. Ten thousand did not reach Camp O'Donnell, and while some of these had no doubt escaped, probably 7,000, among them over 2,300 Americans, died on the march or were killed.[30] A few days before the beginning of the "Bataan death march," as it became known, Colonel Tsuji flew from Singapore to Manila. He quickly found kindred radical officers at Imperial Headquarters who accepted his passionate argument that prisoners should be killed—the Americans as white colonialists, the Filipinos as unworthy Asians. He then issued orders by telephone to Colonel Imai Takeo, hero of the Bataan fighting, to kill all the prisoners under his control. Refusing to believe that any Japanese general would give such an order, Imai demanded the order in writing. Furious, but apparently concerned that the order might be legitimate after all, he ordered all 1,000 prisoners set free, after giving them directions on the best way to escape Bataan. A similar order was relayed to a newly arrived major general, who also doubted its authenticity. The officer who delivered the oral order urged him to comply, saying that his own division was already executing prisoners. The general still demanded a written order.[31]

Angry about Homma's kind treatment of Filipino civilians, General Count Terauchi Hisaichi, commander of the Southern Army, endorsed a pamphlet detailing the horrors of American colonialism in the Philippines. Homma suppressed it, telling Terauchi personally that the American regime had been benevolent and that Japan should try to do even better. Tsuji and his clique sent out orders from headquarters countermanding Homma's benevolent policy. One of the first results was an order to execute Chief Justice José Santos, who was seized and shot by firing squad. The Japanese commander in the area where the execution took place was Major General Kawaguchi Kiyotake. He had served in one of Japan's camps for German prisoners of war during World War I, and he was proud of the compassionate care they had received.[32] When he heard of Santos's execution order, Kawaguchi burst into Homma's office and demanded to know why he had authorized it. Homma knew nothing about the order. Kawaguchi's effort to save the judge failed because, as his former classmate Major General Hayashi later said, Imperial Headquarters was so insistent. When Kawaguchi accused Hayashi of a shameful act, Hayashi admitted that the order had come from Tsuji.[33]

Many senior officers recognized the dangers that fanatical young officers like Tsuji posed. Along with young generals like Ishiwara Kanji, an intellectual beacon for the young officers, and the dashing General Doihara Kenji—known as Doihara of Manchuria, after Lawrence of Arabia—these men represented everything that was brutal to some senior Japanese officers, who saw their influence as ruinous. One senior general urged that "extermination of these poisonous insects should take precedence over all other problems."[34]

As the American and Filipino prisoners settled into the horrific routine of life in various prison camps, and many escaped prisoners joined guerrilla groups in the mountains of Luzon, the war moved to the south. The wealth of the Dutch East Indies, especially its huge oil fields and refineries, had been the main target of the Japanese from the start. With the fall of Singapore and the early successes in the Philippines, Japan turned toward the East Indies. The Dutch had virtually no air force, and the few British, Australian, and American planes that came to their aid were ineffectual. There were over 90,000 men under arms, but most were Indonesians of dubious reliability. There were 25,000 Dutch army troops on Java, the most crucial island, but they had to defend a 500-mile-long northern shoreline, and an equally long expanse of beaches on the south.

On February 15, 1942, Japanese troops landed on Bali and Sumatra. On February 26, two Japanese invasion fleets headed for Java. One invasion force of fifty-six troop transports accompanied by cruisers and destroyers approached western Java, while another force of forty transports with cruiser and destroyer escorts headed for eastern Java. A motley collection of Dutch, British, Australian, and U.S. cruisers and destroyers sailed out to intercept them. The Battle of the Java Sea, as it came to be known, took place at night, when the superior night-fighting skills of the Japanese gave them a decisive advantage. The Allied ships, led by the Dutch admiral Karel Doorman, fought bravely but were older and slower than the Japanese, had weaker firepower, and, unlike them, could not easily be coordinated at night. Doorman, who was killed in the battle, lost two cruisers and three destroyers sunk; other ships suffered heavy damage as well. The Japanese lost no ships and suffered few casualties.[35] Still more Allied ships were sunk in the days to come, and the Japanese transports landed their troops with ease.

The Japanese invasion forces fought with their accustomed skill and courage. Dutch troops fought courageously, too, as did the few British and Australian units there to help them, but greatly outnumbered, they could not save the oil fields. Owing to the hostility of the Indonesian people, they could not slip into the jungle to fight a guerrilla war either. Early in May, they surrendered and began their own experience with Japanese brutality. The Indonesian people initially welcomed the Japanese as liberators but soon found them more brutal than the Dutch. Millions of Indonesians were forced to work under deplorable conditions. After the war, the United Nations estimated that three million died on Java alone, along with another million on neighboring islands.[36]

Dutch commanders and civilian oil field workers managed to set devastating fires when the Japanese arrived. The Japanese responded in terrible anger by machine-gunning and bayoneting at will. The entire white population of Balikpapan was killed in retribution for setting its oil fields on fire.[37] Elsewhere, Dutch and Australian women were repeatedly raped while the Japanese commander looked on with approval. When 2,600 vanquished Allied troops were marched into Cycle Camp in Java, soon to be joined by 500 U.S. and Australian sailors who had survived the sinking of their ships, they were greeted by savage beatings, which would continue, along with virtual starvation and degradation. It was no better for civilian prisoners. When the 65,000 prisoners held in Batavia were released after the Japanese surrender, a British colonel who had seen the good treatment received by Japanese interned in India expected to find the same in Batavia. Instead, he felt as if in another world, speaking to people who had already died. The civilians looked and acted like those released from Nazi concentration camps.[38] They were as skeletal, as diseased, as lifeless. Of the 130,000 civilians interned in Indonesia, 30,000 died.[39]

Throughout March 1942, Japan consolidated her gains in Malaya, Hong Kong, and the Philippines, while heading farther into the South Pacific. She also established a huge naval base at Rabaul, in New Britain, moved into the Solomon Islands and New Guinea, and continued to push deep into Burma. The most extravagantly optimistic expectations of Japan's staff officers had been realized. With Britain on the retreat everywhere, endangered on her home islands, and America badly wounded, Japanese planners discussed possible invasions of Australia, Hawaii, and India.

At the zenith of her power, Japan reveled in her successes. Lantern-light victory parades and self-praise dominated the home islands. In the war zones, Japanese officers threw one party after another. But Japan was soon to be shocked by four major, and wholly unexpected, defeats. Even before those setbacks, she would be shocked out of her complacency by an air raid on Tokyo that her leaders had insisted could not possibly happen. Soon after Pearl Harbor, President Roosevelt told his military leaders that he wanted to strike back against Japan as soon as possible. Admiral King's staff took the challenge seriously, proposing an attack on Tokyo by army two-engined, medium B-25 bombers—launched from an aircraft carrier! The navy had no twin-engined bombers, and no one at the time knew whether B-25's could even lift off a carrier from its 500-foot-long flight decks. Many Army Air Corps fliers qualified for the B-25 volunteered to try, and when one of the volunteers proved to be reserve Lieutenant Colonel James H. Doolittle, he was quickly designated their commander. Then forty-six years old and for some years in private business, Jimmy Doolittle was the first man to perform an outside roll—the cockpit on the outside of the roll rather than on the inside—thought to be impossible, was a former world speed record holder and the first man to fly across the United States in twelve hours.[40]

After training at Eglin Field, Florida, proved that the B-25's could take off in less than 500 feet even when heavily loaded with bombs and gasoline, they flew to San Francisco, where sixteen of them were loaded aboard the new carrier USS *Hornet*. Ominously, it was April Fool's Day. Accompanied by the carrier *Enterprise* as well as an escort of cruisers and destroyers, the task force sailed to within 700 miles of Tokyo, where it was spotted by a Japanese ship that radioed its location. Doolittle had hoped to approach to about 300 miles from the coast where Japan's air defenses began, then attack at night. An American kamikaze, Doolittle had pledged that if his plane were hit badly, he would dive at full throttle into the best available target. Of course, he would prefer that his planes not be shot down, so with the option of night attack gone, he launched immediately. The raiders would reach Japan at about noon. When thirteen of the planes appeared over Tokyo, with three planes bombing three other cities, most people did not notice until bombs fell and even then there was little damage, although fifty civilians were killed and others wounded.[41]

One plane flew to Vladivostok, where its crew was interned. Because the proposed Chinese landing fields were not ready, owing to the usual problems in communicating with the Chinese, the crews either bailed out of their planes or crash-landed. Three were killed on landing and eight captured. All eight were returned to Japan, where they were tortured extensively for information before being sentenced to death. Two pilots and a gunner were beheaded, but five had their sentences commuted, spending the war in prison, where one died.[42]

Three days before the raid, Reuters reported that American planes had bombed Japan. Radio Tokyo ridiculed the report as completely impossible, pointing out that the Japanese were too busy enjoying the fragrance of the cherry blossoms to worry about what could never occur.[43] Reassured by everyone in authority that such a calamity could never take place, the civilian population was stunned by the raid, the government shocked, and the military furious. Yamamoto was so embarrassed that he locked himself in his room, pale and shaken. Newspapers referred to "fiendish" strafing of civilians (which did not occur) during the "inhuman, insatiable" attack "on the sly."[44]

American public opinion went wild with enthusiasm as newspaper headlines gleefully described the raid on "sacred" Japanese soil. Troops were cheered, and even prisoners of war took heart. When Lieutenant Leona Jackson, a U.S. Navy nurse, was taken prisoner on Guam, she observed that the Japanese made their own rules about war and "they aren't pretty."[45] After Doolittle's raid, she joyfully noted that even in Kobe, where she was interned, Japanese morale had been badly shaken. With his usual sense for drama, Roosevelt gave an exultant radio address, puckishly claiming that the planes had taken off from "Shangri-La."

Japan's Imperial General Staff responded with overreactions that would change the course of the war. First, they recalled four badly needed fighter squadrons from China to Japan, and they ordered the destruction of all Chinese air bases in Chekiang. Without delay, 100,000 Japanese troops ravaged everything in their path. They burned, bayoneted, and raped with a savagery that easily rivaled that at Nanking. They also gassed civilians and experimented with biological warfare, killing untold numbers of Chinese with anthrax, typhus, bubonic plague, cholera, and other diseases whose effects on humans were studied in their infamous Unit 731 in Manchuria. When the killing ended, at least 250,000 Chinese civilians lay dead. Chiang had been warned not to cooperate with the Americans again. In fact, he had not cooperated the first time. Fearing Chiang's leaky security, the United Ststes had not informed him about the raid. The already shaky Chinese-U.S. relations were not strengthened.

The most fateful decision came only two days after Doolittle's raid, when the Imperial General Staff approved Yamamoto's proposed attack on Midway. Convinced that Japanese occupation of Midway could prevent a repetition of Doolittle's raid, and concerned about the emperor's safety, Yamamoto set aside plans to invade Australia, Samoa, Fiji, and Hawaii.[46] He now prepared the attack that would result in the calamitous destruction of much of Japan's naval air power.

After Japan's crushing victory at Singapore, the road to Burma—and, beyond it, to India—lay open. While the attack on Midway was being planned, the newly-formed Fifteenth Army under General Ida Shoyin drove rapidly north into Burma, determined to capture the port city of Rangoon and perhaps move into India herself. At the time of Doolittle's raid, General Ida's troops were 200 miles inside Burma, and had taken Rangoon, a respectable performance but not a remarkable one against a badly outnumbered and outgunned force of British, Indian, and Gurkha troops with virtually no air cover or armor. The Imperial General Staff now ordered Ida to spare nothing in an all-out attack to cut the Burma Road and, with it, U.S. lend-lease supplies to Chiang's Nationalists. Led by General William Slim, a tough fighter devoted to Burma and the Burmese, British troops had been slowly withdrawing in 115-degree heat. The three-star U.S. general Joseph Stilwell, with thirteen years experience in China and a good grasp of Mandarin, did his best to convince Chiang that he should send three of his best divisions south to defend the Burma

Road. Grudgingly, Chiang sent only one, and the retreat continued north-west toward Mandalay.

Vinegar Joe, as the sharp-tongued Stilwell was known, had no use for Chiang, whom he referred to as "peanut," and little respect for the British, whom he called "do-nothing Limeys." Tact was not Stilwell's strong suit, but he was a fighter who refused to let Chiang's generals retreat whenever the thought occurred to them. While Ida made ready for an all-out push, Admiral Nagumo, now a good deal less timid than he had been at Pearl Harbor, had easily outmaneuvered a much weaker British fleet in the Indian Ocean, cutting off supplies for Rangoon before it fell. In addition to desperately needed supplies, the First Australian Division, then at sea headed for Burma, was ordered back to Australia. Churchill was horrified, pleading with Prime Minister John Curtin to send his men to Burma, leaving the defense of Australia to the Americans who were on the way. Understandably, Curtin chose to bring his troops back to defend their own country, which was by no means entirely beyond Japan's reach.

Much aided by the Burmese who fought alongside his troops, Ida attacked so furiously that Slim could only retreat and even Stilwell could not hold the Chinese troops together. Surrounded by fleeing civilians, especially almost a million Indians, whose arrogant ways as shopkeepers and low-level government officials had earned Burmese hatred, the Allies retreated to Mandalay, hoping to defend that ancient city. It fell as easily as Rangoon. The only remaining hope was to run for the relative safety of India, but with the roads clogged by desperate Indian civilians and the air in complete Japanese control, even the most skillful rearguard fighting was not enough. The one train line that could have helped was shut down when a cowardly Chinese general commandeered a train for himself and his staff at gunpoint, only to run it head-on into an oncoming train, blocking the single-track line.[47]

With the only available roads choked by ox carts and refugees on foot, Stilwell and his party of 114, including an American doctor and 19 Burmese nurses, set off for India on foot, following elephant trails through the jungle, eating grass, and then rafting across the rapid Chindwin River just ahead of the Japanese. Without the loss of a single person, Stilwell's party made a 50-mile march across a rugged mountain range before reaching the relative safety of India. Only 10,000 of the 100,000 Chinese who attempted to follow ever reached India. All told, 13,000 British troops died during their epic 900-mile retreat. The civilian death toll was about 750,000.[48] Ida's great offensive secured Burma, which actually received independence by Japanese decree on August 1, 1943. Independence proved a sham; Japan ruled Burma in her own interests. Japanese soldiers slapped civilians whenever they felt like it, and conscripted Burmese for heavy labor. As resistance grew, the *kempeitai,* Japan's vicious military police, introduced the Burmese to the same reign of terror and death they established everywhere else the Japanese army had taken control.

The Japanese thrust to the Indian border took her front line so far from supply and troop depots in Bangkok and Singapore that the decision was made to construct a railroad—the Burma–Siam Railroad—from Bangkok to Rangoon. The mountainous jungle cut by deep river valleys would be the most difficult any railroad had ever attempted to traverse. Eventually, 61,000 Allied prisoners, most of them British and Australian, along with 300,000 native laborers would cut huge trees, move tons of earth, and span rivers without any mechanical equipment, although elephants did help in dragging away huge tree trunks. Prisoners worked sixteen-hour shifts with little to eat except rice. They suffered terribly from malaria, dysentery, and cholera, and from the whips and bayonets of sadistic guards. In the end, the 250-mile-long railroad cost the lives of 13,000 Allied prisoners of war, including Americans, and 90,000 native workers.[49]

The end on Corregidor came on May 5, 1942. The final assault cost over 3,000 Japanese lives, with 800 Americans killed before General Wainwright surrendered. One-third of the Americans taken into captivity died in brutal prison camps. MacArthur was furious about Wainwright's surrender, premature as he saw it, but he eulogized the men: "I shall always seem to see a vision of grim, gaunt, ghastly men, still unafraid."[50] With the fall of Corregidor, Allied resistance in the Pacific came to a close. Japan's soldiers were seemingly invincible, and so were her sailors. The Japanese navy had not yet lost a single major ship. Her naval airmen dominated the skies. Defeat was nowhere on the horizon.

On May 4, 1942, a large convoy of troop transports left Rabaul, Japan's large base in New Britain, headed for Port Moresby, in New Guinea, just a few miles off Australia's northeast coast. The Imperial General Staff was divided in its views on whether Port Moresby should serve as a springboard for an invasion of Australia or as an airbase from which to bomb her into military impotence. Thanks to radio intercepts of coded Japanese messages, the Americans knew about the planned invasion force and sent two carriers to intercept it, totally surprising Vice-Admiral Inoue, the operation's commander. Inoue ordered the transports back to Rabaul.

Although their attacks were hampered by poor bombing skills and torpedoes so slow that Japanese ships could evade them, American planes sank a light Japanese carrier, the *Shoho*, the first major Japanese ship lost in the Pacific War. Later in the battle, Japanese planes sank an American carrier, the *Lexington*, and Japanese newspapers declared a devastating victory. The *New York Times* boasted that seventeen to twenty-two Japanese warships had been sunk or severely damaged. Despite this exaggeration, what came to be known as the Battle of the Coral Sea, was a decisive American victory. In addition to the *Shoho*, the Americans damaged two heavy carriers so severely that they were out of service for at least a month. They also prevented the invasion of Port Moresby. The Japanese remained supremely confident, but they would never again achieve a major victory on land, and only partial ones at sea.

"NOT NECESSARILY TO OUR ADVANTAGE"

I n May 1942, Admiral Yamamoto assembled an immense array of naval might for his planned invasion of Midway—8 large aircraft carriers, 11 battleships, including the newly commissioned superbattleship *Yamato*, 22 cruisers, 65 destroyers, and 21 submarines. Despite strenuous objections by some naval staff officers, who thought his plan to divide the fleet into six separate forces too unwieldy and feared that the land-based air power on Midway would be dangerous, Yamamoto was determined to win a huge victory.[1] He believed that he could then persuade Tojo to sue for peace, ending the war while Japan was at the apex of her power. U.S. naval intelligence knew that a huge Japanese fleet was assembling and believed that its target was Midway, but could not be certain. The Japanese naval code referred to the target as AF. Midway was ordered to send a message in plain English that its water distillation plant had broken down. When a decoded Japanese message read that AF was short of water, there was no further doubt.

Only two carriers were in Pearl Harbor to face the Japanese armada until the *Yorktown*, badly damaged in the Coral Sea battle, limped into port on May 26. By all rights, the ship should have gone into a West Coast drydock for a month of repairs. Instead, 1,400 dockyard workmen dropped everything else, laboring around the clock to make the ship seaworthy. On June 1, the *Yorktown* sailed north to rendezvous with the carriers *Enterprise* and *Lexington*, 350 miles northwest of Midway, where they would wait for the Japanese, once again commanded by Admiral Nagumo with his main attack force of four heavy carriers. Thanks to the Americans' effective use of false radio traffic indicating that their carriers were still in the South Pacific, Nagumo moved on toward Midway, which he expected to bomb and then invade without great difficulty. Japanese troops were so confident of victory that they had already arranged for their mail to be forwarded to the "Island of the Rising Sun," Midway's new name.

Japanese carrier planes from one of Yamamoto's forces successfully bombed Dutch Harbor, near the Alaskan mainland, and yet another of his task forces made ready to land troops on Attu, in the Aleutians, where they captured ten U.S. weathermen, then went ashore on a neighbor island, unoccupied Kiska. After Nagumo's initial attack on Midway was only partially successful, some of Midway's land-based planes attacked his carriers. The B-17's hit nothing. Next, obsolete U.S. fighters were shot down like clay pigeons by Zeros before one torpedo plane after another— forty-one in all—was shot down without a single torpedo finding its mark. Fuchida, recovering from an appendectomy on board Nagumo's flagship, admired their courage, as did Genda, who was convalescing from pneumonia. Both men knew that American torpedoes were so slow that they could easily be evaded.[2] Still, the deaths of eighty U.S. torpedo plane aviators were not useless. As Nagumo's Zero fighters swarmed over the painfully slow American torpedo bombers close to the level of the sea, American carrier-based dive bombers came in unseen and unimpeded.

Their bombs smashed the *Akagi, Kaga,* and *Soryu*, leaving them in flames and sinking. Barely escaping death, Fuchida and Genda watched in horror as the *Akagi*'s elevator, "twisting like molten glass," drooped into the hangar below. Planes on deck burned lividly. As Fuchida watched the ship disintegrate, tears streamed down his cheeks.[3]

The *Hiryu* was the next to be fatally hit. Her captain, the brilliant Admiral Yamaguchi Tamon gave an emotional farewell address to his crew, then exchanged ceremonial cups of water (in lieu of sake) with his second in command. Together they sang the national anthem before retiring to their cabins to commit seppuku. Just before killing himself, Yamaguchi paused to admire the beauty of the moon, telling others how magnificent it was.[4]

Hit earlier in the battle, the *Yorktown* appeared to be out of danger when a Japanese submarine's torpedo finished her off. Hoping to escape further damage, Nagumo had turned away from the battle to the north when Yamamoto ordered him to join in a combined attack on Midway, which he hoped would entice the U.S. fleet into an unequal night battle against his powerful battleships. The wary Americans withdrew to the east for the night, not returning to defend Midway until daylight, when their carrier planes could see to operate. By then, Yamamoto had acknowledged defeat. Looking ill, yet taking full responsibility, he ordered his armada back to Japan. In addition to the four carriers, he lost a heavy cruiser, 2,200 sailors, and nearly 250 aircraft with many of the best of his naval aviators. The Japanese Imperial Navy did not inform either the government or the army about the catastrophic loss of the four heavy carriers for several months. Survivors of these ships were sent to remote duty stations, while wounded men were treated incommunicado. Japan's navy was still a more powerful surface force than the U.S. Navy, but this was a war to be won by naval air power and submarines, not by battleships. Japan's naval air power would never recover from Midway.

Japan's first defeat on land came soon thereafter, at Milne Bay near Port Moresby, located in southeast New Guinea. It was a major Allied base only a few hundred miles northwest of Australia's Cape York Peninsula. The loss of four carriers at Midway ended Japan's naval plans to seize Samoa, Fiji, or even the Hawaiian Islands. From now on, the army's strategy would prevail. The Japanese wanted to build such strong defenses all across the Pacific that the United States and Australia would be unwilling to pay the price of assaulting them. In late July, they landed 13,000 men on New Guinea's north coast, at Buna. They would build an airfield at nearby Lae, and a strong detachment under a determined major general named Horii Tomitaro would march south over the 13,000-foot Owen Stanley Mountains to seize Port Moresby. Japanese maps indicated a road from Buna to Moresby. In fact, it was a 2-foot-wide path so overgrown that the jungle often had to be hacked away step by step, and so steep in places that it was almost vertical. To make Horii's task more difficult, a small but determined Australian force challenged his men every step of the way in drenching rain that left almost impassible mud. There was little water or food, and at high altitude the sun made conditions punishingly hot. Nevertheless, Horii pushed his men south as more Australian troops struggled north up the Kokoda Trail—or Bloody Trail, as the Australians called it—to oppose them.

All the while Australian forces were concentrating around Port Moresby, augmented by 1,300 American troops. On August 25, 1942, a force of some 3,000 Japanese marines with light tanks landed to the west of the port at Milne Bay. They launched frontal attacks against the well dug-in Allies, who outnumbered them ten to one, and shot them down in their tracks. After a three-day battle, only 600 Japanese survived to be taken aboard ships. General Horii was stopped too, his starving men at the end of their endurance. Few of them survived the horrendous return march to Buna, followed all the way by relentless Australians. Those who made it back to Buna wore rice bags and blankets, their uniforms long since cast away as rotten rags. They were barefoot, too, most of them barely able to hobble. As a final blow, Horii drowned when he fell off a log raft while crossing a flooding river.[5] Australian and U.S. Army troops now began a siege of Buna that would see some of the most desperate and least-known fighting of the war. The eyes of the United States and Japan were focused elsewhere—on Guadalcanal.

When twenty-three transports carrying U.S. Marines anchored off Guadalcanal, in the Solomon Islands, the night of August 6, 1942, the men were nauseated by the stench of rotting vegetation and miasmatic swamps. Once on shore, they would never learn to live with these smells of decay and death. The next morning, 6,000 men went ashore on the tiny neighbor island of Tulagi, defended by 2,000 Japanese. The fighting involved savage, hand-to-hand killing with no quarter asked or given. Only 23 of the Japanese garrison survived. They had been too badly wounded to resist capture.

The marines then waded ashore unopposed on Long Island–sized Guadalcanal. The unarmed Japanese construction workers building a nearly completed airfield fled into the jungle, leaving still warm rice behind. The marines also welcomed tons of food, a large supply of beer, and an electric generator that powered an ice-making plant. As they dug in around the perimeter of the airfield, they wondered where the Japanese were, a curiosity that led to an incident destined to become one of the Pacific War's best-known goads to savagery. A marine outpost reported seeing a white flag apparently waved by Japanese. A Japanese sailor who had just surrendered to the Americans told them that there were indeed others like him in the jungle who wanted to give up. Lieutenant Colonel Frank Goettge, a marine intelligence officer, organized a patrol of twenty-five volunteers to find these Japanese. The story that grew into mythic proportions was that the Japanese welcomed them with their white flag, only to pull out hidden weapons and slaughter the unsuspecting marines.

From then on, it was "kill or be killed," not only on Guadalcanal but throughout the Pacific. In fact, it appears that the "white flag" was an ordinary Japanese battle flag with the Rising Sun obscured. There was no intention to surrender, no subterfuge.[6] Nevertheless, the story spread, reinforced by numerous legitimate episodes of wounded Japanese using hidden hand grenades to kill their rescuers and themselves. Many marines stenciled "rodent exterminator" on their helmets, and the killing went on.[7] For their part, few Americans on Guadalcanal were taken prisoner by the Japanese. Two who were became victims of vivisection when a Japanese doctor removed their livers without anesthetic. The diary of a Japanese officer on Kawaguchi's staff who witnessed the surgery recorded the event as "very informative." It said nothing about the two men or about what was done with the livers.[8] It is perhaps just as well that Allied soldiers did not find out about this and other acts of vivisection until the war had ended. When Australian soldiers later learned that one of their men in New Guinea had been emasculated and then had "steaks" cut from his body, they took Japanese prisoners up in planes and threw them out. They futhermore killed everyone found alive in a Japanese hospital.[9]

It may also have been fortunate for the Japanese that Allied servicemen had no inkling about the unspeakable horrors inflicted on their former comrades imprisoned in Manchuria and North China. A tall, wealthy Japanese army surgeon named Ishii Shiro returned from a visit to Europe and the Soviet Union in the late 1920s with a report that all these nations were engaged in secret research on biological warfare. Himself an expert on water filtration but fascinated by biological warfare, Ishii soon headed Unit 731, the so-called "Epidemic Prevention and Water Supply Unit" in Manchuria, established by order of Emperor Hirohito in 1936. It is still not certain how much Hirohito knew about what actually took place in this vast, lavishly funded facility. Unit 731, like its sister station Unit 100, in North China, was engaged in research on biological warfare, cruelly using human victims.

Initially the commanders of Unit 731 relied on Chinese and Russian prisoners for their research; after the fall of Singapore and the Philippines, they ordered American and British prisoners driven aboard crowded ships—the Americans enduring the same cruelties that took place during the Bataan death march—en route to Manchuria. Japanese doctors and scientists in Unit 731 were experimenting with diseases such as plague, anthrax, typhoid, dysentery, and cholera as weapons of war. They also developed the capacity to breed fleas—100 million every few days—as carriers of disease. Humans were infected with pathogens and then, after the disease progressed, strapped to operating tables, where surgeons or their assistants cut out their organs for examination. Anesthetics were not used: "I cut him open from the chest to the stomach and he screamed terribly and his face was all twisted in agony. He made this unimaginable sound, he was screaming so horribly. But then finally he stopped. It was all in a day's work for the surgeons, but it really left an impression on me because it was my first time."[10] How many humans were subjected to such torture is not known. Their remains were totally incinerated in an electric furnace.[11]

Other prisoners, including Allied war prisoners, were killed in grisly experiments involving tolerance for freezing temperatures, poison gas, starvation, x-rays, boiling water, and pressure so extreme that their eyes came out of their sockets. Called *marutas*, "logs," they were considered "lumps of meat on a chopping block," not humans.[12] The biological weapons developed at Unit 731 and elsewhere in North China were used against the Chinese on hundreds of occasions, and plans were in place for the use of balloon bombs, already wind-borne across the Pacific, where they killed seven Americans, to infect the West Coast of North America.

Before Soviet troops reached Unit 731, it was totally demolished and all the *marutas* killed. How many prisoners died in all is unknown, but Soviet and Chinese estimates run into thousands. It has been reported that, despite their grotesque crimes, the United States offered Ishii and his associates immunity from prosecution in return for their records. This has been denied, but the fact remains that Ishii was never prosecuted.[13]

Still basking in their sense of invincibility, Japanese commanders repeatedly underestimated the numbers of Americans on Guadalcanal as well as their firepower. The Americans had powerful artillery, tanks, flamethrowers, new semiautomatic rifles, and at least ten times as many machine guns as the Japanese. They also had far more ammunition. Not least, they were determined to win. The first example of Japanese overconfidence came when General Hyakutake, the Japanese commander of the Seventeenth Army in Rabaul, decided to send a 2,500-man detachment under Colonel Ichiki to drive the 10,000 marines into the sea. Ichiki had such contempt for the Americans that he did not even wait for the entire force to land, attacking with only 900 men into massed marine firepower. The Japanese were slaughtered. Marine tanks then encircled the survivors, crushing the dead and wounded under their bloody treads like giant red meat grinders.[14] Ichiki survived long enough to commit seppuku on the battlefield.

The next major attack was led by General Kawaguchi, whose refusal to kill prisoners in the Philippines had brought him into conflict with Colonel Tsuji, who detested him as a "liberal" officer, too kind to the enemy.[15] Like Ichiki, Kawaguchi had too few men, and many of their heavy weapons could not be dragged through the jungle to the marine lines. Worse, Tsuji himself wangled a position as an Imperial General Staff officer assigned to Kawaguchi. Predictably, Tsuji urged a massed frontal attack. Against his better judgment, but stung by Tsuji's insinuations of cowardice, Kawaguchi ordered the attack. During the night, his troops rhythmically slapped the stocks of the rifles and chanted, "U.S. Marines be dead tomorrow." They also shouted, "Babe Ruth eat shit!" The Americans responded with "Tojo eat shit!"[16] When the direct banzai attack finally came, it was Kawaguchi's men who died, in terrible numbers. Those who lived to retreat to the coast were starving because, confident of success, Kawaguchi had left his food supplies at the coast, planning to feed his men on captured marine supplies.

Both Tsuji and Kawaguchi survived to humble themselves before General Hyakutake. Emotionally, Tsuji blamed himself for underestimating "the enemy's fighting powers." Histrionic to a fault, he declared that he deserved a "sentence of ten thousand deaths." Kawaguchi said the blame was his, "feeling as if my intestines had been cut out."[17] Distressed by the defeats and by the open hostility between Kawaguchi and Tsuji (who was packed off to Imperial Army Headquarters, which in turn sent him to Burma), Hyakutake decided to order an entire division to Guadalcanal. By now, the marines had been so greatly reinforced that even the 12,000 men of Japan's Thirty-eighth Division would have had little impact. However, the Japanese division did not land. Its transports were spotted by American planes, which sank most of them. Only about 2,000 men reached shore to join the starving, militarily impotent Japanese forces. By January 19, 1943, when Hyakutake finally decided to concede defeat and evacuate the island, no one among the Japanese garrison had had a bowel movement for three weeks, and all were so salt deprived that the salt water they drank tasted sweet.[18] The Americans did little to disrupt the evacuation, and by February 7 the Japanese were gone. Operating at night, fast destroyers skillfully took away 13,000 men, but 25,000 others lay dead on Guadalcanal, at least 10,000 of them victims of disease or starvation.[19]

As the Japanese Thirty-eighth Division was being destroyed at sea, Admiral William F. "Bull" Halsey, now in command of the South Pacific area, flew to Guadalcanal to promise reinforcements and urge the troops on. The punch line of his speech was "Kill Japs, kill Japs, keep on killing Japs." The slogan caught on with Allied forces throughout the Pacific, and they needed little encouragement. From the first fighting on the Kokoda Trail well into 1944, American, Australian, and some New Zealand troops fought savage battles along New Guinea's north coast and throughout the Solomon Islands. These battles were not as well publicized as the more glamorous invasions of islands such as Tarawa, Saipan, Iwo Jima, and the rest, but they were no less bloody, and certainly no less brutal. Names like Buna, Lae, Munda, Bougainville, and New Britain conjure up ghastly memories for the survivors on both sides who fought there. The weather was appalling, with endless torrents of rain and terrific heat, the jungle even thicker than at Guadalcanal, the swamps larger and more treacherous, and the diseases every bit as bad. The fighting was terrible, too; grenades and bayonets were usually needed to drive the Japanese out of their bunkers. Sometimes Allied and Japanese soldiers fought with knives and fists.[20]

Over the objection of the navy, the Imperial Japanese Army decided that the Solomons and New Guinea must be reinforced. Yamamoto dutifully put together a plan for increased naval and ground strength in the area. In mid-April, he planned a flying tour of inspection, including a visit to sick and wounded in Japanese-held portions of the area. A message announcing the trip was intercepted by U.S. radio operators and decrypted. The decision whether to shoot down Yamamoto's plane was passed all the way to Roosevelt, who approved interception. Shortly before boarding the plane, at the age of sixty, Yamamoto wrote a tender love letter to Chiyoko, ending with "And pressing kisses / upon your picture."[21] He enclosed a small lock of his hair. After his plane was shot down by U.S. fighters, Yamamoto was found still strapped in his seat, a bullet hole through his temple, another in his back.[22]

Over 148,000 Japanese died on New Guinea alone, while another 135,000 were bypassed at Rabaul. Many of these and other bypassed Japanese garrisons starved. Elsewhere, Australian troops attacked them savagely, often taking no prisoners. On Bougainville, a number of wounded Japanese soldiers tried to surrender by raising their hands. The Australian commander, who stood only a few yards away, ordered them shot. When a colonel protested, he snapped, "I want no prisoners. Shoot them all." The order was obeyed.[23] Allied planes routinely strafed life rafts, following a practice begun by the Japanese. The men of the U.S. Forty-first Division—Japanese called them "the butchers"—boasted that they took no prisoners.[24] An officer commented to a visitor that "their favorite occupation" was knocking the gold teeth out of the mouths of Japanese dead.[25] When a U.S. submarine commander torpedoed a Japanese troop transport, then surfaced to machine-gun all the survivors they could, he received a commendation. Charles A. Lindbergh, the aviator, visited a marine unit where reports that Japanese tortured downed U.S. airmen circulated widely. An army sergeant who complained that he had never had a chance to kill a Japanese was invited to go along on a patrol. A prisoner was taken and offered to the sergeant. When the sergeant protested that he could not kill a defenseless prisoner, the soldiers offered to show him how. "One of the patrol members offered the Jap a

Allied airman about to be executed in the South Pacific. (UPI/Corbiss-Bettmann)

cigarette and a light, and as he started to smoke an arm was thrown around his head and his throat 'slit from ear to ear.'"[26]

While this savagery was taking place in the south, the Americans planned to return to the Aleutians to remove the Japanese who had seized U.S. territory. On May 11, 1943, the weather cleared enough to allow 11,000 men of the Seventh Infantry Division to land on Attu. For a week, the 2,500 Japanese fought stubbornly, refusing the appeal of leaflets dropped from planes that they surrender. Finally, over 1,000 Japanese launched a banzai attack, screaming, "Japanese drink blood like wine!" Only 28 prisoners were taken. Attu cost over 1,000 American lives.[27] Kiska was evacuated before any more blood was spilled; when 35,000 American troops went ashore, the garrison of 5,000 Japanese was gone. All that was left was four abandoned dogs.[28]

As the fighting in the South Pacific wore on, the next Allied invasion target was the atoll of Tarawa, in the Gilbert Islands, and the nearby atoll of Makin. Buttressed by reinforced concrete, Tarawa's massive defenses included large British guns brought in from Singapore. Artillery and machine guns covered every yard of approach. Tarawa's commander boasted that its defenses could "withstand assault by a million men for a hundred years."[29] A massive naval bombardment seemed to pulverize the Japanese defenses, but most of its 4,000 Imperial Marine defenders survived to inflict grievous casualties on the Americans as they floundered ashore, victimized by an unpredictable tide as well as Japanese fire. Lightly defended Makin fell with relative ease, but it took 18,000 U.S. Marines three days to subdue Tarawa. Only 1 Japanese officer, 16 enlisted men, and 129 Korean laborers were taken alive, and even this small number was more than many marines would have preferred. Days after the atoll was declared secured, desperate Japanese soldiers continued to emerge from the rubble in doomed banzai charges. Tarawa cost 1,300 marine dead in what the official Marine Corps history declared the "bitterest fighting" in the history of the corps.[30]

In January 1944, the target was Kwajalein, in the Marshall Islands north of Tarawa, a key island controlling the world's largest lagoon. It stood just south of Bikini atoll. Overwhelming U.S. force defeated Kwajalain's garrison of 8,000 men with small loss of American life. The next island prize to be assaulted, Saipan, would not succumb so easily. Its invasion was the costliest operation the United States had yet undertaken. In June 1944, about 20,000 marines came ashore without opposition but soon thereafter the Japanese commander, General Saito Yoshitsugu, ordered a night banzai attack of 1,000 men led by sword-waving officers and thirty-six light tanks. Almost all died before the attack was recalled. The Japanese then fought stubbornly from mountain caves and foxholes, even though they had no chance of victory. When the end seemed near, General Saito ordered the most massive suicide attack yet seen in the Pacific. At dawn, over 4,000 officers and men, some so badly wounded they could barely hobble forward on crutches, threw themselves screaming into American machine-gun fire. When all had been killed, bulldozers buried the bodies in a huge mass grave. Many civilians, along with some Japanese soldiers, hid in caves in the rocky north end of the island. Convinced that the Americans would kill them if they surrendered, many killed themselves with hand grenades, others jumped off 800-foot cliffs to rocks below, and still others swam out to sea with their infants. Some women hid in caves with their infants only to be joined by soldiers. When the infants' cries threatened to reveal their hiding places to the Americans, soldiers ordered the women to kill their children. Several did as they were told.[31] Some civilians were finally induced to surrender; before they did, the death toll had reached about 4,000 men, women, and children. In addition, some 10,000 civilians were killed in battle along with over 41,000 Japanese troops. American casualties topped 18,000, about 3,000 of them killed.[32]

While marines were dying on Saipan, a large Japanese carrier task force was approaching. Only 200 miles west of Saipan, American carriers waited. By this point in the war, the planes of the Americans were superior to those of the Japanese, and their pilots more skillful. So many Japanese planes were shot down that the battle became known as "the Great Marianas Turkey Shoot." Very few Japanese planes survived, and two heavy carriers were sunk along with a light carrier. Two other heavy carriers were badly damaged. The Combined Fleet had lost a third of its surviving carriers and all but thirty-six of its aircraft.[33]

After the fall of Saipan on July 24, a letter-perfect marine landing took place on the island of Tinian, four miles south of Saipan. It fell with the loss of only 400 marine casualties. This was thought to be a small price to pay for another airfield that along with Saipan could provide a base for the B-29 bombers soon to attack Japan's home islands. Guam was next. Even after a two-week naval bombardment, the longest of the war, Guam did not fall easily. After heavy fighting near the beaches, the Japanese fought on from caves in the mountains. Some fighting against Americans and Australians continued until the end of the war, and the last Japanese did not surrender until 1972.[34]

In September 1944, the First Marine Division landed on the island of Peleliu, five miles north of the large U.S. naval base of Ulithi. Thousands of Korean construction workers had turned Peleliu's craggy limestone cliffs into a maze of artillery and machine-gun blockhouses. The 5,000 well-supplied Japanese troops defending Peleliu were confident of holding out against a long siege. And so they did; it took the marines eight weeks of savage, often hand-to-hand fighting to prevail. This time, there were no banzai charges, only desperate fighting to the last man. The marines lost more men here than on Tarawa. Sadly, as almost everyone in authority acknowledged even before the war ended, no military purpose was served by invading Peleliu. It should have been bypassed.[35]

American war planners were torn between next invading the Philippines—"I shall return," as MacArthur insisted—or Taiwan, closer to Japan and a better base for air operations. There were such large Japanese forces in both places that desperate combat would certainly ensue. Relatively little was known about Japanese defenses on Taiwan, which was thus a questionable target. With all of his theatrical power, MacArthur declared that a failure to keep his pledge to return to the Philippines would forever destroy America's credibility in the eyes of all Asians. He prevailed. The Philippines became the chosen target. Before they could be "secured," there would be bitter combat, terrible atrocities, and the almost complete destruction of Manila.

American troops went ashore on Leyte, on October 20, 1944, soon followed by numerous staged photographs of MacArthur's triumphant return, marching majestically through the surf of a pacified Leyte beach. Initially, Japan had only 20,000 inexperienced troops on Leyte to face the 165,000 men MacArthur would put ashore, the largest amphibious operation of the Pacific War. The Americans were attacked by 500 land-based planes, but almost all of them were destroyed in under three days. Before Japanese reinforcements landed and bitter fighting followed, MacArthur announced to the people of Leyte that Sergio Osmeña would be a worthy successor to President Quezon. The next day, MacArthur addressed a large crowd, formally declaring the establishment of the Philippine civil government under President Osmeña. As the Philippine and American flags were raised together, a bugler sounded "To the Colors" and the crowd roared.

MacArthur had experienced the moment of triumph he had longed for since being ordered out of Corregidor, but the success of his Philippines invasion depended on the safety of the troop and supply transports anchored in Leyte Gulf. A large and determined Japanese fleet was under way to destroy them. Four large carriers and two small ones, seven battleships, including the supership *Musashi*, twenty cruisers, and twenty-nine destroyers were at sea. Japan's surface ships were undeniably powerful, but their air cover was slight. Kamikazes would play a part, sinking the U.S. light carrier *Princeton*, but the six Japanese carriers could put only 116 planes in the sky.[36] Waiting for them in Leyte Bay were thirty-two American carriers of various sizes, with 1,400 planes. The *Musashi* was sunk, riddled by bombs and torpedoes, before her eighteen-inch guns could fire a shot. Her captain went down with the great ship. For three days, the battle surged back and forth over a wide area, with many nervous moments for the American transports. When it ended, the strength of American air power had proved devastating. U.S. planes sank four Japanese carriers, three battleships, six cruisers, and twelve destroyers and downed virtually all of Japan's planes. At least 10,000 Japanese died. Fewer than 3,000 Americans died, with the loss of the *Princeton*, two escort carriers, three destroyers, and 200 planes.[37]

On land, the Americans had a much harder time of it. Reinforced Japanese troops fought for every ridge, often inflicting heavy casualties. The Battle of Break Neck Ridge, on the north of Leyte, was especially brutal. The battle for the ridge, held by Japan's elite First Division, forced its American besiegers to suffer a bloodbath before the ridge was finally secured. A Japanese corporal, Kamiko Kiyoshi, described the ferocious combat in vivid images of fear, exaltation, blood, and death. After one battle, Kamiko wrote that shattered American bodies lay everywhere, the cartridges in their ammunition belts detonating like firecrackers.[38] Before the fighting finally ended on Leyte, over 4,000 Americans had died. The Japanese death toll was vastly greater, perhaps 75,000. Civilian casualties were high as well, although large-scale Japanese atrocities did not take place. On nearby Palawan Island, however, when the Japanese commander feared that a U.S. invasion was imminent, he ordered 150 U.S. prisoners to have their hands tied and to be taken to a jungle clearing, doused with gasoline, and set on fire. Those who tried to run were machine-gunned. Three men escaped to tell the gruesome story of men's screams and the smell of burning flesh.[39]

With organized resistance almost ended on Leyte, on January 8, 1945, MacArthur landed 50,000 men on Luzon, determined to free Manila as quickly as possible. General Yamashita's 152,000 men did not yield easily, fighting the Americans to a standstill until two flying columns of tanks dashed past the surprised Japanese into Manila, where they released 5,000 American civilian captives. However, when infantry tried to exploit the success of the tanks, they ran into heavy opposition. A Tsuji-like fanatic, Rear Admiral Sanji Iwabachi, ignored Yamashita's order to make Manila an open city. His 17,000 naval troops, plus 4,000 army troops trapped in the now surrounded city, fought with almost unparalleled savagery. Out of respect for the 700,000 Filipino civilians in the city, MacArthur permitted no bombing, but the Americans were forced to use artillery to dislodge the determined Japanese, who fought off American attacks while raping women with a savagery not exceeded by that at Nanking, bayoneting children, and burning living and dead alike in gasoline-soaked pyres.[40] When the city finally fell, only one-quarter remained relatively intact, the rest lay burned and flattened. Over 100,000 Filipinos were dead, many as a result of Japanese butchery.[41] U.S. airborne troops landed in Corregidor, where with the help of a huge explosion in Malinta Tunnel, they killed the 5,000-man Japanese garrison virtually to the last man.

Even before the loss of Manila and Corregidor, General Yamashita led some 100,000 of his men north into the mountains of Luzon, where they held out until the end of the war. MacArthur's troops now freed the inmates of several prison camps, including Camp O'Donnell. A medical officer, Colonel James O. Gillespie, had watched a new set of prisoners enter a similar camp in 1942: "Limbs grotesquely swollen to double their size. Faces devoid of expression—form or life. Aged incredibly beyond

Filipino victims of Japanese in Manila, 1945. (UPI/Corbiss-Bettmann)

their years. Bare feet on the stony road. Remnants of ragged gunny sacks as loin cloths. Some stark naked. Bloodshot eyes and cracked lips. Smeared with excreta from their bowels." [42] Close to half of these men died during their first year of captivity.

For some who survived, treatment gradually improved. Realizing that these men could be used as laborers or perhaps bargaining chips, many were shipped back to Japan. Some ships were torpedoed; others never made it away. For all, the term "hell ships" was an inadequate condemnation. Packed together in hideously hot holds with no water and little food, some men died and others went mad. Wild with thirst, some slashed the wrists of weaker companions to drink their blood. Others lapped up sewage from open drains.[43]

With the world's attention fixed on the war in Europe and the Pacific, the fighting in Burma received little notice and that in China even less. After Slim and Stilwell managed to withdraw what remained of their forces to India, they launched some small-scale attacks into Burma, without conspicuous success. The most troubling of these for the Japanese were raids deep behind their lines led by the intrepid British jungle fighter Brigadier Orde Wingate and his stalwart "Chindits," named after the stone lions that guarded Burmese temples. The strength of the Allies grew markedly throughout the year, and so did their fighting spirit.

Despite evidence of growing Allied power, Lieutenant General Mutaguchi Renya, a visionary newly appointed to command in Burma, decided that the time had come to invade India. Mutaguchi's operation's officer was horrified. He told Mutaguchi that the Japanese were woefully lacking in the food, ammunition, and medical supplies necessary to maintain a large army as it campaigned across wide rivers and rugged mountains in the face of a now formidable enemy. Mutaguchi brushed his objections off. Having played a catalytic role in starting the China war at Marco Polo Bridge, he now dreamed of a masterstroke that would lead him through all of India and perhaps end the war. Derided throughout the army as a glory seeker, Mutaguchi earned further contempt when he shamelessly paraphrased Togo at Tsushima, declaring, "On this one battle rests the fate of our nation."[44] Three Japanese divisions joined by a division of Chandra Bose's INA troops attacked, 155,000 men in all. One Japanese division and the Indian division assaulted the British stronghold at Kohima. The remaining two Japanese divisions attacked Imphal to the south.

Fierce British resistance at Kohima forced the Japanese to withdraw, and Imphal proved to be an equally tough nut. After two months of desperate, often close-quarters combat, Mutaguchi was forced to withdraw. Caught in monsoon rains, their inadequate supplies now exhausted, his men tried to subsist on monkeys, snakes, lizards—anything. It was a repeat of the Kokoda Trail experience but on a much larger scale. Men threw away their weapons, leaving the retreat route clogged with machine guns, rifles, helmets, gas masks—everything that was heavy and not edible.[45] The sick and wounded killed themselves with grenades, no longer able to stand the maggots that squirmed in their ears, eyes, noses, and mouths. Healthier men fought over food. Before the retreat was over, more than 65,000 Japanese soldiers had died, Mutaguchi was relieved of his command, and Japan's hold on Burma was about to end. Mutaguchi's replacement found that he had only 21,000 effective soldiers to hold off 200,000 men in six British divisions.[46]

Throughout 1943, the war in China continued in its desultory brutality, as the Nationalists avoided combat whenever possible, the warlords sought profit where they could find it, and only the Communists took firm offensive action. To the south, Chinese troops led by Stilwell recaptured much of northern Burma in battles that produced 18,000 casualties. But in 1944, the Japanese prepared to launch a major campaign to destroy Chiang once and for all. Called the ICHI-Go operation, it would shatter Chinese opposition and drive Chiang out of Chungking. ICHI-Go called for an entirely new tactical approach. Huge numbers of pamphlets were dropped, telling anyone who could read them that Japan's enemies were the Americans and British, not the Chinese. It promised that Chinese who offered no resistance would be well treated. What is more, Japanese troops received strict orders that their past fondness for looting, burning, and raping would not be tolerated.[47] As might be expected, the kindness campaign was not a complete success, but Japanese troops nevertheless drove to within 300 miles of Chungking, capturing the rice fields needed to feed the Nationalist army. Just when collapse seemed unavoidable, Major General Fong Hsien-chueh, led the Chinese Tenth Army in a determined attack that drove the Japanese back in retreat after retreat, until they finally withdrew altogether from the land they had taken.

The Japanese soon returned to the attack, however, creating the fear in the United States that Chiang would have to capitulate, releasing almost one million Japanese troops for use elsewhere. In fact, the Japanese no longer sought to drive Chiang out of the war. They settled for capture of the air bases in eastern China used by B-29's to raid Japan. B-29 raids on Japan had indeed been distressingly ineffective, but soon the long-range bombers would fly from Pacific island airfields and, it was hoped, improve their reputation.

In February, 19, 1945, the celebrated Battle of Iwo Jima began. Rejecting wasteful banzai charges, the 21,000 men in the Japanese garrison remained in their labyrinths of underground tunnels complete with food, water, medical supplies, electric lights, telephones, radios, and numerous firing apertures. A tremendous naval bombardment did almost nothing to harm them. Marines had to claw their way across soft lava dunes to kill the defenders where they waited. It was some of the most gory yet dramatic fighting of the war, with the flag raising atop Mount Suribachi caught on film, along with much of the fighting and dying. Before the island was finally neutralized, over 5,000 American marines had been killed and another 25,000 wounded. It was the highest casualty rate in the history of the Marine Corps.

Iwo Jima's elaborate defenses had been designed by Lieutenant General Kuribayashi Tadamichi. He had planned well and now led well, refusing to allow his men to end their lives in banzai attacks while they were still capable of killing Americans. His frequent radio messages to Japan extolled the courage of his men as they faced marine grenades, dynamite charges, and flamethrowers. On March 21, long after Iwo Jima was thought to be secured, he radioed Tokyo that neither he nor his men had eaten or drunk for five days, but he added, "Our fighting spirit is still high."[48] When all hope of killing marines had ended, he finally authorized a banzai charge, but the few survivors were too weak to do more than stagger forward into U.S. guns. Kuribayashi himself ritually stabbed his abdomen before an aide beheaded him. Only 216 men of Iwo Jima's garrison, almost all of them badly wounded, were taken prisoner.[49]

Although its civilian inhabitants were not ethnically Japanese, and not considered social equals as a result, Okinawa was a part of Japan, making up its Forty-seventh Prefecture. Sixty miles in length and two miles wide at its waist, it had room for several airfields that would bring B-29's even closer to mainland Japan. Okinawa's 500,000 civilians proved loyal to Japan, and many would fight to the death in defense of their homeland. But the bulk of the defense would be borne by Japanese troops led by three charismatic officers. The island's commander was Lieutenant General Ushijima Mitsuru. Tall, lean, and self-controlled, he was considerate of others and humorous but iron willed. A former head of Japan's Military Academy, he had fought well in Burma, where he met Cho Isamu, a burly, fiery man with passionate views about samurai honor and the power of attack. Unlike the abstemious Ushijima, Cho, also a lieutenant general but junior to his commander, always managed sumptuous meals, demanded the best sake and whiskey, and even near the end of the battle found ways to have beautiful women visit his quarters.[50] Impetuous and fanatical, Cho was part of a conspiracy during the 1930s to murder the prime minister. Sent to the Kwantung Army rather than to prison, he almost provoked a war with the Soviet Union. Now he was ready for war with the Americans. The chief planning officer for Japan's defense forces on Okinawa was Cho's exact opposite—Colonel Yahara Hiromichi, a tall, patrician officer who had trained for ten months in the United States. He was a thoughtful, careful intellectual who complemented Cho's fervor with his cool, rational style. The three men made a formidable team.

On the morning of April 1, 1945, Easter, the Japanese on Okinawa looked with astonishment at an armada of 1,600 ships that turned the sea dark. By nightfall, 60,000 Americans were on shore without opposition. Ushijima would fight them behind prepared defense lines on the rocky southern tip of the island. The full invasion force numbered 184,000 men, compared with the 150,000 who went ashore at Normandy. At a cost of only 150 killed and wounded, the first wave of U.S. troops captured two airfields and established a beachhead eight miles wide and four deep. As bulldozers worked to make the airfields operational, marines watched in disbelief as a Japanese Zero circled the field before landing. Slipping out of his parachute, the pilot dropped to the runway and began to walk toward a group of marines. He suddenly stopped, an expression of horror on his face. As he reached for his pistol, he was shot dead. As one marine said, "There's always one poor bastard who doesn't get the word."[51]

Eventually, 545,000 marines and army troops would fight on Okinawa, opposing Ushijima's 110,000 troops, some of whom were only partly trained Okinawans. As the fighting spread slowly south, becoming more deadly with each passing week, kamikaze flights roared over the American ships in terrifying displays of suicidal fury. At least 1,900 kamikaze planes were lost. They sank 36 U.S. Navy ships, most of them small, and damaged another 368. Hundreds of "human torpedoes"—torpedoes steered by men—were launched as well. Many malfunctioned but some hit their targets. Even the great *Yamato*, stripped clean of her luxurious appointments, set sail on a kamikaze mission, carrying just enough fuel to reach Okinawa and battle the U.S. fleet. The *Yamato* could outshoot any U.S. ship but never came close enough to one to use her nine 18.1-inch guns. Battered by dozens of bombs and torpedoes, the world's greatest battleship sank, her captain lashed to a compass post.

Suicidal bravery has occurred and been honored throughout the recorded history of warfare. Early in World War II, for example, several American pilots tried to dive their badly damaged planes into Japanese ships, and numbers of men threw themselves on grenades to save others—seven U.S. Marines did so on Okinawa alone.[52] However, these were individual acts, not military policy. For the Japanese, death in battle became a sacred duty. Soldiers and sailors, remembering the imperial rescript "Honor is heavier than mountains and death lighter than a feather," often fought to the last man and, at the very end, usually killed themselves rather than surrender.

From the days of the Russo-Japanese War, fighting spirit was stressed over weapons, a precept devastatingly challenged at Nomonhan in 1939 and later in the Pacific. By late 1944, it was painfully clear to Japanese commanders that their few remaining old planes and young pilots could not hope to halt the American advance toward their homeland. The creation of suicide planes, rockets, and torpedoes was a calculated effort to inflict damage, rationalized as being scarcely more deadly than unarmed aircraft because so very few of them survived. Not all Japanese chosen for kamikaze duty were eager to commit suicide for the emperor; some even refused to fly at the last moment. Others went to their deaths only after leaving poignant letters questioning the meaning of their lives and the nature of death. But thousands of young men eagerly flew suicide planes, ready to give their last breath attempting to crash into an American ship. They accepted this, their final duty, in the spirit of the creator of the Kamikaze Corps, Admiral Onishi Takijiro, who explained his philosophy this way:

> *In blossom today, then scattered;*
> *Life is so like a delicate flower.*
> *How can one expect the fragrance*
> *to last forever?*[53]

The often brutal fighting on Okinawa continued until June 21. American shells, tanks, flamethrowers, satchel changes, grenades, and bayonets killed about 100,000 of Okinawa's defenders. In turn, the Japanese inflicted 49,151 casualties on the Americans, with over 7,500 dead. The navy lost about 5,000 dead and similar number wounded, most of them as a result of kamikaze attacks.[54] Estimates vary, but approximately 150,000 Okinawan civilians died.[55]

Most Okinawan civilians, like almost all Japanese soldiers, believed that the Americans would kill them if they tried to surrender. Many soldiers and civilians fulfilled their vows to kill themselves, often using hand grenades, with predictably grim results. The women had been taught that they would be stripped naked, raped, then run over by tanks.[56] In fact, occasionally soldiers and civilians alike were killed as they tried to surrender. As one Okinawan nurse learned, however, the Americans typically "took care of Okinawans really well," but she learned that only after many of her friends had killed themselves and she had almost done so herself. She, too, was treated properly. After three months, she was reunited with her mother and father. "Mother, barefoot, ran out of a tent in the camp and hugged me to her. 'You lived, you lived!' I still remember her crying out loud."[57]

Among the last to die were Generals Ushijima and Cho. Despite Cho's insistence, Ushijima had repeatedly rejected his officers' requests to die in banzai charges, urging them to keep fighting and killing Americans. After the United States declared the fighting over on Okinawa, Ushijima finally permitted a hundred or so survivors to carry out a suicidal attack. He and Cho would commit seppuku. Yahara asked to join them but was refused, being instead ordered to escape to Japan with a report of the defense of Okinawa. The aristocratic Yahara, who towered over the Okinawans, was easily spotted and captured. That night Cho and Ishijima had an elegant dinner complete with sake and Black and White scotch whisky. Their conversation was lively, with Ishijima cracking jokes to the end. After this final meal, the two men stepped outside in full dress uniforms and sat on a white quilt symbolizing death. As soon as each man's knife was driven into his belly, an adjutant with a sword at the ready delivered the final blow to the back of the neck.[58]

On March 9–10, 1945, over 300 B-29's dropped incendiary bombs on the heart of Tokyo, creating a firestorm of 1,800 degrees Fahrenheit. The

Sumida River boiled, metal melted, and houses and people spontaneously burst into flames. Thousands of burning people ran screaming while others, unhurt, looked on in horror. Bodies burned black lay everywhere—mothers attempting to shield their children, men and women in a last embrace. When the second and third waves of bombs came over Tokyo, a blood-red mist clouded their windshields and the stench was so hideous that crewmen retched until they could put their gas masks on. A sixteen-square-mile area of Tokyo was turned to ashes. Perhaps 100,000 people died. An even longer raid, this time by 562 B-29's, bombed Tokyo again on March 23, and 502 planes struck again thirty-six hours later, this time killing 62 Allied airmen held in a Tokyo prison.[59] General Curtis LeMay's planes also dropped fragmentation bombs "for anti-personnel effect and to discourage fire-fighting."[60]

Between March, when the firebombing began, and Japan's surrender on August 15, 1945, about 40 percent of Osaka had been destroyed, 50 percent of Tokyo, Kobe, and Yokohama, and 90 percent of Aomori.[61] With her shipping decimated by submarine and air attack, raw materials were critically scarce. Aircraft production had virtually ceased, and hunger was widespread. After the fall of Okinawa, there could be no doubt that an invasion of Japan would come soon. American staff officers tortured themselves with the prospect of one million American lives lost while the Japanese prepared the entire population to fight. Old men and women practiced with sharpened bamboo spears, muzzle-loading rifles, even bows and arrows. Children practiced strapping on explosives that would detonate when they crawled under American tanks. It was planned that 28 million men and women aged fifteen to sixty would take up some sort of arms against the invaders. There were over 4,000,000 uniformed men in Japan, 2,335,000 of whom were first-line combat troops. Making use of fortifications all along the coast of Kyushu, these men would meet the Americans on the beaches and smash them if they could. Little could be expected of the remnants of the navy, but 10,000 planes of all sorts, most of them expected to be kamikazes, had been hidden away.[62] An American invasion would lead to a bloodbath—that no one doubted.

The atom bomb made these fears academic. Over the objections of scientists like Edward Teller, then General Eisenhower, who argued vehemently that the war could be ended without the "bomb" and, furthermore, that its use would lead to "world condemnation," it was used

Hiroshima shortly after the atomic bomb blast. (UPI/Corbiss-Bettmann)

nonetheless.[63] On August 8, 1945, a B-29 lifted off from Tinian on its run toward Hiroshima. The atom bomb it dropped killed about 100,000 people, including 22 of 23 American prisoners. The one survivor, dazed and burned, was beaten to death by Japanese.[64] Three days later, a plutonium bomb more powerful than the one dropped on Hiroshima fell on Nagasaki because the primary target, the site of a large army arsenal, was obscured by thick clouds. Thirty-five thousand people died instantly; many others were condemned to linger until dying agonizing deaths weeks and months later. A ring of hills around the city saved others from death, but among the dead were members of a work party of Allied prisoners and an unknown number of other persons held in a prisoner-of-war camp a mile away.[65]

Just hours before Nagasaki was destroyed, Soviet artillery blasted Japanese positions in Manchuria, Soviet planes bombed front lines and rear areas alike, and waves of heavy tanks smashed through Japanese lines. Without tanks of their own, even without antitank guns, and lacking any air cover, the 780,000 Japanese troops in Manchuria, like the 260,000 in Korea, stood little chance against the Soviet invasion force of

1,600,000 men. Soviet tanks and armored personnel carriers moved ahead rapidly, their staff officers following the victorious troops in lend-lease Studebaker sedans.

Even after the two atom bombs and the overwhelming Soviet attack that was crushing Japanese resistance everywhere in Manchuria and Korea, the militarists in the Supreme War Council refused to consider surrender. War Minister Anami insisted that Japan fight to the death, and many radical officers agreed. Wearily, Prime Minister Suzuki announced that he must ask the emperor "to express his wishes." Over the objections of the militants, Emperor Hirohito recorded his famous proclamation of surrender. After observing that the war could not reasonably be continued, he declared that the Allies' surrender terms calling for disarming the military services and punishing war criminals were "unbearable." "Nevertheless," he added, "the time has come when we must bear the unbearable."[66]

The Supreme War Council felt compelled to accept the emperor's wishes. It cabled acceptance of the Allied surrender terms, as long as the emperor retained his authority as sovereign ruler. The emperor recorded a surrender message, which was locked in a wall safe overnight, a wise precaution because fanatical junior army officers were planning to kill the imperial advisers and persuade the emperor to change his mind. Conspirators stormed through the Imperial Palace, shooting and beheading those who opposed them, but they did not find the emperor's recording, and when regular army forces refused to support the coup it soon collapsed. War Minister Anami committed seppuku. On August, 15, 1945, the emperor's speech was broadcast to the nation. After observing that "the war situation has developed not necessarily to our advantage," he acceded to the Allies' demands because, thanks to their "new and cruel bomb," not to do so would "not only result in an ultimate collapse and obliteration of the Japanese nation, but would lead to the extinction of human civilization." Not once did he use the word "surrender."[67]

Most Japanese listened to the surrender proclamation in stunned silence, many in tears. Few had ever before heard the emperor's voice, and to hear it under these circumstances was a profound shock. The emperor spoke in a court dialect fully comprehensible to few Japanese, but the importance of his message was clear. Some radical young officers raved about continuing the fight, but there would be no support for that. A few, like officers in Kyushu, directed their rage at Allied prisoners, brutally hacking to death sixteen newly captured Allied airmen. Eight other U.S. airmen were beheaded in Fukuoka the same day; a similar number had been executed three days earlier.[68]

Other Japanese in the Pacific refused to believe that Japan had surrendered. Many on Iwo Jima stayed in their caves until 1951. A sergeant on Guam held out until 1973, and an officer in the Philippines did so until 1974.[69] When he returned to the Philippines in 1996 to express his regrets for the war and donate $10,000 to a local school, he was not accepted as a hero by the Filipinos, some of whom had lost relatives to him in years past. Seven families accused him of having killed a relative.[70]

After eight days of fighting, when Soviet troops finally accepted a cease-fire—several days after Japan's surrender—the huge Soviet invasion force had killed 80,000 Japanese and taken 594,000 soldiers and civilian prisoners. Some would not return from labor camps for several years, many not ever. In return, Japan's overmatched troops managed to kill 8,000 Soviets and wound 22,000 others, but many Japanese women and children were left to fend for themselves.[71] The surrender of Japanese troops usually proceeded without difficulty, but there were exceptions. On Borneo, Australian troops stood by while several thousand Japanese prisoners were beaten to death by outraged natives.[72] In Burma, just before Japan's surrender, some 30,000 Japanese soldiers tried to break out of a British encirclement. They were slaughtered by massed British fire, many after the armistice was declared. Eventually, 1,400 were taken prisoner, but perhaps 17,000 died at a cost to the British of 97 men. A good many Japanese soldiers who surrendered at war's end were held in British camps, where, although not victims of brutality, they had to work hard for as long as two years before being returned to Japan.[73]

For many Allied prisoners of war, the surrender came just in time. On Java, 100,000 British and Dutch troops were held under the command of General Count Terauchi. Forced to labor under brutal guards on starvation diets until they collapsed or died of disease, these men were also tortured, beaten, and killed at the whim of their guards. Among the prisoners was the author Laurens van der Post, then a Japanese-speaking British officer. As the war wound to an end and Allied troops came closer to Java, General Terauchi issued written orders calling for all the Allied prisoners to be killed before they could be released by Allied forces. Before the order could be carried out, the emaciated, ragged van der Post was summoned to Japanese headquarters, where to his amazement all the Japanese officers rose and bowed. The emperor had announced Japan's surrender. The atom bombs that killed so many Japanese had saved 100,000 Allied prisoners in Java and probably many more of the 250,000 held elsewhere.[74]

Soon after the Japanese surrender, the Allies began to arrest suspected war criminals. Some innocent men were executed, and others received prison sentences. Yet some Japanese guilty of gruesome crimes were never apprehended, and others, like Colonel Tsuji, remained in hiding until after an amnesty was declared in 1948. After the war, he hid first in Thailand disguised as a Buddhist monk and then in Japan. In 1952 he was elected to the Diet. The following year, he founded a militant rearmament association, and attacked the U.S. presence in Japan, vowing to reclaim Japan's sovereignty and rearm Japan for the final inevitable war.[75] In 1956, General Kawaguchi publicly accused him of being a war criminal, but he was nevertheless reelected to the Diet and later to the House of Councillors. In 1961, he vanished during a trip to Southeast Asia, not to be seen again.[76]

FROM CHIVALRY
TO BRUTALITY

J apan's sudden transformation from a country that epitomized military chivalry to one that embodied the depths of armed depravity would seem, on the face of things, to be both baffling and disquieting. To be sure, much about Japan throughout her history has struck Westerners as inexplicable. From the earliest times to the present day, many Western students of Japan have admitted their inability to comprehend one or another aspect of Japanese culture. Nevertheless, Japan's abrupt shift from chivalry to bestiality may not be as puzzling as it first appears.

Many factors combined to bring about this change in Japan's military ethos. Underlying her display of martial savagery in China, and continuing throughout World War II, was a deeply-rooted sense of inferiority, often acknowledged by soldiers and officers alike. For much of Japan's history, her people acknowledged that Chinese culture was superior to their own and, moreover, that in a great many respects the Japanese way of life had been borrowed from China. After the visit of Perry, the Japanese had to admit that Western technology, if not all other aspects of Western culture, was also far superior to her own. Admissions like these would be unsettling for any people, and they were especially galling for the Japanese because, more than most peoples on earth, they were imbued with a sense of the greatness, the inherent superiority, even the divinity of their own "Yamato" race.[1] The ambivalence of the Japanese about their worthiness was palpably painful. Because many felt inferior, they came to fear and hate Westerners as they had earlier feared and hated the Chinese.[2] When Westerners later proved to be vulnerable, the temptation to destroy them grew.

When Western colonial powers finally exposed the weakness of China, Japan's respect for her dwindled, and by the time of the Sino-Japanese War, in 1894–95, Japanese schoolchildren no longer studied the glories of Chinese civilization. Instead, they gloried in lessons about Japan's moral and military superiority over the "despicable," "smelly," and "cowardly" Chinese, typically referred to with a term equivalent to "Chinks."[3]

The Japanese response to Western technology followed a similar course. Intensive efforts to achieve technological parity went hand in hand with racist denunciations. The West was termed "corrupt, soft, and venal," a declining civilization whose animal-like "devil-beast" soldiers would be crushed in battle by Japan's "divine" soldiers. Newspapers, movies, and theaters assaulted the Japanese people with propaganda and, as Prime Minister Tojo admitted, outright lies.[4] Every Allied and Axis power employed film and theater for propaganda purposes, but perhaps none more successfully than Japan, especially her Takarasuka Revue. Like an inverted form of all-male Kabuki theater, this enormously popular all-female theater group skillfully championed Japanese militarism and imperialism at the expense of Westerners. Japan's dedication to Pan-Asian prosperity was dramatized, while the evils of Western colonialism were hammered home. Play after play urged audiences to eradicate "the much-dreaded germs called Anglo-Saxon ideologies."[5]

Changes in national self-concept from inferiority to superiority were facilitated by Japan's use of extensive censorship as well. Censorship, a hallmark of Japan from the start of the Meiji period, became all-pervasive. Publications were closely monitored, while schools promoted changes in how the Japanese should think about themselves and foreigners. During the 1894 war with China, schoolchildren learned songs belittling the Chinese and glorifying Japan, especially her military heroes. By the end of the Russo-Japanese War, the Ministry of Education's control over the minds of Japanese children had become almost total. All elementary school texts were written by the ministry, and children educated during the 1930s firmly believed themselves to belong to a divine race threatened by not fully human Chinese and Westerners. Despite this propaganda onslaught, many Japanese soldiers during World War II still admitted feeling inferior to Westerners, an issue addressed head-on in the pamphlet that Colonel Tsuji distributed to all troops at the start of World War II.

Control over Japanese behavior was remarkable, too. Foreign visitors to Japan around the turn of the century were amazed by the number of precise rules controlling every aspect of Japanese life—how to speak to a superior, how to sit, how to express emotion, how much money could be spent on a gift, how large a person's house could be, and what he could furnish it with.[6] What is more, until 1878 all samurai had the right to kill any nonsamurai who broke any of these rules, or simply behaved in an "unexpected" manner. The specification of rules governing Japanese conduct became somewhat less precise in later years, but the number of rules the Japanese felt compelled to follow continued to be extremely large by Western standards.

The feudal concept of obligation known as *on* also played a part. In medieval Europe, a reciprocal exchange of obligations between lord and vassal assured order. When a Japanese superior, say, a feudal lord or high-ranking samurai, bestowed a favor on a subordinate, however, it forever indebted the latter to a deep, emotional loyalty. Just as children owed everlasting loyalty to parents for the *on* of giving birth to them, all Japanese owed their greatest *on* to the emperor for the privilege of being born his subject. The military not only made use of this indebtedness to the emperor, but lower ranks were regularly made to feel a deep obligation to their seniors.[7] A population long accustomed to precise and stringently enforced rules in everyday life would be at pains not to disappoint friends, kinsmen, or neighbors, especially not those who had bestowed special favors on them. All of these voices were joined by anti-Western slogans and cartoons calling for young people to hate foreigners and to kill them. The effect was powerful.[8]

The training of Japanese soldiers and seamen had always been harsh, even by rigorous German and British standards. As early as 1915, while Japanese forces retained their chivalrous practices, a book describing an army recruit's life was banned.[9] In the 1930s, still more stringent training methods moved into practice, the highest military authorities being determined to overcome the antimilitary mood of the 1920s. Schools had to offer military training, for military service was a man's sacred duty.[10] Students heard again and again that human life was not inviolable; in war it would prove necessary to kill ruthlessly; civilians were no longer to be spared. Boys who left school after finishing the six years of compulsory education had to complete 400 hours of rigorous military training at youth centers established throughout the country. All students who disappointed their teachers were subject to slaps and beatings.[11]

The *kempeitai,* Japan's vicious military police, received sweeping powers to control dissent by any means necessary. Its use of sadistic torture became routine and murder not uncommon. The military schools preparing young men to become officers intentionally obliterated the bond that had previously tied officers and soldiers together in mutual respect as members of a second family. Officers should now be so authoritarian and brutal that soldiers would fear and hate them, a policy reinforced by army training practices encouraging officers and noncommissioned officers to beat their subordinates. It was no different in the navy. A good officer should treat his men with "calculated brutality" to produce vicious fighters who would redirect their pent-up rage against the enemy, including prisoners and civilians. Soldiers came to loathe many of these brutal officers and NCOs, who continued to slap and punch subordinates throughout the war, often so hard they were knocked down, sometimes unconscious. One soldier who remembered being beaten 264 times concluded, "Having been subjected to cruel and irrational punishments we were trained to act without thinking in response to orders."[12]

Officers also enthusiastically read an early-eighteenth-century samurai narrative that encouraged martial virtues and emphasized the honor of death. One admonition was "Every morning be sure to take time to think of yourself as dead."[13] A commitment to *gyokusai*—fighting to the last man—joined with a commitment to seppuku, suicidal charges, and even kamikaze attacks (although not fully institutionalized until 1944) not only enhanced Japanese fighting spirit but also gave many men a fatalistic view of life that made killing easier.

Derisively called "less than a penny" (the price of their draft-notice postcard), soldiers and sailors were hazed, sworn at, slapped, beaten, and forced to complete degrading tasks. They had no privacy, and any form of protest was a capital crime. An officer or NCO who lost his temper might actually beat a recruit to death.[14] One soldier wrote this: "One year's army life has drained the humanity out of everyone. Second-year privates treat us first-year privates as though we were their slaves or rather machines. . . . Were a second-year private to discover that I had written a letter like this in the toilet, I would probably be murdered."[15]

The views of this young soldier, obviously a man of some education, raise an often overlooked point. All Japanese soldiers and sailors received the same brutal training, but they did not all react in the same way. Although the bulk of the men conscripted for service just before and during World War II were the sons of impoverished farmers or fishermen, some were college students from urban backgrounds. These men often detested military life and the brutality that pervaded it, but the sons of peasants and fishermen actually found army life to be easier than the lives they had endured before. Peasant soldiers acknowledged that the first year of training was difficult, but after that they felt well enough treated, had ample free time, and ate better food than they had known earlier. Many actually dreaded a return to farm work after being mustered out of the army.[16] These men were usually perfectly willing to obey orders no matter what they might entail.[17]

It is no accident that the order to all commanders to adhere strictly to international law contained in the imperial rescript issued at the start of the Russo-Japanese War, as well as World War I, was omitted from the rescript that began World War II in the Pacific.[18] From primary schools to the Imperial Palace, Japanese authorities ignored their past commitment to chivalry. Early in the Pacific War, soldiers carried with them a field service code exhorting them not to commit atrocities, but most officers did nothing to reinforce this message.[19] Even before World War II erupted, Japanese soldiers, sailors, and airmen had been indoctrinated with "facts" proving that their enemies, whether Chinese or European, were inferior, even subhuman creatures for whom no respect was possible. When those enemies were so easily defeated, they received even less respect. When they surrendered, as they did in such large numbers early in the war, that lack of respect intensified into disgust. The Japanese did not surrender, because anyone who did so was considered dead. They could not return to their families. When Japanese officers ordered that these enemies, civilian as well as military, be killed for any number of reasons—to punish, to intimidate survivors, to vent rage—most of their men obeyed.

It should not be overlooked that many Japanese soldiers and sailors as well as their leaders considered Japan's reason for initiating the war in China and the Pacific to be entirely just. Japan's continuing inability to feed her impoverished population led many Japanese to believe that acquiring overseas land was essential. Japanese leaders argued that the only difference between Japan and the Western colonial nations was Japan's limited natural resources and her late entry into colonial competition.

Had Japan chosen to pursue imperial expansion in the late sixteenth or early seventeenth century when her large, well-armed, and superbly disciplined army put her near the pinnacle of world power, she could easily have colonized the Philippines, Indonesia, and much of southeast Asia. She might well have occupied Australia, New Zealand, and Hawaii as well. She might not have been able to take India, but she stood at least an even chance of driving the Chinese out of Korea and holding several Chinese sea ports. She might even have colonized the west coast of North America. At the very least, she could have developed trade throughout Asia and the Pacific. Japan did none of these things. She closed her harbors, destroyed her firearms, and lived in splendid isolation from the world until the middle of the nineteenth century.

By the time Japan had rearmed sufficiently once again to entertain any serious thoughts of colonial expansion, the nineteenth century was almost over. The European powers had already claimed all of Africa, most of Asia, and every place of value in the Pacific. Blocked at every turn by European and U.S. military power, Japan could have followed the lead of other formerly powerful states like Sweden by relying on her own territory and resources, content to live on at the sufferance of greater powers. She did not take this course, perhaps because her belief in her divine origins drove her to achieve more power, and perhaps because her great military past would not allow her to take a more peaceful path. But she was also driven by the painful realization that her population was too large for her small, almost entirely mountainous islands, and that she was too poor in natural resources for her easily to ally herself with a greater military power that would protect her.

At the turn of the century, with the partial exception of silk and tea, Japan had no products or raw materials the rest of the world wanted. In retrospect, it is easy enough to say that Japan should have made herself into a peace-loving economic power by manufacturing goods that the rest of the world did want, but there is no guarantee that the rest of the world would have fostered her independence and economic growth then as the United States did after 1945. Without a strong military, she might not have survived as an autonomous state, and Japan did not have the resources to be both a dominant military power and an economic power during the first half of the twentieth century.

The simple truth is that Japan came onto the world scene at the wrong time—too late for colonialism and too early for economic power based on the electronics revolution. And in choosing to create a powerful army and navy, she inevitably put herself on a collision course with the West, particularly the major powers in the Pacific—America, Britain, the Netherlands, and Russia. Once the United States demanded that Japan withdraw from China and orchestrated an oil embargo against her, as occurred only four months before Pearl Harbor, Japan had two choices: withdraw from China and negotiate with the West from a position of weakness, or seize a major source of oil before her existing two-year reserve was exhausted.

Given the total control that Japan's military had over her government, the first choice was impossible to accept. The Japanese military had long been determined to expand either north or south. Despite last-minute American attempts to achieve a compromise that would avert war, the oil embargo imposed by the Dutch and Americans made war almost certain; the American demand that she leave Manchuria became the casus belli.

Japan's desire for world domination no doubt influenced many Japanese leaders over the course of their lives, but when the decision to bomb Pearl Harbor was made these men thought in far more limited terms—withdraw from China and become a "slave state," as they often put it, of the Western forces that "encircled" her, or go to war with

America, Britain, and the Netherlands in the hope that they might have enough early success to negotiate peace on more favorable terms. Britain's will to fight was thought to be destroyed by German successes, while America was expected to deploy her strength helping Britain, not fighting in the Pacific.[20] No senior military officer seriously believed that the Japanese could win the war, but few anticipated that the Allies would demand unconditional surrender either.

Many of Japan's military leaders, especially her young officers, had long advocated war. Eager to use Western economic pressure to excuse their belligerency, these men had engineered the "tripartite" military alliance with Germany and Italy signed in September 1940. In 1941, convinced that the Axis powers would easily defeat Britain and the Soviet Union, they declared it imperative for Japan to enter the war before it ended in order for Japan to claim Southeast Asia and Indonesia as her share of the spoils.[21] Beginning in 1939, German newsreels of Hitler's military triumphs were shown in Japan every day, reinforcing this sense of urgency.[22]

Unlike Western soldiers who often professed to believe that God or Christian doctrine were moral authorities standing above their officers or political leaders, most Japanese recognized no moral authority higher than the emperor. When officers told their men that they must act brutally in the name of the emperor, as they often did, few Japanese would resist the order. Despite the growing brutality of officers, the Imperial Japanese Army was still organized as a family, with small groups of recruits from the same town or village relating to one another as "brothers." As a result, peer pressure to behave as ordered—and as the other men actually did—had even more power here than it had in other armies. And peer pressure in any army is great. A sense of guilt relating to universal values such as human life or dignity was not as powerful an emotion for most Japanese as it could be for some Christian soldiers. This allowed many men to kill and rape without guilt or remorse. More specific forms of guilt did exist, but these referred to failing the emperor, one's family, one's comrades, or some other reference group. Some college-educated soldiers were restrained in the use of brutality by a more universal sense of guilt, but these men were a minority. However, like their samurai ancestors, virtually all who served in the Japanese military were acutely sensitive to feelings of shame that could dishonor their family, platoon, or regiment, and the military was skilled in the use of shame to induce men to behave as needed, including sadistically.

These many factors combined to create a climate in which wartime atrocities were a likely outcome. However, the reality of Japan's World War II sadistic brutality is more complex than this simple overview would suggest. First, different kinds of atrocities occurred for quite different reasons. Second, not all Japanese committed wartime atrocities even when ordered to do so. Finally, some Allied officers also ordered atrocities, and some Allied soldiers behaved brutally without orders.

Different kinds of brutal behavior that took place throughout the Pacific War tend to be lumped together. For example, many individuals, acting alone and without apparent premeditation, behaved in bestial ways. A Japanese soldier in China demanded that villages provide him with a young woman; when no young woman was made available, he killed a three year-old.[23] Other Japanese killed prisoners, raped women, or burned seemingly without provocation or without the collaboration of others. For example, without orders, some Japanese doctors routinely shot Chinese patients, then tried to save them to improve their surgical skills. Allied soldiers sometimes acted similarly, gratuitously killing a prisoner or, in one instance, machine-gunning a large number of men in an apparent fit of rage.[24]

On many occasions, small groups of men committed atrocious acts. These acts were sometimes planned and sometimes not. Armed Japanese in groups looted, raped, and killed wantonly—usually they were drunk, but not always. Now and then, they threatened and even attacked Japanese officers. This kind of behavior was common, and so troubling that Japanese military courts frequently prosecuted offenders. An investigation found that most of the offenders were reservists, not first-time combat troops, and that most were drunk at the time. Many of the crimes were said to result from a sense of contempt for "inferior" native peoples. The reality that brutal officers were targeted was not addressed.[25] Allied atrocities of this sort rarely involved native peoples but were not uncommon where Japanese were concerned. Charles Lindbergh, then serving as a combat flier in the South Pacific, was appalled by the atrocities of Allied servicemen as well as by their total contempt for the Japanese. "What is courage for us is fanaticism for him. We hold his examples of atrocity screamingly to the heavens while we cover up our own and condone them as just retribution for his acts."[26]

Atrocities committed by small groups of men were terrible enough, but those ordered by high-ranking officers were particularly dreadful because they typically involved large numbers of victims and represented cold, calculated sadism. Well-documented Japanese atrocities of this sort were many and inconceivably ghastly. Although Allied commanders could not match the scope or sadism of their Japanese counterparts, some did order the killing of prisoners and the strafing of Japanese survivors in boats, in life rafts, or clinging to wreckage. Some also insisted that all wounded Japanese be killed. Many of these brutal acts were justified as retribution for Japan's atrocities. Weak as that argument may be morally, sometimes there could be no such justification at all. For example, in 1941, French troops in Vietnam arrested 8,000 civilians, including children and the elderly. After tying these people together by running wires through their heels or palms, they exposed them to the sun for several days.[27]

Just as it is true that some Allied servicemen committed atrocities during the Pacific War, at times under orders, some Japanese refused to behave brutally, even when ordered to do so. To be sure, most Japanese who were ordered to kill, rape, or burn did so, often with joyous zeal, but some soldiers refused orders to bayonet prisoners and yet survived the war to talk about it.[28] Numerous Japanese officers, including some executed as war criminals, refused orders to kill prisoners or mistreat civilians. Many Japanese took great pleasure in killing, often as painfully as possible. Others did so without a second thought. But some Japanese surprised Allied prisoners by being gentle and kind.[29]

It is worth noting that appalling as the behavior of many Japanese units during the war in China and the Pacific was, it was hardly unprecedented. As we have seen, China's treatment of prisoners in earlier wars was appalling. Terrible as they were, examples of Chinese cruelty to prisoners in earlier years were duplicated throughout human history in most parts of the world, where warfare often led to wholesale slaughter.[30] In modern times, the Turkish massacre of perhaps one million Armenians is a particularly horrific example. Later, the Spanish civil war set a grim standard for the world as fascist planes bombed undefended cities. The Italian use of poison gas against Ethiopians marked another hideous episode in pre–World War II history. In Russia before the revolution of 1917, Cossacks quite frequently slaughtered unarmed Jews. In the 1930s, Stalin's forces tortured and killed millions of Soviet citizens. During World War II, German soldiers shot and hanged Soviet civilians in vast numbers, while Soviet troops murdered thousands of Polish officers, and when Soviet troops entered Germany, they took terrible revenge on German civilians. Germans more than once killed every man, woman, and child in Czech and French villages, and the British Royal Air Force aided by U.S. planes firebombed the medieval city of Dresden, killing tens of thousands, including Allied prisoners, in this undefended nonmilitary target. Since the end of World War II, no year has passed without reports of military and police atrocities somewhere in the world. What was done in Argentina, Bosnia, Cambodia, Haiti, Iraq, Rwanda, and Sudan, to name but a few places, and what is still being done in many other places is a painful reminder that the savagery can continue.

Consider, too, how very easy it is to persuade Westerners, including Americans, to hate and kill their enemies. In 1941, most Americans had little reason to hate the Japanese. To be sure, anti-Asian racism still existed, especially on the West Coast, but many Japanese-Americans had by then become U.S. citizens who were law-abiding and respected residents of West Coast cities and towns. Some Americans knew about Japanese atrocities in China, but this was long before television images could rapidly transform public opinion. Millions of Americans had seen photographs of Chinese victims of Japanese bombs in *Life* magazine, and most of them must have been appalled, but on the eve of Pearl Harbor there cannot have been more than a few thousand people in the entire United States who wanted to go to war with Japan.

Yet in a matter of only days after Pearl Harbor, Americans were referring to Japanese as "yellow monkeys," calling them "vermin," and recommending the use of unlimited force against them. Japanese-American citizens on the West Coast were rounded up, usually with the loss of everything they owned, many at first incarcerated in hurriedly and only partially cleared-out stockyards, pigpens, and horse stalls at race tracks before being moved to internment camps, where they lived in what might charitably be characterized as spartan conditions. Authorities explained that this was necessary to protect the defenseless West Coast. However, in equally defenseless Hawaii, U.S. naval and military bases could not be maintained without local Japanese-American labor. That these Japanese-Americans were not interned was an act of hypocrisy that came to the attention of few Americans at the time, except, of course, the Japanese-Americans themselves.

After the war, the Allies put many Japanese military leaders on trial for war crimes, accusing some of them of having engaged in a conspiracy to commit atrocities that led to the "wholesale destruction of human life, not alone on the field of battle . . . but in homes, hospitals, and orphanages, in factories and fields; and the victims would be the young and the old, the well and the infirm—men, women and children alike."[31] That many of these Japanese had been guilty of atrocious acts was obvious, but the war had been so brutal on both sides that, as more than one observer has pointed out, this same eloquent accusation could have been made against the Allies, including the Americans.

The Allies could not deny that, among other things, some members of their armed forces had mutilated Japanese corpses for souvenirs, killed Japanese wounded on the battlefield, shot prisoners, killed the Japanese crews of torpedoed ships, firebombed civilian targets, and, finally, dropped two atom bombs on Japanese cities. Now, there is more than a grain of truth to the Allied claim that Japanese atrocities had drawn the Allies into retaliation. It is probably true that Allied behavior would have been less brutal had the Japanese not behaved so savagely at the war's outset, but that is not the whole story. When Japan began bombing Chinese cities in 1937, just a few months after Picasso painted *Guernica*, the world condemned her actions. The U.S. Department of State declared such bombing to be "contrary to principles of law and humanity" and, in 1938, added that these attacks were "barbarous." When German planes engaged in widespread bombing of civilian populations in 1939, President Roosevelt said that this bombing "has sickened the hearts of every civilized man and woman, and has profoundly shocked the conscience of humanity."[32]

Yet in November 1941, weeks before Japanese planes attacked Pearl Harbor, the U.S. Army chief of staff, George C. Marshall, ordered his aides to prepare plans for "general incendiary attacks to burn up the wood and paper structures of the densely populated Japanese cities."[33] When U.S. planes finally had the opportunity to bomb Japan in late 1944, the initial attacks largely avoided civilian centers, but when these high-level bombing raids proved to be ineffective and costly, the U.S. Army Air Corps in May 1945 turned to low-level incendiary raids on Japanese cities. General Curtis LeMay, who planned the raid and said that he wished he could have led it in person, later proudly declared, "We scorched, and boiled and baked to death more people in Tokyo on that night of May 9–10 than went up in vapor at Hiroshima and Nagasaki."[34] General Tommy Powers, who actually led the incendiary raid on Tokyo, said that it caused "more casualties than . . . any other military action in the history of the world."[35] He neglected to mention that most of the victims were civilians, including many women and children. Tokyo was not the only Japanese city to be firebombed, and by the end of the war firebombs made up nearly two-thirds of the total tonnage of bombs dropped on Japan.

One of the men closest to General Douglas MacArthur was General Bonner Fellers. In June of 1945, he sent MacArthur a confidential memo describing the American firebomb raids as "one of the most ruthless and barbaric killings of non-combatants in all history."[36] Later two atom bombs were dropped on Japanese cities. The alternative of dropping the first atom bomb in Tokyo Bay, on an unpopulated center rather than a city, or so high above Tokyo that few casualties would result, as was urged by Edward Teller, was not seriously debated in the U.S. government. There is some reason to believe that the bombs were dropped as much to impress Stalin as to end Japanese resistance.[37] What is more, while the Japanese were actually signing the peace treaty, over 1,000 U.S. planes vengefully firebombed what remained of Tokyo. Some of these planes were still in the air when President Truman announced the Japanese surrender. About 400,000 Japanese men, women, and children—"in homes, hospitals, and orphanages" died in these air raids on Tokyo, as well as in others in the smaller cities of Osaka, Nagoya, Kobe, and Yokohama. The total loss of American life in the Pacific theater was only one-fourth of this number, while Japanese military and naval deaths against U.S. forces were just under 900,000.

Many Japanese atrocities were more personal than firebombing. Rape, bayoneting helpless men, women, and children, torture, starving prisoners, infecting them with lethal microorganisms, and performing surgery on prisoners without anesthesia may very well be more bestial than firebombing, but burning hundreds of thousands of helpless civilians to death in their homes did not bring Americans any closer to God. Had Japan won the war, a Japanese war-crimes tribunal would certainly have found senior U.S. officers and government officials guilty of war crimes, and it is not difficult to imagine that an impartial tribunal of neutral countries would have agreed with them soon after the war or, for that matter, even today.

The conclusion should not be drawn that Americans are unusually vicious. Men from all countries, particularly men of different races, can be induced to kill one another in bestial ways with relative ease. With a far briefer period of preparation for hatred than the Japanese experienced, many individual Americans, Australians, and Britons also behaved savagely. The war in the Pacific was one of the most brutal ever fought, on both sides. When the enemies are from another race, the likelihood that warfare against them and their countrymen will be brutal is greatly increased. One atrocity usually leads to another, and the result is a rage for revenge. None of this should be even remotely strange. Perhaps we need only remember the killing of women and children at My Lai and then recall that it was not an isolated incident in the Vietnam War. An American officer explained how it was possible for otherwise "decent" American young men to commit atrocities like this one.

> You put those same kids in the jungle for awhile, get them real scared, deprive them of sleep, and let a few incidents change some of their fears to hate. Give them a sergeant who has seen too many of his men killed by booby traps and by lack of distrust, and who feels that Vietnamese . . . are not like him. Add a little mob pressure, and those nice kids who accompanied us today would rape like champions. Kill, rape and steal is the name of the game.[38]

WHY CHIVALRY?

If this is so, if brutality is so easily learned, then the most intriguing question to be addressed here is not why the Japanese, or any other nation, behaved so appallingly during World War II or any other war. Horrible as military brutality certainly is, it is commonplace, as the war in Vietnam must surely remind us, or the savage war in Korea before that. It is the all too uncommon occurrence of chivalry in warfare that requires an explanation, not brutality. The real puzzle is why Japanese troops behaved so decorously throughout most of the war of 1894–95 against China and during the Boxer Rebellion. Why, again, throughout the brutal, often hand-to-hand killing of the Russo-Japanese War, did their chivalry win the admiration of the world? And why was there no brutality against the Germans in 1914 and very little against Soviet troops in 1939?

The Chinese mutilated Japanese prisoners throughout the war of 1894–95, but only at Port Arthur did Japan's soldiers behave barbarously in return. The Boxer Rebellion provided ample provocation for both Russian and Japanese troops to seek terrible vengeance for Chinese atrocities. The Russian massacre of Chinese men, women, and children at Blagoveshchensk was unprovoked, but the Chinese soon afterward inflicted unspeakable torture on Russian soldiers, and the Russians responded with more terror. The Japanese had as much reason to seek revenge as the Russians did. Their diplomat Sugiyama had been murdered and mutilated, Japanese troops had taken heavy casualties at Tientsin, and some had been tortured and mutilated by Chinese as they marched on Peking. Yet the behavior of Japanese soldiers toward the Chinese remained as consistently restrained as that of the Russians was brutal.

The conditions necessary for Japanese brutality were present in abundance before and during the Russo-Japanese War. The Russians thought themselves so superior to the Japanese that they would smash them like mosquitoes, as they were fond of saying, and they did not care if the Japanese heard it. Russian racial slurs were public as well. While it is true that most Russian soldiers did not hate the Japanese, many of their officers did. Just before the war broke out, officers of the Russian navy almost universally expressed such contempt and hatred for the Japanese that they swore they would never surrender to them under any circumstances and would instead blow up their ships.[39] And early in the land war, at least one officer carried dumdum bullets, and wounded Russian officers were known to kill Japanese medical corpsmen after they had treated them.[40] Cossacks killed Japanese prisoners throughout the war, and on occasion so did Russian infantry. There is also no doubt that many Japanese officers and most of their men hated the Russians before the war broke out. They had been taught over and over that Russia had deprived Japan of her rightful gains in the 1894–95 war against China, had ridiculed Japanese soldiers during the Boxer Rebellion, and still contemptuously referred to them as "yellow monkeys."[41] When orders came to march against Russia, many Japanese officers and men wept with joy.[42]

In addition, the war was fought under appalling conditions of extreme heat and cold, torrential rains, dust storms, plagues of flies, and endemic diseases. There was terrible slaughter by artillery, rifle fire, and mines, while men frequently fought hand to hand with bayonets, clubbed rifles, knives, rocks, and even their teeth. Men on both sides were frequently so exhausted that they could sleep through the heaviest artillery barrages. As casualties mounted, both armies had reason to seek revenge for the deaths of so many of their friends.

Yet the Japanese did not behave brutally. Occasional stories of alleged Japanese atrocities were investigated by the many European newsmen and military attachés, who found no evidence to sustain any of these charges.[43] As we have already seen, instead of committing atrocities, the Japanese treated the bodies of dead Russians with respect and showed wounded Russians exceptional kindness. For the most part, the Russians avoided atrocities against the Japanese as well, although they were often brutal to the Chinese.

A British newsman wrote, "The chivalry displayed by the Japanese soldier to a fallen foe has been demonstrated on innumerable occasions since the momentous crossing of the Yalu. I have witnessed the considerate treatment accorded to Russian prisoners which could not be excelled in point of consideration by any army in the world."[44] Surprisingly, instead of becoming inured to death as soldiers usually do, veteran Japanese soldiers could be moved to tears by the suffering of their enemies. When a badly wounded Russian soldier died shortly after saying that he did not know why he had been sent to war, and asked that the Japanese let his wife and child know how he died, many men wept in sympathy.[45] Russian soldiers were often equally kind to wounded Japanese.

There can be no easy explanation for the conspicuous display of chivalry by these two so very different armies. Part of the answer must lie in the refusal of officers on either side to order the execution or mistreatment of enemy prisoners. Their proper behavior may have resulted in part from a desire not to be discredited in the eyes of the many foreign observers who accompanied both armies, but these foreign eyes could not be everywhere at once, and there is no evidence to suggest that atrocities took place when an observer was not present. What is more, with a few exceptions on the part of the Russians, troops on either side did not commit brutal acts when their officers were not there to control them. Also, none of the foreign observers made any note of Japanese officers' having to restrain their men from harming enemy prisoners. Somehow, common soldiers on both sides felt sympathy for one another, and this sympathy grew as the war continued. Only one man, a British observer with the Russians, implied that the Japanese were behaving under unnatural restraint when he wrote sarcastically that the next time Japan went to war "she will permit herself to indulge in the usual barbarities of Christian nations."[46] He was wrong. The next time was against the Germans in World War I, and, as we have seen, the Japanese once again were chivalrous. And although Japanese troops had brutalized the Chinese since 1932, when they fought Russian troops in 1939, they again behaved correctly.

It may be tempting to explain away the humane behavior of the Japanese military at the turn of the century as the product of a gentler, more humane era, but while the fin de siècle saw wondrous achievements in technology, medicine, and even social programs, it was not a time when warfare was synonymous with chivalry. An obvious example of Western military barbarity took place during the Boxer Rebellion when all the Western armies, led by the Germans and Russians, brutalized innocent Chinese civilians. And this was not a unique expression of Western barbarism. A few years later, U.S. troops in the Philippines used torture to defeat the Filipino rebels.[47] In fact, Western troops repeatedly used brutal means to defeat and control "native" peoples in their far-flung colonies. To mention only two examples among many, in 1900, British troops finally put down a military uprising by the Asante in Ghana by ruthlessly burning crops and actually allowing their African allies to enslave Asante women and children who fell into their hands.[48] In 1904, some 20,000 imperial German troops under General von Trotha were sent to Namibia (then South-West Africa) to quell a rebellion by the Herero. Von Trotha announced that it was his "policy to use force with terrorism and even brutality," and he meant what he said.[49] After heavy fighting against the poorly armed Herero, German troops engaged in an orgy of shooting, bayoneting, and burning alive women and children as well as men. It is probable that over 50,000 people died, many of them after Herero resistance had ended.

Barbarous acts were not confined to fighting between European troops and Chinese or Africans; they also took place when Europeans fought one another. The well-publicized Boer War in South Africa, which began in 1899 and lasted into 1902, was fought by British troops against well-armed but outnumbered Boer farmers. Any African who aided the British was shot out of hand by the Boers, and some British troops were found guilty of killing Boer prisoners as well, but the worst outrages occurred by order of Lord Kitchener, Britain's famous field marshal. Unable to defeat the highly mobile Boer guerrilla cavalry, Kitchener not only ordered that Boer farms be burned and their livestock driven off, he interned some 110,000 Boer women and children in "concentration camps," where lacking all medical care, exposed to the elements that ranged from great heat to frost, without clean water, and intentionally fed a starvation diet, many thousands died of disease, more than 3,000 in one month alone. Kitchener's intent was to use these pathetic civilian hostages to compel a Boer surrender. Instead, he so outraged world opinion that the British government was forced to provide more humane living conditions. Kitchener responded by bringing no more civilians into his camps but instead burning their houses, leaving them without food or shelter in the veldt, hoping that their menfolk would leave the fighting zone to care for them.[50]

Despite these less than ideal models for Western military conduct, one reason for the exemplary behavior of Japan's military earlier in the century is the training the Japanese received from the French, Germans, and British. While it is apparent that the armies and navies of these three Western nations were not always chivalrous in battle, they indoctrinated their Japanese pupils with the ideal of humane warfare, deploring the exceptions to the ideal that sometimes led to barbarity. It is true that Japan was determined to impress Western observers by her "civilized" conduct in order to take a place among them as a great power worthy of respect— and of bank loans—but those cynical considerations seemingly had little influence on the conduct of Japanese officers.[51] Japanese officers earlier in this century held themselves, and their men, to a high standard of chivalry because anything less would be unworthy of them.

Their chivalrous behavior was not solely a product of Western values and practices, or of a desire to impress Westerners, it was also related to Japan's code of Bushido (the "way of the warrior"). The chivalrous ideals that underlay Bushido can be traced to early Chinese philosophy, especially Zen Buddhism, which came to Japan from China in the late twelfth and thirteenth centuries, but the name itself was not used before the seventeenth century, during the period of Tokugawa isolation. It was then, in peacetime, that samurai attempted to refine their code as warriors.[52] The military virtues it espoused were not unlike those that guided the knights errant of Christendom. In addition to ennobling samurai loyalty to their lord and courage in battle, this refined code of Bushido valued aesthetic achievements, especially in poetry and literature, called for compassion for the weak, including wounded enemies, and allowed for honorable surrender. The failure to follow these precepts dishonored a samurai, leading to an unbearable sensation of shame.[53] It is this code that animated

Japanese warriors until some time after World War I. The "Imperial Precepts to Soldiers and Sailors," issued in 1882, exhorted them to exhibit valor, loyalty, righteousness, simplicity, respect for superiors, and consideration for inferiors.[54]

The evolution of the concept Bushido is inordinately complex, but some of its stages are clear. Before the Tokugawa era of seclusion, warfare was the province of samurai, and these men were devoted to the arts of war, from swordsmanship and the most ingenious use of armor to the use of any ruse or deception that could lead to victory. Clan warfare was constant with chivalry; loyalty and even courage were often sacrificed to expediency.[55] During the relatively peaceful Tokugawa period, samurai reflected on the way of the warrior and became increasingly self-conscious about a warrior's ideal code of behavior. Bravery was thought essential, and an honorable death became idealized as a means by which a man's spirit could become a god, eternally to protect his family or clan. Suicide emerged as an honorable way to die, but the Japanese insisted that suicide—by disembowelment—be painful. Loyalty and integrity were stressed as well.[56] A somewhat idealized version of this code, originally published in English, became a best-seller in the West. President Roosevelt personally purchased sixty copies.[57]

It is not correct to say, as some scholars have done, that the way of the samurai warrior did not stress compassion and kindness until the Meiji restoration in 1868.[58] The "Regulations" for samurai warriors, written by a famous general in 1412, proscribed the wanton taking of a life and called for humane, courteous, and kind behavior. These writings were required reading in the Japanese military until the 1930s.[59] After the Meiji restoration, the code of Bushido increasingly stressed the knightly virtues of compassion, kindness, and consideration for one's enemies. By this time, the samurai made up only 5 percent of the population, but their code—Bushido—became the ideal for all military men, no matter their class. During the early years of the twentieth century, Japanese officers, soldiers, and sailors consciously referred to this code to guide their behavior in warfare. As we have seen, when they found themselves unable to measure up, their sense of shame could be acute.

By the 1930s, all of that had changed. The military reforms of that time not only stressed brutal discipline in Japan's armed forces; it increasingly emphasized hatred of the enemy. The code of Bushido changed as well.

Loyalty now belonged to the emperor alone and was unquestioned. No longer could surrender be an option for a Japanese soldier or sailor, and enemies who chose surrender were beneath contempt. Compassion for wounded enemies was discouraged, even forbidden. Death was now likened to the fall of cherry blossoms, as beautiful as it was inevitable. Victory would no longer be sought within honorable rules of war but by any means, no matter how bestial or deceitful. As a result, the white flag of surrender, which had hitherto been honored by Japanese forces, could now be used to lure enemies into the open where they could be killed. Corpses would be booby-trapped to kill enemy burial parties. Wounded men would use hidden hand grenades to kill those who attempted to help them. And all of the atrocities that Japanese forces inflicted on military prisoners or civilians would now be justified under Bushido's new insistence on victory by any means.

War-crimes tribunals after the Japanese surrender regularly condemned this new code of Bushido and the practices it legitimized, and they were right to do so. Many Japanese military men in China and World War II dishonored themselves by any standard. That we can understand the circumstances that brought about these wartime atrocities makes them no less appalling. But perhaps all of us, especially the Japanese, can find solace by remembering that the fathers and grandfathers of those men who behaved so atrociously themselves fought in terrible wars with bravery and compassion that earned them the respect of the world. What those hundreds of thousands of Japanese did at the start of this century not only brings honor to them, it should bring a new way of thinking about Japan to people around the world as they prepare to close that century and enter one in which Japan's military is once again likely to play a crucial role.

EPILOGUE

A fter her defeat in World War II, Japan adopted a constitution renouncing recourse to war as her sovereign right and pledging not to maintain sea, land, or air forces. The new democracy of Japan would be defended, if the need arose, by the might of her conqueror, the United States. Some Japanese were humiliated by this American-imposed constitution, but many others were so weary of war that they gladly accepted pacification. Her economy shattered, her military gone, Japan watched warily as the Soviet Union tested her own nuclear weapons, while the tension that had existed between the West and the

Soviet Union even before World War II ended became the ever-dangerous Cold War. The outbreak of the Korean War in 1950 brought that danger very close to Japan, but it also rejuvenated Japan's shattered economy as the U.S. Army, Navy, Marines, and Air Force returned to the Far East in large numbers with a huge appetite for labor and supplies.

The Korean War instantly demonstrated that America's insistence on Japan's demilitarization was elastic. MacArthur not only ordered Japan to form a police reserve force, the precursor to its Self-Defense Force (SDF) of later years; he also asked the Japanese to use their surviving small naval and coast guard vessels to sweep mines off the Korean coast, an assignment carried out surreptitiously throughout the war. By 1952, Japan's defense forces had expanded to 110,000 men, and the Americans provided them with tanks, artillery, frigates, landing ships, and light aircraft. In the following year, the United States asked the Japanese to increase their land forces to 325,000 men; their navy would add eighteen destroyers and their air force expand to 800 war planes served by 30,000 men.[1] After much negotiation between the Americans, who wanted Japan to shoulder a larger share of the cost of her own defense, and the Japanese, who were reluctant to do so, a compromise was reached. It set Japan's ground SDF at 150,000 men, her maritime SDF at 15,808 and her air SDF at 6,287.[2]

In 1953, a new Defense Academy was founded. Unlike the academies of the former Imperial Army and Navy, which emphasized spiritual power, surprise, and hand-to-hand combat, this academy's four-year curriculum would emphasize science and technology. The school set itself the task of training "civic-minded gentlemen," not military men "of the old type." Its graduates were not required to serve in the SDF, and many have chosen not to do so. When the first class of 400 entered the academy, its members were told that they would be given a "firm understanding of the democratic system" and be trained as "balanced human beings."[3] The demand for absolute loyalty that had dominated the Imperial Army and Navy was abolished. Because graduates could choose to join the army, navy, or air branches of the SDF, the academy also eliminated much of the competition that had driven the Imperial Army and Navy on so many adventures. Japan's new ethic of pacifism was not only a product of its new constitution, it was inculcated into its new officers from the very beginning.

The U.S.-Japan Security Treaty gave Japan a nuclear shield at very low cost to her, but it also created the perception that the SDF was little more than an American pawn in the Cold War. In 1970, when Prime Minister Nakasone attempted to make the SDF more autonomous under the treaty, loud protests arose within Japan, and both China and North Korea accused the Japanese of a revival of militarism. The proposal was shelved, but the so-called Nixon shock of 1971 forced Japan to reassess the role of her armed forces. Nixon's recognition of China without consulting Japan left her feeling vulnerable. Later that same year, Nixon announced that he would defend the dollar by halting the conversion of dollars for gold. Again, the Japanese government was shocked. The oil crisis of 1973 plunged the oil-dependent Japanese economy into crisis and convinced the government that Japan's vulnerability meant that the SDF would have to be augmented. The navy, in particular, would have to be strengthened to protect oil tankers. Later, when the Soviet Union invaded Afghanistan and moved additional air power along with a powerful aircraft carrier to the Far East, Japan's military leaders called not only for still more defensive strength but for an offensive capability as well. The Reagan years of military confrontation with the Soviet "evil empire" encouraged further Japanese rearmament, and defense spending rose again.

With the end of the Cold War and the dismantling of the Soviet Union, the United States and other Western nations began to reduce their military spending, but Japan's military expansion accelerated. Like the Pentagon, Japan's Defense Agency preaches military preparedness as a virtue in itself, but even the sternest critics of Japan's defense buildup could not deny that Japan now faces chilling threats in the Far East. The greatest danger may come from China.

The performance of high-technology British, French, and U.S. weaponry in the Gulf War shocked China's complacent military leaders into launching a vast program of modernization. In 1993, the International Monetary Fund declared that China had the third-largest gross national product in the world.[4] Since 1988, China has spent a larger percentage of her GNP on weapons procurement than any other nation, raising her military budget by 75 percent, after adjustment for inflation, over the last seven years.[5] In 1995, China's military budget rose to a whopping 6 percent, half again as much as the United States's 4 percent military budget and more than six times as much as Japan's of less than 1 percent. With this money, China purchased large numbers of the most modern aircraft and surface-to-air missiles in Russia's arsenal.[6] China's 3-million-man People's Liberation Army is being reequipped with the most advanced weapons, including Russia's newest tanks, while her navy is being greatly expanded and modernized for long-range operations that may include the use of an aircraft carrier.[7]

A recent classified book called *Can China's Armed Forces Win the Next War?*—apparently written by Chinese admirals—emphasizes the need to avoid direct military conflict with the United States for the foreseeable future but points to numerous trouble spots where China may soon use her military power effectively.[8] The most immediate target may be the oil-rich South China Sea, which China claims as her own.[9] Japan accepted China's claim to these islands in 1993 in return for fishing rights, but Brunei, Vietnam, Indonesia, Taiwan, Malaysia, and the Philippines all dispute China's sovereignty and all but Brunei maintain small military forces on some of the Spratlys, just as China does.[10] The book argues that China must seize the islands of the South China Sea by the year 2000 before the area is internationalized.[11] This threat is being taken very seriously by the Southeast Asian nations, which are rearming at a rapid pace.[12]

In 1995, a Chinese government publication, *Military Secrets*, added fuel to the fire by writing, "It is a top priority for China to have air support for the possible battle in the Spratly Islands."[13] This same book also points to Japan, South Korea, India, Taiwan, Russia, and Vietnam as nations that pose a threat to China's interests. In 1994, India's air chief marshal expressed his concern about China's military buildup this way: "On the one hand, the probability of an armed conflict with China has been reduced in the short term, but in the long term, by 2005, the threat from China will be of a different magnitude altogether."[14] India has reason for concern about China's growing military power, and so does the United States. It has been reported that when the U.S. Naval War College in 1995 carried out a computer simulation of a war against China in Asia in 2010, China was the victor. When the CIA conducted its own simulation of such a war in 2005, China won that as well.[15]

Russia also has concerns about possible Chinese expansion in Siberia, Mongolia, and Central Asia. One hot spot among many is the small republic of Kyrgyzstan, bordering Russia and China, and previously a part of the Soviet Union. Some 21 percent of its 4.5 million people are Russian, the remainder being Muslims with ties to China and hostility toward Russia. The country possesses enormous wealth. In addition to rich deposits of oil, gas, silver, zinc, tin, and mercury, Kyrgyzstan possesses the seventh-richest gold mine in the world.[16] Although it has been weakened, Russia still has great military strength, much of which is deployed in Siberia, which Russia has sworn to defend. And Sakhalin Island remains a bone of contention with Japan. Japan's century-long conflict with Russia has not yet ended.

The Korean Peninsula is another obvious danger zone. It is dangerous not only because North Korea's large, well-armed army and air forces are on the brink of attaining nuclear capability with a long-range, Rodong-I, ballistic missile delivery system.[17] A task force of the House Republican research committee concluded that the U.S.-brokered agreement to neutralize their nuclear potential actually increased their potential for nuclear brinkmanship because it helped solve their energy and food needs without effectively controlling their nuclear weapons.[18] To make matters worse, South Korea remains highly suspicious of Japanese intentions and both Koreas are embittered about Japan's past actions toward them. A recent novel that became an instant best-selling thriller in Korea has Japan invading South Korea, threatening her with annihilation. When the United States fails to meet her treaty obligations to South Korea, North Korea uses its nuclear might to defeat the Japanese.[19]

Trouble lurks to the south as well. Not only could conflict in the Spratly Islands involve several nations, including Japan, whose oil-supply sea-lanes would be threatened; a shooting war between China and Taiwan could have a similarly dangerous outcome. During the fall of 1995, after the Clinton administration granted a visa to Taiwan's president, Lee Teng-hui, despite China's protests, several American visitors to China were warned by high-ranking Chinese military officials that China might use force to recapture Taiwan. One former top Pentagon official was bluntly warned that China was willing to sacrifice millions of her people to reunite Taiwan and China. With the warning came the remark that the United States would not intervene because she would not be willing to sacrifice Los Angeles to save Taiwan, a clear reference to China's nuclear ICBMs.[20] In mid-December 1995, when China threatened Taiwan by conducting a series of military exercises and missile tests in and near the Taiwan Strait, the United States responded by sending the aircraft carrier *Nimitz* and several other warships through the strait in an obvious show of force. This war scare was averted, but the Chinese government rarely misses an opportunity to warn Taiwan, and the West, that any Taiwanese declaration of independence from China could lead to China's use of force.

Conflict in South Asia or the Middle East could bring about a wider war. To consider just one potential trouble spot among several, in April 1995, U.S. Assistant Secretary of State for Asian Affairs Robin Raphael warned that the dispute over Kashmir between India and Pakistan could lead to a ballistic missile race between the two adversaries, which have already fought three wars against each other and very nearly fought several others.[21] Pakistan can easily assemble nuclear weapons that can be delivered by her U.S.-built F-16 fighter-bombers, and it is generally thought that she has received M-11 medium-range missiles from China. India, too, has nuclear weapons that can be fired from highly mobile missile launchers mounted on trucks. India's aging Soviet-built air force, now being fitted with the latest radar systems and most sophisticated missiles, can carry nuclear weapons as well. India also has one of the world's strongest navies.On Friday, January 26, 1996, a missile struck a crowd gathered outside a mosque in Kashmir, killing over twenty people and wounding another twenty-five. Pakistan accused India of firing the missile. In response, India blamed Pakistan for the rocket and the next day conducted the fifteenth test of her new nuclear-capable, medium-range rocket.[22]

Japanese leaders well realize the potential dangers that face Japan in the Far East, just as they are concerned about the potential loss of Middle Eastern oil supplies, should war break out again in that tormented region. Although Japan's Self-Defense Force is still small compared with that of her potential adversaries, she now has more tanks than Great Britain and her new Model 90 Tank is a match for any in the world. Japan has the world's best coastal defense navy, and her Aegis destroyers permit her to convoy supply ships 1,000 miles beyond Japan. Her ships have the most modern radar and ship-to-ship missile systems. She also has sixteen submarines, more Patriot missiles than Israel, more high-quality jet fighters than any other country except the United States, and superb defensive weapons systems. The government has spent over $30 billion in the development of the FSX, the next generation of fighter aircraft being produced jointly by Mitsubishi Heavy Industries and General Dynamics.[23] Money has been budgeted for an aircraft carrier as well. And even though the Japanese people continue to express strong reservations about developing an independent nuclear deterrent, Japan could easily utilize plutonium 239 from its thirty-seven nuclear power plants to produce such weapons, a possibility that greatly concerns her neighbors, who fear Japanese rearmament. Japan's domestically produced H-2 rocket, which launched a two-ton satellite in 1993, could readily be converted for use as an intercontinental ballistic missile. It is a point of no small significance that in 1994 Japan was the only Western nation without a plan to reduce the size of her military. Instead of military reductions, Japan's military budget for that year rose to become the second largest in the world, behind only that of the United States.[24] Japan's military budget in 1995 was again the second-largest in the world.

In 1992, Japan sent over 1,200 armed engineers to Cambodia as part of the United Nation's peacekeeping mission, the first armed Japanese troops to serve outside Japan since 1945. It is certain that Japan will be asked to serve in other UN missions in the future. In a part of the world so heavily armed and so politically unstable as the Far East, Japan's armed forces may well find themselves involved in a regional conflict, perhaps a very deadly one. If Japan's military power continues to grow and if she develops a nuclear deterrent, it is quite possible that she will reasonably soon replace the United States as the guarantor of peace in that part of the world.

During the first half of this century, Japan's military forces won stupendous victories before suffering devastating defeat in World War II. It may not be merely an oddment of history that when they won those great victories, their chivalry earned them the respect of the world and that when they were defeated, their barbarism led to the world's contempt. Perhaps this knowledge will guide Japan's military leaders as they prepare to confront the challenges that face them in the next century.

NOTES

INTRODUCTION

1. Braddon 1983.
2. Ibid.; Russell 1958. Both Braddon and Russell have been criticized for taking a one-sided view of World War II atrocities.
3. Russell 1958.
4. Harris 1994; *Los Angeles Times*, March 20, 1995. In return for classified documents regarding biological warfare, the U.S. government is reported to have granted the Japanese camp commander and his staff immunity from prosecution.
5. Ienaga 1978, 189.

6. Harries and Harries 1991.

7. Russell 1958.

8. Cook and Cook 1992, 155.

9. Russell 1958.

10. Ibid.

11. Ibid., 224.

12. Ibid.

13. Ibid.

14. Ibid., 240.

15. Ibid., 242–43.

16. Ibid., 259.

17. Dower 1986, 53.

18. Ibid., 33.

19. Seaman 1905, 71.

20. *Illustrated London News*, January 5, 1905.

21. Randall 1985.

CHAPTER 1: THE CRUCIBLE OF CONFLICT—NORTHEAST ASIA

1. Ballard 1921.

2. Perrin 1965.

3. Turnbull 1977, 198; Berry 1989.

4. Turnbull 1977, 199.

5. Hsu 1995.

6. Turnbull 1977, 228.

7. Buruma 1995, 26.

8. Sansom 1962; Calman 1992.

9. Hsu 1995.

10. Ibid., 217.

11. Holt 1964, 67.

12. Waley 1958, 170.

13. Ibid., 109.

14. Hsu 1995, 237.

15. Ibid., 240; Holt 1964, 79.

16. Montgomery 1989, 21.

17. Holt 1964, 71.

18. Hsu 1995, 262.

19. Holt 1964, 245.

20. Ibid.

21. Wolseley 1903, 2:27.

22. Rennie 1863.

23. Ibid.

24. Ibid.

25. Ibid., 184.

26. Swinhoe 1861, 95–96.

27. Lehmann 1964, 96.

28. Rennie 1863, 126–27.

29. Swinhoe 1861, 114.

30. Wolseley 1972, 139.

31. Allgood 1901, 48.

32. Swinhoe 1861, 119.

33. Wolseley 1972, 180–81.

34. Swinhoe 1861, 261.

35. Lehmann 1964, 107.

36. Knollys 1875, 202.

37. Hsu 1995, 264.

38. Warner and Warner 1974, 115.

39. Hsu 1995.

40. Perrin 1965.

41. Wheeler 1946, 69.

42. Hackett 1971.

43. Perry 1968.

44. Ibid., 192.

45. Montgomery 1989, 30.

46. Palmer 1932, 211; Jansen 1995.

47. Hane 1982; Jansen 1995.

48. Harries and Harries 1991, 9.

49. Hane 1982, 150–51.

50. Harries and Harries 1991, 33.

51. Hane 1982.

52. Harries and Harries 1991, 57–58.

53. Falk 1936.

54. Montgomery 1987; Jansen 1975.

55. Hsu 1995.

56. Christie 1914, 93.

57. Barry 1905, 209; Allan 1898.

58. Warner and Warner 1974, 6.

59. Wright 1961, 100.

60. Weale 1904, 307–8. Red Cross observers with the Japanese army agreed (Harries and Harries 1991).

61. Lone 1994.

62. Hsu 1995; Jansen 1975.

63. Okamoto 1970, 48; Jansen 1995.

64. Montgomery 1987, 151.

65. Okamoto 1970, 49.

66. Quested 1982, 28.

67. Warner and Warner 1974, 105.

68. There are many romanized versions of the names of these bandits, each with strong support for authenticity. I have chosen this version because it was the most common spelling in use around the turn of the century.

69. Mutsu 1982.

70. Quested 1982, 27.

71. White 1964; Quested 1982.

72. Quested 1982, 109.

73. Lensen 1967.

74. Kushakov 1902.

75. Lensen 1967, 49.

76. Ibid., 40.

77. McCully 1977, 222; Lensen 1967, 69.

78. Lensen 1967, 101.

79. Ibid., 103.

80. Witte 1921, 114.

81. Lensen 1967, 120.

82. Kushakov 1902.

CHAPTER 2: THE BOXER REBELLION

1. For a review of this new evidence, see Seagrave 1992.

2. Ibid., 190.

3. Rasmussen 1925, 50.

4. Seagrave 1992.

5. Ibid.

6. Keown-Boyd 1991, 27.

7. Seagrave 1992, 288.

8. Keown-Boyd 1991, 43.

9. Ibid., 90.

10. Hoover 1951–52.

11. The Japanese did not have a marine corps in the American sense; their so-called marines were sailors who had received some training as infantrymen (Hayashi and Coox 1958).

12. Keown-Boyd 1991, 57.

13. Hooker 1987, 14.

14. Giles 1970.

15. Keown-Boyd 1991, 66.

16. Ibid., 80.

17. Brown 1902, 31.

18. Keown-Boyd 1991, 95.

19. Hoover 1951–52, 52.

20. Butler 1933.

21. Rasmussen 1925, 156.

22. Butler 1992, 47.

23. Keown-Boyd 1991, 98.

24. Ibid., 127.

25. O'Connor 1973, 157.

26. Palmer 1932, 185.

27. Keown-Boyd 1991.

28. Palmer 1932; Landor 1901.

29. Palmer 1932, 178.

30. Nish 1966, 88.

31. Keown-Boyd 1991, 143.

32. Seagrave 1992, 336.

33. Hooker 1987, 95.

34. Weale 1907, 126.

35. Hooker 1987, 162.

36. Ibid.

37. Seagrave 1992.

38. Giles 1970, 130.

39. Ibid., 127.

40. Hooker 1987, 96.

41. Seagrave 1992, 338. This acceptance of the Chinese was due to the compassionate leadership of Colonel Shiba. Most Japanese continued to detest the Chinese.

42. Weale 1910, 44–45.

43. Giles 1970, 148.

44. Seagrave 1992, 396–97.

45. Palmer 1932, 174.

46. Keown-Boyd 1991, 157.

47. Butler 1933, 67.

48. Steel 1985, 22.

49. Ibid., 17; Brown 1902, 85.

50. Palmer 1932, 196; Lynch 1901.

51. Butler 1933, 70.

52. Palmer 1932, 200.

53. Brown 1902.

54. Palmer 1932, 200; Lynch 1901.

55. *Illustrated London News*, December 29, 1900.

56. Palmer 1932, 201.

57. Steel 1985, 79.

58. Ibid., 21.

59. Keown-Boyd 1991, 167.

60. Seagrave 1992.

61. Hooker 1987.

62. Seagrave 1992, 363.

63. Palmer 1932, 201.

64. Esherick 1987, 297.

65. Ibid.

66. Seagrave 1992, 363.

67. Fleming 1959, 229.

68. O'Connor 1973, 292.

69. Keown-Boyd 1991; 207.

70. Waldersee 1924, 238.

71. Ibid.

72. Keown-Boyd 1991, 207.

73. Steel 1985, 54.

74. Dillon 1901, see Lensen.

75. Seagrave 1992, 365; Esherick 1987.

76. Brown 1902, 526–27.

77. Lynch 1901.

78. Nish 1966, 89; Jansen 1975.

79. Hsu 1995, 481.

80. White 1964, 21.

81. Montgomery 1989, 183. See also Jansen 1975.

82. Nish 1966, 275.

83. White 1964, 112.

84. Ibid., 121.

85. Nish 1966, 285.

86. Okamoto 1970.

CHAPTER 3: "AND WHERE MAY JAPAN HAPPEN TO BE?"

1. Palmer 1932, 136.
2. Ignatyev 1944, 119.
3. Rodzianko n.d., 99.
4. Custine 1989.
5. Ignatyev 1944; Rodzianko n.d.
6. Bushnell 1985, 16.
7. Veresaev 1917, 159.
8. McCormick 1909, 2:278.
9. Rodzianko n.d.
10. Baring 1905, 148.
11. Veresaev 1917, 268.
12. Seaman 1905, 71.
13. Rodzianko n.d., 87.
14. Taburno 1905, 103.
15. Reichman 1906, 245.
16. Quested 1982, 69; Baring 1905.
17. Palmer 1904, 135–36.
18. Scidmore 1907, 37.
19. Baring 1905; Brooke 1905; Hamilton 1906; Waters 1906.
20. Soloviev 1906, 37.
21. Hamilton 1906.
22. Waters 1907, 3:112.
23. Hamilton 1906, 325; Soloviev 1906.
24. McCullagh 1906, 168.
25. Hamilton 1906, 331.
26. Kuropatkin 1909, 2:271.
27. Schuyler 1906–07, 153–55.
28. Harvard 1906, 24–25.
29. Ibid., 51–53.
30. *Cassell's* 1905, 3:263.
31. March 1906–7, 54–60.
32. Veresaev 1917.
33. Baring 1905, 128.
34. Kuropatkin 1909, 1:281.
35. Ignatyev 1944, 229.
36. Falk 1936, 5.
37. Noel 1937.
38. White 1964.

39. Kuropatkin 1909, 2:217.

40. Hearn 1959, 25; Iritani 1991.

41. Palmer 1932, 128.

42. Ashmead-Bartlett 1906.

43. Palmer 1904, 115.

44. Hamilton 1906, 16.

45. Ibid., 277, 312, 354.

46. March 1906–7, 53.

47. McCormick 1909, 2:326.

48. Seaman 1905.

49. Hamilton 1906, 8–9.

50. Brindle 1905, 9.

51. Hamilton 1906, 315.

52. Quested 1982, 111.

53. McCullagh 1906, 22.

54. Weale 1904.

55. Nojine 1908.

56. Brindle 1905; McCullagh 1906, 22.

57. Warner and Warner 1974, 261; Klado 1905.

58. Semenoff 1913, 19–20.

59. Greener 1905, 51.

60. McCormick 1909, 1:35.

61. Greener 1905, 82.

62. Ibid., 98.

63. *Illustrated London News*, April 2, 1904, 501.

64. Ibid., April 9, 1904, 531.

65. McKenzie 1905, 27; Warner and Warner 1974, 91.

66. Connaughton 1988, 24.

67. McKenzie 1905, 55.

68. *Illustrated London News*, April 2, 1904, 485; Checkland 1994.

69. Tyler 1905, 302.

70. *Cassell's* 1905, 4:339. This report has not been verified by other sources.

71. Hargreaves 1962, 19.

72. Weale 1904, 371–72.

73. Ignatyev 1944, 169.

74. Veresaev 1917.

75. *Illustrated London News*, April 16, 1904, 567.

76. McCully 1977, 14; Semenoff 1913, 5.

77. Connaughton 1988; Warner and Warner 1974; Hamilton 1906.

78. Sakurai 1912, 7ff., 23ff.
79. Tyler 1905, 175.
80. Palmer 1904, 163.
81. Cordonnier 1912, 119.
82. Palmer 1904, 316–17.
83. *Illustrated London News*, October 8, 1904, 507.
84. Warner and Warner 1974, 287.
85. Ignatyev 1944.
86. Seaman 1905, 11.
87. Warner and Warner 1974.
88. Palmer 1904.
89. Brindle 1905.
90. Waters 1905, 128.
91. Brindle 1905, 117–18.
92. Ibid., 8.
93. Lynch 1901.
94. Warner and Warner 1974, 254.
95. Woodward 1965, 130.
96. Scidmore 1907, 218.
97. Warner and Warner 1974, 262–63.
98. Sakurai 1912, 57.
99. Nojine 1908, 122.
100. Connaughton 1988, 77.
101. Hargreaves 1962, 83.
102. Nojine 1908.
103. Hamilton 1906, 127.
104. Ibid., 128.
105. Brooke 1905, 35.
106. Ignatyev 1944, 196.
107. Brooke 1905, 232.
108. Palmer 1932, 249.
109. McKenzie 1905, 153–54.
110. Scidmore 1907, 124.
111. Palmer 1904, 97.
112. Soloviev 1906, 28.
113. Ibid.
114. Hamilton 1906, 198.
115. Ibid., 6.

116. Veresaev 1917, 47; *Cassell's* 1905, 5:535.
117. Wincelberg 1976, 167.

CHAPTER 4: "BRUTE FORCE, ANGUISH, AND HUMILIATION"
1. Steer 1913, 72.
2. Warner and Warner 1974, 370.
3. Sakurai 1912, 148.
4. Warner and Warner 1974, 374.
5. Sakurai 1912, 143.
6. Ibid.
7. Ashmead-Bartlett 1906.
8. Hargreaves 1962, 99.
9. Ibid., 75.
10. Baring 1905, 143.
11. Soloviev 1906, 45.
12. McCully 1977, 38.
13. *Cassell's* 1905, 3:257.
14. Soloviev 1906, 43.
15. Taburno 1905; Veresaev 1917, 61.
16. Warner and Warner 1974, 383.
17. *Cassell's* 1905, 4:350.
18. Taburno 1905.
19. Ibid., 105.
20. Veresaev 1917, 303.
21. Warner and Warner 1974, 416.
22. Veresaev 1917, 303.
23. Ignatyev 1944.
24. Kuropatkin 1909, 2:227.
25. Hamilton 1906, 16.
26. Palmer 1932, 244–45.
27. Villiers 1905.
28. Brooke 1905, 40.
29. Ignatyev 1944, 168.
30. Brooke 1905, 96.
31. Taburno 1905, 121.
32. Sakurai 1912, 126–27.
33. Brooke 1905, 107.
34. Connaughton 1988, 145.

35. Baring 1905, 132.
36. Ignatyev 1944, 220.
37. Brooke 1905, 219.
38. Ignatyev 1944, 226.
39. Soloviev 1906, 48.
40. Ignatyev 1944, 240; *Illustrated London News*, September 24, 1904, 438.
41. Soloviev 1906, 42.
42. Brooke 1905, 167.
43. Wincelberg 1976, 147.
44. Ignatyev 1944.
45. Hamilton 1905, 285.
46. Ibid., 147.
47. Christie 1914, 105.
48. Ashmead-Bartlett 1906, 194.
49. Ibid., 296.
50. *Cassell's* 1905, 4:458.
51. Steer 1913.
52. Warner and Warner 1974, 461.
53. Sakurai 1912, 160.
54. *Cassell's* 1905, 4:391–92.
55. Villiers 1905, 43–44, 143–44.
56. Seaman 1905, 93.
57. Taburno 1905, 158.
58. Ashmead-Bartlett 1906, 295.
59. Barry 1905, 312.
60. Ibid.
61. Warner and Warner 1974, 466.
62. Tretyakov 1911, 264.
63. Ashmead-Bartlett 1906, 329.
64. *Cassell's* 1905, 4:447.
65. Wheeler and Rives 1965.
66. Wood 1905, 209.
67. *Cassell's* 1905, 4:442.
68. Warner and Warner 1974, 476.
69. *Nation* 78 (1904): 229.
70. Harvard 1906, 258.
71. James 1905, 275.
72. Ibid., 281.
73. Ashmead-Bartlett 1906, 407.

74. Ibid., 419–20.
75. McCullagh 1906, 95.
76. Ignatyev 1944, 243.
77. Connaughton 1988, 208.
78. Waters 1906.
79. Brooke 1905, 254.
80. Ignatyev 1944, 242.
81. Menning 1992, 152.
82. Akashi 1988.
83. Palmer 1904, 57.
84. Hamilton 1906, 252–53.
85. Ibid., 242.
86. Baring 1905, 169.
87. Ibid., 176–77; McCullagh 1906, 114.
88. Taburno 1905, 33.
89. Ibid., 59.
90. McCormick 1909, 2:327, 1:335.
91. *Cassell's* 1905, 4:359–60.
92. Ibid.
93. Ignatyev 1944, 240.
94. Veresaev 1917.
95. McCullagh 1906, 246–48.
96. Ibid., 259.
97. Ignatyev 1944, 261.

CHAPTER 5: "YOU CAN KEEP TOKYO FOR YOURSELF"

1. White 1964, 179.
2. Westwood 1986, 66.
3. Esthus 1988, 4.
4. Jane 1904, 519.
5. Westwood 1986, 151.
6. Klado 1906.
7. Westwood 1986. The name of this ship is often spelled *Orel* in English, but this transliteration is inaccurate.
8. *Cassell's* 1905, 3:286.
9. Hough 1958, 58.
10. White 1964, 181.
11. Semenoff 1909, 304.
12. Westwood 1986.

13. Semenoff 1909, 325.

14. Hough 1958, 101.

15. Semenoff 1909, 363.

16. Westwood 1986, 140.

17. Ogasawara 1934.

18. Falk 1936, 18.

19. Westwood 1986, 227.

20. Warner and Warner 1974, 344.

21. Novikoff-Priboy 1937, 144.

22. Ibid., 401.

23. Ibid., 173.

24. Ibid., 219.

25. Ibid.

26. Ibid., 218.

27. Warner and Warner 1974, 548.

28. Novikoff-Priboy 1937, 370.

29. Warner and Warner 1974, 54.

30. Novikoff-Priboy 1937, 316.

31. Ibid., 369.

32. Busch 1969, 200.

33. Hough 1958, 190.

34. Westwood 1986.

35. Ibid., 282.

36. Warner and Warner 1974, 551.

37. Ibid., 555.

38. White 1964, 208.

39. Westwood 1986, 286.

40. McCullagh 1906, 332.

41. Seaman 1905, 68.

42. Scidmore 1907.

43. Ibid., 214.

44. *Illustrated London News*, December 3, 1904, 832.

45. Richardson 1905.

46. D'Anethan 1912, 388.

47. Ibid., 429.

48. *Illustrated London News*, March 18, 1905, 390.

49. Ibid., August 13, 1904, 227.

50. Seaman 1905, 62–63.

51. Ibid. 65.

52. Novikoff-Priboy 1937; Rodzianko n.d.

53. Novikoff-Priboy 1937, 396.

54. Semenoff 1913, 353.

55. Esthus 1988, 165.

56. Cordonnier 1912, 68.

57. Witte 1921, 135.

58. Randall 1985.

59. Witte 1921, 142.

60. Randall 1985, 49.

61. Witte 1921.

62. Ibid., 289.

63. Randall 1985, 87.

64. September 6, 1905.

65. Warner and Warner 1974, 573.

66. Ibid., 574.

67. Esthus 1988, 1.

68. Kokovtsov 1935, 60; Harcave 1964; Fuller 1985.

69. Warner and Warner 1974, 554.

70. Falk 1936, 457.

CHAPTER 6: "TO HELL WITH BABE RUTH"

1. Lo 1976, 287.

2. *Illustrated London News*, January 14, 1905, 42.

3. Kitahara 1989, 65.

4. Ibid., 58.

5. Ogasawara 1934, 433.

6. Ibid., 442–43.

7. Falk 1936.

8. Kitahara 1989, 66.

9. Wheeler 1946, 104.

10. Lea 1942.

11. Ibid.; Schiffrin 1968.

12. Storry 1957, 3.

13. Hane 1986; Montgomery 1989.

14. Montgomery 1989, 212.

15. Nish 1972, 135.

16. Burdick 1976, 239; Tarnstrom 1992.

17. Burdick 1976, 239.

18. Ibid., 111.

19. Ibid., 112, 239.
20. Ibid., 160; Harries and Harries 1991, 112.
21. Burdick 1976, 352.
22. Jones 1915, 111–13.
23. Ibid., 142.
24. Burdick 1976; 184.
25. Ibid., 190.
26. Jones 1915, 196.
27. Burdick 1976, 240.
28. Jones 1915, 119.
29. Burdick and Moessner 1984, 13.
30. Ibid., 48.
31. Ibid., 66.
32. Ibid., 99.
33. Ibid., 103.
34. Montgomery 1989, 232; Humphries 1995.
35. Harries and Harries 1991, 124.
36. Hopkirk 1984.
37. Morley 1957. A huge arms stockpile in Vladivostok disappeared about this time. It has been speculated that the Japanese received a good portion of it (Harries and Harries 1991, 124).
38. Storry 1957, 3; Kitahara 1989, 69; Peattie 1975, 5.
39. Hane 1982, 7.
40. Ibid., 44, 115.
41. Ibid., 118; Toland 1971, 68.
42. Hane 1982, 117.
43. Ibid.
44. Ienaga 1978, 5.
45. Kitahara 1989, 71.
46. Shigemitsu 1958, 29.
47. Ibid.
48. Wheeler 1946, 192.
49. Humphries 1995; Coox 1964, 39.
50. Storry 1957, 24, 43.
51. Ienaga 1978; Jansen 1975, 337.
52. Wheeler 1946, 210.
53. Drea 1981.
54. Ibid.
55. Ibid., 46.

56. Ibid., 78.
57. Coox 1985, 915.
58. Drea 1981.
59. Coox 1985.
60. Russell 1958, 234–35.
61. Coox 1985, 951.
62. Harries and Harries 1991, 161.
63. Coox 1964.
64. Hayashi and Coox 1958, 196.
65. *Life Goes to War* 1977. For a discussion of the opium trade, see Harries and Harries 1991, 244.
66. Shigemitsu 1958, 45.
67. Ienaga 1978, 186.
68. Coox 1964, 96.
69. Wilson 1982.
70. Ibid.
71. Lin 1995, 10; for other graphic accounts see Iritani 1991.
72. Timperley 1938, 152.
73. Coox 1964; 76. See also Humphries 1995, 216.
74. Hayashi and Coox 1958, viii.
75. Ibid., viii.
76. *Los Angeles Times*, July 7, 1994.
77. Ienaga 1978; Wilson 1982; Cook and Cook 1992.
78. Ienaga 1978, 167.
79. Cook and Cook 1992, 43.
80. Ibid., 151.
81. Harries and Harries 1991, 235.
82. Ibid., 261.
83. Ibid., 320.
84. Coox 1964.

CHAPTER 7: "REMEMBER PEARL HARBOR"

1. Rusbridger and Nave 1992.
2. Iritani 1991, 94. Bergamini's argument that the emperor championed the war and micro-managed it is not accepted by most historians (Bergamini 1991).
3. Toland 1970, 133.
4. Ibid., 140–41.
5. Ibid., 145; Costello 1981, 116.

6. Agawa 1979, 228–29.
7. Ibid., 173.
8. Harries and Harries 1991, 298; Cook and Cook 1992, 83.
9. Agawa 1979, 130.
10. Ibid., 254.
11. Prange 1982, 275.
12. Agawa 1979, 265.
13. Prange 1990.
14. Schultz 1979.
15. Ibid., 173; Cressman 1995.
16. Costello 1981, 146.
17. Dower 1986, 44.
18. Costello 1981, 178, 216.
19. Russell 1958, 98.
20. Tsuji 1961, 65–66.
21. Ibid.
22. Zich 1977, 123.
23. Tsuji 1961, 35.
24. Ibid.
25. Hall 1983, 101–2.
26. Russell 1958, 96.
27. Ibid., 171–72.
28. Hall 1983; Reel 1949.
29. Toland 1970, 260.
30. Ibid., 300.
31. Ibid., 296.
32. Harries and Harries 1991, 338.
33. Toland 1970, 318.
34. Harries and Harries 1991, 334.
35. Van der Vat 1991.
36. Dower 1986, 296.
37. Costello 1981, 216.
38. Russell 1958, 209; Haney 1991.
39. Dower 1986, 296.
40. Toland 1970, 305.
41. Costello 1981, 235.
42. Ibid., 235.
43. Toland 1970, 305.
44. Ibid., 309.

45. Van der Vat 1991, 27.

46. Prange 1990, 64.

47. Costello 1981, 243.

48. Ibid., 244.

49. Ibid., 397; La Forte and Marcello 1993.

50. Costello 1981, 267.

CHAPTER 8: "NOT NECESSARILY TO OUR ADVANTAGE"

1. Agawa 1979.

2. Prange 1990.

3. Ibid.; Costello 1981, 296.

4. Costello 1981, 302.

5. Ibid., 376.

6. Frank 1990, 130–31.

7. Dower 1986, 92.

8. Van der Vat 1991, 219; see British reference WO 208/4605 PW JA 100037, p. 37.

9. Lindbergh 1970, 902.

10. Kristoff 1995, A1.

11. Williams and Wallace 1989, 32.

12. Ibid., 44; Harris 1994.

13. Williams and Wallace 1989; Harris 1994.

14. Costello 1981, 330.

15. Toland 1970, 399; Frank 1990.

16. Toland 1970, 404.

17. Costello 1981, 359; Frank 1990.

18. Toland 1970, 392.

19. Harries and Harries 1991, 400; Frank 1990.

20. Costello 1981, 420.

21. Agawa 1979, 310.

22. Hoyt 1990.

23. Warner and Warner 1982, 36.

24. Dower 1986, 69.

25. Lindbergh 1970, 882.

26. Ibid., 853.

27. Costello 1981, 405.

28. Ibid., 406.

29. Ibid., 431.

30. Ibid., 438.

31. Cook and Cook 1992, 289.

32. Ibid., 291; Costello 1981, 484.

33. Costello 1981, 483.

34. Ito 1967.

35. Costello 1981, 497.

36. Toland 1970, 546.

37. Costello 1981, 501.

38. Kamiko 1966.

39. Steinberg 1979, 151.

40. Iritani 1991, 292.

41. Costello 1981, 533.

42. Toland 1970, 598.

43. Ibid., 1970, 601.

44. Harries and Harries 1991, 409.

45. Hayashi and Coox 1958, 97.

46. Costello 1981, 522.

47. Toland 1970, 618.

48. Costello 1981, 547.

49. Toland 1970, 669.

50. Leckie 1995.

51. Ibid., 76.

52. Toland 1970, 665.

53. Inoguchi et al. 1958, 187; Naito 1989.

54. Leckie 1995, 202.

55. Cook and Cook 1992, 367.

56. Ibid., 360.

57. Ibid., 362.

58. Leckie 1995, 205.

59. Toland 1970, 744.

60. Harries and Harries 1991, 446.

61. Ibid., 445–46.

62. Toland 1970, 756.

63. Ibid., 771.

64. Ibid., 790.

65. Ibid., 805.

66. Costello 1981, 593.

67. Ibid., 596.

68. Ibid., 597; Dower 1986, 300.

69. Onoda 1974.

70. CNN, May 26, 1996.

71. Hayashi and Coox 1958, 175; Cook and Cook 1992.

72. Harries and Harries 1991, 459.

73. Aida 1962.

74. Van der Post 1995.

75. Peattie 1975.

76. Toland 1970, 915.

CHAPTER 9: FROM CHIVALRY TO BRUTALITY

1. Peattie 1975. For an instructive perspective on Japanese views of their inferiority see Aida 1962.

2. Kitahara 1989, 45; Tanaka 1993, 187; Ikegami 1995, 321; Giffard 1994.

3. Ienaga 1978, 7; Mitchell 1976.

4. Kitahara 1989, 76; Iritani 1991.

5. Robertson 1995.

6. Hearn 1959.

7. Tsurumi 1970.

8. Cook and Cook 1992.

9. Ienaga 1978, 17.

10. Ibid., 262.

11. Ibid., 29; Tsurumi 1970; Iritani 1991.

12. Ienaga 1978, 53; Cook and Cook 1992; Aida 1962; Hane 1982, 60; Iritani 1991, 191–92.

13. Quoted in Ikegami 1995, 281.

14. Checkland 1994, 122.

15. Tsurumi 1970, 117.

16. Hane 1982, 32.

17. Tsurumi 1970, 119, 126.

18. Ienaga 1978, 136.

19. Dower 1986, 61.

20. Ibid., 58; Iritani 1991, 264.

21. Shigemitsu 1958.

22. Cook and Cook 1992, 51.

23. Harries and Harries 1991, 242.

24. Cook and Cook 1992, 149; Manchester 1979.

25. Harries and Harries 1991, 320–21; Hanayama 1950.

26. Lindbergh 1970, 880.

27. Vu 1984.

28. Cook and Cook 1992, 272

29. For examples, see Dower 1986; Ienaga 1978; Harries and Harries 1991; Cook and Cook 1992.

30. Howard, Andreopoulos and Shulman 1994; Keeley 1996.

31. Justice Joseph B. Keenan, quoted in Pritchard and Zaide 1981, 1:390.

32. Dower 1986, 38.

33. Costello 1981, 105.

34. LeMay and Kantor 1965, 387.

35. Ibid., 10.

36. Dower 1986, 41.

37. Ienaga 1978; Blackette 1949; Alperovitz, et al. 1995.

38. Holmes 1986, 392.

39. Jane 1904, 586–87.

40. Sakurai 1912, 238.

41. Hamilton 1906, 9.

42. Sakurai 1912.

43. Brindle 1905.

44. Ibid., 108.

45. Sakurai 1912, 69.

46. McCullagh 1906, 375.

47. Linn 1989, 23, 145.

48. Edgerton 1995.

49. Bridgeman 1981, 103.

50. Pakenham 1991.

51. Palmer 1932, 237.

52. Friday 1994.

53. Tsurumi 1970; Ikegami 1995.

54. Hane 1982, 59.

55. Friday 1994.

56. Nitobe 1969; Cleary 1991.

57. Nitobe 1969; Harries and Harries 1991, 96.

58. Turnbull 1977.

59. Wilson 1982a; Sadler 1941.

EPILOGUE

1. Maeda 1995, 72; Perry 1980.

2. Maeda 1995, 76.

3. Ibid., 54.

4. *China Information*, February 1994, 5.

5. Kristof 1995a, 49.

6. *Aviation Week and Space Technology*, July 10, 1995, 30.

7. Ibid., April 17, 1995, 68; Farmer 1996.

8. Lin 1994.

9. *Aviation Week and Space Technology*, April 17, 1995; *Inside China Mainland*, June 1995, 29.

10. Hyer 1995, 45; *Asian Defense Journal*, June 1995, 70; Kristof 1995a, 51.

11. Munro 1994.

12. *Asian Defense Journal*, April 1994.

13. Hyer 1995, 34.

14. Bain 1994, 131.

15. Kristof 1995a, 50.

16. *Asian Defense Journal*, January 1995, 67.

17. *Aviation Week and Space Technology*, July 10, 1995, 30; Kihl 1994.

18. *Asian Defense Journal*, January 1995, 103.

19. Funabashi 1994.

20. *Los Angeles Times*, January 27, 1996.

21. *Asian Defense Journal*, April 1995, 87.

22. Ibid.

23. *Aviation Week and Space Technology*, May 1, 1995, 26.

24. *Los Angeles Times*, January 28, 1996; Simon 1993.

BIBLIOGRAPHY

Aida, Y. *Prisoner of the British: A Japanese Soldier's Experience in Burma*. London: Cresset, 1962.

Agawa, H. *The Reluctant Admiral: Yamamoto and the Imperial Navy* (trans. by J. Bester). Tokyo: Kodansha, 1979.

Akashi, M. *Rakka Ryusui: Colonel Akashi's Report on His Secret Cooperation with the Russian Revolutionary Parties During the Russo-Japanese War*. Helsinki: Finnish Historical Society, 1988.

Allan, J. *Under the Dragon Flag: My Experiences in the China-Japanese War*. London: W. M. Heinemann, 1898.

Allgood, G. *China War, 1860: Letters and Journal.* London: John Murray, 1901.

Alperowitz, G., et. al. *The Decision to Use the Atomic Bomb and the Architecture of an American Myth.* New York: Knopf, 1995.

Asakawa, K. *The Russo-Japanese Conflict: Its Causes and Issues.* London: W. M. Blackwood and Sons, Shannon: Kennikat Press, 1904.

Ashmead-Bartlett, E. *Port Arthur, The Siege and Capitulation.* London: W. M. Blackwood and Sons, 1906.

Ballard, G. A. *The Influence of the Sea on the Political History of Japan.* London: John Murray, 1921.

Bain, W. M. "Sino-Indian Military Modernization: The Potential for Destabilization." *Asian Affairs: An American Review,* 21:131–147, 1994.

Baring, M. *With the Russians in Manchuria.* London: Methuen, 1905.

Barr, Pat. *Foreign Devils: Westerners in the Far East.* Harmondsworth, England: Penguin, 1970.

Barry, R. *Port Arthur: A Monster Heroism.* New York: Moffat, Yard & Co., 1905.

Beasley, W. G. *Japanese Imperialism, 1894–1945.* Oxford: Clarendon Press, 1987.

Berger, G. M. *Parties Out of Power in Japan, 1931–1941.* Princeton, NJ: Princeton University Press, 1977.

Berry, M. E. *Hideyoshi.* Cambridge: Harvard University Press, 1989.

Blackette, P. M. S. *Fear, War and the Bomb: Military and Political Consequences of the Bomb.* New York: Whittlesey House, 1949.

Braddon, R. *The Other Hundred Year's War: Japan's Bid for Supremacy, 1941–2041.* London: Collins, 1983.

Bridgeman, J. M. *Revolt of the Hereros.* Berkeley: University of California Press, 1981.

Brindle, Ernest. *With Russian, Japanese and Chunchuse.* London: John Murray, 1905.

Brooke, Lord. *An Eye-Witness in Manchuria.* London: Eveleigh Nash, 1905.

Brown, F. *From Tientsin to Peking with the Allied Forces.* New York: Arno Press and the New York Times, 1970.

Burdick, C. B. *The Japanese Siege of Tsingtao.* Hamden, CT: Archon Books, 1976.

Burdick, C. and U. Moessner. *The German Prisoners-of-War in Japan, 1914–20.* Lanham, MD: University Press of America, 1984.

Buruma, I. *Memories of War in Germany and Japan.* New York: Farrar, Straus & Giroux, 1994.

Buruma, I. "The War over the Bomb." *New York Review of Books,* 44:26–34, 1995.

Busch, N. F. *The Emperor's Sword: Japan vs. Russia in the Battle of Tsushima.* New York: Funk and Wagnalls, 1969.

Bushnell, J. *Mutiny Amid Repression: Russian Soldiers in the Revolution of 1905–1906.* Bloomington: Indiana University Press, 1985.

Calman, D. *The Nature and Origins of Japanese Imperialism: A Reinterpretation of the Great Crisis of 1873.* London: Routledge, 1992.

Cassell's History of the Russo-Japanese War, 5 vols. London, 1905.

Checkland, O. *Humanitarianism and the Emperor's Japan, 1877–1977.* New York: St. Martin's Press, 1994.

Christie, D. *Thirty Years in Mukden, 1883–1913, Being the Experiences and Recollections of Dugald Christie, C.M.G., F.R.C.S., F.R.C.P.* London: Christie and Co., 1914.

Cleary, T. *The Japanese Art of War: Understanding the Culture of Strategy.* Boston: Shambhala, 1991.

Clubb, O. E. *China and Russia: The Great Game.* New York: Columbia University Press, 1971.

Collier's Weekly, Russo-Japanese War, Photographic and Descriptive View. New York, undated.

Connaughton, R. M. *The War of the Rising Sun and the Tumbling Bear: A Military History of the Russo-Japanese War 1904–5.* London: Routledge, 1988.

Cook, H. T., and T. F. Cook. *Japan at War: An Oral History.* New York: The New Press, 1992.

Coox, A. D. *Year of the Tiger.* Tokyo: Orient/West, 1964.

Coox, A. D. *Nomonhan: Japan Against Russia, 1939*, 2 vols. Stanford: Stanford University Press, 1985.

Cordonnier, E. L. V. *The Japanese in Manchuria*, 2 vols. London: Hugh Rees, 1912.

Costello, J. *The Pacific War, 1941–1945.* New York: Quill, 1981.

Cressman, R. J. *Magnificent Fight: A Battle for Wake Island.* Annapolis, MD: Naval Institute Press, 1995.

Curtiss, J. S. *The Russian Army Under Nicholas I, 1825–1855.* Durham, NC: Duke University, 1965.

Custine, the Marquis de. *Empire of the Czar. A Journey through Eternal Russia.* New York: Anchor Books, 1989.

d'Anethan, Baroness A. *Fourteen Years of Diplomatic Life in Japan.* London: Stanley, Paul and Co., 1912.

de Negrier, General. *Lessons of the Russo-Japanese War*, London: Hugh Rees, 1906.

Dennett, T. *Roosevelt and the Russo-Japanese War.* Gloucester, MA: Peter Smith, 1959.

Dillon, E. J. "The Chinese Wolf and the European Lamb." *The Contemporary Review*, 74:1–31, 1901.

Dower, J. D. *War Without Mercy: Race and Power in the Pacific War*. New York: Pantheon Books, 1986.

Dower, J. D. *Japan in War and Peace: Selected Essays*. New York: New Press, 1993.

Drea, E. J. *Nomohan: Japanese-Soviet Tactical Combat, 1939*. Fort Leavenworth, KS: Combat Studies Institute, Leavenworth Papers, No. 2, 1981.

Edgerton, R. B. *The Fall of the Asante Empire: The Hundred-Year War for the Gold Coast*. New York: The Free Press, 1995.

Elegant, R. *The Centre of the World: Communism and the Mind of China*. London: Methuen, 1963.

Esherick, J. W. *The Origins of the Boxer Rebellion*. Berkeley: University of California Press, 1987.

Esthus, R. A. *Double Eagle and the Rising Sun: The Russians and Japanese at Portsmouth in 1905*. Duke University Press, 1988.

Falk, E. A. *Togo and the Rise of Japanese Sea Power*. New York: Longmans, Green and Co., 1936.

Farmer, M. "Fire of the Dragon," *Popular Science*. August 1996, pp. 79–82.

Fleming, P. *The Siege at Peking*. London: Nicholas Fleming, 1959.

Fox, J., Jr. *Following the Sun Flag*. New York: Scribner's Sons, 1905.

Frank, R. B. *Guadalcanal: The Definitive Account of the Landmark Battle*. New York: Random House, 1990.

Friday, K. F. "Bushido or Bull? A Medieval Historian's Perspective on the Imperial Army and the Japanese Warrior Tradition." *The History Teacher*, 27:339–349, 1994.

Fuller, W. C., Jr. *Civil-Military Conflict in Imperial Russia, 1881–1914*. Princeton, NJ: Princeton University Press, 1985.

Funabashi, Y. "A Nuclear North Korea on the Israeli Model." *New Perspectives Quarterly*, Fall 1994, pp. 58–61.

German General Staff. *The Russo-Japanese War*, 5 vols., prepared by the Historical Section, authorized translation by Karl von Donat. London: Hugh Rees, 1909–10.

Giffard, S. *Japan Among the Powers, 1890–1990*. New Haven, CT: Yale University Press, 1994.

Giles, L. *The Siege of the Peking Legations: A Diary*. Perth: University of Western Australia Press, 1970.

Greener, William. *A Secret Agent in Port Arthur*. London: Archibald Constable & Co., 1905.

Hackett, R. F. *Yamagata Aritomo in the Rise of Modern Japan, 1838–1922*. Cambridge: Harvard University Press, 1971.

Haldane, A. L. *Reports From British Officers Attached to the Japanese and Russian Forces in the Field*. London: H.M. Stationery Office, 1908.

Hall, T. *The Fall of Singapore*. Sydney: Methuen Australia, 1983.

Hamilton, Lieutenant-General Sir Ian. *A Staff Officer's Scrap Book During the Russo-Japanese War*. 2 vols. London: Edward Arnold, 1906.

Hanayama, S. *The Way of Deliverance: Three Years with the Condemned War Criminals* (trans. by H. Suzuki, E. Nada, J. Sasaki, and H. Collins.). New York: Scribners, 1950.

Hane, M. *Peasants, Rebels and Outcastes: The Underside of Modern Japan*. New York: Pantheon Books, 1982.

Hane, M. *Modern Japan: A Historical Survey*. London: Westview Press, 1986.

Haney, R. E. *Caged Dragons: An American P.O.W. in World War II Japan*. Ann Arbor, MI: Sabre Press, 1991.

Harcave, S. *First Blood: The Russian Revolution of 1905*. London: The Bodley Head, 1964.

Hargreaves, R. *Red Sun Rising: The Siege of Port Arthur*. New York: S. B. Lippincott, 1962.

Harries, M. and S. Harries. *Soldiers of the Sun: The Rise and Fall of the Imperial Japanese Army*. New York: Random House, 1991.

Harris, S. H. *Factories of Death: Japanese Biological Warfare 1932–1945 and the American Cover-Up*. London: Routledge, 1994.

Hart, R. A. *The Great White Fleet*. Boston: Little, Brown, 1965.

Harvard, V. *Report of Col. Valery Harvard Reports of Military Observers*. Washington, DC: Government Printing Office, 1906.

Hayashi, S., and Coox, A. D. *Kogun: The Japanese Army in the Pacific*. Westport, CT: Greenwood Press, 1958.

Hearn, L. *Japan: An Attempt at Interpretation*. Tokyo: Charles E. Tuttle, 1959.

Heine, W. *With Perry to Japan*. Honolulu: University of Hawaii Press, 1990.

His Majesty's Stationery Office. *The Russo-Japanese War, Reports from British Officers Attached to the Japanese and Russian Forces in the Field*, 3 vols., and 3 vols. of maps and appendices. London: H.M. Stationery Office, 1908.

Historical Section of the Committee of Imperial Defense. *The Official History of the Russo-Japanese War (Naval and Military)*, 3 vols., and 3 vols. of maps and appendices. London: Harrison and Sons, 1909.

Holmes, E. *Acts of War: The Behavior of Men in Battle*. New York: The Free Press, 1986.

Holt, E. *The Opium Wars in China*. London: Putnam, 1964.

Hopkins, P. *Setting the East Ablaze: Lenin's Dream of an Empire in Asia*. London: John Murray, 1984.

Hooker, M. *Behind the Scenes in Peking*. New York: Oxford University Press, 1987.

Hoover, H. *The Memoirs of Herbert Hoover*. 3 vols. New York: Macmillan, 1951–52.

Hough, R. *The Fleet That Had to Die*. New York: The Viking Press, 1958.

Howard, M., G. J. Andreopoulos, and M. R. Shulman (eds.) *The Laws of War: Constraints on Warfare in the Western World*. New Haven, CT: Yale University Press, 1994.

Hoyt, E. P. *The Fall of Tsingtao*. London: Arthur Barker, 1975.

Hoyt, E. P. *Yamamoto: The Man Who Planned Pearl Harbor*. New York: McGraw-Hill, 1990.

Hsu, I. C. Y. *The Rise of Modern China*. New York: Oxford University Press, 1995.

Humphries, L. A., *The Way of the Heavenly Sword: The Japanese Army in the 1920's*. Stanford: Stanford University Press, 1995.

Hyer, E. "The South China Sea Disputes: Implications of China's Territorial Settlements," *Pacific Affairs*, 68:34–54, 1995.

Ienaga, S. *The Pacific War, 1931–1945*. New York: Random House, 1978.

Ignatyev, A. A. *A Subaltern in Old Russia*. New York: Hutchinson, 1944.

Ikegami, E. *The Taming of the Samurai. Honorific Individualism and the Making of Modern Japan*. Cambridge: Harvard University Press, 1995.

Inoguchi, R., Nakajima, T., with R. Pineau. *The Divine Wind: Japan's Kamikaze Force in World War II*. Annapolis, MD: U.S. Naval Institute, 1958.

Iritani, T. *Group Psychology of the Japanese in Wartime*. London: Kegan Paul, 1991.

Ito, M. *The Emperor's Last Soldiers*. New York: Coward-McCann, 1967.

Ito, M. with R. Pineau. *The End of the Imperial Japanese Navy*. New York: W. W. Norton, 1956.

James, D. H. *The Siege of Port Arthur, Records of an Eye-witness*. London: T. Fisher Unwin, 1905.

Jane, F. T. *The Imperial Japanese Navy*. London: Conway Maritime Press, 1904.

———. *The Imperial Russian Navy*. London: Conway Maritime Press, 1904.

Jansen, M. B. *Japan and China: From War to Peace, 1894–1972*. Princeton: Chicago: Rand McNally, 1975.

Jansen, M. B. *Japan and Its World: Two Centuries of Change*. Princeton: Princeton University Press, 1995.

Jones, F. C. *Shanghai and Tientsin*. New York: American Council, Institute of Pacific Relations, 1949.

Jones, J. *The Fall of Tsingtao: With a Study of Japan's Ambitions in China*. Boston: Houghton and Mifflin, 1915.

Jukes, G. *The Soviet Union in Asia*. Berkeley: University of California Press, 1973.

Kamiko, K. *I Didn't Die on Leyte*. Tokyo: Shuppan Kyodo Sha, 1966.

Keeley, L. H. *War Before Civilization: The Myth of the Peaceful Savage*. Oxford: Oxford University Press, 1996.

Keown-Boyd, H. *The Fists of Righteous Harmony: A History of the Boxer Uprising in China in the Year 1900*. London: Leo Cooper, 1991.

Kihl, Y. W. (ed.) *Korea and the World: Beyond the Cold War*. Boulder, CO: Westview Press, 1994.

Kinai, M. *The Russo-Japanese War, Official Reports*. 3 vols. Tokyo: Simbashido.

Kitahara, M. *Children of the Sun: The Japanese and the Outside World*. New York: St. Martin's Press, 1989.

Klado, Captain N. L. *The Russian Navy in the Russo-Japanese War*, translated by L. J. H. Dickinson. London: G. Bell, 1905.

——. *The Battle of the Sea of Japan*, translated by L. J. H. Dickinson and F. P. Marchant. London: Hodder and Stoughton, 1906.

Knollys, H. *Incidents in the China War of 1860*. London: William Blackwood and Sons, 1875.

Kokovtsov, Count. *Out of My Past: The Memoirs of Count Kokovtsov*. Stanford: Stanford University Press, 1935.

Kristof, N. D. "Japan Confronting Gruesome War Atrocity," *The New York Times*, March 17, 1995.

Kristof, N. D. "The Real Chinese Threat," *The New York Times Magazine*, August 27, 1995, pp. 49–51.

Kuropatkin, A. N., General. *The Russian Army and the Japanese War*. 2 vols. New York: E. P. Dutton, 1909.

Kushakov, K. *Yushno-Manchzhurskie Bezporiadki v 1900 godu*. Ashkabad, 1902.

La Farge, T. E. *China and the World War*. Stanford: Stanford University Press, 1937.

La Forte, R. S. and R. E. Marcello (eds.) *Building the Death Railway: The Ordeal of American POWs in Burma, 1942–1945*. Wilmington, DE: SR Books, 1993.

Landor, A. H. S. *China and the Allies*. 2 vols. London: William Heinemann, 1901.

Lattimore, O. *Manchuria: Cradle of Conflict*. New York: Macmillan, 1935.

Lea, H. *The Valor of Ignorance*. New York: Harper & Brothers, 1942 (orig. 1909).

Leckie, R. *Okinawa: The Last Battle of World War II*. New York: Viking, 1995.

Lehmann, J. H. *All Sir Garnet: A Life of Field-Marshal Lord Wolseley*. London: Jonathan Cape, 1964.

LeMay, C. E., with M. Kantor. *Mission with LeMay: My Story*. New York: Doubleday, 1965.

Lensen, G. A. *The Russian Push Toward Japan*: Princeton: Princeton University Press, 1959.

Life Goes to War: A Picture History of World War II. New York: Simon and Schuster, 1977.

Lin, C. P. "The Stealthy Advance of China's People's Liberation Army." *American Enterprise*, January/February, 29–35, 1994.

Lin, J. H. "Nanjing Massacre: The Forgotten Holocaust," *The Rice Paper*, Winter, 1995.

Lindbergh, C. A. *The Wartime Journals of Charles A. Lindbergh*. New York: Harcourt, Brace, Jovanovich, 1970.

Linn, B. A. *The U.S. Army and Counterinsurgency in the Philippine War, 1899–1902*. Chapel Hill: University of North Carolina Press, 1989.

Lloyd, A. *Every-Day Japan*. London: Cassell and Co., 1909.

Lobanov-Rosktovsky, Prince. *Russia and Asia*. Ann Arbor, MI: G. Wahr Pub. Co., 1951.

Lockhart, R. H. *The Two Revolutions*. London: Phoenix House, 1957.

Lo, H-M. *The Correspondence of G. E. Morrison, 1895–1912*. Cambridge: Cambridge University Press, 1976.

Lone, S. *Japan's First Modern War: Army and Society in the Conflict with China, 1894–95*. New York: St. Martin's Press, 1994.

Lynch, G. *The War of the Civilizations, Being the Record of "Foreign Devils'" Experiences with the Allies in China*. New York: Longman's Green, 1901.

MacKinnon, S. R. *Power and Politics in Late Imperial China*. Berkeley: University of California Press, 1980.

McCormick, F. *The Tragedy of Russia in Pacific Asia*. 2 vols. London: Grant, Richards, 1909.

McCullagh, F. *With the Cossacks, Being the Story of an Irishman Who Rode with the Cossacks Throughout the Russo-Japanese War*. London: Eveleigh Nash, 1906.

McCully, N. A. *The McCully Report: The Russo-Japanese War*. Annapolis, MD: Naval Institute Press, 1977.

McCune, S. *Korea's Heritage: A Regional and Social Geography*. Tokyo, Rutland, VT: C. E. Tuttle Co., 1956.

McKenzie, F. A. *From Tokyo to Tiflis: Uncensored Letters from the War*. London: Hurst and Blackett, 1905.

Maeda, T. *The Hidden Army: The Untold Story Of Japan's Military Forces*. Chicago: edition q, 1995.

Malozemoff, A. *Russian Far Eastern Policy, 1881–1904*. Berkeley: University of California Press, 1958.

Manchester, W. *Goodbye Darkness: A Memoir of the Pacific War*. Boston: Little, Brown, 1979.

March, P. C. *Reports of Military Observers (U.S.) During the Russo-Japanese War*. Washington: Government Printing Office, 1906–7.

Massie, R. K. *Peter the Great: His Life and World*. New York: A. A. Knopf, 1980.

Menning, B. W. *Bayonets Before Bullets: The Imperial Russian Army, 1861–1914*. Bloomington, IN: 1992.

Mitchell, R. H. *Thought Control in Prewar Japan*. Ithaca, NY: Cornell University Press, 1976.

Montgomery, M. *Imperialist Japan: The Yen to Dominate*. London: Christopher Helm, 1989.

Morley, J. M. *The Japanese Thrust into Siberia, 1918*. New York: Columbia University Press, 1957.

Munro, R. H. "Eavesdropping on the Chinese Military: Where it Expects War— Where it Doesn't." *Orbis*, Summer, 355–372, 1994.

Mutsu, M. *A Diplomatic Record of the Sino-Japanese War, 1894–1895*. Princeton, NJ: Princeton University Press, 1982.

Naito, H. *Thunder Gods: The Kamikaze Pilots Tell Their Story*. New York: Kodansha, 1989.

Nish, I. *The Anglo-Japanese Alliance: The Diplomacy of Two Island Empires, 1894–1907*. London: Athlone Press, 1966.

———. *Alliance in Decline: A Study of Anglo-Japanese Relations, 1908–1923*. London: Athlone Press, 1972.

Nitobe, I. *Bushido: The Soul of Japan*. Rutland, VT: Charles E. Tuttle, 1969.

Noel, P. *When Japan Fights*. Tokyo: The Hokuseido Press, 1937.

Nojine, E. K. *The Truth About Port Arthur*, translated and edited by Captain A. B. Lindsay and Major E. D. Swinton. London: John Murray, 1908.

Norregaard, B. W. *The Great Siege, The Investment and Fall of Port Arthur*. London: Methuen, 1906.

Novikoff-Priboy, A. S. *Tsushima*. New York: A. A. Knopf, 1937.

O'Connor, R. *The Spirit Soldiers: A Historical Narrative of the Boxer Rebellion*. New York: G. P. Putnam's Sons, 1973.

Ogasawara, N. *Life of Admiral Togo*. Tokyo: Seito Shorin Press, 1934.

Okamoto, S. *The Japanese Oligarchy and the Russo-Japanese War*. New York: Columbia University Press, 1970.

Onoda, H. *No Surrender: My Thirty-Year War*. Tokyo: Kodansha, 1974.

Palmer, Frederick. *With Kuroki in Manchuria*. New York: Charles Scribner's Sons, 1904.

———. *With My Own Eyes*. Indianapolis: Bobbs-Merrill, 1932.

Peattie, M. R. *Ishiwara Kanji, and Japan's Confrontation with the West*. Princeton: Princeton University Press, 1975.

Perrin, N. "Giving Up the Gun." *New Yorker*, November 20, 1965.

Perry, J. C. *Beneath Eagle's Wings: Americans in Occupied Japan*. New York: Dodd, Mead, 1980.

Perry, M. C. *The Japan Expedition, 1852–1854: The Personal Journal of Commodore Matthew C. Perry,* Roger Pineau (ed.). Washington, DC: Smithsonian Institute Press, 1968.

Politovsky, E. S. *From Libau to Tsushima, A Narrative of the Voyage of Admiral Rojestvensky's Fleet to Eastern Seas*, translated by Major F. R. Godfrey. London: John Murray, 1906.

Prange, G. W. *Miracle at Midway*. New York: Penguin, 1982.

Prange, G. W. *God's Samurai: Lead Pilot at Pearl Harbor*. New York: Brasseys, 1990.

Pritchard, R. J. and S. M. Zaide (eds.). *The Tokyo War Crimes Trial: The Complete Transcripts of the Proceedings of the International Military Tribunal for the Far East*. 2 vols. New York: Garland, 1981.

Quested, R. K. I. *"Matey" Imperialists? The Tsarist Russians in Manchuria, 1895–1917*. Hong Kong: University of Hong Kong.

Randall, P. E. *There Are No Victors Here! A Local Perspective on the Treaty of Portsmouth*. Portsmouth: Peter E. Randall, 1985.

Rasmussen, O. D. *Tientsin: An Illustrated Outline History*. Tientsin: The Tientsin Press, 1925.

Rennie, D. F. *The British Arms in North China and Japan*. London: John Murray, 1863.

Reel, A. F. *The Case of General Yamashita*. New York: Octagon Books, 1949.

Reichmann, C. *Reports of Military Observers (U.S.) During the Russo-Japanese War*. Washington, DC: U.S. Government Printing Office, 1906–7.

Reports of Military Observers attached to the Armies in Manchuria during the Russo-Japanese War. Part I. Washington, DC: Government Printing Office, 1906.

Richardson, T. E. *In Japanese Hospitals During War-time*. London: William Blackwood and Sons, 1905.

Robertson, J. "Mon Japan: The Revue Theater as a Technology of Japanese Imperialism." *American Ethnologist*, 22:970–996, 1995.

Rodzianko, P. *Tattered Banners—An Autobiography*. London: Seeley Service, n.d.

Rusbridger, J. and E. Nave. *Betrayal at Pearl Harbor: How Churchill Lured Roosevelt into World War II*. New York: Simon & Schuster, 1992.

Russell, E. F. L. (Lord). *The Knights of Bushido: A Short History of Japanese War Crimes*. London: Cassell, 1958.

Sadler, A. L. *The Code of the Samurai*. Tokyo: The Japan Foundation, 1941.

Sakurai T. *Human Bullets*. Tokyo: Teibi, 1912.

Salisbury, H. E. *War Between Russia and China*. New York: Norton, 1969.

Sanders, J. L. *The Moscow Uprising of December, 1905: A Background Study*. New York: Garland, 1987.

Sansom, G. B. *Japan: A Short Cultural History*. New York: Appleton-Crofts, 1962.

Schiffrin, H. Z. *Sun Yat-sen and the Origins of the Chinese Revolution*. Berkeley: University of California Press, 1968.

Schram, S. *Mao Tse-tung*. New York: Simon and Schuster, 1966.

Schuyler, W. S. *Reports of Military Observers (U.S.) During the Russo-Japanese War*. Washington, DC: Government Printing Office, 1906–7.

Scidmore, E. R. *As the Hague Ordains: Journal of Russian Prisoner's Wife in Japan*. New York: Henry Holt, 1907.

Schultz, D. *Wake Island*. Chicago: Playboy, 1979.

Seagrave, S. *Dragon Lady: The Life and Legend of the Last Empress of China*. New York: A. A. Knopf, 1992.

Seaman, L. L. *From Tokyo Through Manchuria with the Japanese*. London: D. Appleton and Co., 1905.

Semenoff, Captain V .I. *Rasplata* ("The Reckoning"). New York: E. P. Dutton, 1913.

———. *The Battle of Tsushima*, translated by Captain A. B. Lindsay. New York: E. P. Dutton, 1913.

Shigemitsu, M. *Japan and her Destiny: My Struggle for Peace* (ed. by Maj. General F. S. G. Piggott). New York: E. P. Dutton, 1958.

Simon, S. W. (ed.) *East Asian Security in the Post-Cold War Era*. Armonk, N.Y.: M. E. Sharpe, 1993.

Smith, W. R. *The Siege and Fall of Port Arthur*. London: Eveleigh Nash, 1905.

Soloviev, Z. *Actual Experiences in War*. Washington, DC: Government Printing Office, No. 9, 1906.

Steel, R. A. *Through Peking's Sewer Gate: Relief of the Boxer Siege, 1900–1901.* New York: Vantage, 1985.

Steer, A. P. *The "Novik" and the Part She Played in the Russo-Japanese War.* New York: E. P. Dutton, 1913.

Steinberg, R. *Island Fighting.* Chicago: Time-Life, 1978.

Steinberg, R. *Return to the Philippines.* Chicago: Time-Life, 1979.

Story, D. *The Campaign with Kuropatkin.* London: T. W. Laruie, 1904.

Storry, R. *The Double Patriots: A Study of Japanese Nationalism.* London: Chalto and Windus, 1957.

Swinhoe, R. *Narratives of the North China Campaign of 1860.* London: 1863.

Taburno, J. *The Truth About the War.* Kansas City, MO: Franklin Hudson, 1905.

Tanaka, S. *Japan's Orient: Rendering Pasts Into History.* Berkeley: University of California Press, 1993.

Tani, T. Lieutenant-General. *Kimitsu Nichi-Ro-Sen-shi* ("Intelligence History of the Japano-Russian War"), lectures at the War College, Inaba Masao, ed. Tokyo: Hara Shobo, 1966.

Tarnstrom, R. L. *The Wars of Japan.* Lindsborg, Kansas: Trogen Books, 1992.

Tasaki, H. *Long the Imperial Way.* Boston: Houghton, Mifflin, 1950.

Thomas, L. *Old Gimlet Eye: The Adventures of Smedley P. Butler.* New York: Farrar & Rinehart, 1933.

Timperley, H. J. *Japanese Terror in China.* New York: Modern Age Books, 1938.

Toland, J. *The Rising Sun: The Decline and Fall of the Japanese Empire, 1936–1945.* New York: Random House, 1970.

Tretyakov, Lieutenant-General N. A. *My Experiences at Nan-shan and Port Arthur With the Fifth East Siberian Rifles.* London: H. Rees, Ltd., 1911.

Tsurumi, K. *Social Change and the Individual: Japan Before and After Defeat in World War II.* Princeton, NJ: Princeton University Press, 1970.

Tsuji, M. *Singapore: The Japanese Version.* New York: St. Martin's Press, 1961.

Turnbull, S. R. *The Samurai: A Military History.* New York: Macmillan, 1977.

Tyler, S. *The Japan-Russia War.* Philadelphia: P. W. Ziegler, 1905

Van Der Post, Laurens. "The Prisoners and the Bomb." *The American Enterprise,* 6:70–73, 1995.

Van der Vat, Dan. *The Pacific Campaign: The U.S.-Japanese Naval War of 1941–1945.* New York: Simon & Schuster, 1991.

Veresaev, V. *In the War.* New York: Mitchell Kennerley, 1917.

Villiers, F. *Port Arthur, Three Months with the Besiegers.* London: Longmans, Green & Co., 1905.

Vu, C. *Political and Social Change in Viet-Nam Between 1940 and 1946*. Ph.D. Dissertation, University of Wisconsin, 1984.

Waldersee, A. Count von. *A Field-Marshal's Memoirs*. London: Hutchinson and Co., 1924.

Waley, A. *The Opium War Through Chinese Eyes*. Stanford: Stanford University Press, 1958.

Warner, D. and P. Warner. *The Tide at Sunrise: A History of the Russo-Japanese War, 1904–05*. New York: Charter House, 1974.

Warner, D. and P. Warner. *The Sacred Warriors: Japan's Suicide Legions*. New York: Van Nostrand, 1982.

Waters, Colonel W. H.-H. *Reports From British Officers in the Field With the Russian and Japanese Forces*. London: War Office, 1906.

Watts, A. J., and B. G. Gordon. *The Imperial Japanese Navy*. New York: Doubleday & Co., 1971.

Weale, B. L. Putnam (Bertram Lenox Simpson). *With Manchu and Muscovite*. New York: Dodd, Mead and Company, 1910.

Weinberg, R. *The Revolution of 1905 in Odessa: Blood on the Steps*. Bloomington: Indiana University Press, 1993.

Westwood, J. N. *Russia Against Japan, 1904–05: A New Look at the Russo-Japanese War*. New York: Macmillan, 1986.

————. *Witnesses of Tsushima*. Tokyo: Sophia University, 1970.

Wheeler, P. and H. M. Rives. *Dome of Many-Colored Glass*. Garden City, NY: Doubleday & Co., 1955.

White, J. A. *The Diplomacy of the Russo-Japanese War*. Princeton: Princeton University Press, 1964.

Wilson, D. *When Tigers Fight: The Story of the Sino-Japanese War, 1937–1945*. New York: The Viking Press, 1982.

Wilson, W. S. *Ideals of the Samurai: Writings of Japanese Warriors*. Burbank, CA: Ohara, 1982a.

Williams, P. and D. Wallace. *Unit 731: The Japanese Army's Secret of Secrets*. London: Hodder and Stoughton, 1989.

Wincelberg, S. *The Samurai of Vishnograd: The Notebooks of Jacob Marateck/retold by Shimon and Anita Wincelberg*. Philadelphia: Jewish Publication Society of America, 1976

Witte, S. *The Memoirs of Count Witte* (Trans. by A. Yarmolinsky). London: Heinemann , 1921.

Wolseley, G. J. *The Story of A Soldier's Life*. 2 vols. Westminster: Archibald Constable, 1903.

Wolseley, G. J. *Narrative of the War with China in 1860*. London: Longman, Green, Longman and Roberts, 1962.

Wood, O. L. *From the Yalu to Port Arthur*. Kansas City, MO: Franklin Hudson, 1905.

Woodward, D. *The Russians at Sea*. London: William Kimber, 1965.

Wright, H. C. S. *With Togo, the Story of Seven Months Under His Command*, London: Hurst and Blackett, 1961.

Zich, A. *The Rising Sun*. Alexandria, VA: Time-Life Books, 1977.

INDEX

Numbers in *italics* refer to illustrations.

German West Africa, 195
Germany, imperial, 101, 237, 318
    in Boxer Rebellion, 17, 60, 64, 65, 67, 70,
        72, 73, 75, 79–80, 81, 84, 86, 87, 88,
        90, 94–95
    Dogger Bank incident as viewed in, 194
    Japanese military trained by, 44, 322
    looting by forces of, 81
    navy of, 227
    Portsmouth treaty as viewed in, 219
    pre-World War I Japanese imperialism
        and, 223
    Sino-Japanese War and, 49
    treatment of civilians by forces of, 93–94,
        321
    in World War I, 227–32, 261, 320–21
Germany, Nazi, 14, 238, 243, 251, 253, 312,
        314–15, 316
Ghana, 321
Gilbert Islands, 289
Giles, Lancelot, 84
Gillespie, James O., 293–94
Gilyak, 74
Gneisenau, 227
Goettge, Frank, 283
Graham, Billy, 261
Grant, Sir James Hope, 30, 31, 32, 33,
        34–35, 36
Great Britain:
    African imperialism of, 237
    in Boxer Rebellion, 17, 60, 61, 64–65, 67,
        72–78, 80, 84, 86, 90, 93, 94, 95
    China aided by, 243
    China-based traders from, 27–28
    China dominated by, 25, 27–38
    Dogger Bank incident and, 192–94
    Indians in military of, 15, 264, 267–68
    as Japanese ally, 96–98, 216, 223
    Japanese military trained by, 32
    looting by forces of, 93
    navy of, 192–94, 202, 206, 223, 246, 266,
        272, 276
    Nicholas II's view of, 50
    in 1927 Nanking, 245
    in opening of Japan, 42
    Pearl Harbor and, 252–53
    in Persian Gulf War, 327
    pre-World War I Japanese imperialism
        and, 223

Russo-Japanese War and, 99, 130, 180, 194
Sikhs in military of, 14, 31, 32, 36, 228
Sino-Japanese War and, 46
Togo's visit to, 223
treatment of civilians by forces of, 61, 74,
    79, 94, 321–22
treatment of prisoners and wounded by
    forces of, 33, 34, 36, 272, 321
treatment of prisoners and wounded
    from, 14, 34, 36, 37, 192, 264, 267–68,
    277, 284, 303
Vladivostok intervention of, 234
in World War I, 226–32, 234
in World War II, 252–53, 264–68, 271,
    272, 275, 276–77, 295, 303, 312, 315,
    318
Greener, William, 120, 121
Gribski, K. N., 55–56
Grippenberg, Oscar, 179, 181
Gromov, Colonel, 128–29
Guadalcanal, Battle of, 282–85
Guam, 261, 274, 290, 303
Guernica (Picasso), 316
Gurkha troops, 275
gyokusai, 309

Halsey, William F. "Bull," 286
Hamilton, Sir Ian, 142, 165, 179
Hankow-Wuhan industrial complex, 250–51
Hashimoto, Colonel, 246
Hawaii, 223, 237, 273, 275, 281, 315
Hay, John, 97–98
Hayashi Senjuro, 239, 271
Hearst, William Randolph, 224, 225
Henry, Paul, 92
Herero, 321
Heston, Charlton, 60
Hideyoshi, Toyotomi, 22–23, 39, 46, 236
Hirohito, emperor of Japan, 177, 239
    Nanking and, 245
    surrender and, 302
    Unit 731 established by, 284
    war opposed by, 253
Hiroshima, bombing of, 301–2, *301,* 317
Hirota Koki, 253
Hiryu, 281
Hitler, Adolf, 238
Holland, 223, 237
    in Boxer Rebellion, 64

Kamranh Bay, 200–201
K'ang-hsi, Chinese emperor, 25
Kaulbars, Baron A. V., 184
Kawaguchi Kiyotake, 271, 283, 285, 286, 304
Kawai Chiyoko, 257
Kawane Yoshikata, 270
Keller, Count Fyodor, 143–44
kempeitai, 308
Kempff, Louis, 73
Ketteler, Baron Clemens Freiherr von, 65, 70, 82, 95
Ketteler, Maud von, 65
Khalkhin Gol, 239–42
King, Ernest, 273
Kitchener, Horatio Herbert, 1st earl, 321–22
Klado, Nikolai, 195–96, 197
Kobe, 300
Kodama Gentaro, Baron, 132, 140
    in journey to Mukden, 177
    at Liaoyang, 151, 155–56
    Port Arthur battle led by, 169, 170–71
kokutai, 235
Komei, emperor of Japan, 42
Komura Jutaro, Marquis, 216, 217, 218–20
Kondratenko, General, 167
Kongo, 228
Konoye, Prince, 239, 253, 265
Korea:
    Anglo-Japanese accord on, 216
    "comfort women" from, 16, 226, 251
    conscripts from, 226
    early Japanese conflicts with, 22–23
    forced workers from, 226, 290
    Japanese annexation of, 226
    Japanese brutality in, 242
    Japanese control of, 97, 223, 226
    in Russo-Japanese War, 121–30, 217
    Sino-Japanese conflicts over, 45–47, 48–49
    U.S.-Japanese accord on, 226
    in World War II, 302
Korea, North, 329
Korea, South, 328, 329
Korean War, 326
Koreyetz, 121
Kowshing, 45–46
Kuang Hsu, emperor of China, 62–63
Kublai Khan, 22
Kung, Prince, 31, 37–38
Kuribayashi Tadamichi, 296

Kuroki Tametomo, 126, 127, 128, 129, 130, 141, 144
    at Liaoyang, 152, 153, 156–57, 159–60, 161
    at Mukden, 183
    at Rice Cake Hill, 161
    at Tashihchaio, 144
Kuropatkin, Alexei, 112, 123, 124, *124,* 125–26, 127, 130, 139, 140, 141
    Boris sent to Russia by, 155
    Grippenberg's denunciation of, 181
    indecision of, 155
    at Liaoyang, 151, 153, 154, 156, 157, 158, 162, 163, 164
    at Mukden, 178, 182, 183
    and Nogi's journey to Mukden, 177
    removed from command, 186
    San-de-pu and, 179, 180
    Tashihchaio defended by, 142–43, 144
    in withdrawal to Tieh-ling, 184–86
Kursel, Werner von, 208, 209
Kwajalein, 262, 289
Kwantung Army, 239
Kyrgyzstan, 328–29

Ladybird, 246
Lae, 286
Landor, Henry Savage, 80–81
Latin America, 237
Lea, Homer, 225
League of Nations, 235, 237
Lee Teng-hui, 329
LeMay, Curtis, 300, 316–17
Lenox-Simpson, Bertram, 83, 85
Lexington, 278, 280
Leyte, 269, 291
Liaotung Peninsula, 48, 49–50, 98
    in Boxer Rebellion, 50–58
    description of, 50–52, 241
Liaoyang, Battle of, 147, 151–65
    beginning of fighting in, 158
    description of forces at, 151–56
    lessons of, 162–63
    number of troops at, 157–58
    Rice Cake Hill in, 160–61
    Russian retreat to Mukden in, 161–62
    Sha-ho River in, 163–64, 179
    transport to, 151–52
liberals, Japanese, 239
Life, 244, 257, 315

pillaging, *see* looting
Poland, 101, 315
Poles, in Russian military, 110, 153
Port Arthur, 48–49, 96, 98, *117,* 118–21, *119,*
    132–33, 135–36, 147–48
  carnage at, 172
  description of, 116–18
  Japanese assault on, 147–51, 156, 157,
    165–73, *170,* 222
  Japanese surprise attack on, 116, 118,
    123, 255
  Japanese tunneling at, 165–66, 171
  Russian departure from, 175–76
  Russian surrender of, 173–77
  203–Meter Hill fighting and, 170–71,
    172, 173
Portsmouth, Treaty of (1907), 216–20, 224, 225
Portugal:
  China-based traders from, 27
  early Japanese contacts with, 22, 23, 39
  Russo-Japanese War and, 194
Prince of Wales, 266
Princeton, 291, 292
prisoners:
  anti-Boxer allies' treatment of, 85
  British treatment of, 33, 34, 321
  Chinese treatment of, 34, 36, 37, 53–54,
    56, 58, 314
  French treatment of, 85
  German treatment of, 14
  Italian treatment of, 14
  U.S. treatment of, 321
prisoners, Japanese:
  Allied treatment of, 313, 316
  Australian treatment of, 283, 303
  British treatment of, 272
  Chinese treatment of, 318
  Russian treatment of, 146, 319
  Soviet treatment of, 241–42, 303
  U.S. treatment of, 287–88
prisoners of Japanese:
  Chinese as, 48, 88–89, 244–47, *248,* 249
  Germans as, 230–33
  Russians as, 17–18, 129, 144, 175, 181,
    211–15, 320
prisoners of Japanese, in World War II, 317
  Americans as, 15, 261, 263–64, 269–70,
    271, 272, 274, 277, 283, 284, 285, 292,
    293–94, 302–3
  Australians as, 15, 277

biological experiments on, 14–15, 284–85,
    313, 317
  British as, 14, 264, 267–68, 277, 284, 303
  Chinese as, 14–15, *250,* 284
  Dutch as, 303
  Europeans in Indonesia as, 272
  Filipinos as, 15, 269–70, 271
  Indians as, 15, 268
  Soviets as, 14–15, 241, 284
propaganda, 306
prostitutes:
  forced, *see* "comfort women"
  Russian frequenting of, 117, 120, 137, 154,
    167, 196
Putilov, Admiral, 42
pyroxylin, 205

Quezon, Manuel Luis, 291

Raden, Baron von, 67–68, 84
Radziwill, Prince, 174–75
Raggi, Marquese di Salvago, 65
rape:
  by Bolsheviks, 234
  in Boxer Rebellion, 54, 61, 81, 85, 94, 95
  in Russo-Japanese War, 165, 178
rape, by Japanese:
  in 1930s China, 14, 244, 246, 247–49
  in Sino-Japanese War, 48
  in World War II, 16, 17, 264, 265, 267,
    268, 272, 275, 293, 312, 317
Raphael, Robin, 330
Reagan, Ronald, 327
Red Cross, 109, 122, 137, 138, 241
religion:
  in Japanese military, 113, 322
  in Russian military, 110
Rennenkampf, Pavel Karlovich, 57
Repulse, 266
Retvizan, 135, 148, 173
Roosevelt, Franklin D., 253–54, 316
  on Doolittle raid, 274
  Pearl Harbor and, 252–53, 265
Roosevelt, Theodore, 98, 137, 226, 323
  immigration policies of, 224
  Russo-Japanese War and, 211, 216
  Togo's visit with, 224
  U.S. fleet tour ordered by, 225
Rozhdestvensky, Zinovi Petrovich, 189, *189,*
    190, *193*

Rozhdestvensky, Zinovi Petrovich,
continued
descriptions of, 188, 194
in Madagascar, 196, 198
relief from command sought by, 196
at Tsushima, 203–9
after Tsushima defeat, 215
in voyage to Far East, 187–203, *193, 200*
wounding of, 208–9
Rudnev, Captain, 122
Rurik, 122–23
Russ, 181
Russia, imperial, 314
in Boxer Rebellion, 17, 53–58, 60, 64,
67–68, 72, 73, 74, 75, 77, 78, 79–80, 81,
84, 87, 88, 90, 92, 94, 96
Chinese conflicts with, over Manchuria,
24, 25, 26, 29, 38, 50–58, 95, 96, 97
Liaotung Peninsula leased to, 50
loans to China from, 48
in opening of Japan, 42
rape by forces of, 54, 95, 165, 178
Sino-Japanese War and, 49
Trans-Siberian railroad built by, 49,
50–53, 103
treatment of civilians by forces of, 54–56,
58, 74, 87, 89, 94, 319, 321
treatment of dead by forces of, 129
treatment of prisoners by forces of,
146, 319
treatment of prisoners from, 17–18,
53–54, 56, 58, 129, 144, 175, 181,
211–15, 320
see also Manchuria; Russo-Japanese War;
Soviet Union
Russia, post-Soviet, 328, 329
Russian military, in Russo-Japanese War,
100–111, 144–45, 152–55
conscripts in, 104–6
Cossacks in, 108–9, 110, 114, 142, 146, 153,
156, 177–78, 180, 319
drinking by, 152–53, 161–62, 164, 167,
174, 183
ethnic makeup of, 110, 153
food of, 167, 185–86
intelligence of, 101, 116, 157, 182
looting by, 131–32, 165, 174, 178, 183
medical care in, 109, 167–68, 182–83
morale of, 110–11, 155, 162, 164, 181

officers in, 103–6, 153–54, 157, 163, 164
petty regulations observed by, 154–55
regional organization of, 109
religion in, 110
Siberians in, 106, 142, 143, 145, 161
training of, 135
treatment of civilians by, 121, 131, 178,
183, 192, 320
treatment of dead from, 129, *145,* 177,
181, 320
treatment of wounded by, 146, 168–69,
192, 213
treatment of wounded from, 17–18, 122,
139, 144, 175, *180,* 181, *212,* 213, 320
uniforms of, 106–7
U.S.-Japanese Siberian intervention and,
233–34
weapons of, 107–8, 114
wives of, 154, 168
Russian navy, in Russo-Japanese War, 120,
121–23, 133–35, 136, 147–49, 172–73,
187–215
in Dogger Bank incident, 192, 193
drinking in, 190, 196, 197, 203
in Madagascar, 195–99
makeup of, 188, 191, 199
medical care in, 199, 205, 207, 210
morale of, 190
mutiny in, 198
officers in, 188–89, 190
recoaling of, 194–95, 200
sailors in, 188–89, 190
"self-sinkers" (Third Pacific Reinforcing
Squadron) in, 196, 197, 199, 200, 201
torpedo boats feared by, 191–92, 195
torpedo practice by, 198–99
treatment of shipwrecked sailors by, 74,
122–23, 137
at Tsushima, 203–12, 216, 222
in voyage to Far East, 187–203, *193, 200*
Russo-Japanese War, 78, 307, 309, 318
casualties in, 130, 132, 139, 149, 159, 162,
180, 186, 241
events leading to, 96–99
explanations of chivalry in, 319–20
Japanese financial condition in, 215–16,
236
Japanese intelligence in, 116, 132, 157
Japanese journey to, 126–27

World War II, continued
explanations of causes of, 311–12
Iwo Jima in, 286, 296
Japan after, 325–31
Japanese celebrations in, 273
Japanese opposition to, 253, 257, 269
Japanese pessimism on, 257
looting in, 264, 267, 268
Midway battle in, 279–81
Okinawa in, 296–99
Philippines in, 15, 17, 261, 262, 269–71,
273, 291–94, 303
rape in, 16, 17, 264, 265, 267, 268, 272, 275,
293, 312, 317
Southeast Asia in, 265–69, 271–78, 294–95
South Pacific in, 281–91
spies in, 260, 265
summary of, 13–14
surrender in, 302–3
treatment of civilians in, 16, 17, 268, 269,
270, 272, 275, 277, 292, 293, 299, 312,
313, 314, 316–17
treatment of dead in, 241, 265, 285, 287,
316
treatment of prisoners in, 14, 241–42, 272,
283, 287–88, 288, 303, 313, 316, 321;
see also prisoners of Japanese, in
World War II
treatment of shipwrecked sailors in,
15–16, 314
treatment of wounded in, 264, 283, 285,
287, 316, 324
U.S. code-breaking in, 254, 277–78
Wake Island in, 261–64
see also Pearl Harbor, attack on
wounded:
in Anglo-French-Chinese War of

1859–60, 33, 36
in Boxer Rebellion, 94
in Dogger Bank incident, 192

wounded, Japanese:
in Russo-Japanese War, 146, 168–69, 213
in World War II, 283, 285, 287, 316
wounded, Japanese treatment of, 324
in Russo-Japanese War, 17–18, 122, 139,
144, 175, 180, 181, 213, 320
in World War II, 264

Yahara Hiromichi, 297, 299
Yalu, Battle of the, 126–30, 127, 320
Yamagata Aritomo, 39, 40, 47, 97, 173
Yamaguchi Motoomi, 82, 87
Yamaguchi Tamon, 281
Yamamoto Isoroku, 207, 256, 274, 275, 279
background of, 256–57
death of, 287
Pearl Harbor attack planned by, 256–57
second Pearl Harbor attack rejected by,
260–61
Yamashita Tomoyuki, 266–67, 268, 269, 292
Yamato, 279, 298
Yellow Sea, Battle of the, 46–47
Yokohama, 115, 300
Yorktown, 280, 281
Yoshida Shoin, 42
Yuan Shih-k'ai, 69, 94

Zasulich, M. I., 127–29
Zen Buddhism, 322
Zhukov, Georgi K., 240–41